Ethnic Diversity and Economic Instability in Africa

There is a growing consensus in the development economics literature that ethnic diversity is a significant factor in explaining Africa's poor economic performance. *Ethnic Diversity and Economic Instability in Africa* challenges this conventional wisdom. Drawing on the insights of historians, anthropologists and political scientists, as well as development economists, this book questions whether ethnicity is the most useful organising principle by which to examine the economic development of Africa, arguing that it is a more fluid and contingent concept than economic models allow. Instead, the authors explore the actual experience of ethnicity in Africa and propose new methods of measuring ethnic diversity and inequalities. Finally, some tentative conclusions are reached regarding appropriate policy reforms.

HIROYUKI HINO is Economic Advisor to the Prime Minister of the Republic of Kenya.

JOHN LONSDALE is Fellow of Trinity College and Professor Emeritus of Modern African History at the University of Cambridge.

GUSTAV RANIS is Frank Altschul Professor Emeritus of International Economics at Yale University.

FRANCES STEWART is Professor Emeritus of Development Economics at the University of Oxford.

Ethnic Diversity and Economic Instability in Africa

Interdisciplinary Perspectives

Edited by

HIROYUKI HINO

JOHN LONSDALE

GUSTAV RANIS

FRANCES STEWART

CAMBRIDGE
UNIVERSITY PRESS

CAMBRIDGE
UNIVERSITY PRESS

University Printing House, Cambridge CB2 8BS, United Kingdom

One Liberty Plaza, 20th Floor, New York, NY 10006, USA

477 Williamstown Road, Port Melbourne, VIC 3207, Australia

314-321, 3rd Floor, Plot 3, Splendor Forum, Jasola District Centre, New Delhi - 110025, India

79 Anson Road, #06-04/06, Singapore 079906

Cambridge University Press is part of the University of Cambridge.

It furthers the University's mission by disseminating knowledge in the pursuit of education, learning and research at the highest international levels of excellence.

www.cambridge.org
Information on this title: www.cambridge.org/9781107025998

© Cambridge University Press 2012

First published 2012
Reprinted 2012
First paperback edition 2014

A catalogue record for this publication is available from the British Library

Library of Congress Cataloging in Publication data
Ethnic diversity and economic instability in Africa : interdisciplinary perspectives /
Hiroyuki Hino . . . [et al.].
    p. cm.
  Includes bibliographical references and index.
  ISBN 978-1-107-02599-8 (hardback)
  1. Cultural pluralism – Economic aspects – Africa. 2. Africa – Ethnic relations –
Economic aspects. 3. Africa – Economic conditions – 1960– I. Hino, Hiroyuki,
1945–
  HN780.Z9M8448 2012
  305.80096–dc23
  2012016900

ISBN 978-1-107-02599-8 Hardback
ISBN 978-1-107-44300-6 Paperback

Contents

Figures

Tables

Contributors

BRUCE J. BERMAN is Professor Emeritus of Political Studies and History and Director and Principal Investigator of the Ethnicity and Democratic Governance Program at Queen's University, Ontario, Canada. He was educated at Dartmouth College (BA, International Relations), the London School of Economics (MA, Social Anthropology) and Yale University (M.Phil., Ph.D., Political Science). He has served as the President of the Canadian Association of African Studies in 1990–1 and the African Studies Association in the US in 2004–5.

GRAHAM K. BROWN is Director of the Centre for Development Studies and a senior lecturer in International Development at the University of Bath, UK. In 2011–12 he was the Lee Kong Chian Distinguished Visiting Fellow at Stanford University and the National University of Singapore. His research is concerned with the nexus of inequality, identity, and development, with an empirical focus on Southeast Asia, and has been published in leading disciplinary journals, including *World Development* and *Oxford Development Studies*.

YASH PAL GHAI is a legal scholar. He has lectured in the leading law schools including Warwick, Yale, Harvard and University of Hong Kong. He has been involved in constitution-making in various countries throughout the world. He was the Chairman of the Kenya constitution review process, heading the Constitution of Kenya Review Commission and the Kenya Constitution Conference (2000–4). More recently he was consultant to the Somali Constitution Commission on the preparation of the Somali draft constitution.

NOBUAKI HAMAGUCHI is Professor of the Research Institute for Economics and Business Administration, Kobe University, Japan. He graduated from the Osaka University of Foreign Studies and has a Ph.D. from the University of Pennsylvania. His research interests include economic development, regional economics and international trade and investment.

HIROYUKI HINO is a professor at Kobe University, Special Fellow at the Japan International Cooperation Agency Research Institute (JICA-RI) and currently serving as Economic Advisor to the Prime Minister of the Government of Kenya. After he received a Ph.D. in Economics at the University of Rochester, he joined the International Monetary Fund (IMF) and worked on IMF policy issues in its Exchange and Trade Relations Department. He was Assistant Director of the African Department and Director of Regional Office for Asia and the Pacific.

ARNIM LANGER is Director of the Centre for Research on Peace and Development (CRPD) and University Lecturer in International Relations at the University of Leuven in Belgium. His research areas include causes and consequences of conflict, post-conflict economic reconstruction, inequality, group behaviour and identity formation.

JOHN LONSDALE is Emeritus Professor of Modern African History and a Fellow of Trinity College Cambridge. Among his books are (as co-author) *Unhappy Valley: Conflict in Kenya and Africa* (1992); (as co-editor) *Mau Mau and Nationhood* (2003); (as co-editor) *Writing for Kenya: the Life and Works of Henry Muoria* (2009); and (as co-editor) *Trinity: a Portrait* (2011).

BETHWELL A. OGOT is Chancellor of Moi University and Professor Emeritus of History at Maseno University, Kenya. He is author of over twenty books and eighty articles and book chapters on Kenyan and African history. His latest works include *History as Destiny and History as Knowledge* (2005), *History of the Luo-Speaking Peoples of Eastern Africa* (2009), and *Who, if Anyone, Owns the Past?* (2010). He was President of the International Scientific Committee for the Preparation of a General History of Africa for the United Nations Educational, Scientific and Cultural Organization (UNESCO).

GUSTAV RANIS is the Frank Altschul Professor Emeritus of International Economics at Yale University. He was Assistant Administrator for Program and Policy at the Agency for International Development (AID) for the Department of State in 1965–7, Director of Yale's Economic Growth Center in 1967–75, Director of the Yale Center for International and Area Studies from 1995 to 2003 and a Carnegie Corporation Scholar in 2004–6. He has more than twenty books and 200 articles on theoretical and policy-related issues of development to his credit.

KEN-ICHI SHIMOMURA is Professor of Economics and Director of the Research Institute for Economics and Business Administration at Kobe University. He obtained a Ph.D. in Economics from the University of Rochester. His research fields are economic theory and experimental economics.

PARKER SHIPTON is Professor of Anthropology and Research Fellow in African Studies at Boston University. He has written extensively on farming and herding people of Africa, particularly on customs involving kinship, land tenure, ritual and money and exchange.

FRANCES STEWART is Emeritus Professor of Development Economics and Director of the Centre for Research on Inequality, Human Security and Ethnicity (CRISE) at the University of Oxford. A pre-eminent development economist, in 2010 she received the Mahbub ul Haq award from the United Nations for Lifetime Services to Human Development. She has an honorary doctorate from the University of Sussex.

TAKEHIKO YAMATO is Professor in the Graduate School of Decision Science and Technology, Tokyo Institute of Technology. He received his MA and Ph.D. in Economics at the University of Rochester. His fields of specialisation include microeconomic theory, experimental economics, game theory, mechanism design, public economics and industrial organisation.

Foreword

Over the last decade, we have witnessed greater political stability and higher economic growth in Sub-Saharan Africa. While expectations seem to be forming that Africa could be a new growth centre in the decades to come, there remains the risk of political instability and economic downturn. The recurrence of military coups, continued semi-authoritarian rule and weak governance are still observed in some parts of the continent.

Many previous studies attribute these risks to political mobilisation brought by ethnic as well as religious division in African societies. However, African history demonstrates that ethnic diversities do not necessarily cause political conflicts and economic instability. A more sophisticated approach is necessary to gain a better understanding of the conditions under which ethnic diversity could be a source of political and economic instability, and the factors that contribute to nation-building with social harmony and economic prosperity in the long run.

The Japan International Cooperation Agency (JICA) Research Institute adopted 'Ethnic diversity and economic instability in Africa' as one of its major research projects upon its establishment in October 2008. This project was organised in collaboration with the Research Institute for Economics and Business Administration of Kobe University, and led by Dr Hiroyuki Hino, Special Fellow of JICA Research Institute and Professor of Economics at Kobe University.

The research team comprises internationally renowned scholars from diverse disciplines including economics, political science, history, anthropology and law. This composition facilitated the research and analyses of the nature and consequences of interaction between ethnicity and economy that critically depend on historical contingencies, political structure, constitutional design and economic circumstance. I am gratified that scholars of such prominence have worked together as a team for two years.

This book is the first of a series of publications generated by this project. Each chapter discusses different aspects of understanding complex relationships between ethnic diversity and economic performance. One of the main findings is the existence of a vicious circle between ethnic isolationism and economic uncertainty, implying that the causal relations between the two are not one-way but circular. This finding confirms the importance of improving people's economic conditions so that their ethnic identities cannot be manipulated and exploited by political leaders for their own gain. For this purpose, inclusive development that mitigates both horizontal and vertical inequalities among ethnic communities and other groups must be achieved.

This orientation coincides with JICA's basic policy. Since I assumed the presidency of this organisation in 2003, it has incorporated the concept of 'human security' into its core principles and guidelines for aid programming and implementation. To empower people to live with dignity by providing basic economic means is a fundamental condition if we are to prevent recurrence of conflict and bring long-term political stability and sustained economic development to conflict-prone or -affected countries.

I believe that this book demonstrates the potential of interdisciplinary research in identifying the root causes of instability and in elaborating practical policies to transform ethnic diversity into a positive force for inclusive development in Africa. I hope that this volume will help to generate further interest in economic development in Africa in general and the influences of ethnicity in particular, among researchers, practitioners and policy makers.

Sadako Ogata
President
Japan International Cooperation Agency

Preface

Over the last two decades, the macroeconomic performance of most countries in Sub-Saharan Africa has improved substantially, with higher economic growth, lower inflation and improved balance of payments. Over the same period, however, income disparities have widened and poverty has remained entrenched. Social friction associated with greater inequality, as well as pervasive unemployment and underemployment, population growth and increasingly scarce land and water resources, have made many African economies potentially unstable and vulnerable to political and other shocks. Ethnic diversity, highlighted by socio-economic and political inequality, has contributed to ethnic clashes.

Empirical work in development economics has generally shown that ethnic diversity, i.e. the co-existence of numerous distinct ethnic communities in a country, has significantly lowered economic growth in Africa, possibly because it has led to sub-optimal provision of public goods. Moreover, it is generally assumed that ethnic diversity also contributes to heightened economic instability.

But we still need to ask if it can be shown empirically or theoretically that the observed instability of African economies can be attributed to the co-existence of ethnically distinct communities. Other equally important factors may also be at play. It is possible, for example, that it is the political exploitation of ethnic diversity, not diversity in itself, which makes such economies more unstable. One must also ask how far market forces are dominant in African economies, or whether the powers of the state remain even more pervasive than is often assumed. Further still, how fundamental are the differences between the preferences of a country's ethnic communities? Are they different enough to disrupt the ways in which one would normally expect an economy to work?

With a view to providing answers to these difficult questions, the Japan International Cooperation Agency Research Institute (JICA-RI) and the Kobe University Research Institute for Economics and Business

Administration (RIEB) initiated a joint research project in the Spring of 2009. A team of economists, political scientists, economic historians and anthropologists from Africa, Asia, Europe and North America was formed to undertake this research. Since then, this research team has held four conferences at which relevant papers were presented for debate. The first conference was held at Kobe University in July 2009, the second at Yale University in January 2010, the third in Naivasha, Kenya, in November 2010, and the fourth at Oxford University in July 2011. The members of the project team are listed in the Appendix.

This volume represents the first of a collection of papers presented at our conferences. It aims principally to arrive at a diagnosis of the aforementioned issues. A sequel to this volume will be devoted to policies that can help to transform ethnic diversity from a negative to a potentially positive influence, thus contributing to building nations where ethnic communities can work harmoniously to reap the fruits of economic development with growth, stability and equity.

We hope that this book will serve as catalyst, to stimulate further interest in interdisciplinary studies on the subject of ethnicity and development in Sub-Saharan Africa.

Hiroyuki Hino, John Lonsdale,
Gustav Ranis and Frances Stewart

Acknowledgements

This book is a product of a research project entitled 'Ethnic diversity and economic instability in Africa: policies for harmonious development', which was organised and funded jointly by the Japan International Cooperation Agency Research Institute (JICA-RI) and Kobe University Research Institute for Economics and Business Administration (RIEB). We are most grateful to the JICA-RI for financing most of this project, and taking care of its administrative and logistical arrangements. The project was also partly funded by a Grant-in-Aid for Scientific Research from the Ministry of Education, Culture, Sports, Science and Technology, Japan (grant number: 22330085). Views and opinions expressed in the book are those of the authors, and do not necessarily reflect those of JICA or Kobe University.

We would like to express our sincere gratitude to Dr Keiichi Tsunekawa, former Director of JICA-RI, for his support of this project, and especially to Dr Chris Harrison, the Publishing Director of Social Sciences of the Cambridge University Press, for his encouragement, guidance and patience during the preparation of this book. Our thanks also go to the anonymous readers for their most helpful comments. Finally, we wish to thank Ms Elizabeth Wellman for her editorial assistance, Ms Takako Kitano of RIEB for her assistance in the overall management of this research project and Ms Eva Gladwell Mithamo of the Office of the Economic Advisor to the Prime Minister of the Republic of Kenya for her administrative assistance.

Hiroyuki Hino, John Lonsdale,
Gustav Ranis and Frances Stewart

Introduction: Findings of development economics and their limitations

GUSTAV RANIS

Introduction

There seems to be a general consensus in development economics, based on both cross-country regressions and individual country studies, that ethnic diversity, especially in the Sub-Saharan African context, is one of the causal factors behind relatively poor development performance. While much of the past relevant literature focuses on diversity's impact on economic growth, we also have evidence that it adversely affects income distribution and poverty as well as human development. But much less is known about the impact of such diversity on economic stability or instability in Africa.

It is generally accepted that more than two thousand ethnic groups, usually lacking the ability to exit from poverty, find themselves in Sub-Saharan Africa. Although some have expressed the view that land-locked conditions may have contributed to such marked ethnic diversity, the development economics literature generally takes ethnicity as exogenous and invariable over time. Indeed, most of the major findings of development economics fundamentally rest on the assumption that ethnicity is exogenous to democracy, geography and other factors that affect economic development. This is because those findings are derived mostly from the applications of statistical methods (cross-country regressions) which are invalid if this assumption does not hold. This is but one of the reasons why such regressions are, at best, the beginning, not the end, of wisdom.

Economic historians and anthropologists have long argued – correctly – that ethnicity is an identity that evolves over time in response to economic, demographic and political developments. To a large degree,

Paper presented at the Kobe Conference on Ethnic Diversity and Economic Instability in Africa: Policies for Harmonious Development, July 2009. The author would like to thank Hino Hiroyuki for his helpful comments and Yanjing Huang for her competent research assistance.

1

ethnicity is 'constructed' as evidence in Kenya and elsewhere amply demonstrates. Where there is no economic growth or where the economy is unstable, new ethnic alliances may emerge or ethnic antagonisms may be heightened. In other words, ethnicity and economic development (or growth) are mutually dependent – there is no simple, one-way causal relationship as commonly assumed in development economics.

We all agree that it would be a mistake to talk about 'the' African economy. Much of the development economics literature distinguishes African economies between natural-resource-rich country cases, coastal cash crop exporters and land-locked, internally oriented economies, each encompassing approximately one-third of the total population of Sub-Saharan Africa. But to economic historians and political scientists, such a demarcation is inadequate and could mask more fundamental differences.

Historians and anthropologists argue, again correctly, that economic characteristics of African countries – and their relative development – cannot be understood without reference to the impact of colonial administrations on the political and economic institutions in the post-colonial regime in each country. For example why have Botswana and Sierra Leone – both equally rich in diamonds – followed such sharply divergent post-colonial development paths? Equally important, interactions between ethnicity and the market – through trade of natural resources and labour and through contests for land – historically have shaped much economic development in Africa, with influences still in evidence today.

Therefore, long-term economic performance of African economies can be fully understood only on the basis of proper dialogue between economics, history, political science and anthropology. The purpose of this introduction is to provide a starting point for such a dialogue. In what follows we will offer (1) a summary of some of what seems to be known in the development economics literature with respect to the impact of diversity, however defined, on development; and (2) some preliminary hypotheses about diversity and economic volatility. Finally, we will provide a quick guide to the book, and briefly summarise and suggest some future research priorities.

Diversity and development

Following Barro's lead (Barro 1991), some economists have detected no unique African explanation for Africa's poor performance but blame it all on poor policies and the well-known violations of Washington Consensus strictures – including the lack of openness, low savings rates and flawed monetary and fiscal policies – as well as lack of access to the sea, a tropical climate, Dutch disease, corruption and sometimes even the kitchen sink. Sachs and Warner (1997), for example, follow this line of reasoning.

On the other hand, Paul Collier (2007), as well as Collier and Gunning (1999) and Easterly and Levine (1997) point to the importance of ethnic diversity. Collier and Gunning, for example, claim that ethno-linguistic fractionalisation (ELF), accounts for 35 per cent of the growth shortfall in Sub-Saharan Africa, or for 45 per cent if closely linked poor policies are included.[1] José Garcia Montalvo and Marta Reynal-Querol (2005) prefer polarisation as the measure of diversity of greatest relevance in most country cases but share the general view of the importance of diversity's impact on growth.[2]

The main argument being put forward by such authors as Easterly and Levine is that polarised societies cannot agree on needed public goods and are more likely to engage in rent-seeking activities. Collier (1998) similarly points to ELF as reducing trust, increasing transaction costs and adversely affecting development generally. Bates (2000) does not embrace the ELF measure in the same way but agrees to emphasise that contacts and contracts, implicit or explicit, can be quite strong and can promote both human capital and human development within but not across groups. Habyarimana *et al.* (2009) provide a framework for examining ethnic versus rival explanations for the lack of productive collective action.

Most specialists on the subject seem to hold the view that Africa's generally low population density makes it difficult to generate the kind of trust which crosses ethnic boundaries that is required for the provision of public goods. Frequent human contact ensures the creation of the required social capital. Individuals as well as entire clans tend to look at each other and worry about patent inequalities, vertical as well as horizontal, rather than about their absolute levels of welfare. It is in this sense that, in ethnically divided societies, each group has its own

---

[1] ELF is measured by the probability that two randomly chosen individuals in a given country do not belong to the same ethnolinguistic group.
[2] Polarisation is measured by the degree of homogeneity within groups, the degree of heterogeneity across groups plus, most importantly, the small number of similarly sized groups.

egalitarian impulse, but that impulse does not extend across ethnic lines, either by virtue of insurance or altruism. This is in sharp contrast to the case of some of the more densely populated countries of Asia, where land scarcity and labour abundance have led to co-operation across ethnicities, especially in the case of intensive agriculture.

Development economists also argue that strong, within-group loyalty can hurt growth in another way. Namely, it does not pay for the individual member of a clan to be a successful stand-out, i.e. do well or get promoted, if this results in the rest of his extended family descending on him. Anthropologists too find this proposition rather convincing.

To measure ethnic diversity, Alesina *et al.* (2003) favour the ELF, while Reynal-Querol (2002) as well as Esteban and Ray (1994) prefer the concept of polarisation, a closely balanced, and therefore contested, ethnic majority dominance. There are findings showing that low levels of ELF as well as very high levels do not pose as much of a threat to development as intermediate levels. Others conclude that we should really be counting much more on polarisation when two contending parties are very close in terms of their power, which may lead not only to bad policy and bad development outcomes but also to less stability. The correlation between fractionalisation and polarisation is apparently positive and very high at low levels of ELF but zero or even negative at intermediate and high levels.

Diversity and democracy

While many authors have discussed the underlying causes of adverse development outcomes, many issues remain open for discussion, and some of these are by no means irrelevant to understanding the relationship between ethnicity and economic development. Issues which remain open for debate include the importance of initial conditions, including colonial heritage, natural resource endowment, the role of institutions, broadly defined, as well as the relevance of the extent of democracy (or lack thereof) in affecting the relationship linking diversity, growth and stability.

With respect to the initial conditions, the relative abundance of land and the low level of population density have already been mentioned. While economists are generally ready to accept kinship relationships as exogenously given, there can be little doubt that they are a substitute for social security networks and that any inequality in the initial distribution of land and other assets has historically permitted clan elites to capture the commanding heights of politics. Unlike the case of the more homogeneous Asian superfamilies, we have here smaller kinship-loyal families, sustaining co-operation within the group, but without altruism travelling across ethnicities. Consequently, increased diversity leads to less collective action with respect to public goods and, at the aggregate level, to more engagement in free-riding, consequent lower growth and some of the other aforementioned adverse developmental outcomes.

As Avner Greif (1993) has also emphasised, citing European historical evidence, legal and political institutions foster intra-elite co-operation but inter-group non-co-operation. The same asymmetry exists with respect to social capital, relatively strong within ethnic groups but not extending across these groups. Within groups, there is bonding going on, which is relatively weak across groups. Bridging across groups is, of course, difficult, even if better for optimisation in the economic sense. The greater the extent of diversity, the more internal bonding occurs, with less bridging.

The strength of natural resource endowments represents another important dimension of the initial conditions. Natural resources are an important cause of the likely asymmetry between different ethnic groups, depending on the vagaries of nature and culminating in the reduced incentive of those blessed with relative abundance to provide public goods to others. In Nigeria, for example, a minority ethnic group sitting on oil is demanding a larger provision of national public goods, currently creating conflict. Moreover, resource-dominant groups are likely to suffer from some manifestation of the so-called natural resource curse, encouraging rent-seeking and weakening the pressure for economic or institutional reforms, all of which, of course, contribute to sustained unequal distributions of income, both of the vertical and horizontal type.

In this setting, local public goods are always preferred over national public goods and the same sort of asymmetries affect the overall quality of social capital which is based on intensive trust within rather than across groups. As Jonathan Temple (1998) points out, an initial unequal distribution of income generally affects development negatively. Similarly, Knack and Keefer (1997) support the position that trust is more pronounced, *ceteris paribus*, when incomes are more equally distributed.

Clearly, the spillover of social capital across ethnic boundaries, as well as the willingness to provide national public goods, depends very much on the overall distribution of income, both of the vertical and horizontal types, which are, to some extent, overlapping. As Fosu *et al.* (2006) point out, heterogeneous societies are better at private goods provision, working through the market, but not very good at providing public goods. Greif emphasises that land or mineral rights are usually critical and are not at all helped by dysfunctional institutions which obstruct egalitarian outcomes. Kinship groups can be useful in the private sector, as ethnic minorities benefit. But in the public sector they can be harmful because ethnic majorities benefit. What is not clear and what is worthy of investigation is whether diversity improves the quality of private goods via an increase in variety.

All of this argues for the possible importance of decentralisation. There exists, of course, a large volume of literature concerning vertical decentralisation, both pro and con, with the pros emphasising that local communities have more information and that they are likely to contain much less ethnic diversity than those at the centre, and the cons pointing to the greater likelihood that local elites will dominate. Vertical decentralisation is seen as reducing friction but may also, as some authors point out, lead to the creation of regional parties with less interest in public goods at the national level. In other words, if too many groups form at the local level, none is strong enough to control the state and none is in a position to mobilise an 'encompassing interest', *à la* Mancur Olson, at the national level. Diversity fosters trust within groups and, while vertical decentralisation is helpful at the local level, it reduces trust at the national level, as well as the provision of public goods, with results already referred to.

Others, including Bardhan and Mookherjee (2000), express some concern about the enhanced possibilities for corruption at the local level, often dominated by local elites. But the comparison between corruption at central and local levels is an unresolved issue that can only be settled by empirical, individual country analysis. In any case, with vertical decentralisation leading to smaller jurisdictions exhibiting less diversity, ELF is reduced, but there is a greater danger of polarisation with, for example, a large minority opposing the central government, as pointed out by Yuichi Sasaoka (2007). The fact is that most central governments are in the hands of a small elite using public goods to exercise patronage of one kind or another, mostly in the form of civil service employment.

Much less attention is devoted in the literature to another kind of decentralisation – the horizontal type – shifting power from the executive, especially the finance ministry, to other ministries, to the legislative branches at all levels, as well as to the judiciary, thus providing greater access for minorities, which can make a large difference (Brancati 2006). Trust can be strongly influenced by such an independent judiciary, a feature rarely in evidence.

As far as I can surmise, the jury is still out with respect to the impact of democracy on all this. Alesina *et al.* (2003) have reported diversity as less serious in democracies because minorities are more likely to feel represented. Barro (1996) finds that democracy enhances growth at low levels of income and depresses it at intermediate levels. Most of the parliamentary systems turn out to be more stable than presidential ones, especially when there are many clans represented by various political parties. With ethnic diversity more pronounced at the centre, a diverse society benefits more from democracy, and a more competitive political system lowers rent-seeking and increases efficiency. Bates *et al.* (2004) report that authoritarian governments lower innovative capacity (TFP) and thus impede growth as well as development in other dimensions.

On the other hand, Besley and Kudamatsu (2007) point out that autocratic regimes may be extremely effective, possibly performing better than democracies if the electorate is sufficiently well organised. If central government elites are sedentary bandits, this may lead to resistance, possibly violence and lower growth, something that Bates *et al.* call 'a political trap'. But if the bandits are of the roving type, this is more likely to generate instability as public goods become exceedingly scarce and are fought over. To conclude that democracy has little impact on growth but could have an impact on stability is a subject to which we shall return.

The role of markets in development in Africa is another open issue. In the private sector, minority kinship groups benefit from its relative impersonality while, in the public sector, minority kinship groups are disadvantaged and majorities benefit. Therefore, the ruling elite usually prefer the public sector, even if it is less efficient. With respect to particular production sectors, in agriculture the majority of kinship groups usually eschew social capital beyond their own jurisdiction. In industry, to which minority groups are likely to gravitate, they benefit from the relatively larger, more urban, private activity. Hence, for any given distribution of political and economic resources, one might expect a more market-oriented, arm's length, impersonal system to be superior in terms of developmental outcomes. However, markets may also accentuate or even create horizontal inequalities, especially given an initial unequal distribution of natural resources (Mukherji 2009). Moreover, a strong market orientation is often associated with a lower level of public goods. It therefore gives minorities less of an obligation to respect the state in terms of taxes or any other indication of support.

Diversity and volatility

In contrast to the nexus of diversity, democracy and development discussed above, very little research to date has focused on the relationship between diversity and instability. We therefore present a number of preliminary hypotheses which may hopefully help stimulate future research.

There can be little doubt that the unequal distribution of natural resource wealth across different clans can be a cause of instability, as those who are not favoured by nature are likely to object and provoke political instability, leading to economic instability. There is clearly a tendency for those blessed by nature to deny public goods to the rest of the body politic across ethnic borders, if only to yield sporadically, when under pressure. This may be one reason why it has been found in several empirical studies that the intermediate level of diversity, as measured by the ELF, leads to the worst case of political instability and, therefore, economic instability.

Terms-of-trade fluctuations are likely to be another major source of instability, especially affecting the commercially advantaged clans relative to those which are less advantaged. There is ample evidence that terms-of-trade fluctuations have very much affected growth in Sub-Saharan Africa. It would not require much additional research to show that, within particular countries, the more diverse the society, the more likely that terms-of-trade fluctuations will lead to fluctuations in development, including growth, poverty and income distribution outcomes, since they are bound to affect different groups differently. Exposure to terms-of-trade volatility indeed is 50 per cent higher in Sub-Saharan

Africa than in other developing countries, after controlling for differences in income per capita. Food insecurity, also unequally affecting different clans and currently on the rise, can similarly enhance economic volatility and therefore demands analysis.

In addition, terms-of-trade fluctuations are usually managed poorly by governments (Ranis 1991). During downturns a government typically tries to supplement demand via government budget deficits and monetary expansion, while, during upturns, it becomes very bullish and tries to further enhance growth by means of foreign borrowing and, once again, domestic expansionary fiscal and monetary policies. Such asymmetry over the cycle often ultimately leads to crisis, to the imposition of import restrictions, to devaluations, and to other sudden changes in overall policy, all in a system under duress, all of which has the effect of generating instability. Easterly *et al.* (1993) indicate that terms-of-trade shocks explain much of the growth fluctuation in Africa. Country characteristics matter of course, but policies matter less than the extent of externally caused volatility, affecting different groups differently. Internal policies may add to the problem. For example, export marketing boards, which are still prevalent in some countries, have erratic price-setting policies, often favouring the commercialised regions of a country and contributing to overall volatility. To reduce such boom-and-bust oscillations one needs a democracy with relatively strong checks and balances, as, for example, in the Botswana diamond case.

It can also be assumed that frequent political turnover and regime change, which has been an endemic feature of much of Sub-Saharan Africa, leads not only to political but also to economic instability. It should not be difficult to trace the number of coups, changes in government and even ministers of finance, as causal agents in this respect. Oscillation between a market orientation and a controls orientation in policy, which is often referred to as sub-optimal for development generally, can also be considered a likely cause of instability, especially if these decisions are the result of continuous bargaining between different ethnic groups and the central government. Power-sharing as a solution, via proportional representation, mutual veto and decentralisation (Lijphart 1977) has not been much in evidence in Africa.

Decentralisation may also be a cause for concern. If it takes the usual form of delegation or deconcentration, instead of true devolution to local bodies in the form of fiscal decentralisation, reliance on the centre's funds for public goods is retained. This maintains power in the hands of those who control lives and is likely to lead to lobbying, continuous bargaining, uncertainty, conflict and economic fluctuations. As Kimenyi (2006) points out, ethnic heterogeneity leads to the under-provision of non-excludable public goods, but it favours excludable patronage goods. Resistance against this system from minorities risks higher instability, especially if combined with the central government's inequitable tax and other direct interventions in favour of the elite, permitting trust to fluctuate and decline over time. Of course, if clan population proportions change, especially in closely split polarised societies, another reason for volatility makes its appearance. The possibility of alternating roving and stationary bandit regimes is not at all unrealistic and is also relevant to the issue of instability.

Another source of instability results from the gradual shift in much of Sub-Saharan Africa from traditional communal land ownership, with virtually unlimited supplies of land, to private ownership and modern property rights, as land shortage, combined with population increase, leads to titling, insecurity and volatility.

Finally, agents of globalisation may well contribute to economic instability. Examples here include the following:

(1) Remittances from abroad may be aggravating horizontal and vertical inequality because certain better-off ethnic communities are more able to adapt and migrate abroad.

(2) Unequal development of private capital markets is also likely to have a differential impact on different ethnic groups.

(3) It is no secret that foreign aid agencies often play favourites, supporting natural resource-rich regions or politically attractive clans from their own foreign policy points of view, thus exacerbating both horizontal and vertical inequalities and causing political as well as economic instability. More generally, multilateral financial institutions and bilateral aid agencies have not been sufficiently aware of or sensitive to the impact of the policies they advocate and the projects they implement on the provision of public goods to different communities, causing horizontal inequalities. Aid-funded projects are likely to induce rent-seeking, favour the affluent, weaken the social fabric and represent instability – creating political and economic shocks. Moreover donors are often driven to make abrupt changes in the priority they attach to different sectors or regions.

(4) Non-governmental organisations (NGOs), which are increasingly numerous in quantity and influential in terms of resources, but weak in terms of cohesion and accountability, are also often found to be competing with each other and jockeying for favour among privileged ethnic groups, thus making a contribution to an increase in volatility.

(5) Finally, it is generally acknowledged that global warming has been associated with an increased incidence of different kinds of natural disaster. As such exogenous shocks become more frequent they are prone to contribute increasingly to instability in Sub-Saharan Africa, customarily affecting the poorer groups as well as different ethnic groups disproportionately. Receding rangelands, a consequence of desertification, is threatening the livelihood of pastoralists. Drying rivers are reducing cultivable lands. The frequency of tsunamis and the threat of rising ocean levels are increasing. Such shocks are sure to cause inter-community or ethnic conflicts, and to produce 'climate change refugees'. In other words, climate change will likely increase economic instability in the ethnically diverse countries of Africa.

Introduction to the book and some concluding thoughts

In the overview of the development economics literature presented above, I have tried to cite as many as possible of the known facts and conclusions that have come to my attention from research on the subject of the impact of diversity on growth. I have also presented best guesses, not yet based on the literature, of what causal links between diversity and instability might be worthy of future examination.

This book offers to move beyond the main findings of development economics, begins to broaden the scope and depth of analyses and elaborates new hypotheses. We will do so by generating a dialogue among economics, economic history, political science and anthropology.

In Part I, we seek to gain a fuller understanding of ethnicity as it relates to the economy. John Lonsdale (Chapter 1) sees himself as providing the historian's contingent piece of grit in the economists' model oyster. Believing in the unpredictable interdependence of ethnicity and economy, and in the different implications of different markets (in land, labour, power, foodstuffs etc.), he rejects the utility of ELF, arguing that new vertical inequalities within intra-ethnic moral economies are as politically significant as new inter-ethnic horizontal inequalities, and suggests that the modern reversal of Africa's factor values between land and labour needs to be at the centre of analysis. Brown and Langer, economists, then show that how diversity is best measured clearly depends on the empirical reality and the question being asked (Chapter 2). Surveys (e.g. Afro Barometer) have also revealed that while ethnicity is one of the important identities in most African countries, its relative prominence shifts over time, depending on political and economic circumstances (e.g. Chandra 2009). Bethwell Ogot, an African historian (Chapter 3), then argues that 'negative ethnicity', comprising ethnic characteristics that negatively affect politics and economy, is by no means a universal quality of ethnicity in Africa, and subsequently explains how it arose historically.

In Part II, we investigate whether ethnic diversity is indeed a causal factor of the poor economic performance of Africa. We offer three distinct perspectives from constitutionalism, political history and spatial economics. Yash Ghai, constitutional scholar, reviews the history and the current state of constitutionalism in Africa (Chapter 4). His review leads to a conclusion that true respect for constitutionalism has largely been absent in Africa because ethnic trust and allegiances allowed post-colonial elites to create nationhood where economy – and civil society – was subordinated by the state. Under such conditions, market economy has remained unable to function since independence. Bruce Berman, political scientist and historian (Chapter 5), argues that one must understand ethnicity and markets in historical context since there is no straightforward causal relationship between ethnicity and economic instability. One must analyse the impact of colonial and post-colonial states on the construction of markets and ethnic communities, including the horizontal inequalities between and the vertical inequalities within ethnic groups. More recently, neo-liberal structural adjustment policies have both undermined states and sharpened the economic inequalities and instabilities that have in turn exacerbated inter-ethnic conflicts.

On the other hand, armed with district level data of actual ethnic composition in Kenya, Nobuaki Hamaguchi, an economist (Chapter 6), finds that the existence of ethnically similar communities in proximity raises the per capita income of that district, which suggests that ethnic diversity could potentially be welfare enhancing due to gains from trade between ethnic communities with different economic strengths.

But because of territorial confinement, ethnic dissimilarity works like physical distance, and thus limits gains from trade to a cluster of ethnically similar communities.

In Part III, we attempt to gain a more cohesive understanding of the relationship between ethnic diversity and stability, based on inferences from anthropology, quantitative analyses and economic experiments. Parker Shipton, an anthropologist, argues that territorial confinement of ethnic communities has exacerbated the pressures of a rapidly rising population, increasingly scarce land and eroding soil fertility, and has aggravated already severe economic hardship (Chapter 7). This has led ethnic communities to become even more inward-looking and to seek protection of their own interests, which further raises economic instability and uncertainty. Shipton's hypothesis is that the restriction of movement of Africans – imposed by the national borders of rich countries and harsh geography – is a major contributor to the territorial confinement.

Brown and Stewart (Chapter 8) model a number of relationships that may determine economic instability as I conjectured above. They find that ethnic diversity itself does not appear to be correlated with instability. Rather, it is the degree of inequality among ethnic groups (horizontal inequality) that is closely correlated with instability. To test whether ethnicity influences stability and the welfare quality of the market economy, Shimomura and Yamato (Chapter 9) conduct market experiments in which individuals belonging to two ethnic groups exchange two goods. The preferences of the people engaged in exchange and the distribution of the initial endowments are controlled in order to derive the pure effects of ethnicity. The experiments were conducted in Kenya. The results showed that trading between ethnic groups can stabilise markets and also bring about a more equitable outcome. However, more thorough experiments will have to be conducted before definitive conclusions can be derived.

Looking further ahead, it is suggested that careful attention be given to decentralisation, which may be stabilising if it is accompanied by fiscal devolution, but not if the centre retains the bulk of resources and is able to favour culturally aligned groups and those already favoured by nature at the local level. Thus, the best sequence seems to be economic reforms followed by both political and fiscal decentralisation. Comparative studies of constitutions and the extent of adherence to them are relevant. The role of foreign capital, especially foreign aid and NGO flows – possibly, but not necessarily contributing to instability – must be examined.

The basic normative issue before us is how enhanced and non-volatile trust can be generated in the presence of diversity and how the related issue of sustainably encouraging the provision of national public goods can best be tackled. This is where economic historians, anthropologists, political scientists and development economists can most usefully apply their combined talents. As Platteau and Baland (1994), aptly put it 'how generalized trust … can be established … is probably one of the most challenging questions confronting development scholars'.

References

Alesina, Alberto, Devleeschauwer, Arnaud, Easterly, William, Kurlat, Sergio and Wacziarg, Romain 2003. *Fractionalization*. NBER Working Papers 9411. Cambridge, MA: National Bureau of Economic Research.

Bardhan, Pranab K. and Mookherjee, Dilip 2000. 'Capture and Governance at Local and National Levels', *American Economic Review* 90: 135–9.

Barro, Robert J. 1991. 'Economic Growth in a Cross Section of Countries', *The Quarterly Journal of Economics* 106: 407–43.

    1996. 'Democracy and Growth', *Journal of Economic Growth* 1: 1–27.

Bates, Robert H. 2000. 'Ethnicity and Development in Africa: a Reappraisal', *American Economic Review* 90: 131–4.

Bates, Robert H., Greif, Avner, Humphreys, Macartan and Singh, Smita 2004. *Institutions and Development*. Center for International Development Working Paper 107 (September), Harvard Kennedy School, Cambridge, MA.

Besley, Timothy J. and Kudamatsu, Masayuki 2007. *Making Autocracy Work*. Centre for Economic Policy Research Discussion Paper 6371 (June), London.

Brancati, Dawn 2006. 'Decentralization: Fueling the Fire or Dampening the Flames of Ethnic Conflict and Secessionism?', *International Organization* 60: 651–85.

Brown, Graham and Langer, Arnim 2010. *Conceptualizing and Measuring Ethnicity*. Japan International Cooperation Agency Research Institute (JICA-RI) Working Papers 9, JICA-RI, Tokyo, Japan.

Chandra, Kanchan 2009. 'Design Measures of Ethnic Identity: the Problems of Overlap and Incompleteness', *Qualitative and Multi-Method Research* 7 (1), 36–40.

Collier, Pau. 1998. *The Political Economy of Ethnicity*. Working Papers Series 98, Centre for the Study of African Economies, Oxford University.
2007. *Growth Strategies for Africa*. A Paper Prepared for the Spence Commission on Economic Growth (January), Centre for the Study of African Economies, Department of Economics, Oxford University.
Collier, Paul and Gunning, Jan-Willem 1999. 'Explaining African Economic Performance', *Journal of Economic Literature* 37: 64–111.
Easterly, William and Levine, Ross 1997. 'Africa's Growth Tragedy: Policies and Ethnic Divisions', *The Quarterly Journal of Economics* 112: 1,203–50.
Easterly, William, Kremer, Michael, Pritchett, Lant and Summers, Lawrence H. 1993. 'Good Policy or Good Luck?: Country Growth Performance and Temporary Shocks', *Journal of Monetary Economics* 32: 459–83.
Esteban, Joan and Ray, Debraj 1994. 'On the Measurement of Polarization', *Econometrica* 62: 819–51.
Fosu, Augustin, Bates, Robert and Hoeffler, Anke 2006. 'Institutions, Governance and Economic Development in Africa: an Overview', *Journal of African Economies* 15: 1–9.
Greif, Avner 1993. 'Contract Enforceability and Economic Institutions in Early Trade: the Maghribi Traders' Coalition', *American Economic Review* 83: 525–48.
Habyarimana, James, Humphreys, Macartan, Posner, Dan and Weinstein, Jeremy 2009. *Coethnicity: Diversity and the Dilemmas of Collective Action*. New York: Russell Sage Foundation.
Kimenyi, Mwangi Samson 2006. 'Ethnicity, Governance and the Provision of Public Goods', *Journal of African Economies* 15 (1), 62–99.
Knack, S., and Keefer, P. (1997). 'Does Social Capital Have an Economic Payoff? A Cross-country Investigation', *Quarterly Journal of Economics* 112 (4): 1,251–88.
Lijphart, Arend 1977. *Democracy in Plural Societies: a Comparative Exploration*. New Haven, CT: Yale University Press.
Montalvo, José G. and Reynal-Querol, Marta 2005. 'Ethnic Polarization, Potential Conflict, and Civil Wars', *American Economic Review* 95 (3): 796–816.
Platteau, Jean-Phillipe and Baland, J. M. 1994. *Does Heterogeneity Hinder Collective Action?* Papers 146, Notre-Dame de la Paix, Sciences Economiques et Sociales.
Ranis, Gustav 1991. 'The Political Economy of Development Policy Change', in *Politics and Policy Making in Developing Countries: Perspectives on the New Political Economy*, Meier, G. (ed.). San Francisco, CA: International Center for Economic Growth, ICS Press.

Reynal-Querol, Marta 2002. 'Ethnicity, political systems and civil wars', *Journal of Conflict Resoultion* 46 (1): 29–54.

Sachs, Jeffrey D. and Warner, Andrew M. 1997. 'Sources of Slow Growth in African Economies', *Journal of African Economies* 6 (3): 335–76.

Sasaoka, Yuichi 2007. 'Decentralization and Conflict', presented at Wilton Park Conference on Conflict Prevention and Development Cooperation in Africa, UK (8–11 Nov.).

Temple, Jonathan 1998. 'Initial Conditions, Social Capital, and Growth in Africa', *Journal of African Economies* 7 (3): 309–47.

PART I

Demystifying ethnicity

1 | Ethnic patriotism and markets in African history

JOHN LONSDALE

Introduction: the contingencies of history

My purpose is to warn against any 'law' claiming to relate ethnicity and markets. I offer, instead, complexity, contingency and context – and for three reasons. Firstly, I am an historian and attempts to devise 'laws of history' have ended in analytical tears, while attempts to bend history to any such law end in monstrous regimes. Secondly, both the idea of ethnicity and the experience of ethnic groups resist definition or prediction, as other contributors agree. Finally, markets differ in their social impact according to what is traded and how it is produced.

My first reason for caution, then, is disciplinary. Economists – although my fellow contributors show admirable caution – like to devise algebraic models of causation and then 'shock' them with awkward facts. Historians know that the past delivers shocks as a matter of course. History may appear to show us similarities or analogies and to teach lessons but appearances deceive; the past obeys no law nor does it repeat itself. History, as Bethwell Ogot, Kenya's senior historian has said, is a discipline of contexts, and all contexts differ (Falola and Odhiambo 2002).

Historians have learned from the fate of the two schools of history with the most ambitious causal models, Marxist historiography and its antithesis, *Annales*. Marxists believed history moved, indeed advanced, thanks to a contradiction between successive modes of production, pre-capitalist and capitalist for example, and their social relations, such as feudal and bourgeois. Their dialectical opposition inflamed class struggle. This would bring in proletarian dictatorship and then the withering away of the state on a global scale. Actual history has not been like that. The most persuasive attempt to correct this

I am grateful for comments from colleagues: David Anderson, Bruce Berman, Phil Bonner, Hino Hiroyuki, Carola Lentz, Enocent Msindo, Henry Oyugi, Frances Stewart and Richard Waller. None bears responsibility for my conclusions.

teleology – by invoking Gramsci's concept of 'hegemony' or popularly acceptable inequality – has been the most contradictory in rescuing materialist history with a lifeline of ideas.

The French *Annales* school, by contrast, was largely anti-Marxist in origin. It emphasised not history's dynamics but its continuities because, it was argued, friction between three different layers of time hindered all change. Economic geography filled the bottom layer of time; it was almost immobile. Human *mentalités* at a middle level, therefore, were slow to change, only in the *longue durée* – as, for instance, from an age of faith to one of reason. At the top, on the surface of history, people imagined they exercised rational choice in pursuing their strategic advantage, but that was because they mistook daily 'events' for significant change. Even 'great men' were constrained in their choices by the time-lags beneath them. It was an interesting approach but could not explain the revolutionary changes of modern times. The *Annales* school has in consequence had more influence in medieval rather than modern European history.

A third grand theory, 'modernisation' – a Marxist heresy in which markets, literacy, wage labour and other modern goods would, without class conflict, cause small ethnic loyalties to surrender to large national ones – has been refuted by the widespread local, more often than national, resistance to globalisation.

Many historians have reacted to these disappointments in determinism by taking up 'history from below', and this interest in the lives of the disregarded people of the past further reinforces a focus on difference and detail at the expense of structure and strategy. I myself take what seems useful from the first two opposed schools of history while also exploring history 'from below'. From *Annales* I borrow immobile history and the *longue durée* to discuss how ecology and demography affect power, markets and ethnic *mentalités*. From my earlier Marxism I still think class formation to be an historical force but, in another heresy, one that acts only within specific cultures that one can call ethnic or national. Their culture is what teaches people the value of their labour power in Marxist terms or, more simply, their human dignity (Kenyatta 1938; Marx 1973: 105, 283–7, 325–6, 408–9, 494–5). It is the loss or threatened loss of that dignity through the alienation of one's labour that fires up self-defence. Marxists thought ethnicity a 'false consciousness', in the misguided belief that culture was not a relation of production. But one's ethnicity is a 'language of class', since cultures are shaped by 'moral economies' – all those presumed rights and duties that, despite social inequality, carry sufficient legitimacy (Gramsci's hegemony) to shape people's rational choices in their pursuit of a material gain that is worthless without security and trust, honour and reputation (Siméant 2010; Stedman Jones 1983; Thompson 1993).[1]

To sum up my historian's approach, I visualise three levels of causation. At the bottom, almost immobile before the twentieth century, Africa's demography put a high price on scarce labour while holding abundant land cheap.[2] At a middle level, political power before, during and after colonial rule affects social mobility and regional inequality and, therefore, ethnic *mentalités* or discursive traditions. Finally, on history's surface but informed by the moral criteria of their traditions, people seek self-mastery, clientelist equity, or neighbourly trust – subject only to the one law all historians accept, that of unintended consequences. Historians are Keynesian; we assume that 'animal spirits' enliven all allegedly impersonal markets. Our models are agent-based and unpredictable. History's grit may shock the economists' model oyster, but that is how pearls are made.

Secondly, to get closer to our topic, *ethnicity* takes many different forms, like 'the joker in a card-game'.[3] It is a relational concept of social belonging that adjusts to changing situations. Like *annalistes'* time, belonging is layered. We all have several identities – ethnic, national, gendered, generational, religious, occupational, class and so on. Our ethnicity, although often our most deeply felt community of belonging, interacts with our other identity layers or hyphenated attributes.[4] Which one occupies our self-interested imagination at any time will vary. How far we are aware of our ethnicity varies too. It is a universal quality: it civilises us, each in our culturally distinctive way, but it is often unconscious, as we strive to live up to the only social norms we know. Conscious ethnicity is Janus-faced, like nationhood. It may be a productive, inclusive instinct for inter-ethnic civility or market gain. It can as well instil a destructively exclusive sense of belonging that

---

[1] See also my next section and Chapter 5 by Bruce Berman.
[2] See the Introduction by Gustav Ranis.
[3] Lentz (1995: 304). For successive literature surveys, see Young (1982: 71–98); Lentz (1995); Berman (1998); Spear (2003); Bates (2006); Waller (2011).
[4] See Chapter 8 by Graham Brown and Frances Stewart for ethnicity's varied contextual value by comparison with religion, occupation and gender.

defies all arguments for seemingly more rational constructs of self-interest and social trust.

In Africa, ethnic hostility often stems from regional or 'horizontal' inequalities in wealth, power, education or reputation, since ethnic groups, not least in Kenya, generally retain regional 'homelands' even when these exist only in the folk-memory of migrant townspeople.[5] But, as some of my case studies show, changes in social differentiation or 'vertical' inequality within an ethnic group can cause still fiercer conflict about how to reinterpret moral economy. Internal stress may foster external aggression, as a form of political displacement. The ethnic groups we seek to understand have not only external relations but also internal histories. To measure only a country's ethnic fragmentation or its demographic polarity – both external relations – in order to predict economic effects, is a risky, one-eyed enterprise.[6]

Analysts of ethnicity are commonly divided into three schools – primordial, instrumental and constructivist. *Primordialists* think in terms of separate origins, unchanging 'custom' and bounded distinctiveness over time, not least in language. *Instrumentalists* think ethnic groups act mainly as competitive teams – recruited by elite strategists who appeal to fictive kinship as the most efficient bond of solidarity. Marxists argued that black bourgeoisies, like white rulers or capitalists before them, used ethnic division to break up hostile lower-class solidarities. But in 'subaltern instrumentalities' the poor can also press claims for generous patronage on their elite 'kin' (Bates 1974). *Constructivists*, the most recent school of analysis, observe that ethnic groups change in consciousness and composition thanks less to strategic need than to social processes that generate norms of moral economy, to which even elites must respond.

But, again, analytical impurity has its advantages. These approaches offer more insight in combination than singly. Ethnic groups acquire internal cohesion and a sense of difference from – not always hostile to – 'others' in countless negotiations of innovation and resistance that change their moral and social markers over time (Feierman 1990). This socially constructed cohesion is available for instrumental use by political or economic entrepreneurs whose most seductive, if

---

[5] For horizontal and vertical inequalities see Chapter 8 by Brown and Stewart; for Kenya's ethnic 'blockiness', Chapter 7 by Parker Shipton.
[6] See Chapter 2 by Graham K. Brown and Arnim Langer.

misleading, call to solidarity is that 'we' are all one family, despite our inequalities and conflicts – and always have been. Readiness to form rival teams of common 'blood' seems to be a primordial human instinct, against the complex grain of history and often against our apparent self-interest, especially when invited to become cannon fodder for the sake of 'king and country'. Yet, crucially – something neglected by all three interpretive schools – ethnic groups are also moral communities, potentially able to resist instrumental exploitation and to re-examine moral economy.

It was partly because it suggested that Africans, like others, had multiple identities with debatable possibilities that scholars preferred the term ethnicity to tribe. 'Tribe' suggests a primordial backwardness hostile to both social change and plural identity. It also, equally misleadingly, suggests a small group of men directly descended from one ancestral core and obedient to a common 'tradition', hostile to 'others'. Such groups seem naturally adapted to frontier isolation, but appearances deceive. They are more likely to be frontier splinters of larger language-groups or culture-groups, or composites of several such pioneer fragments (Kopytoff 1987). Linear descent is a convenient myth so long as inter-ethnic marriage is a necessary insurance policy. Seemingly simple tribes are best seen as masks for complexity. In any case they represent but one end of a social spectrum, using frontier inaccessibility to prevent some larger power from exploiting them. At the other end of the spectrum stand the three main language groups of Nigeria – Hausa, Igbo and Yoruba – each of around 30 million people. Their members cannot possibly know each other, they have overlapping identities unrelated to their ethnicity; they are an 'imagined community' as much as any nation – which is what they call themselves. Yet within the still larger Nigerian composite nation they are 'tribes'. Segmentary opposition between nation and tribe can cascade still further down, so that within the Yoruba or Igbo nations, smaller 'tribes' cluster round their respective 'hometowns' which, being markets, are cosmopolitan. Ethnicity resists definition because it is a sliding scale.

Finally, to conclude my introduction, *markets* are social and political rather than impersonal institutions. As a West African informant told a researcher half a century ago: '[W]hen I get [to the market] I look for three persons: my girl friend, my debtor, and my enemy ... And when I go to the market and do not see them all, the market is not good' (Skinner 1962: 270). Markets are as subjectively varied as ethnicity. They can encourage inter-ethnic co-operation as well as competition. Wide ethnic diaspora and tight ethnic protection of specialised skills can both promote market trust. Production of human capital is equally contradictory. It seems best built within an ethnic community that learns ecological wisdom through time or collectively pays the next generation's school fees – but such continuity is often mothered by inter-ethnic marriage. Markets in foods, tools and cloth, perhaps in consequence, have flourished in multi-ethnic contexts. Labour markets, slave or free, as my case studies show, can argue for inclusive, porous ethnic identity in one era and exclusive chauvinisms in another. All markets are different: 'not everything is ultimately interchangeable for everything else'.[7]

Markets may transform social relations vertically, between rich and poor or old and young, and horizontally, between ethnic groups. Analyses of how inter-ethnic relations affect economic development focus on horizontal inequalities. I attach more importance to how changing vertical inequalities disturb the internal moral economies that are Africa's main indigenous source of political thought (Lonsdale 2004).

It would be possible to sum up my approach with contingent dichotomies that portray ethnic groups as small bands of seemingly primordial origin *and/or* as nations of millions, multi-ethnic in origin; as inclusive diaspora, associations of international trust *and/or* the embodiment of regional rivalry for power within a nation-state; as paper categories of population, language and civil law invented for the bureaucratic convenience of tax-collectors, biblical translators and employers, *and/or* historically imagined moral communities, cradles of self-discipline and social responsibility; as mutual aid societies for urban security and improvement *and/or* warlord-led mafias; as competitive electoral constituencies *and/or* vote-banks intimidated by autocratic bosses with vigilante 'youth wings' at their heel.

One could rest content with these complications. Or one might protest that ethnicity is only one, dependent, variable in Africa's disappointing economic history. Other less mobile factors may be of greater significance: an old continent's eroded soils, scarce minerals (until modern mining capital or today's oil), few navigable rivers, tropical diseases unchecked by annual winters, volatile climate, demographic

---

[7] To quote Shipton, in Chapter 7.

weakness, and, now, the contradiction between neo-liberal economic conditionality and obstacles put in the path of labour migration, once Africa's most dynamic economic activity.[8, 9] Or, despite my cautions, my *annaliste*-Marxist mix may suggest an argument. How far it offers guidance for future policy is, naturally, debatable.

Moral ethnicity and political tribalism: patriotisms in the *longue durée*

My argument is that in the past three centuries there has been one fundamental change in African history, what *annalistes* call a 'conjuncture', when different layers of time changed together: population, power and the ethnic *mentalités* underlying political choice. But there have been other, less profound, conjunctures, too (Braudel 1973 [1949]: 892–900).

The chief conjuncture occurred in the short century of colonial rule from c. 1885 to c. 1975. I say 'occurred in' since the building of colonial conquest-states was not the only change that forced Africans to reconsider their ethnically constitutive moral economies and strategic politics. Of arguably equal importance were peace, accelerating population growth, the rising value of land, new forms of urbanisation and labour mobility, and the expansion of (largely Christian) literacy. Together, these changes raised awareness of ethnic difference, hardened boundaries and stimulated inter-ethnic competition. Just as importantly, they also made ethnic publics more critically aware of their internal moral economies. The most decisive conjunctural element was, very probably, the reversal in factor values between land and labour, as the one rose and the other fell in price.

To take these five changes in turn: peace, first, made social boundaries still more porous than before, even dangerously so. In past centuries 'big men', chiefs and kings had exercised some control over the assimilation of dependent strangers, as war captives, nubile women, famished pawns or useful clients. The colonial pax now freed or forced large numbers of virile young men to cross boundaries in search of the means to marry or pay tax. They could be disturbingly less subservient to local norms and hierarchies. By the 1950s population growth, next,

---

[8] Iliffe (1995); and Chapter 6, by Nobuaki Hamaguchi.
[9] Compare Chapter 5 by Berman and Chapter 7 by Shipton.

had in any case made people less willing to absorb immigrants. Wealth had once lain in the control of scarce people, kin or client, slave or free, raided or traded for their skills and sweat (Guyer and Belinga 1995; Miller 1988). Now agrarian capitalism, thirdly, placed a premium on titled ownership of land, to defend it against the claims of juniors or migrant strangers.[10] But the continuing loss of labour power from rural households to alien towns added a fourth, gendered, context in which to re-think belonging: the urban freedoms available to unruly women made men nervous. Finally, if ethnicity constitutes a moral community, then literacy extended the number of public moralists and the range of comparisons they could draw with other peoples and periods (not least the biblical children of Israel), in judging their own situation.[11] Each local realm of the word was more sharply defined by a print vernacular standardised by African and missionary translators (Landau 1995) – but Europeans could never enter nor control these intimate societal conversations.

Alien rule did, however, help to shape discursive arenas.[12] Power tends to divide. It is a scarce good that exists by excluding others; it is dangerous. But it works by offering opportunity, sharing authority and privilege with a few. Colonial power was more exclusionary and divisive than most other forms of rule but needed African allies. White officials sought legitimacy by treating 'tribes' as nations, co-opting chiefs as 'tribal' patrons. This use of African division helped, conversely, to shape the ethnic colonisation of the state apparatus from below. But Africans had to re-imagine for themselves the inner morality and external politics of their new strategies of belonging and opportunity. The once-supposed colonial ability to 'invent' African ethnicities is increasingly under question.[13] African imaginations could also take directions contrary to those of their rulers. To take three examples from colonial Kenya: the British distrusted the Kikuyu Central Association mainly because it tried to unite a people the British ruled in three separate districts. The Luyia, comprising over one dozen 'tribes' of heterogeneous origin, first united to resist the official policy that subjected them to a

---

[10] Kuba and Lentz (2006); Mackenzie (1998); and Chapter 7 by Shipton.
[11] Lonsdale (2009); for the Bible's political influence: Walzer (1985); Hastings (1997); Barber (2006); Muoria Sal *et al.* (2009).
[12] As emphasised in Chapter 5 by Berman.
[13] See Terence Ranger's substitution of 'imagination' (1993) for his earlier, if still more often quoted 'invention' (1983).

single ruling dynasty and then to denounce a white-settler land-grab. The Kalenjin, known to the British as 'Nandi-speaking peoples', pioneered their ethnic co-operation in the unwelcome form of inter-district cattle theft. Their collective name was their own idea, *Kalenjin* meaning 'I say to you', first broadcast on local radio during the Second World War (Anderson 1993; Lynch 2008; MacArthur 2009; Spencer 1985).

The twentieth century was not the only time African history underwent rapid change. In earlier centuries, in general, ethnicity was only one loyalty among many that included Islamic brotherhoods, prophetic cults, trading partnerships, 'snowball states' in which mobile war-leaders accumulated multilingual subjects, river-bank chains of villages and, perhaps most commonly, 'houses' led by 'big men' who prized skills of immigrant origin. Nonetheless, ethnic groups existed; their rituals of harvest, chiefship, initiation and so on provided theatres of social memory, of political accountability and norms of civilised behaviour (Connerton 1989). Their cultural boundaries might well be porous but that was the point: they welcomed more people. Multilingualism was proof of both population mobility and its ethnic diversity. Flexibility in diversity remains today. Situational ethnicity has outlived both colonial rule and the one-party state. Conflicts of autochthony, wars of 'who is who', show how population growth and the rising value of land have increased the perils in belonging but they are not the only post-colonial form of ethnic relations.[14]

If ethnic fluidity remains today, historians can, conversely, find moments when ethnic relations became more clearly defined in pre-colonial times – by resistance to state-building, for example, by commercial trust and industry, or by new cultures of progress born out of social disruption. In the early nineteenth century, for instance, state-building among the Nguni-speakers of southern Africa brought inequalities, seen as ethnic, between core supporters of the upstart Zulu dynasty and its peripheral tributaries; and resentment of group subjection then marched north with the Ndebele kingdom that seceded from Zululand (Msindo 2004; Wright and Hamilton 1990). A possibly more common form of resistance to royal power created the people of Uganda now called Acholi, whose chiefs organised a community of solidarity that refused to kneel to the King of Bunyoro (Atkinson

---

[14] For which, again, see Chapter 5 by Berman.

1994). Commercial trust, next, defined 'Hausa' as an urban civilisation, so named by their trading partners in the seventeenth century (Haour and Rossi 2010). As my Fulani case study will show, such a geographically dispersed population could become a self-conscious people, assimilating others. But it was, thirdly, in their disrupted diaspora, in Cuba, Brazil or Sierra Leone, as slaves or Christian freed slaves, that people from western Nigeria first saw themselves as 'Yoruba': their earliest communal riot with members of the similar Igbo diaspora was in 1843. African-led Christianity later absorbed the civic virtues of what became 'Yorubaland', so that different townspeople learned to be Yoruba, years before British rule (Peel 2000: 283–4).

The colonial era was, therefore, only one conjuncture among many, if also the most profound, in African social history. The next stage of my argument is that the colonial conjuncture stimulated two sides of ethnic patriotism that had clearly existed in some form before, in the Acholi, Hausa, Nguni and Yoruba cases: the internal argument I call 'moral ethnicity' and the external rivalry I call 'political tribalism' – or, in Kenyan parlance, positive and negative ethnicity (Lonsdale 1992: 461–8, 1996). African ethnicities were and are 'states of mind' as much as 'actual social organisations' (Roberts 1976: 65).

The distinction between moral ethnicity and political tribalism may help us analyse the limits of cultural change in the face of new horizontal or vertical market inequality. For the former is a *mentalité*, slow to change, the latter a strategy, alert to opportunity or threat. Both can be called patriotic – since 'patriotism' is a slippery term. Internal patriotism is historically informed and comparatively aware (Lonsdale 2009). It prompts the question 'Does the self-government of my country (*patrie*) – or what I imagine to be my country – itself respect the rights hard-won by our ancestors while deserving the respect of the wider world?' The answer will inform what chief Awolowo called a 'searching self-examination', to ensure that the community deserves well of nature, 'heals the land' and protects posterity (Awolowo [1947] 1966: 34; Feierman 1990). Self-critical patriotism implies an awareness of 'others' but has no need to be their enemy. But patriots also declare: 'My country, right or wrong.' Such unquestioning loyalty is likely to characterise 'political tribalism', an externally focused, often defensive, energy mobilised when a region or its leaders fear exclusion from power and its fruits – often, therefore, before general elections. But it may also be drummed up as a means to placate the angry, frustrated, moral ethnicity of clients who feel ignored or exploited by their patrons.

The idea of moral ethnicity is derived from the concept of 'moral economy'. Moral economies place prudential, civilising limits on market economy. As webs of trust and obligation, they sustain social order and trustworthy, repeatable, market transactions. In unequal societies, as all are, moral economy represents the market in which to barter terms of legitimate authority, reliable knowledge, marriage, responsible power, honour and the just reward of loyal labour, permitting a subsistence to the deserving poor. In Africa it is the arena in which clients negotiate the co-operative, if subservient, creation of well-being against its private appropriation by their patrons (Ensminger 1992). Their debate concerns civic virtue, making ethnic identity a contentious achievement as much as a comforting inheritance. Rich and poor are both subject to judgement. Wealthy polygynous householders had the hospitable capacity to manage public well-being; to refuse the responsibility of patronage risked a charge of selfish sorcery. Since landlessness used to be unknown in most of pre-colonial Africa outside Ethiopia, poverty was, equally, a failing rather than a misfortune (for exceptions, Iliffe 1987). Moral ethnicity has stern criteria of personal responsibility and may be less alert to structural injustice.

Moral ethnicity reflects the scarcely moving bottom layer of African history, economic or ecological geography. One can indeed identify 'ecological ethnicities' in pre-colonial times. Botanical identities emerged from the knowledge that mastered changing climatic seasons (Feierman 1974: 17–22), pastoral societies demanded generational discipline (Baxter and Almagor 1978; Kurimoto and Simsonse 1998), cavalry cultures elevated warrior nobility above peasantry (Goody 1971; Iliffe 2005: ch. 2; Law 1980), river-bank language-chains practised a cosmopolitan tolerance (Brinkman 2006: 27–34; Harms 1981) and forest-clearing agrarian civilisations prized household responsibility and its meritorious sweat (Beidelman 1986; Kershaw 1997). Ethnic cultures celebrated what best represented their productive relationships. In modern times ecological ethnicity was often reinforced by colonial cash-cropping policy, another formative aspect of the colonial conjuncture. Some ethnic groups became cocoa or cotton tribes, coffee, cashew-nut or ground-nut tribes. In the late colonial period their marketing co-operatives and para-statal exporting monopolies provided ethnicities with market-orientated political strategies. But new skills and employments, unrelated to ecology but products of the colonial conjuncture such as Christian literacy, schoolteaching or midwifery (Thomas 2003), also made such strategies more disputatious. Untried clerks could have a hard struggle against the environmental wisdom of unlettered elders (Lonsdale 2005).

A further consequence of the continent's immobile but unreliable ecological history has been the necessity of inter-group co-operation for survival. Cohesive groups were often very small societies. That forced them to create wide networks – for marriage, to exchange specialised products or ritual skills and to insure against drought or disease. Small groups, and especially their 'big men', had to keep their horizontal relations with 'others' in good repair under a surface of periodic friction (Ambler 1988). Economically destructive warfare often accompanied African state-building (Austin 2004: 24–5), but constant 'tribal war' was not something from which colonialism had to liberate Africans. It might be more true to say that the colonial conjuncture generalised such hostility. In contemporary Africa, especially in a previously stateless area such as Kenya, ethnic discourse is split between this older patriotic desire to preserve relations of trust with neighbouring 'others' and the unprecedentedly desperate, equally patriotic, need to compete 'horizontally', for a share of the national cake. State power might, generously, be seen as an attempt to defy Africa's immobile historical geography with 'development'. No wonder that inter-ethnic distrust is driven, above all, by fear of exclusion from such power – a power quite unattainable in pre-colonial times.

This fear is the chief stimulus to political tribalism. The most precious quality of moral ethnicity – as for a nation – is eternal vigilance. Political tribalism, especially at elections, expects unquestioning loyalty. It is the only kind of ethnicity that Western journalists see in Africa; it is the kind measured by the ethno-linguistic fractionalisation (ELF) index. It reflects the political segmentation of the nation-state. Representatives who appeal for ethnic solidarity in national politics are no longer untried clerks but patrons, and patrons no longer judged by their domestic skills of management but by their cunning in the selfish, sorcerous, national arena in which competition is based on the zero-sum premise that, to the extent that one group makes 'horizontal' gains, the others will lose. In electoral contests people are expected to line up behind their 'big man' patrons, no matter how much they may question those patrons' behaviour towards internal clients. If constituents do not provide a reliable vote bank, they cannot expect to 'eat' at the high-political table at which the national cake is shared. Such behaviour – from which the average voter rarely benefits – is the product of a political system, not inherent in ethnic difference. It also tends to be self-fulfilling, destructive both of market trust and the rule of law, forcing people to seek still more protection and co-operation at the hands of their ethnic kin (Mueller 2008, 2010).

To sum up, internal patriotism, moral ethnicity, is neither primordially inherited nor politically invented but historically constructed, argumentative, vigilant and historically disposed to inter-ethnic social, cultural and material exchange. External patriotism, political tribalism, is contingent on immediate contexts, mainly those which seem to spell danger, and so tends to do as it is told; it is inclined to ethnic mercantilism. Moral ethnicity asks how to live well together in the modern world (Iliffe 1979: ch. 10), how to translate into moral economy the new vertical inequality, the social mobility, of the colonial conjuncture. It provides Africans with a public sphere (if a local one), a materially based language of class, a moral test of accountability and, now that power structures are more visible, an alert political eye. Political tribalism shows determination to exploit or resist the regional inequalities characteristic of narrowly based colonial development. Both forms of local patriotism, like nationalism, represent modern enlargements of social scale – from 'house', lineage or clan to conscious ethnic commitment – enlargements that 'modernisation theory' misunderstood as a clinging to pre-modern tradition.

Perhaps the key question to ask is how, when and to what political effect, moral ethnicity and political tribalism affect each other. Moral ethnicity is a constitutive element, the critical self-examination, of ethnic belonging. Political tribalism, like international aggression, is contingent on wider political and economic processes. But leaders who face trouble in their backyard are often tempted to strangle internal dissent with the solidarity of external crisis. This observation applies as much to ethnic groups as to nation-states. And Kenya, as we shall see, offers a striking contrast with which to explore relations between ethnicity's external and internal dimensions. In the colonial conjuncture Kikuyuland experienced the sharpest reversal in factor values between labour and land, when the labour of even industrious clients lost its value as patrons favoured by the state pursued agrarian profit on land hemmed in by white settlement. The agriculture of Luoland stagnated by contrast, further from markets, less fertile and less reliably watered. Rising tension between Kikuyu clients and patrons, culminating in Mau Mau, forced elites to recover their reputation by seizing state power for ethnic benefit. Luo tenant rights were safer; their leaders, less pressured from below, did not have the same urgent need to dominate national politics.

Other cases, I intend, will suggest other relationships.

Case studies: an outline

My case studies, chosen to demonstrate difference, straddle the nineteenth and twentieth centuries. This is to show how the *longue durée* has affected the political and economic 'events' that are scorned by *annalistes* but are the policy makers' chief concern. The changes to look out for are: the displacement of ethnic *diaspora* by colonial and post-colonial states as suppliers of public goods (with arguably greater transaction costs); the decreasing value of labour (even, recently, educated labour) against the rising value of property; the spread and intensification of divisive political power, from the scatter of former kingdoms to the present continental state system; and the growing politicisation, therefore, of markets. The end product, not prime cause, of these changes has been political tribalism, competition for state power. More deeply, such horizontal conflict may in part respond to the growing vertical inequalities of intra-ethnic class formation – to the rising crisis, therefore, of moral ethnicity.

From *West Africa* my cases contrast the ethnicities of savannah and forest, interior and coast, Muslim and Christian, and so between Fulani and Asante peoples, as just one example. Fulani history shows how ethnic *diaspora* could supply such public goods as trust, protection and enforceable contracts over wide areas, although their customers arguably had to pay the rental costs of their market monopoly. Markets may also bring new vertical inequalities and the rupture of previous networks of trust, betrayals felt more deeply within peoples than between them – as in Asante (Austin 2004: 15; Hopkins 2009: 172, citing Ahlerup and Olsson 2007).

In *East Africa* – the region I know best – I will attend to five points of contrast: the first is between states, Uganda's Great Lakes kingdoms, and stateless peoples in what are now Kenya and Tanzania. Kingdoms faced internal tension with the coming of long-distance trade. The highland peoples in what became Kenya tell a different story, how inter-ethnic economic specialisation promoted commerce, like medieval European craft guilds or as in international trade theory. Secondly, one must distinguish between those stateless peoples, now Tanzanians, who in the nineteenth century were most involved in Zanzibari commerce and those who were peripheral, now Kenyans. Thirdly, in the twentieth century, one can contrast those who, like the Kikuyu, produced for the export market or fed centres of employment and others, like the Luo, whose distance from markets forced them to sell their labour elsewhere. Next, there could be a wide gulf between labour-exporters whose literacy enabled them to enter the skilled job market and those who had little to offer other than their 'martial qualities'. Finally, one might explain the different fortunes of Kenya and Tanzania in the first years of independence by contrasting the respect for moral ethnicity that gave Kenyatta his skill in political tribalism, with the fear of political tribalism that led Nyerere to offend Tanzanian moral ethnicities.

In *southern Africa* the main market influence on ethnicity has been labour migration to the mines and commercial farms. The labour market's political character changed radically with a late-twentieth-century conjuncture: the transfer of white minority power to African majorities. Black xenophobia seems to have taken over from white racism as a result. Inter-ethnic conflict had previously existed but it was largely between young migrant workers, in ritual contests of manliness as much as expressions of ethnic competition in the labour market. Political context matters.

West Africa

West Africa's ethnic relations are governed – as *annalistes* would expect – by economic geography. The region has three ecological zones, stretching horizontally across the map. Its northern frontier is the Sahara, a sand ocean navigated by the Touareg peoples who also controlled the slave-production of salt. The middle zone of savannah grasslands is fairly well watered in some places and largely free of the tsetse fly, friendly therefore to horses and cattle. Its dry seasons were as good for trade as for cavalry warfare. Barges carrying 60 tons of goods navigated its main artery, the river Niger. Ethnic trading *diaspora* – or linguistic networks that acquired an ethnic character: Hausa,

Malinke/Mande and Fulani/Fulbe/Peul – controlled savannah trade. The region's southern frontier was the Atlantic Ocean, fringed by forests that needed large concentrations of labour to exploit. This need stimulated the rise of some of Africa's strongest kingdoms, which supplied that other, notorious, demand for labour – from the trans-Atlantic slave plantations at the core of Europe's empires.

West Africa was one vast market; its geographical zones traded goods and services according to their comparative advantage (Austin 2004; Hopkins 1973). The Sahara was the gateway to Mediterranean and Islamic trade. Its salt, essential to life further south, was worked by slaves supplied by the horsemen of the savannah. The savannah itself supported towns, fed by slave-worked farms, whose artisans made textiles and leather goods prized throughout the region and beyond. The forest zone produced timber, gold and kola, all welcome in the savannahs, as well as the palm-oil that accompanied and in time supplanted overseas slave exports, which in turn financed the import of domestic hardware, cheap textiles and guns from the maritime Europeans.

What ethnic relations grew out of and governed this commercial activity? As suggested, African ethnicities were often founded on the special skills needed to exploit different ecological niches. My West African case focuses on two such skills. First, Fulani were originally cattle-keepers, too loose-knit to be called an ethnic group, who in their seasonal search for grazing became active in long-distance trade. This required trust between strangers, often separated by months of travel. The savannah was also on the outer fringes of the Islamic world. Its state structures had declined since West Africa's Islamic golden medieval age, so Sufi brotherhoods organised (and divided) the community of faith. Islam provided commerce with a common culture of trust and a literacy as good for drafting contracts as for religious learning. The brotherhoods also provided the public goods of long-distance market intelligence, places of refreshment, protective companions and business partners (Cohen 1969).

Fulani traders were Muslim by 1750. Literacy made them welcome at the courts of pagan kings. Market, religious, and political contradictions, together with knowledge of upheavals elsewhere in the Islamic world, combined to instigate a series of Muslim revolutions in the early nineteenth century in which Fulani took the lead. Their largest, most lasting, revolution overturned the Hausa kingdoms in what is now northern Nigeria (Hiskett 1973). In this wealthy urban region

Fulani success attracted ambitious migrants from elsewhere. 'Fulani' became more diverse; they grew in confidence. Their historians imagined a suitably glorious past. Perhaps to counter their growing complexity they told Fulani they were all descended from tight-knit Berber clans who first brought Islam across the Sahara to western Africa.

As Fulani civilisation absorbed more strangers, so 'the' Fulani came to see themselves as a primordial tribe (Robinson 1985). But this self-placement in global history also gave their bookish leaders a self-critical patriotism that asked if Fulani rule was equal to the best in the history of Islam, a politically censorious faith. The first caliphs of the Fulani empire of Sokoto despaired of the venal ambitions of their lieutenants (Last 1967). It was from this supposedly natural 'race' of rulers that the British co-opted their leaders to exercise 'indirect rule' over northern Nigeria, and it is as a political tribe that Fulani have dominated the vote-banks of the Nigerian Republic ever since, not simply as Fulani but as Hausa-Fulani, a culture that has joined conqueror and conquered. Nor do the complications end there. Other branches of the Fulani, further west, have been politically marginalised as a minority of former slave-owning aristocrats, without a Nigerian ability to assimilate a formerly subject local culture (Schmidt 2005: 145–56).

It was not 'the market' that made these different Fulani identities but a long history that reinforced commerce with religious fervour, literacy and revolutionary success; with ambitious immigrants aspiring to become Fulani; with the different 'tribal' preconceptions of their British and French rulers, and then the economic changes over which colonial rule presided. For these many reasons Fulani patriotism today is divided between conservative and radical readings of proper Islamic rule. On the one hand Fulani notables still assert dynastic authority; on the other the Islam of the streets from time to time breaks into riotous protest at the loss of brotherhood among the local community that is part Fulani, part Islamic *'umma*. Their fear of the radical Islamic poor, hit by vertical market inequalities, makes Nigeria's Muslim elite the more determined to pursue the oil-fuelled competition in political tribalism that lies at the root of Nigeria's economic stagnation.

The Asante, my second example of economic specialisation, were a nation created by the labour of forest-clearance. For the past three centuries their market-related history has been very different from that of the Fulani. The Asante kingdom was founded around 1700 as a military confederation, to control the interior and oceanic slave trades. Its political culture was formed not only in trade but also in war and production. All demanded massive investments of labour, to police trade-routes and to hack forest into an agrarian civilisation able to support an urban regime. Separate clans could not by themselves recruit and control that labour. That was possible only in coalition, a military confederacy under a succession of kings, Asantehenes.

Asante patriotism therefore subordinated private wealth to an ethic of service to the state, without which neither private nor public wealth could be accumulated. Royal officials also had to swear not to reveal their subjects' ethnic origins: Asante had absorbed too many 'strangers', often descended from slaves, who feared discrimination. Asante's labour needs forced the kingdom to be as welcoming as Fulani revolutionaries to ethnic 'others'. But in modern times Asante patriotism has differed from Nigeria's Fulani patriotism in two ways, in refusing to continue to absorb strangers, and in its mass rather than elite political tribalism (Arhin 1983; McCaskie 1995; Wilks 1975, 1993).

The first difference stems from the way Asante, like other coastal peoples, recruited labour for their family cocoa farms, small capitalist firms (Hill 1963; Hopkins 1973: 216–18). In the early twentieth century, migrant workers from the land-locked French colonies of Upper Volta and Soudan (Burkina Faso and Mali), sold their labour to the petty capitalists of the coastal colonies, in numbers as large as those employed in South Africa's mines. With their history of scarce labour and abundant land, Asante farmers welcomed in these strangers who, over time, often negotiated a rise in status from visiting worker to resident share-cropper (Austin 2005; Iliffe 1983: 24–9). The cocoa export market was opening the frontiers of ethnicity, as the military recruitment of labour had done earlier. But in the colonial conjuncture, that relationship changed as population grew and land became scarce. Today, people of distant origin, previously integrated vertically as clients, are horizontal strangers once again. Patriotism has become less inclusive, more 'tribal' than regional (Kuba and Lentz 2006, ch. 6. by Amanor and ch. 8 by Austin). But that is also due to another stimulus, found in Asante's constitutional history. The labour market alone is not sufficient explanation.

Constitutional history is often thought old-fashioned but it can be a passionate patriotic concern in Africa, especially in societies created by pre-colonial kingdoms. For another effect of the cocoa trade was increased vertical tension between Asante chiefs and their commoners, as chiefs exploited pre-capitalist privileges for capitalist market advantage. The breaking of local reciprocities between chief and commoner, along what became class lines, made Asante commoners appeal to their king for redress – as we shall also find in Buganda. As petty capitalists themselves they also feared rule by the supposedly socialist Kwame Nkrumah. On both counts commoners called for a federal, not unitary, post-colonial Ghanaian state: their king would protect their private enterprise from chiefs and socialism, each as greedy as the other. But commoner discontent so frightened both Asantehene and chiefs that the kingdom's elite submitted themselves to the new Ghanaian state, for protection against their people's class-antagonism (Allman 1993). Elites can fear, as well as use, the strategic instrument of a patriotic ethnicity.

East Africa

My first East African case contrasts the changing economics of social relations as experienced between kingdoms and then between stateless peoples. In Uganda, market relations with ethnicity have been devastating, thanks to the friction between the Buganda kingdom and the rest of Uganda – a colonially fabricated mix, like Ghana, of kingdoms and stateless peoples (Low 2009). The story is complex. Its relevance to our enquiry stems from the way in which, in the nineteenth century, the Uganda area was penetrated by two very different Arab commercial interests, from Khartoum to the north and Zanzibar to the east. Khartoum traders were poorly financed but had relatively secure communications up the river Nile. The first fact forced, the second allowed them to use coercion in their search for slaves. The Great Lakes kingdom most damaged by their intrusion was the most northerly one, Bunyoro, which concluded that foreigners were dangerous. It resisted all later intruders, which included, fatally, its British colonial rulers (Doyle 2006, ch. 2).

Zanzibaris, by contrast, were well financed by British Indians; and on their long marches into the interior they had to negotiate with communities along the route. For ivory and slaves they exchanged textiles, ornaments and guns. The first Great Lakes kingdom they met was Buganda. Its chiefs competed for Zanzibar's trade between themselves and with their king or *kabaka*. Access to external commerce weakened the vertical ties between chiefs and king and therefore between chiefs and their peasant followers, since previously chiefs could win royal favour and promotion only by providing loyal soldiers for the king's wars and labourers on his roads. Buganda's politics became more volatile. This historical contingency allowed the British to win control over Buganda in the 1890s, simply by backing the winning side in one of the kingdom's civil wars. This Anglo-Ganda alliance conquered the rest of Uganda – an alliance cemented in 1900 by an agreement that distributed freehold land in Buganda to its chiefs. Secure property liberated them from the royal market in reputation and loyalty. They could demand more from their peasants than before – in forced labour on cotton and coffee for export. Ganda peasants, like Asante commoners, accused their chiefs of breaking their patriotic moral economy, under which patrons had had to nurse the needs of followers who might otherwise line up behind a rival chief. The markets in land, no longer dependent on royal favour, and in exportable goods, had subverted the political market in reputation (Hanson 2003; Waller 1971).

During the remaining sixty years of British rule, peasant populism looked to the king for defence against over-mighty chiefs. This constitutional protest, Buganda's version of moral ethnicity, was more passionate than any nationalism felt for Uganda as a whole. Buganda's monarchy, feeling secure in its British alliance (which Asante never enjoyed), allowed itself to be pushed from below into demanding a federal status within Uganda. Nationalism in the rest of Uganda was as determined to overturn Buganda's advantage as to get rid of British rule (Gertzel 1974; Leys 1967; Low 1971, chs. 5–7). So there are two points to make here in conclusion. One is that outraged moral ethnicity from below, pitching peasant rights against propertied chiefs, can drive elite politics into political tribalism – although Ganda nationalists would never see Buganda as a 'tribe'. The other stems from the long-term inter-ethnic, or inter-kingdom, effects of the market. Those who first encountered the outside world through the Khartoumers' brutality wanted to get even with the Baganda, whose openness to Zanzibar's free-traders had paid such rich dividends. This market-based flaw in Uganda's politics needed, as we shall see, only the political irruption of my fourth East African market contrast to complete the country's post-colonial tragedy.

If relations between long-distance trade and kingdoms could have such far-reaching consequences, what of the contrasting case, regional trade between stateless peoples? A classic example is found in Kenya's highlands, in the triangular commerce between hunting, herding and farming, between the Okiek, Maasai and Kikuyu peoples.[15] Here it appears that there had been increasing specialisation of production in earlier years, so that by the late nineteenth century Okiek, Maasai and Kikuyu were trading complementary goods and services, each buying from the other what they did not produce themselves (Iliffe 1987: 68–70; Spear and Waller 1993: 1–18, 290–302).

The key complementarity lay between agriculture and pastoralism. Kikuyu farming had reasonably secure returns; these were banked in livestock, the reserve currency of reputation and power. The Maasai, bankers to the highland market, could make spectacular returns in cattle-rearing but were vulnerable to equally spectacular crashes in droughts, when they had to turn to their kin among the Kikuyu for grain and vegetable rations in return for various forms of service. Okiek hunters occupied an ambiguous position, despised as the stockless poor by Maasai, as idle non-cultivators by Kikuyu, but suppliers of ritual goods to both. Each group retained cultural boundaries that protected the allocation of productive assets – farm-gardens, hunting estates, cattle and grazing rights – but allowed the passage of people over these boundaries on condition of some fee payment, a temporary element of submission and respect for one's ecologically governed new culture. The links between growth, insurance and diversity seem to have been exemplary here. And after the colonial conjuncture the negotiation of horizontal inequalities has been easier than between Buganda and its neighbours. It is true that the Rift Valley, the arena of inter-ethnic exchange in pre-colonial times, has seen terrible violence and forced evictions in recent years (see Chapter 3). But it is also the case that wealthy Maasai and Kikuyu have come together to exploit the agricultural potential of formerly pastoral lands. Inter-ethnicity retains its market attraction, at least for elites; and inter-ethnic violence has thus far been under elite control, ordered when politically necessary (Anderson and Lochery 2008; Oucho 2002).

My second eastern African contrast, between Tanzania's stateless peoples who were previously engaged in the Zanzibar trade and those now in Kenya who were less involved, goes far to explain the differences between their modern nationalisms. The key contrast lies in the link between market and language, and therefore between commerce

[15] Compare the farming Fur and pastoral Baggara of the Sudan: Haaland (1969).

and the flow of ideas, a critical matter in the construction of nationalism. The language of Zanzibar's 'informal empire' of free trade
(Gallagher and Robinson 1953) was Swahili, its culture of trust Islam.
In the twentieth century Swahili became more widely used in Tanzania
than in Kenya – even if Islam was politically insignificant in both. This
linguistic contrast goes far to explain Tanzania's greater unity in both
nationalist and post-colonial eras. The rhetoric of nationhood came
easily to Nyerere; Kenyatta spoke more readily of a Kenya that was a
'kind of United Nations in miniature' (Kenyatta 1964: 57).

Not the least important aspect of this contrast in Swahili usage
has been that Tanzanian Christians more commonly read a Swahili
Bible while Kenyan Christians started their literate lives more often
by reading the Bible in their local vernacular. For Christians the Bible
is a primer in nationhood (Hastings 1997). Kenyan 'readers' – as they
called themselves – could readily compare their own ethnic group
with the children of Israel; many local historians today claim that
their ethnogenesis originated in exodus from Egypt, like the Israelites.
Tanzanian Swahili readers could more easily imagine themselves to
have a national destiny. A Tanzanian patriotism is, however, by no
means universal (Maddox and Giblin 2005), perhaps because of the
further contrast between Kenya and Tanzania which rounds off my
discussion of East Africa, below.

But why, in Kenya, should Kikuyu, not Luo, take the lead in radical
nationalist politics – a contingency that still splits Kenya fifty years
later? For an answer we need my third East African contrast, between
those who sold food or export crops and those who sold, chiefly, their
labour power. This economic difference shaped the relative anger of
their moral ethnicities and, therefore, the unequal energies of their political tribalism.

Kikuyu, 20 per cent of Kenya's population, occupy the centre of the
country, bordering its capital Nairobi. At the hub of the communications network they enjoy reliable rainfall on high, relatively disease-
free, formerly forested land.[16] What caused them angry patriotic debate
was change in their vertical inequalities, thanks, again, to the reversal
in values between labour and land. Production of food and charcoal

---

[16] Kikuyu exposure to malaria is increasing, since global warming allows
the anopheles mosquito to thrive at higher altitudes: *The Times* (London,
31 December 2009: 16).

for Nairobi subverted relations between patrons and clients; property became more profitable than patronage. What mattered now was an elder's control of his land, worked by his wives; and not consideration for clients with whom his fathers would have shared usage of the land, in return for their support in litigation and war.

How could those thrown off their patron's land secure the house-holder's self-mastery which lay at the heart of Kikuyu moral economy? Fear of social extinction thanks, as in Buganda, to betrayal by one's patron, generated the radicalism of the Mau Mau movement. 'Moral outrage' gave 'excellent motivation for resolute action' (Moodie and Ndatshe 1994: 281). The outraged moral ethnicity of discarded clients divided Kikuyu between Kenya's most militant nationalists, Mau Mau, and its most convinced conservatives, the 'loyalists' who backed the British and then inherited the state's coercive powers at independence. Both were patriots; both believed Kikuyu citizenship was earned by sturdy, sweaty, self-reliance. But generous patronage, which had once offered respectability to all prepared to sweat, had become a selfish interest in property, not people. Mau Mau members feared that the industrious client's road to civic virtue had closed. Loyalists considered it was still open – except to those who had disqualified themselves as clients by becoming Mau Mau 'hooligans'. Kikuyu elites have since used the state to protect their conservative ethnic patriotism against its no less Kikuyu but dangerously radical opponents (Branch 2009; Lonsdale 1992; Mackenzie 1998). This ideological rift in patriotism explains the ruthlessness of Kikuyu elites, more like Fulani than Asante.

Luo patriotism was less divided within and less forceful, therefore, in the national arena. Fifteen per cent of Kenya's population, Luo live on low-lying, irregularly watered, rather infertile, malaria-prone land in the far interior. Lacking agrarian potential, they enjoyed two advantages in the labour market, paralleled by the Scots throughout the British empire. One was their early acquisition of mission literacy. The other was their muscular build, allegedly nourished by the protein their fishermen harvested from Lake Victoria. Both qualities created a reputation that took Luo youths and, increasingly, their families, far from their impoverished homeland. They became East Africa's chief railway tribe, with Luo ticket clerks, stationmasters and engineers scattered from Uganda to the Kenyan and Tanzanian coasts. They led Kenya's trade unions, a role that favoured negotiation rather than conflict, especially when the chief negotiator was that genius, Tom Mboya (Cooper 1987; Goldsworthy 1982; Grillo 1973; Parkin 1969).

This migrant colonisation of colonial market economy meant that Luo knew less of the propertied social differentiation that poisoned Kikuyu politics. When the British pressed them to reform their land tenure in the 1950s Luo elders showed a degree of concern for their tenants' rights that the market had driven from many Kikuyu patrons' minds (Shipton 1989, 2007, 2009). Luo patriotism remained united behind the rustic figure of Oginga Odinga to an extent that no Kikuyu leader, not even Kenyatta, could hope to attain. (Tom Mboya remained a man of the town until after his assassination when Luo, suspicious of his urban cunning in life [Parkin 1978: 217–28], reclaimed him in death.) Horizontal, external Luo politics was not fired up by the vertical, internal friction that propelled the Kikuyu. Odinga's moderate, naively socialist, politics was outbid by Kikuyu conservatives, toughened by fear of their own radicals. Land conflict and crop marketing trumped the relatively untroubled ethnic patriotism of the Luo and their trade unionist culture of negotiation, learned in the labour market (Bates 1989: 41–4; Odinga 1967).

It took my fourth contrast, between those such as the Luo with skills to sell and those with nothing to offer the labour market but their supposed martial qualities, to create East Africa's darkest modern tragedy – Idi Amin's 1971 coup in Uganda. Uganda's politics, split between Buganda and the rest, was sufficiently volatile for President Obote, a man of the stateless north, to place more reliance than Nyerere or Kenyatta on his army. His army also came mainly from the north, recruited among people distant from export markets and mission literacy, whose sole opportunity for power came from casting their military strength into the political arena. No scholar has yet suggested that Idi Amin was driven by his ethnic (Kakwa) or even Ugandan patriotism. Self-preservation seems a more likely motive, more so than a military class-consciousness. But patriotism is not to be expected behind every political action derived from one's privileged or, in this case, marginal market position (Hansen and Twaddle 1988; Parsons 2003).

The most intriguing question to be asked of East African markets and ethnicity is the last. How much, in the early years of independence, was the relative economic success of capitalist Kenya and the relative failure of socialist Tanzania due to their presidents' understanding of moral ethnicity and fear of political tribalism, those twin patriotisms?

Kenyatta was unafraid of political tribalism; indeed, he used it to stitch together a ruling coalition with non-Kikuyu that defeated his internal Kikuyu radicals. But that political skill was founded on his respect for the disciplines of tradition that taught men and women how to strive for self-respect, the core of moral ethnicity (Lonsdale 2002). Nyerere dismantled chiefship, the focus of ethnicity; he also misunderstood the moral ethnicity of the past, seeing it as an altruistic communalism rather than the lop-sided reciprocity, the unequal moral economy, that allowed wealth and poverty to co-exist. It is not surprising, although it was to Nyerere, that Tanzanians resisted the new, enforced communalism of *Ujamaa vijijini*, village collectivisation, so destructive of self-mastery (Scott 1998: ch. 7). Patriotic thought matters.

Southern Africa

Johannesburg's *Weekly Mail and Guardian* runs a strip cartoon called 'Madam and Eve'. Madam is the white housewife, at leisure in the front room, Eve her black servant, at work at the back. In one episode a few years ago, Eve looks up from the newspaper to ask, 'Madam, what is xenophobia?' Madam replies, at first at a loss for the appropriate word, 'Fear of, ... fear of ... *Nigerians*!' (date lost). South Africa, as Africa's land of opportunity, feels itself to be full of increasing numbers of stranger Africans, especially the Nigerians and Congolese who are said to run the rackets and, more recently, Zimbabweans fleeing tyranny and starvation. There have been street riots against this foreign influx, ever more competitors for scarce jobs and services.

But South Africa has been full of stranger Africans since the 1890s, when more Mozambicans than South Africans worked in the gold mines. Mozambique remained the single largest source of mineworkers into the 1960s (Harries 1994; Wilson 1972: 70). The enormous migrant labour market of southern Africa, from the copper mines of Katanga and Zambia in the north to the gold mines of the south, has certainly witnessed inter-ethnic competition over jobs, housing, women and the petty trade, often in liquor, that has supplied the immigrants' basic needs. Periodic riots and so-called 'faction-fights' made the mining towns much like those of the US at a similar time. But they lacked the intensity and generality of the recent xenophobia.

This earlier violence was far from a matter of clashing primordialisms or of its converse, the anomic, normless 'detribalisation' once feared by colonial officials and anthropologists alike. What migrant labour encouraged was an enlargement of the moral imagination of ethnicity and its patriotic obligations (Beinart 1982; Bonner and Nieftagodien 2001a and 2001b; Moodie and Ndatshe 1994; van Onselen 1976). The first scholars to study this labour market in the 1950s, the 'Manchester School', were more impressed by the 'super tribes' that emerged on the way to work and in the workplace than by the clashes between them (Lentz 1995: 308–10). Young men, 'peasants raiding the cash economy for goods' (Max Gluckman, Foreword to Watson 1958: x), came from small, discrete, rural communities but then allied themselves in town or down the mine with others who spoke more or less the same language, or who took the same bus or train between work and home. In South Africa a 'Nyasa' was anyone who came from Nyasaland (Malawi) for work, irrespective of his ethnic origin. The most visible evidence of their various patriotisms was not fighting but the dance ceremonies they used so extravagantly to perform, competing in their mastery of the rituals of urban civilisation in order to win the respect of urban strangers (Ranger 1975).

The expansion and contraction of ethnic consciousness in southern Africa, as in the rest of Africa, can in any case be observed long before the inception of the migrant labour market and colonial state-building. The construction, destruction and expansion of ethnic identity in nineteenth-century South Africa's 'time of troubles' and state-building, referred to earlier, is known to all undergraduate students of African history (Etherington 2001). A study of ethnic relations further north, in what is now Zimbabwe, has shown how Kalanga and Ndebele people oscillated between mutual assimilation and hostility according to changing contexts. Internal and external conceptions of patriotism also varied over time. In the late nineteenth century, before the European conquest, Ndebele commoners' resistance to royal claims influenced the missionary choice of dialect in translating the Bible, what became the language of Ndebele moral ethnicity. A generation or two later commoners developed a less questioning, more aggressive, ideology of Ndebele identity when facing horizontal competition in the urban labour market of Bulawayo (Msindo 2004; Ranger 2010). We need to keep a sharp eye on such changing contexts before judging the labour market's role in ethnic consciousness.

For labour market competition alone did not create the ethnic patriotisms of southern Africa. Probably more important in most workers' strategies of investment in social security was the relative health of their rural political economies of origin – to continue a discussion begun with the Kikuyu–Luo contrast. The labour market was for many years a risky and racially oppressive arena of African enterprise. By comparison – in a region where white-settler protectionism denied agrarian profit to Africans – rights to cultivable or pastoral land 'at home' were relatively secure, so long as one paid one's obligations in the rural moral economy. This consideration remained true probably until the later twentieth century when, on different time-scales, rural economies became over-burdened with people on over-worked land. Until that time, when peasants ceased to make brief raids on the urban labour market and began to rely on it for subsistence, the need to maintain rural property rights was the main incentive to honour the many-stranded reciprocities inherent in one's ethnic identity, often romanticised in an exile imagination.

Southern Africa's labour market has therefore had varied effects on ethnic sentiment. Books have explored the complexities. But recent studies have focused on the need to understand the moral economies of personal integrity that carry men and women through often contradictory phases of their life cycle, at times beholden to ethnic kin and traditionalised rural authorities responsible for allocating land, at others proving their manhood or womanhood in townships or labour compounds where moral community stems from a shared need to overcome humiliation. 'Manhood is hard', runs a Sotho proverb; 'it is dug out from the rocks' (Iliffe 2005: 287; Moodie and Ndatshe 1994). The most consistent street violence of late-twentieth-century South African towns seems to have had nothing to do with ethnicity. *Tsotsi* gangs were created by youths born in town, based on entirely urban perceptions of territory and male property in women. Rival gangs spoke a lingua franca, *tsotsitaal*, based on Afrikaans, with borrowings from Zulu, Xhosa and English in a fine display of multi-ethnicity. Tsotsis assessed each others' cultural status by reference not to ethnicity but to the way different townships developed their own dialect of *tsotsitaal* (Glaser 2000: 70–1). In a rapidly urbanising Africa, will ethnicity elsewhere also cease to be the deepest community of belonging?

Other South African evidence suggests otherwise. An increasingly common form of violence seems, as Africans began to glimpse the possibility of power, to have expressed vertical grievance within ethnic groups – which is not to deny that horizontal, inter-ethnic violence could at times be brutal and bloody. But the internal tension situates the labour market more firmly in the realm of moral ethnicity. For two centuries, patriotic debate had simmered between Xhosa 'reds' who stayed to mind the cattle and 'schools' who 'absconded' from home to work in East London (Mayer [1961] 1971). In the 1970s, young township 'comrades' turned the tables on their elders in the Cape. The antagonists were all Xhosa. The young taunted their elders: 'We asked for freedom and [the whites] gave you beer!' Comrades burned down elders' liquor stores. When they cornered a drinker they might wash out his beery mouth with soap or force him to vomit. One cannot imagine a fiercer disagreement over how to construct patriotic manliness in town (*Report* 1980: 309–31). In the dying days of apartheid there was comparable violence between fellow Zulu, largely rural supporters of the Inkatha Freedom Party on one hand and urban members of the African National Congress on the other. Unlike the Luo experience, selling one's labour outside the household domain seems to have caused as much vertical tension within ethnic groups as, horizontally, between them – but not as lethal as the expropriation of dependents from one's land had caused among Kikuyu.

That reflection on antagonisms stirred by the migrant labour market applies to the period before 1994, before Africans could wield much power over each other and when many had common enemies in both the white regime and the social alienations of city life.[17] What introduced xenophobia in the South African labour market, then, was both the end of the apartheid influx controls that previously imposed some (if not much) control over the supply of labour and, perhaps still more importantly, the inherent divisiveness of state power that became available to Africans. This brings us back to end with another conjuncture, a peculiarly South African one this time, when slow-growing demography has been overtaken by massive immigration, when urbanisation is no longer subject to pass controls, and when African access to political power exploded almost overnight.

Conclusions

Throwing all caution aside, let me start with a generalisation: patriotic ethnic thought matters. In historical kingdoms it was constitutional

---

[17] Many urban, 'section 10' Africans, the 'Drum generation', exempted from movement controls, found town life exciting and fulfilling, but that is another story.

thought. Championed by commoners in Asante or Buganda, it decided relations between Asante and Ghana, Buganda and Uganda. Its varied intensity – as between Kikuyu and Luo – underlay the inequalities of Kenyatta's Kenya; its resistance to egalitarianism helped to bring down Nyerere's Tanzania. Ethnic patriotism is worth studying.

Secondly, patriotic ethnicity is as much a language of class as a provocation to ethnic competition. Changing vertical inequalities are as hurtful as horizontal ones. A moral ethnicity outraged by class formation and the devaluation of clientage can propel frightened elites into political tribalism. The instrumentality of ethnicity is not a simple matter of elite manipulation.

These conclusions, thirdly, are based on assumptions about the internal moral economy of ethnicity. One's ethnicity is a moral community in which people debate their rational choices under stern reputational criteria shaped over the *longue durée* by ecological and political context. Economic modellers seem, rather, to work on the twin assumptions that political tribalism is both a constant and the only relevant aspect of ethnicity. Such assumptions surely need to be reconsidered.

But fourthly, even if patriotic ethnic thought is worth studying, there is still a question, how far it is an independent causal factor, how far a dependent variable. I have three doubts in mind. I have earlier cited other, natural, reasons for Africa's poor economic performance in what *annalistes* would call its immobile history. I also argued that the conjunctural colonial linkage of demographic and political change, the reversal in factor values between labour and land, and the advent of literacy and peace, all helped to harden ethnic boundaries and enliven internal ethnic debate more or less contemporaneously with the growth of anti-colonial nationalism. So a third doubt arises from the realisation that the distinction between 'nations' as legitimately sovereign and ethnic groups as problematic 'sub-nations' is a matter of contingent historical process. One must ask, again, how far ethnicity is necessarily an obstacle to market-based 'development' or, instead, how far certain modes of nation building or trajectories of development have made it so. My case studies suggest that it is best to keep this an open question. By itself ethnicity explains nothing; its salience in any particular transaction has to be explained. Nor can the relation between ethnicity and markets be studied in isolation.

Markets themselves, fifthly, must be specified, both in commodity and in their relative freedom of price movement. Luo dependence on the labour market fostered a politics very different from that which came out of the Kikuyu experience of social differentiation by property, driven by market production on their own land. The freedom of the Zanzibar market gave Buganda great advantages – if indirect and unintended, as historians would expect – over Bunyoro, whose trade with Khartoum lay under the threat of force.

African ethnic groups have changed boundaries and 'custom' throughout history. They '[made] up the rules as they [went] along' (Marshall Sahlins, in Spear and Waller 1993: 302). But it has also been suggested that ethnic connections with commerce could create a general, cyclical, pattern, setting rules that nobody makes up but to which all must respond.[18] Ethnicity may initially facilitate trade by providing market intelligence and trust, as in the Fulani case or in the different logic of the triangular market of producer protection and banking insurance in highland Kenya. Should trade prosper it may change both vertical and horizontal inequalities. This may in turn disturb internal moral ethnicity and destabilise relations between ethnic groups. These changes may, finally, damage the trust on which alone markets can thrive. Economists might consider the utility of such a cyclical model, if only to shock and then discard it.

That history cannot repeat itself is perhaps shown by asking if Africans might try to replicate what appear to be two promising precedents in socio-economic diversity, namely, the heterogeneous composition of entrepreneurial 'houses' and the public service ethic of nineteenth-century Asante. Each precedent was flawed. 'Houses' rarely survived the succession disputes that followed the death of a 'big man' founder; their meritocratic basis of recruitment was also premised on a labour scarcity that no longer exists. And Asante's political culture split, before colonial rule, into a civil war between a so-called 'capitalist', private, business interest pursued by royal trade officials, a 'war party' of army commanders, and a republican mob on the streets of Kumasi, the Asante capital (Wilks 1975: ch. 12–15; McCaskie 1995: ch. 2). There is little historical comfort to be found in either case.

If, finally, one generalises about African ethnicity and markets, let it be with a keen eye to its diverse contexts and changing circumstances.

---

[18] Professor Hino Hiroyuki, in a comment on an earlier draft.

The ELF index, which assumes ethnicity to be both hard of boundary and constant in intensity, should be replaced. More indeterminate models are needed, in which economic agents exercise rational choice not only in uncertain contexts but also with more regard to the patriotisms that are re-interpreted from slower-moving pasts, open to interethnic co-operation and disciplined by internal reputation.

References

Ahlerup, Pelle and Olsson, Ola 2007. *The Roots of Ethnic Diversity*, Working Papers, School of Business, Economics and Law, Göteborg University.

Allman, Jean M. 1993. *The Quills of the Porcupine: Asante Nationalism in an Emergent Ghana*. Madison, WI: The University of Wisconsin Press.

Ambler, Charles H. 1988. *Kenyan Communities in the Age of Imperialism: the Central Region in the Late Nineteenth Century*. New Haven, CT: Yale University Press.

Anderson, David M. 1993. 'Black Mischief: Crime, Protest and Resistance in Colonial Kenya', *Historical Journal* 36: 851–77.

Anderson, David M. and Lochery, Emma 2008. 'Violence and Exodus in Kenya's Rift Valley, 2008: Predictable and Preventable?', *Journal of Eastern African Studies* 2: 328–43.

Arhin, Kwame 1983. 'Rank and Class among the Asante and Fante in the Nineteenth Century', *Africa* 53: 2–22.

Atkinson, Ronald R. 1994. *The Roots of Ethnicity: The Origins of the Acholi of Uganda before 1800*. University of Pennsylvania Press.

Austin, Gareth 2004. *Markets with, without, and in spite of States: West Africa in the Pre-colonial Nineteenth Century*, GEHN Working Paper 03/04, London School of Economics.

2005. *Labour, Land and Capital in Ghana: From Slavery to Free Labour in Asante, 1807–1956*. Rochester, NY: University of Rochester Press.

Awolowo, Obafemi 1966 [1947]. *The Path to Nigerian Freedom*. London: Faber.

Barber, Karin (ed.) 2006. *Africa's Hidden Histories: Everyday Literacy and Making the Self*. Bloomington, IN: Indiana University Press.

Bates, Robert 1974. 'Ethnic Competition and Modernization in Africa', *Comparative Political Studies* 6: 457–84.

1989. *Beyond the Miracle of the Market: the Political Economy of Agrarian Development in Kenya*. Cambridge University Press.

2006. 'Ethnicity', in *The Elgar Companion to Development Studies*, Clarke David (ed.). Cheltenham: Elgar.

Baxter, P. T. W. and Almagor, Uri (eds.) 1978. *Age, Generation and Time: Some Features of East African Age Organizations*. London: Hurst.

Beidelman, Tom 1986. *Moral Imagination in Kaguru Modes of Thought*, Bloomington, IN: Indiana University Press.

Beinart, William 1982. *The Political Economy of Pondoland, 1860–1930*. Cambridge University Press.

Berman, Bruce 1998. 'Ethnicity, Patronage and the African state: the Politics of Uncivil Nationalism', *African Affairs* 97: 305–41.

Bonner, Philip and Nieftagodien, Noor 2001a. *Kathorus: a History*. Cape Town: Maskew Miller Longman.

2001b. *Alexandra: a History*. Johannesburg: Wits University Press.

Branch, Daniel 2009. *Defeating Mau Mau, Creating Kenya: Counter-insurgency, Civil War, and Decolonization*. Cambridge University Press.

Braudel, Fernand 1973 [Paris 1949]. *The Mediterranean and the Mediterranean World in the Age of Philip II*, 2 volumes. London: Collins.

Brinkman, Inge 2006. *A War for People: Civilians, Mobility, and Legitimacy in South-East Angola During the MPLA's War for Independence*. Cologne: Rüdiger Köppe Verlag.

Cohen, Abner 1969. *Custom and Politics in Urban Africa: a Study of Hausa Migrants in Yoruba Towns*. London: Routledge and Kegan Paul.

Commission of Enquiry 1980. *Report of the Commission of Enquiry into the Riots at Soweto and Elsewhere from 16 June 1976 to 28 February 1977, Vol I*. Pretoria: Government Printer.

Connerton, Paul 1989. *How Societies Remember*. Cambridge University Press.

Cooper, Frederick 1987. *On the African Waterfront: Urban Disorder and the Transformation of Work in Colonial Mombasa*. New Haven, CT: Yale University Press.

Doyle, Shane 2006. *Crisis and Decline in Bunyoro: Population and Environment in Western Uganda, 1860–1955*. Oxford: James Currey.

Ensminger, Jean 1992. *Making a Market: the Institutional Transformation of an African Society*. Cambridge University Press.

Etherington, Norman 2001. *The Great Treks: the Transformation of Southern Africa, 1815–1854*. Harlow: Pearson Education.

Falola, Toyin and Odhiambo, Atieno (eds.). 2002. *The Challenges of History and Leadership in Africa: the Essays of Bethwell Alan Ogot*. Trenton, NJ: Africa World Press.

Feierman, Steven 1974. *The Shambaa Kingdom: a History*. University of Wisconsin Press.

1990. *Peasant Intellectuals: Anthropology and History in Tanzania*. University of Wisconsin Press.

Gallagher, J. A. and Robinson, R. E. 1953. 'The Imperialism of Free Trade', *Economic History Review*, 2nd series VI: 1–15.

Gertzel, Cherry 1974. *Party and Locality in Northern Uganda, 1945–1962*. London: Athlone Press.

Glaser, Clive 2000. *Bo-Tsotsi: the Youth Gangs of Soweto, 1935–1976*. Portsmouth, NH: Heinemann.

Goldsworthy, David 1982. *Tom Mboya: the Man Kenya Wanted to Forget*. London: Heinemann.

Goody, Jack 1971. *Technology, Tradition, and the State in Africa*. London: Oxford University Press.

Grillo, R. D. 1973. *African Railwaymen: Solidarity and Opposition in an East African Labour Force*. Cambridge University Press.

Guyer, Jane and Belinga, Samuel E. 1995. 'Wealth in People as Wealth in Knowledge: Accumulation and Composition in Equatorial Africa', *Journal of African History* 36: 91–120.

Haaland, Gunnar 1969. 'Economic Determinants in Ethnic Processes', in *Ethnic Groups and Boundaries: the Social Organization of Culture Difference*, Fredrik Barth (ed.). Bergen: Universitets Forlaget, 58–73.

Hansen, Holger Bernt and Twaddle, Michael (eds.). 1988. *Uganda Now: Between Decay and Development*. London: James Currey.

Hanson, Holly E. 2003. *Landed Obligation: the Practice of Power in Buganda*. Portsmouth, NH: Heinemann.

Haour, Anne and Rossi, Benedetta (eds.) 2010. *Being and Becoming Hausa: Interdisciplinary Perspectives*. Leiden: Brill.

Harms, Robert 1981. *River of Wealth, River of Sorrow: the Central Zaire Basin in the Era of the Slave and Ivory Trade 1500–1891*. New Haven, CT: Yale University Press.

Harries, Patrick 1994. *Work, Culture, and Identity: Migrant Laborers in Mozambique and South Africa, c. 1860–1910*. Portsmouth, NH: Heinemann.

Hastings, Adrian 1997. *The Construction of Nationhood: Ethnicity, Religion and Nationalism*. Cambridge University Press.

Hill, Polly 1963. *The Migrant Cocoa-Farmers of Southern Ghana*. Cambridge University Press.

Hiskett, Mervyn 1973. *The Sword of Truth: the Life and Times of the Shehu Usman Dan Fodio*. Oxford University Press.

Hopkins, A. G. 1973. *An Economic History of West Africa*. London: Longman.

2009. 'The New Economic History of Africa', *Journal of African History* 50: 155–77.

Iliffe, John 1979. *A Modern History of Tanganyika*. Cambridge University Press.

1983. *The Emergence of African Capitalism*. London: Macmillan.

1987. *The African Poor: a History*. Cambridge University Press.

1995 [2007]. *Africans: the History of a Continent*. Cambridge University Press.

2005. *Honour in African History*. Cambridge University Press.

Kenyatta, Jomo 1938. *Facing Mount Kenya: the Tribal Life of the Gikuyu*. London: Secker and Warburg.

1964. *Harambee! The Prime Minister's Speeches 1963–4*. Nairobi: Oxford University Press.

Kershaw, Greet 1997. *Mau Mau from Below*. Oxford: James Currey.

Kopytoff, Igor 1987. 'The Internal African Frontier: the Making of African Political Culture', in *The African Frontier: the Reproduction of Traditional African Societies*, Igor Kopytoff (ed.). Bloomington, IN: Indiana University Press, 3–84.

Kuba, Richard and Lentz, Carola (eds.) 2006. *Land and the Politics of Belonging in West Africa*. Leiden: Brill.

Kurimoto, Eisei and Simsonse, Simon (eds.) 1998. *Conflict, Age and Power in North East Africa*. Oxford: James Currey.

Landau, Paul 1995. *The Realm of the Word: Language, Gender, and Christianity in a Southern African Kingdom*. Portsmouth, NH: Heinemann.

Last, Murray 1967. *The Sokoto Caliphate*. London: Longmans.

Law, Robin 1980. *The Horse in West African History*. Oxford University Press.

Lentz, Carola 1995. '"Tribalism" and Ethnicity in Africa: a Review of Four Decades of Anglophone Research', *Cahiers des Sciences Humaines* 31: 303–28.

Leys, Colin 1967. *Politicians and Policies: an Essay on Politics in Acholi, Uganda, 1962–5*. Nairobi: East African Publishing House.

Lonsdale, John 1992. 'The Moral Economy of Mau Mau', in *Unhappy Valley: Conflict in Kenya and Africa*, Bruce Berman and John Lonsdale. London: James Currey, chs. 11–12.

1996. 'Moral Ethnicity, Ethnic Nationalism and Political Tribalism: the Case of the Kikuyu', in *Staat und Gesellschaft in Afrika: Erosions- und Reformprozesse*, Peter Meyns (ed.). Hamburg: Lit Verlag, 93–106.

2002. 'Jomo Kenyatta, God, and the Modern World', in *African Modernities: Entangled Meanings in Current Debate*, Jan-Georg Deutsch, Peter Probst and Heike Schmidt (eds.). Oxford: James Currey, ch. 3, 31–66.

2004. 'Moral and Political Argument in Kenya', in *Ethnicity and Democracy in Africa*, Bruce Berman, Dickson Eyoh and Will Kymlicka (eds.). Oxford: James Currey, ch. 5, 73–95.

2005. '"Listen while I Read": Patriotic Christianity among the Young Gikuyu', in *Christianity and Social Change in Africa: Essays in Honour* of *J. D. Y. Peel*, Toyin Falola (ed.). Durham, NC: Carolina Academic Press, ch. 24, 563–93.

2009. 'Writing Competitive Patriotisms in Eastern Africa', in *Recasting the Past: History Writing and Political Work in Modern Africa*, Derek Peterson and Giacomo Macola (eds.). Athens, OH: Ohio University Press, 251–67.

Low, D. A. 1971. *Buganda in Modern History*. London: Weidenfeld and Nicolson.

2009. *Fabrication of Empire: the British and the Uganda Kingdoms, 1890–1902.* Cambridge University Press.

Lynch, Gabrielle 2008. 'Kenyan Politics and the Ethnic Factor: the Case of the Kalenjin', Ph.D. thesis, Oxford University.

MacArthur, Julie 2009. 'Mapping Political Community among the Luyia of Western Kenya 1930–63', Ph.D. thesis, Cambridge University.

Mackenzie, Fiona 1998. *Land, Ecology and Resistance in Kenya, 1880–1952*, Edinburgh: Edinburgh University Press.

Maddox, Gregory H. and Giblin, James L. (eds.) 2005. *In Search of a Nation: Histories of Authority and Dissidence in Tanzania*. Oxford: James Currey.

Marx, Karl 1973. *Grundrisse: Foundations of the Critique of Political Economy*. Harmondsworth: Penguin.

Mayer, Philip 1971 [1961]. *Townsmen or Tribesmen: Conservatism and the Process of Urbanization in a South African City*. Cape Town: Oxford University Press.

McCaskie, T. C. 1995. *State and Society in Pre-colonial Asante*. Cambridge University Press.

Miller, Joseph C. 1988. *Way of Death: Merchant Capitalism and the Angolan Slave Trade c. 1730–1830*. London: James Currey.

Moodie, Dunbar with Ndatshe, Vivienne 1994. *Going for Gold: Men, Mines and Migration*. Berkeley, CA: University of California Press.

Msindo, Enocent 2004. 'Ethnicity in Matabeleland, Zimbabwe: a Study of Kalanga-Ndebele Relations, 1860s–1980s', Ph.D. thesis, Cambridge University.

Mueller, Susanne 2008. 'The Political Economy of Kenya's Crisis', *Journal of Eastern African Studies* 2: 185–310.

2010. *Dying to Win: Elections, Political Violence, and Institutional Decay in Kenya*, Working Paper 263, African Studies Center, Boston University.

Muoria Sal, Wangari, Frederiksen, Bodil Folke, Lonsdale, John and Peterson, Derek, (eds.) 2009. *Writing for Kenya: The Life and Works of Henry Muoria*. Leiden: Brill.

Odinga, Oginga 1967. *Not Yet Uhuru*. London: Heinemann.

Oucho, John O. 2002. *Undercurrents of Ethnic Conflict in Kenya.* Leiden: Brill.

Parkin, David 1969. *Neighbours and Nationals in an African City Ward.* London: Routledge and Kegan Paul.

   1978. *The Cultural Definition of Political Response: Lineal Destiny among the Luo.* London: Academic Press.

Parsons, Timothy H. 2003. *The 1964 Army Mutinies and the Making of Modern East Africa.* Westport, CT: Praeger.

Peel, J. D. Y. 2000. *Religious Encounter and the Making of the Yoruba,* Bloomington: Indiana University Press.

Ranger, T. O. 1975. *Dance and Society in Eastern Africa, 1890–1970: the Beni 'Ngoma'.* London: Heinemann.

   1983. 'The Invention of Tradition in Colonial Africa', in *The Invention of Tradition,* E. J. Hobsbawm and T. O. Ranger (eds.). Cambridge University Press, 211–62.

   1993. 'The Invention of Tradition Revisited: the Case of Africa', in *Legitimacy and the State in Twentieth Century Africa,* Terence Ranger and Olufemi Vaughan (eds.). London: Macmillan, 62–111.

   2010. *Bulawayo Burning: the Social History of a Southern African City 1893–1960.* Woodbridge: Currey.

Roberts, Andrew 1976. *A History of Zambia.* London: Heinemann.

Robinson, David 1985. *The Holy War of Umar Tal.* Oxford University Press.

Schmidt, Elizabeth 2005. *Mobilizing the Masses: Gender, Ethnicity, and Class in the Nationalist Movement in Guinea, 1939–1958.* Portsmouth, NH: Heinemann.

Scott, James C. 1998. *Seeing Like a State: How Certain Schemes to Improve the Human Condition Have Failed.* New Haven, CT: Yale University Press.

Shipton, Parker 1989. *Bitter Money: Cultural Economy and Some African Meanings of Forbidden Commodities.* Washington, DC: American Anthropological Association.

   2007. *The Nature of Entrustment: Intimacy, Exchange and the Sacred in Africa.* New Haven, CT: Yale University Press.

   2009. *Mortgaging the Ancestors: Ideologies of Attachment in Africa.* New Haven, CT: Yale University Press.

Siméant, Johanna 2010. '"Economie Morale" et Protestation – détours Africains', *Genèses* 4 (81): 118–36.

Skinner, Elliott P. 1962. 'Trade and Markets among the Mossi People', in *Markets in Africa,* Paul Bohannan and George Dalton (eds.). Evanston, IL: Northwestern University Press, ch. 9.

Spear, Thomas 2003. 'Neo-traditionalism and the Limits of Invention in British Colonial Africa', *Journal of African History* 44: 3–27.

Spear, Thomas and Waller, Richard (eds.) 1993. *Being Maasai: Ethnicity and Identity in Eastern Africa.* London: James Currey.

Spencer, John 1985. *KAU: The Kenya African Union.* London: KPI.

Stedman-Jones, Gareth 1983. *Languages of Class: Studies in English Working-class History 1832–1982.* Cambridge University Press.

Thomas, Lynn M. 2003. *Politics of the Womb: Women, Reproduction and the State in Kenya.* Berkeley, CA: University of California Press.

Thompson, E. P. 1993. *Customs in Common.* Harmondsworth: Penguin.

van Onselen, Charles 1976. *Studies in the Social and Economic History of the Witwatersrand 1886–1914,* 2 volumes. London: Longman.

Waller, R. D. 1971. 'The Traditional Economy of Buganda', M.A. thesis, University of London.

　　2012. 'Ethnicity and Identity' in *The Oxford Handbook of Modern African History,* Richard Reid and John Parker (eds.). Oxford University Press.

Walzer, Michael 1985. *Exodus and Revolution.* New York: Basic Books.

Watson, William 1958. *Tribal Cohesion in a Money Economy: a Study of the Mambwe People of Northern Rhodesia.* Manchester University Press.

Wilks, Ivor 1975. *Asante in the Nineteenth Century: the Structure and Evolution of a Political Order.* Cambridge University Press.

　　1993. *Forests of Gold: Essays on the Akan and the Kingdom of Asante.* Athens, OH: Ohio University Press.

Wilson, Francis 1972. *Labour in the South African Gold Mines 1911–1969.* Cambridge University Press.

Wright, John and Hamilton, Carolyn 1990. 'The Making of the Amalala: Ethnicity, Ideology and Relations of Subordination in a Precolonial Context', *South African Historical Journal* 22: 3–23.

Young, Crawford 1982. 'Patterns of Social Conflict: State, Class, and Ethnicity', *Daedalus* 111: 71–98.

2 The concept of ethnicity: strengths and limitations for quantitative analysis

GRAHAM K. BROWN AND ARNIM LANGER

Introduction

In the previous chapter, John Lonsdale (Chapter 1) argued that ethnicity is a sense of belonging that influences, and is influenced by, a number of factors, and hence its defining characteristics can, and are indeed likely to, change over time. He goes on to argue that relations between ethnicity and markets vary, depending on what is traded, where it is traded and who is doing the trading. From this perspective, ethnicity is seen as inherently difficult to measure, and its relation with the economy cannot be represented by a simple algebraic equation. Lonsdale thus calls for extreme caution in interpreting, or even in accepting, the claims of an increasing number of political scientists and economists who have incorporated ethnic groups into their (empirical) analyses or use ethnic diversity as an independent variable for explaining a range of social and economic outcomes, most notably relating to violent group mobilisation, secessionist movements and economic growth differences (see, for example, Collier and Hoeffler 1998; Easterly 1997; Rodrik 1999; Sambanis 1999). This skepticism towards quantitative approaches is widely shared among historians and anthropologists, including Berman (Chapter 5) and Shipton (Chapter 7). Martin Doornbos has strikingly captured this position as follows: 'Ethnicity does not explain anything, it needs to be explained' (Doornbos 1991: 19).

This chapter takes a different perspective and shows how economists and political scientists are increasingly developing and deploying new techniques and more sophisticated measures of ethnicity that are more commensurate with theoretical perspectives on ethnicity. This chapter takes a step further in this direction, and proposes a conceptual framework based around the notion of 'social distance' that provides, we suggest, a convincing way to blend theoretically rich perspectives on ethnicity, such as those proposed by Lonsdale, with careful and serious quantitative analysis.

The chapter proceeds as follows. In the first section we will discuss different definitions of and approaches to ethnicity. The second section discusses how ethnicity is generally operationalised in the quantitative literature, explores the tensions between these approaches and the historical perspectives on ethnicity highlighted in the first section and proposes an alternative conceptual framework for quantitative analyses which, we suggest, substantially overcomes these tensions. The third section presents and discusses a range of measures that can be used to quantify and compare the degree of diversity and disparity across different countries and societal contexts. In the final section, we will draw some conclusions with regard to the usability and limitations of ethnicity and ethnic diversity as explanatory variables in social and economic research, with a particular focus on policy relevance.

What is 'ethnicity'?

While there is no universally accepted definition, ethnicity is generally characterised as a sense of group belonging, based on ideas of common origins, history, culture, language, experience and values (see, for example, Anderson 1983; Bates 2004; Glazer and Moynihan 1976; Horowitz 1985; Varshney 2001). In addition to real or putative common descent, most definitions of ethnicity emphasise 'the sharing of a "culture", the most notable aspect of which is language' (Bates 2004: 5). Three analytical approaches have emerged from the debates on the character of ethnicity: primordialism, instrumentalism and constructivism.

There appears to be a clear distinction between the ways in which people in non-scholarly and scholarly circles think about ethnicity and ethnic differences. The view that is popular in non-academic circles has been termed 'primordialism'. The primordialist view emphasises the 'affective properties of ethnicity' and asserts that people's ethnic consciousness is 'deeply embedded in the constitution of the self' (Young 2003: 13). Ethnicity is regarded as a *natural* result of biological differences or a long historical process (see, in particular, Van den Berghe 1978). Primordialists generally claim that ethnicity is unchanging and unique. While newspapers and magazines as well as politicians often take a primordialist view in order to explain the emergence of ethnic conflicts, among academics this is increasingly discredited. Consequently, as Kanchan Chandra notes, 'it is now virtually impossible to find a social scientist who *openly* defends a primordialist position' (Chandra 2001: 8, emphasis added).

In the academic literature, the primordialist view is usually associated with Edward Shils and Clifford Geertz (see Geertz 1963; Shils 1957). Yet, as Robin Cohen argues, Shils and Geertz's 'primordial' argument should not be equated with the political *practice* of primordialism and is hence rather more sophisticated and difficult to refute than might appear at first glance (see Cohen 1999). Geertz understood primordialism thus: 'By a primordial attachment is meant one that stems from the 'givens' of social existence ... congruities of blood, speech, custom and so on, *are seen* to have an ineffable, and at times overpowering, coerciveness in and of themselves. One is bound to one's kinsman, one's neighbour, one's fellow believer, *ipso facto* [by that very fact]; as the result not merely of personal affection, practical necessity, common interest, or incurred obligation, but at least in great part by virtue of some unaccountable absolute import attributed to the very tie itself' (Geertz 1963, quoted in Cohen 1999: 4, emphasis added). Thus, as Cohen points out, Clifford Geertz does not assert (as is often argued by anti-primordialists) that common blood, kinship and beliefs are primordial givens of social existence, but instead he argues that these things 'are seen' to be primordial.

From the beginning of the 1970s, the primordialist view of ethnicity was challenged by so-called 'instrumentalists' or 'functionalists'. The instrumentalists' main criticism focused on the primordialists' inability to see that certain episodes of apparently ancient hatred were 'selectively retrieved by the knowledge elite, ignoring the many instances of cooperation and coexistence' (Varshney 2001: 812). Moreover, most ethnic groups interact in a co-operative and peaceful rather than violent way (Fearon and Laitin 1996). Another weakness of the primordial view is its inability to explain why ethnic groups change over time.

The instrumentalist view emphasises the importance of ethnicity and ethnic affiliations in social, political and economic competition. Instrumentalists particularly focus on the role of elites in this respect. According to instrumentalists, ethnicity is a *resource* used by elites to define group identity, regulate group membership and boundaries and make claims and extract (state) resources (see, for example, Brass 1985; Glazer and Moynihan 1976; Hardin 1995; Rabushka and Shepsle 1972). Another reason why ethnic elites sometimes use and accentuate ethnic differences is 'to transfer potential hostility from inequalities and power disparities *within* their communities to the elites and subjects of other communities' (Nafziger and Auvinen 2002: 159, emphasis added).

Since the early 1980s, the constructivist perspective has probably become the most influential perspective in the study of ethnicity. In contrast to primordialists, constructivists tend to focus on the processes through which ethnic groups have emerged and have gained social significance (Ukiwo 2005). However, as Robert Bates argues the constructivist approach to ethnicity combines elements of both the primordial and instrumentalist approaches: 'In keeping with the primordialists, constructivists view ethnic identities as a cultural endowment; but in keeping with instrumentalists, they view ethnic identities as malleable. Distinguishing their position is the belief that while identities can be reshaped, they can be altered only at significant cost' (Bates 2004: 5).

In the process of identity construction, a crucial role is played by so-called 'cultural entrepreneurs who codify and standardise a language, equipping it with a written form, create an ethnos-centred historical narrative, populated with internal heroes and external villains, and build a literary tradition' (Young 2003: 14). In many African countries, the colonial regimes played an important role in the 'promotion', 'systematisation' and in some cases the actual 'invention' of ethnic groups and identities (see Ranger 1983; Young 1985).

While ethnic identities once constructed tend to endure and can arouse deep attachments from the people involved, the boundaries of ethnic groups remain fluid and situational. As Ralph Premdas puts it, 'the maintenance of boundaries is situationally determined, may shift over time and context, and generally serves to differentiate members dialectically and oppositionally from other groups in terms of "we–they" antipathies' (Premdas 1995: 4). However, the 'delineation' of ethnic groups is often quite arbitrary and can be the result of external processes or decisions taken by people who are not part of a group. Ukoha Ukiwo notes that 'ethnic groups may be "objectified" by recognition and classification by the state, religious institutions and the intelligentsia as well as by self-identification and recognition by others' (Ukiwo 2006: 21).

How do we operationalise 'ethnicity'?

There is, then, a clear academic consensus that the extreme primordialist position that views ethnic affiliation as fixed and unchanging is no longer tenable, if indeed it ever was thought to be so. What is less clear is the extent to which this renders quantitative inquiries that utilise 'measures' of ethnicity problematic. This debate is rendered more difficult to navigate because it often falls along disciplinary and methodological lines. Opposition to 'measuring' ethnicity is often bundled together with a broader opposition to quantitative methods and to positivist epistemologies in social science. In introducing their insightful collected volume examining the politics of census classifications from an anthropological perspective, for instance, David Kertzer and Dominique Arel (2002: 19) assert that the 'notion that cultural categories can be reduced to an objective core ... is dangerously close to the primordialist notion of timeless identities'.

It is clearly beyond the scope of this chapter to resolve these larger disputes, but before proceeding to discuss different specific measures of ethnicity, in this section we defend the proposition that while any measurement of ethnic diversity for quantitative inquiry may be *practically difficult*, it is not *conceptually impossible*. We can draw a parallel here with the quantitative measurement of democracy. As Gary Goertz (2006) discusses extensively, there are a range of measures of democracy available for quantitative inquiry, but what is important from a methodological perspective is what he terms 'concept–measure consistency'. Thus, for instance, while the common Polity dataset may be a useful measure of democracy if we are concerned with a conceptualisation of democracy that places emphasis on party competitiveness and balance of powers, it is less useful as a measure if we are concerned with the emancipatory dimension of democracy. This is because this latter dimension is not well coded in the Polity dataset – Switzerland, in the Polity dataset, is coded with a full ten points on democracy since 1848, despite not granting women the vote at the federal level until 1971.

From this perspective, the charge against quantitative measures of ethnicity is that they are employing data (usually census or survey responses) that are 'dangerously close' to primordialism to measure a concept ('ethnicity') that is generally agreed to be socially constructed – there is not good concept–measure consistency, in Goertz' terminology. Our claim in this section is that we *can* reconcile the concept and measurement in a consistent way, but that it requires critical and explicit attention to this relationship. In fact, such critical attention is present to some degree in the contemporary quantitative literature. In this section we first review the steps that have been taken to improve concept–measurement consistency in dealing with ethnicity and then proceed to make a more general argument about how to improve this consistency.

Until quite recently, these problems have been insufficiently acknowledged and addressed in most quantitative studies focusing on the implications of ethnic diversity on different social and economic outcomes. An important issue that illustrates this lack of methodological rigour is the fact that many scholars who have analysed statistically the relationship between ethnic diversity and violent conflict or economic growth have failed to define the concept of ethnicity, even though they were generally quite careful in defining other terms and concepts (Green 2004). Thus, for instance, William Easterly and Ross Levine, in their influential article 'Africa's Growth Tragedy: Policies and Ethnic Divisions', offer no definition of ethnicity and ethnic diversity is simply 'operationalised' by using the ethno-linguistic fractionalisation (ELF) data set (see Easterly and Levine 1997). Similarly, in Collier and Hoeffler's quantitative studies of violent conflict and civil war, ethnicity also remains undefined and again the ELF index is used to 'operationalise' ethnic diversity (see Collier and Hoeffler 1998, 2002). In both these studies the ELF index is only discussed in passing, without linking the composition of the data set to a particular perspective on ethnicity. Yet, as Elliot Green rightly notes, 'while many authors do not offer their own definition of ethnicity, they do, however, draw upon data sets of ethnic groups that needed to be based upon some objective criteria' (Green 2004: 16).

While some scholars ignore the definitional aspects of the concept of ethnicity altogether, others pay lip-service to a constructivist approach to ethnicity. Rogers Brubaker has argued in this respect that while the mainstream scholarship on ethnic politics has by and large moved away from the kind of ethnic primordialism associated with the works of Clifford Geertz, this has resulted nonetheless in the kind of '*clichéd constructivism*' in which broadly constructivist onto-logical pronouncements are followed by 'groupist' empirical analy-sis, which take the ethnic group as an essentially primordial given (Brubaker and Cooper 2000). While Brubaker's critique is valid and very important, we argue that his solution – that we should ana-lyse 'ethnicity without groups' and focus on the social *processes* of ethnicisation, social mobilisation and organisation, and *identifica-tion* (rather than 'identity') – seems to throw out the baby with the bathwater.

While quantitative studies of ethnic diversity are inherently prob-lematic because they require the reduction of ethnicity into exhaustive and mutually exclusive ethnic groups (something sophisticated theo-ries of ethnicity militate against), as long as the results are interpreted while cognisant of the limitations of this kind of categorisation, quan-titative analysis can provide a useful systematic form of comparison. Indeed, within the econometric and quantitative literature on ethnic conflict, there appears to be a shift towards taking such concerns into consideration through more nuanced 'measures' of ethnicity (Posner 2004). There are a number of other problems which make the con-struction of a cross-national data set of ethnic groups an inherently tricky exercise and which complicate the interpretation of significant correlations between a particular measure of ethnic diversity (based on these data sets) and some other 'dependent' variable (such as the emergence of political violence and positive economic growth). The two main problems relate to the following questions: (1) how can we identify the (main) ethnic groups of a country? and (2) how do we deal with changes in ethnic demography over time?

With regard to the first problem, James Fearon has emphasised the difficulty of coding ethnic groups and finding the 'right' list of ethnic groups: 'Anyone with primordialist leanings should be quickly disa-bused of them by undertaking to code "ethnic groups" in many differ-ent countries. It rapidly becomes clear that one must make all manner of borderline-arbitrary decisions, and that in many cases there is no single right answer to the question "What are the ethnic groups in this country?" Constructivist or instrumentalist arguments about the contingent, fuzzy, and situational character of ethnicity seem amply supported' (Fearon 2003: 197). Take, for example, Ghana. What is the most appropriate ethnic classification for this country? Should we distinguish between the four major ethno-linguistic groups (i.e. the Akan, Ewe, Ga-Dangmes and Mole-Dagbanis) or should we also take into account sub-divisions within these groups (the Akan, for example, consist of twenty smaller ethnic sub-groups of which the Ashantis and Fantis are demographically the most important ones)? Clearly, the approach we take in this respect will have a major impact on the 'measured' level of ethnic diversity, and consequently may have an important effect on the relationships we aim to test. Moreover, considering that there might be more than one 'plausible' ethnic classificatory scheme in certain countries, 'we must be careful that we do not, in effect, choose the coding that best supports our theory, after the fact' (Fearon 2003: 197).

While scholars such as James Fearon have addressed a pragmatic problem in 'listing' ethnic groups, however, there remains a concern that whatever 'level' one codes at, the ethnic groups that are coded for are those which have already been bestowed *political* significance through (usually, in the developing world) colonial processes of identity formation, bureaucratisation and census definition. The charge here is one of selection on the dependent variable: in using existing 'bureaucratic identities' to code ethnicity, we are using those identities that are already politicised to some degree.

With regard to both this issue and the issue of demographic changes over time, Daniel Posner identifies two different kinds of ethnic demographic changes; the first one relates to a change in the salient 'ethnic cleavage', while the second one involves 'changes in the number and relative sizes of groups' (Posner 2005: 2–3). With respect to the first type of ethnic demographic change, it is important to note that 'societies contain multiple dimensions of ethnic cleavage, each of which can be salient in different settings and historical moments' (Posner 2005: 2–3). India's 'ethnic' landscape, for example, looks quite different when defined in terms of ethnic, religious, language or caste differences (Posner 2005: 2–3). With respect to the second type of ethnic demographic change, it is important to note that changes in the number and relative sizes of ethnic groups can be the result of differences in natural growth patterns across groups, 'internal redefinitions' (as with the redefinition of Isaaqs and Hawiyes as separate ethnic groups in Somalia) and migration flows (Posner 2005: 2–3).

The way one deals with these issues (for example, whether one decides to enumerate groups on the basis of language, religion or caste differences) will again have a major impact on the 'measured' degree of ethnic diversity in a particular country.

Scholars such as Fearon and Posner, then, are usefully problematising the quantification of ethnicity and, in doing so, contributing towards bridging the concept–measurement divide. Here, however, we wish to propose a more general claim about the way in which we can conceptualise quantitative enquiries into 'ethnicity' in order to accommodate both the criticisms of data primordialism and the existing concept–measurement divide. Our claim is that in quantitative analysis of 'ethnicity', the concepts we are dealing with should *not* be conceived of as 'ethnicity' *per se*, but as 'diversity' and 'disparity', which can also be seen usefully together as a second-level conceptual dimension of a broader top-level concept of 'social distance'. This perspective that the concepts we are interested in quantitatively are not 'ethnicity' or 'religion' but more abstract notions of social distance is in fact more-or-less explicit or implicit in many of the proposed measures we discuss in the next section, which are concerned with concepts such as 'fractionalisation' and 'polarisation'. These latter concepts can in turn be seen as third-level conceptualisations of particular *forms* of social distance.

If the concepts we are dealing with quantitatively can be brought together under the broad notion of 'social distance', what role *does* 'ethnicity' play? Our suggestion is that in this scheme 'ethnicity' is an *indicator* that can be usefully operationalised, along with other forms of identity cleavage such as 'religion', 'gender' and so forth and along with indicators of disparity such as distribution of socio-economic and political resources, for the measurement of social distance. This does not mean that theoretical, conceptual and empirical enquiry into the nature of 'ethnicity' itself is not necessary or useful, but that insofar as we are interested in examining quantitatively the relationship between 'ethnicity' and different economic and political outcomes such as the provision of public goods, violent conflict and economic growth, a theoretical stance that posits 'ethnicity' as an indicator of the concept of 'social distance' appears both to be closer to the way in which these measures are already implicitly constructed, and to resolve many of the theoretical objections to the use of purportedly primordial data sets for the construction of these measures.

To expand upon this latter claim, if we reconceive of ethnicity as an indicator of social diversity and disparity, the fact that the data we typically employ in the measurement of this indicator are neither as fluid nor as multidimensional as theorists of ethnicity *qua* ethnicity contend is less problematic because we may regard this as an issue of measurement bias and measurement error. Bias, because the categories we use are acknowledged to be those legitimised by historical state practices. Error, because the exclusive and exhaustive codings employed do not fully capture the nuance of ethnic identity. It may seem perverse to contend that some of the theoretical problems with measuring 'ethnicity' are resolved by acknowledging measurement bias and measurement error, but our contention is that this is less problematic than reconciling 'primordial' data with constructivist concepts. Measurement error and measurement bias are inherent features of virtually all quantitative variables – even something as apparently uncontentious as gross domestic product (GDP) is subject to bias – the exclusion or underestimation of the informal sector and other productive activities such as housework – and measurement error – as witnessed by the often large statistical discrepancy between the different methods of calculating GDP. One of the advantages of quantitative methods is that the accumulation of multiple observations allows us to minimise problems of measurement error in the examination of causal relationships and correlations.

To summarise, then, within a Goertz-style schema we suggest that the various measures discussed below be understood as measures of different sub-concepts of diversity and disparity – for instance, fractionalisation or horizontal inequality – and that these two in turn can be seen as sub-concepts of a broader notion of social distance. Crucially, however, we treat 'ethnicity' in this formulation as an *indicator* of diversity in the same way that land-ownership or income is an indicator of disparity. This conceptual map is depicted schematically in Figure 2.1.

How do we measure diversity and disparity?

In the previous sections, then, we defended conceptual notions of diversity and disparity and argued that they were consistent with sophisticated theories of ethnicity as long as we treat the categorical 'ethnic' data employed in these measures as indicators of social

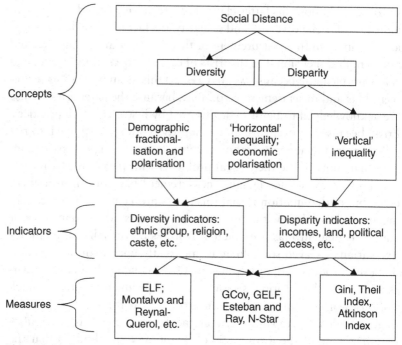

Figure 2.1. Conceptual map of social distance

distance rather than as ethnicity *qua* ethnicity. In this section, we
review the range of measures of 'ethnicity' available in the quantitative literature. In accordance with our conceptual mapping, however,
we treat these as different measures of social distance which may
combine aspects of diversity and of disparity. We hence distinguish
between 'pure' measures of diversity that measure (ethnic) diversity
alone – that is, the measure has only one type of input: the number or
population proportion of each group – and what we term 'synthetic'
measures – measures that incorporate information on ethnic diversity
with other information on between-group *disparity*, particularly geographical location, economic resources and political power. Clearly, a
third class of measures is possible, incorporating information about
disparity but not about diversity; into this class of measures would fall
various traditional indicators of inequality such as the Gini coefficient
and the Atkinson index, which are extensively discussed and debated
elsewhere. It is important here to note that many of the measures we
discuss in the synthetic section are flexible enough to be used in other

ways – the indices of geographical segregation that we discuss below, for instance, can easily be adapted as measures of occupational or educational segregation in the economic sphere.

Pure diversity measures

Leaving aside classificatory schemes (Bangura 2001) or 'dummy' variables for certain patterns of ethnic diversity such as Collier and Hoeffler's 'ethnic dominance' dummy, the most common and longest-used 'pure' measure of ethnic diversity is the notion of ethnic 'fractionalisation'. Fractionalisation purports to capture statistically the degree to which a population is divided into a large number of small groups. Statistically, the index used to measure fractionalisation can be intuitively interpreted as the probability that two randomly selected individuals from the entire population belong to different groups (see Appendix 2.1 for details). The measure hence scores zero in a perfectly homogenous population (i.e. all individuals belong to the same group) and reaches its theoretical maximum value of 1 where an infinite population is divided into infinite groups of one member.

The fractionalisation index is often criticised but this critique usually relates to the *data* employed to construct the index rather than the index itself. The data originally used to construct the ELF measure, the *Atlas Naradov Mira*, were based on a worldwide survey of ethnic diversity by a group of Soviet ethnologists in the early 1960s and published as an atlas (Bruk and Apenchenko 1964). As James Fearon further notes: 'The Soviet team mainly used language to define groups, but sometimes included groups that seem to be distinguished by some notion of race rather than language, and quite often used national origin (e.g. Anglo-Canadians are listed in the United States)' (Fearon 2003: 196).

While the ELF is easy to use, different scholars have pointed out serious faults and weaknesses of the index (see, in particular, Chandra 2001; Green 2004; Laitin and Posner 2001; Posner 2004). While some of these criticisms are specific to the ELF index, others focus more generally on the limitations of measuring ethnic diversity (Posner 2004). First, the ELF index has been criticised for not accurately representing ethnic diversity for at least three reasons: (1) it is actually predominantly based on linguistic categories, and it therefore misses 'multiple dimensions of ethnic identity in all countries' (Laitin and Posner 2001: 14); (2) it is out of date and thus unrepresentative both of demographic changes over the past four decades and the realignment of country boundaries over the same period; and (3) it 'also suffers from a number of basic coding inaccuracies' (Posner 2004: 850).

Second, and more fundamentally, it is argued that the use of frac-tionalisation in econometric analysis is problematic as it assumes that the political outcomes we are interested in vary with the level of fractionalisation rather than some other diversity measure. This lat-ter critique gave birth to the concept of (demographic) polarisation. Daniel Posner identifies a number of other problems with summarising a country's 'ethnic landscape with a single index of fractionalisation', including the problem that the Herfindahl formula (which underlies the ELF index) is 'insensitive to a great deal of potentially relevant variation in the ethnic landscapes of the countries being compared', the problem 'that ethnic fractionalisation indices such as the ELF fail to incorporate potentially relevant information about the spatial dis-tribution of groups around the country' and the problem that frac-tionalisation indices 'convey no information about the *depth* of the divisions that separate members of one group from another' (Posner 2004: 851). The serious shortcomings of the ELF index have driven a number of scholars to attempt to construct new measures and indices (see, for example, Alesina *et al.* 2003; Fearon 2003; Posner 2004). While these new ethnic diversity measures, such as Fearon's index and Posner's politically relevant ethnic groups (PREG) index, are very good at addressing some of the major faults of the ELF index, a major 'problem' with them is that they are no longer 'pure' demographic measures. Thus, for instance, Posner's PREG index is 'an index of fractionalisation that reflects the groups *that are actually doing the competing over policy*, not the ones that an ethnographer happens to identify as representing distinct cultural units' (Posner 2004: 853, original emphasis).

Dissatisfied with the assumption that fractionalisation is the most important type of ethnic demography, Montalvo and Reynal-Querol (2005) have developed an index of demographic *polarisation* rather than fractionalisation. Working particularly within the context of ethnic conflict, the assumption behind their measure is that while the fractionalisation–conflict matrix rightly attributes a low chance of eth-nic conflict to homogenous populations, highly fractionalised societies are also less likely to be conflictual as no group has the 'critical mass'

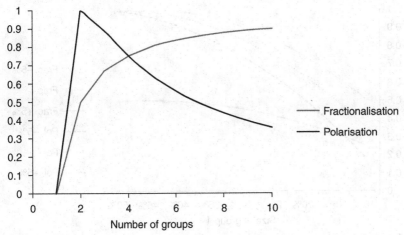

Figure 2.2. Pure demographic measures for evenly sized groups

necessary for conflict. Instead, they postulate that conflict is more likely the more a population is polarised into two large groups.

Like the fractionalisation index, this measure scores zero in a homogenous population, but also tends towards zero in highly fractionalised populations, reaching its maximum instead at the point of even distribution between two groups. The relationship between fractionalisation and polarisation is thus broadly quadratic, taking the form of an inverse U-curve, with greater variation at the peak of the curve. Comparing their measure against the fractionalisation index, Montalvo and Reynal-Querol (2005) find a statistically significant relationship between religious polarisation and conflict, but no such relationship with religious fractionalisation. The different relationships the fractionalisation and polarisation indices pick up can be illustrated graphically by comparing the results they produce for populations divided into different numbers of evenly sized groups (see Figure 2.2). Both measures score zero where there is only one group, but whereas the fractionalisation index increases at a declining speed as the number of groups in increased, the polarisation index jumps to its maximum with two groups and then declines away as the number of groups increases.

The fractionalisation and demographic polarisation indices discussed here have several significant advantages for econometric analysis of ethnicity. Firstly, they are both intuitively and easily interpreted.

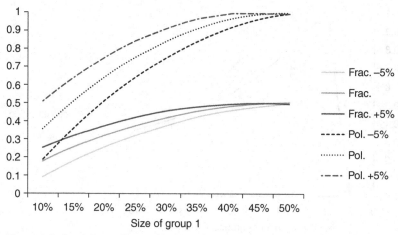

Figure 2.3 Sensitivity of pure demographic measures to variation in group size

Secondly, they are not data hungry and can be calculated with bare population proportions, which are widely available for most countries and, in many cases, sub-units of countries (regions, cities, etc.). Of course, these measures are still subject to the criticism that they do not cater to the fluidity and vagueness of ethnic identities, but if we interpret them, as proposed above, as *indicators* of social diversity, then this is less problematic. Moreover, because these measures are surprisingly *insensitive* to small variations in group size, the reduction of ethnic diversity into an exclusive and exhaustive category set is less problematic: we can tolerate a degree of measurement error (groups are not in actuality the same size as suggested in the data, or have changed composition over time) and arbitrary categorisation (a small proportion of individuals do not 'fit' properly into the categorical framework) and still have confidence that the measure produces a reasonable estimation of diversity. Figure 2.3 demonstrates the sensitivity of the two measures in a two-group scenario. Each measure is calculated for different distributions, where Group 1 is from 10 per cent of the population to 50 per cent and where Group 2 from 90 per cent to 50 per cent. We then recalculate the measures assuming a 5 per cent error both positively and negatively. It can be seen that where both groups are at least reasonably sizable, the variation in the index is relatively small, even with a sizeable measurement error of 5 per cent.

Synthetic measures of ethnic disparity

Geographical distribution and ethnic diversity: segregation indices

The measures of ethnic diversity discussed thus far have related to national-level functions of population distribution. Yet there is reason to suppose that the way in which groups are geographically concentrated may have important ramifications for ethnic politics, including conflict and economic development. There is intuitively a much greater risk of political instability if a 5 per cent minority group is concentrated in one particular region of the country than if it were dispersed evenly across the country.

While segregation indices have only been used recently in the study of ethnicity in the developing world (see Kasara 2010), within the sociological literature on race relations in the US extensive use has been made of such indices of segregation focusing, for instance, on educational establishments. These indices measure how far different ethnic groups are concentrated across particular 'units' – schools, geographical regions, occupations, etc. (Coleman *et al.* 1982; Reardon and Yun 2001). There is not one established or dominant index, however. Reardon and Firebaugh (2002) review the available sets of segregation indices in depth and distinguish four different analytical components of segregation, which are catered for in various combinations by existing indices, two of which are of particular importance:

- Disproportionality – segregation as 'a function of the disproportionality in group proportions across organizational units' (Reardon and Firebaugh (2002: 39). Thus, for instance, if Group A constitutes 10 per cent of the overall population but 40 per cent of one particular unit (e.g. geographical region), that group is disproportionately represented in the unit.
- Association – segregation as 'association between groups and organizational units', producing measures related to basic statistics such as the χ^2.

In addition, Reardon and Firebaugh identify a number of axiomatic principles that a segregation index should satisfy, including the transfer principle, which states that the segregation index should show a reduction if a person is moved from one unit to another unit in which the person's group is less predominant than in their original unit. This principle turns out to be of particular pragmatic importance because only one measure, which they term H, satisfies this principle; H also incorporates both the disproportionality and the association components of segregation (see Appendix 2.1 for details).

To operationalise the segregation index for measuring geographic segregation, we need to identify the appropriate 'unit' across which group distributions are to be measured. An intuitively plausible option is the primary administrative divisions (PADs) of the country in question – usually states in federal systems (e.g. the US, Nigeria, etc.) and provinces (e.g. Indonesia, Canada), regions (UK) or *départements* in unitary states.

Using the PADs of a country as the basis for computing an ethnic segregation index presents two interlinked problems, however. Firstly, the size of PADs varies considerably from country to country, both in relative terms – the average proportion of the total population in each PAD – and in absolute terms – the absolute number of inhabitants in each PAD. Indeed, such size variation can occur within the same country, as well as across countries. To give an extreme example, the Indonesian province of East Java contains around 35 million inhabitants, or 17 per cent of the national population; in contrast, the province of North Maluku has around 800,000 inhabitants, less than 0.5 per cent of the national population. Clearly, the larger the proportion of the total population contained with one subdivision, the larger the amount of segregation that could be 'hidden' within that province. We can demonstrate this with the two simple examples below. In scenario 1, three groups are distributed across three states, each group slightly concentrated in a different state, producing a segregation index (using *SEGH*) of 0.054. Scenario 2 describes the same population, but with states B and C merged to form state D. By combining these two states, the segregation measure is reduced by a half to 0.028, even though the 'actual' physical segregation of the groups has not altered, merely the administrative calculus (see Table 2.1).

A second problem relates to the *way* in which countries are subdivided. Assuming that the 'actual' spatial distribution of (ethnic) groups is relatively segregated, administrative boundaries can be drawn in a way that either accentuates or minimises the calculation of segregation. Administrative boundaries drawn 'around' (ethnic) groups will accentuate the measure of segregation; boundaries drawn

Table 2.1. *Scenarios of geographical segregation*

Scenario 1	Group 1	Group 2	Group 3
State A	10	10	20
State B	20	10	10
State C	10	20	10
Scenario 2	**Group 1**	**Group 2**	**Group 3**
State A	10	10	20
State D	30	30	20

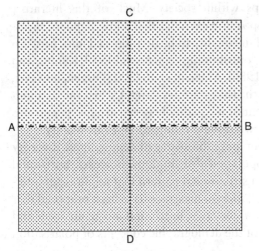

Figure 2.4 Schematic diagram of segregation

'through' ethnic groups will minimise the measure. An extreme, sim-
plified version of this problem is portrayed in Figure 2.4, which depicts
a 'country' physically segregated into two groups, one of which occupies the 'north' of the country, the other the 'south'. If the country is
divided into two administrative zones along the 'east–west' axis (line
AB), segregation is complete – such a situation would score 1 on all
six segregation measures. If, on the other hand, the country is divided
along the 'north–south' axis (line CD), the *administrative* segregation
of the country would score 0; each zone would be equally balanced
between the two groups.

Segregation indices have not been employed extensively in development literature related to ethnic diversity, but Kasara has shown that it is a powerful tool for analysing ethnic conflicts. The segregation indices also have clear potential applications in investigating regional dynamics of economic growth and service provision. Moreover, in line with our observation above about the flexibility of synthetic measures, segregation indices may prove useful in exploring economic and sociological ramifications of ethnic segregation across non-geographical units, such as the industrial sector.

Economic distribution and ethnic diversity

There is a growing literature on different measures of 'horizontal' inequality between groups within society. Much of this literature relates to technical decomposition exercises that allow standard measures of individual 'vertical' inequality to be decomposed into 'between group' and 'within group' contributions (e.g. Anand 1983; Kanbur and Zhang 1999; Maasoumi 1986). Mancini *et al.* (2008) argue, however, that such decomposition measures are less useful when one is interested primarily in the extent of inequality between groups *qua* groups because they conflate the two different dimensions of inequality.

Just as there are different 'pure' measures of demographic diversity that pick up different population distributions, however, horizontal *inequality* is not the only distributional pattern that might be of interest in diverse populations. Different measures have been proposed that capture different patterns of disparity: horizontal inequality itself and two economic extensions of the demographic concepts of polarisation and fractionalisation.

In fact, in terms of horizontal inequality, there are a range of possible measures that largely correspond to horizontal extensions of the traditional range of vertical inequality measures. After a review of different available 'direct' measures of horizontal group inequality, Mancini *et al.* conclude that the best available measure, which they term the GCov, is the simple population-weighted coefficient of variation in group means to the overall average – one of the measures proposed by Williamson in his early study of regional inequality (Williamson 1965; see Appendix 2.1 for statistical details). Intuitively, this can be interpreted as the extent to which group mean incomes (or other variables) vary from the overall mean. It is weighted for population size, which means that a large group with a mean income far from the overall mean has a proportionately larger effect on the inequality measure than a smaller group with the same mean income.

An alternative approach to measuring horizontal disparity between groups has been proposed by Esteban and Ray. The approach captures *economic* polarisation rather than the purely demographic polarisation captured by Montalvo and Reynal-Querol (Duclos *et al.* 2004; Esteban and Ray 1994; see Appendix 2.1 for statistical details). Esteban and Ray argue that economic polarisation (which we term here 'ER'), defined as the extent to which a population 'is grouped into significantly sized "clusters" such that each group is very "similar" in terms of the attributes of its members, but different clusters have members with very "dissimilar" attributes' (Esteban and Ray 1994: 819), is an important and both qualitatively and quantitatively different dimension of distribution than inequality. They go on to argue that polarisation may be high even when inequality is low and hence may provide a better correlate of conflict. Their measure can be interpreted as an extension of the Montalvo and Reynal-Querol measure of demographic polarisation, with distances weighted by relative economic distance; if economic distances are ignored, the measure collapses to the demographic polarisation index.

A final measure of horizontal disparity we discuss here is the generalised fractionalisation index (GELF) proposed by Bossert *et al.* (2011). This measure is slightly more complex than the previous two, but is very flexible in its application (see Appendix 2.1 for details). Whereas the ELF can be interpreted as the probability that two randomly chosen individuals belong to different ethnic groups, then, the analogous intuitive interpretation of the GELF is simply the average expected *level of dissimilarity* between two individuals drawn at random from the population.

The great flexibility of the GELF measures is that potentially any number of dimensions – cultural, geographical, socio-economic, political, etc. – can be incorporated into the measure. In addition, it does not dictate *how* entries into the similarity matrix are to be computed, although one could easily stipulate certain intuitive limitations upon the calculation, e.g. that an increase in 'distance' between two individuals on any one dimension should, *ceteris paribus*, result in a decrease

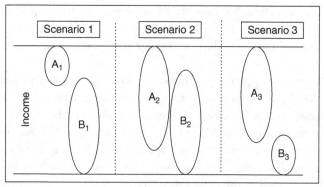

Figure 2.5 Scenarios of inter-group disparity

in 'similarity'. As we explore below, however, this also renders the measure arguably *too* flexible and possibly arbitrary.

The three measures described above (i.e. GCov, ER and GELF) all synthesise dimensions of socio-economic disparity with measures of demographic distribution, but purport to capture different relationships – inequality, polarisation and fractionalisation, respectively. In an inter-group context, however, none of these has an immediately intuitive interpretation. To elucidate this, Figure 2.5 depicts three stylised distributional scenarios. In scenario 1, a relatively small group, A_1 is much richer on average than the larger group, B_1. Scenario 2 shows two evenly sized groups, one of which is slightly richer than the other. Finally, scenario 3 reverses scenario 1, with a large wealthy group and a small poorer one. How would one intuitively rank these in terms of horizontal inequality, economic polarisation and generalised fractionalisation (assuming, in this latter case, no within-group heterogeneity)? Scenario 2 clearly has the highest level of *demographic* polarisation and would score a maximum 1.0 on the demographic measure discussed above, but how does it rank in terms of economic polarisation? This clearly depends to some degree on how much 'weight' we assign to each of the different dimensions of polarisation – economic and demographic – in the computation of the measure, a task performed by the α variable in the equation, as well as on how big the actual economic distance is. Similarly, we could reasonably assert that scenario 2 is the least unequal, but selecting which of scenarios 1 and 3 are the most unequal is more difficult. Moreover – and this point we will return to in some depth below – whichever measure we choose, we need to be aware that different scenarios such as those laid out below might have radically different implications in terms of political economy – for instance, group competition versus co-operation, as well as conflict potential – which cannot necessarily be neatly ordered by a single synthetic measure.

In the first place, however, we compare how these different measures rank different distributions. We do this by comparing stylised distributions. To compare stylised distributions, we systematise the type of scenario depicted above by calculating each different measure in two group scenarios with five different income ratios between the richer and the poorer group: 2, 4, 6, 8 and 10. We calculate each measure for all possible demographic distributions, from the richer group constituting 1 per cent of the population to 99 per cent of the population. To give some idea of what these ratios mean in the real world, in South Africa at the height of Apartheid in 1970, the dispersion ratio of average incomes between Whites and Blacks was 13:1 (van den Berg and Louw 2004), while the politically sensitive Chinese–Malay income ratio in Malaysia has varied between around 3:1 and 2:1 since 1970.

For the GCov, we need no further information to compute the measure. For the economic polarisation index ER, we need to set the free variable α, which we set near its maximum 1.5, following other implementations of the measure (e.g. Ezcurra 2009); we discuss later the impact of varying α. For the GELF measure, we need to define the similarity matrix. With two variables of interest – 'ethnic' group and income – we operationalise the matrix by giving equal weight (0.5) to each dimension. The ethnic dimension is a simple dummy – 'individuals' of the same group score the full value (i.e. 0.5); those of different groups score the minimum value 0. For the income dimension, we take the reciprocal of the income ratio. Again, we assume no within-group income variation.

Figure 2.6, Figure 2.7 and Figure 2.8 below exhibit the results of these scenario calculations. At the lowest income ratio of 2:1, the curve traced by all three measures as we increase the proportion of the population in the richer group is broadly similar, tracing out an inverse-U curve. While the GELF measure produces an exactly symmetrical curve, with its maximum point at the 50:50 distribution, the other two measures are skewed towards higher results where the richer group is less than half the population; the GCov reaches its maximum where

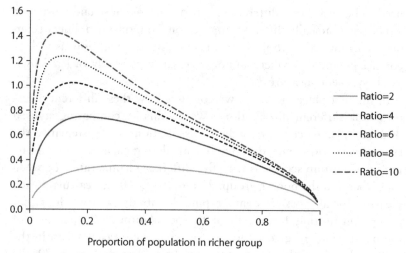

Figure 2.6 Scenarios of horizontal inequality in a two-group context

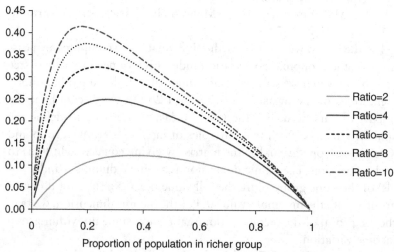

Figure 2.7 Scenarios of economic polarisation in a two-group context

the rich group constitutes one-third of the population; the ER where it constitutes slightly over one-third at 36.666 per cent.

As we increase the between-group income ratio, the GELF measure remains symmetrical with the peak tending asymptotically towards 0.50. Where there is a theoretical complete economic as well as

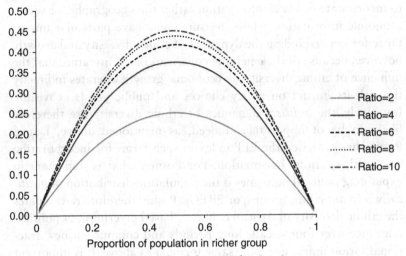

Figure 2.8 Scenarios of generalised fractionalisation in a two-group context with no within-group inequality

cultural distance between the two groups, the measure would collapse into the ethnic fractionalisation index, which gives a result of 0.50 for a population distribution of 50:50. For the other two measures, however, as the disparity ratio increases, the peak of the curve becomes increasingly skewed towards reporting higher levels of inequality/polarisation in the population distributions with a smaller rich group: at the highest income ratio calculated here, 10:1, the GCov reaches its maximum where the rich group constitutes around 10 per cent of the population; the ER polarisation index at around 18 per cent. While the GCov and ER measures clearly behave differently from the GELF at high inequality ratios, then, it is less clear that they are picking up qualitatively different distributions as claimed by Esteban and Ray. Moreover, the differences between these curves and the GELF measure only really emerge at high levels of inequality which we would rarely see in the real world, although it must be borne in mind that the GELF measure is also able to incorporate dimensions of within-group heterogeneity, which we have presumed to be zero here.

Political distribution and ethnic diversity

Less well developed in the literature, but nonetheless worth reviewing briefly, are measures of ethnic diversity that have been developed to incorporate *political* information rather than geographic or socio-economic information. These measures may have particular importance for understanding the dynamics of ethnic diversity and growth, however, because of the emerging consensus in the literature that the influence of ethnic diversity on economic growth operates indirectly through its impact on policy choices and public goods provision. Intuitively, the *political* dynamics of ethnic diversity are therefore likely to be of importance. Indeed, as mentioned above, Daniel Posner has criticised the ELF index in such terms for incorporating too much spurious information. For Posner, what is important in explaining political outcomes is the population distribution of *politically relevant* ethnic groups, or PREGs. Posner therefore re-estimates the ethnic diversity of African countries based on criteria of political relevance over four decade-long periods and computes a new fractionalisation index, using the same formula as above. It is important to distinguish between Posner's PREGs and other attempts to re-estimate the ELF, such as that of Alesina *et al.* (2003). Alesina *et al.* are concerned with the *quality* of data going into the ELF formula, but still describe a 'pure' measure of fractionalisation. By excluding politically irrelevant groups, Posner's PREGs constitute a 'synthetic' measure in so far as there is a non-demographic (i.e. political) dimension in the computation of the index, even if this is simply what is 'left out', so to speak.

Lars-Erik Cederman and Luc Girardin (2007) develop a synthetic measure of ethnic diversity aimed at capturing both the importance of *dyadic* relationships and the importance of political power, which they term N* (N-star). Primarily aimed at mapping ethnic conflict rather than ethnic politics and developmental performance, Cederman and Girardin envisage ethnic politics as a 'star-like' constellation in which the overall level of diversity or polarisation is less important than the interaction between the group(s) that control the state, and group(s) that do not control the state. Their measure stipulates the attribution of ethnic groups in power (EGIP) and assumes that those groups lie at the centre of a 'star-like' configuration, whereby the total risk of conflict is a multiplicative function of the risk of conflict between the EGIP and *each* other group separately.

Figure 2.9 schematically depicts the calculation of the N* index for a hypothetical country with one group in power that constitutes 30 per cent of the population (A), and three other groups, B, C and D,

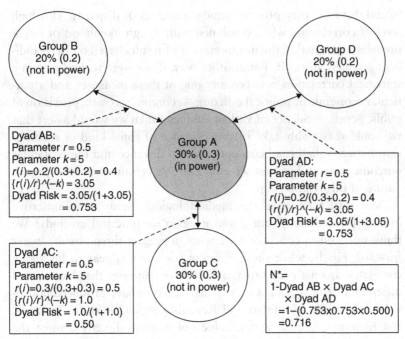

Group B
20% (0.2)
(not in power)

Group D
20% (0.2)
(not in power)

Group A
30% (0.3)
(in power)

Dyad AB:
Parameter $r = 0.5$
Parameter $k = 5$
$r(i) = 0.2/(0.3+0.2) = 0.4$
$\{r(i)/r\}^\wedge(-k) = 3.05$
Dyad Risk = 3.05/(1+3.05)
= 0.753

Dyad AD:
Parameter $r = 0.5$
Parameter $k = 5$
$r(i) = 0.2/(0.3+0.2) = 0.4$
$\{r(i)/r\}^\wedge(-k) = 3.05$
Dyad Risk = 3.05/(1+3.05)
= 0.753

Dyad AC:
Parameter $r = 0.5$
Parameter $k = 5$
$r(i) = 0.3/(0.3+0.3) = 0.5$
$\{r(i)/r\}^\wedge(-k) = 1.0$
Dyad Risk = 1.0/(1+1.0)
= 0.50

Group C
30% (0.3)
(not in power)

N*=
1-Dyad AB × Dyad AC
× Dyad AD
=1−(0.753×0.753×0.500)
=0.716

Figure 2.9 Graphical representation of Cederman and Girardin's N* measure

which constitute respectively 20 per cent, 30 per cent and 20 per cent
of the population.

Conclusions

In this chapter, we have reviewed the ontological debates over the
nature of ethnicity and the different ways in which it is operationalised and 'measured' for quantitative research. In the first two sections, we defended the use of such measures by arguing that while the
apparently 'primordial' implications of the ethnicity data that form the
basis of such measurements are incommensurate with the complexity
of ethnicity in reality, their employment in quantitative measures can
be reconciled in so far as we treat 'ethnicity' as an indicator of concepts of diversity and social distance, rather than as the concept being
measured in itself. In the latter two sections, however, we identified a
more practical problem with these measures: while they purport to
capture very different distributional relationships and dimensions of

'social distance' they produce similar rankings of disparity. This high level of correlation, when combined with a high likelihood of measurement error, makes the interpretation of results based on these indices extremely difficult. Put another way, if we were to find a strong statistical correlation between any one of these measures and a particular economic or political outcome – economic growth, provision of public goods, incidence of violent conflict – then we would assert that we could reasonably take this as evidence of some kind of relationship between the broad concept of social distance and the particular outcome we test, but that we could be less certain about the precise nature of this relationship.

Does this, then, save the methodological rigour of quantitative inquiry into ethnicity, but doom it again on practical grounds? We think not, and in conclusion we wish to suggest three possible ways forward. Firstly, while these different measures appear to be highly correlated against each other, quantitative enquiries that have tested different measures against a particular outcome *have* produced noticeable differences. Montalvo and Reynal-Querol (2005), for instance, test their measure of demographic polarisation directly against the fractionalisation index, using the same data, and find that polarisation is a significant correlate of ethnic conflict where fractionalisation is not. Similarly, Posner (2004) is able to use the differences between the significance of the ELF and his PREG index to explore the precise mechanisms through which ethnic diversity affects economic growth in Africa. The high empirical correlation between these various measures demonstrated here certainly cautions us to be extremely careful in interpreting such results, but as data improve and the possibility emerges of meta-analyses that compare the same equations across different data sets, we may gain more confidence in such results.[1]

Secondly, we suggest that the results reported here encourage us towards more theoretically sophisticated measures such as the N^* that not only 'map' social distance but also incorporate a specific theorised *mechanism* linking social distance to a specific outcome. While

[1] Brown and Langer (2011), for instance, replicate Sambanis' (2005) meta-study of civil war incidence across different conflict data sets with critical attention to the passage of time, and find – in qualified support of Montalvo and Reynal-Querol – that while ethnic fractionalisation does not provide a strong correlate of conflict in any time period across any definition of conflict, ethnic polarisation does appear to provide a consistent correlate in a particular time period.

data limitations prevented us from comparing the N* measure with the other measure of political disparity review, the PREG, Cederman and Girardin themselves compare the N* with the basic ELF, finding that N* is a significant correlate of ethnic conflict, where ELF is not. Crucially, the direct correlation between their measure and N* is very low (correlation coefficient 0.42). In this case, then, we have strong evidence of a particular mechanism translating social distance in a particular political outcome, and the low correlation between this theoretically rich 'process' measure and the less sophisticated 'mapping' measure should comfort us that we have, indeed, identified something specific. This is encouraging, but it also clearly calls more attention to development of such sophisticated measures and less 'off-the-shelf' (Kalyvas 2008) style analyses that combine existing data sets with different outcomes. As noted above, the advantage of some of the measures discussed, such as the GELF and the segregation indices, is their flexibility. The advantage of the N* measure, however, is its *inflexibility* – it purports to capture a precise relationship between a particular form of social distance and a particular outcome. Furthermore, it can be tested as such.

The final conclusion that we can draw from this review of quantitative approaches to ethnicity is the need for more engagement with qualitative analyses such as those presented in Chapter 1 (Lonsdale), Chapter 5 (Berman) and Chapter 7 (Shipton). Where data or theoretical limitations are substantial, or where we can only use indices that are highly correlated empirically but purport to pick up different relationships, a properly iterative combination of quantitative and qualitative enquiry can be expected to provide better insights into the particular mechanisms at work.

Appendix 2.1: statistical measures

Fractionalisation

Where a population is divided into N groups, each of which constituting proportion p_i of the population, the fractionalisation index is given as the following equation:

$$FRAC = 1 - \sum_{i=1}^{N} p_i^2$$

Demographic polarisation

Where a population is divided into N groups, each of which constituting proportion p_i of the population, the fractionalisation index is given as:

$$MRQ = 4 \sum_{i=1}^{N} p_i^2 (1 - p_i)$$

Segregation

Derived from the Theil information index, the formula for H (here termed $SEGH$) is given as:

$$SEGH = \sum_{m=1}^{M} \sum_{j=1}^{J} \frac{t_i}{TE} \pi jm \ \text{In} \ \frac{\pi jm}{\pi_m}$$

where:

$$E = \sum_{m=1}^{M} \pi_m \ \text{In} \ \frac{1}{\pi_m}$$

and:

- j and m respectively denote index units and groups;
- t_j stands for the number of individuals in unit j;
- π_{jm} is the proportion of unit j constituted by group m;
- π_m is the proportion of group m in the overall population; and
- T is the total population.

Horizontal inequality (GCov)

Where n ethnic groups have a mean income (years of education, etc.) y_i, with an overall mean of $\bar{y}$, and which constitute proportion p_i of the total population, then we have the following:

$$GCov = \left(\sum_{i=1}^{n} p_i (y_i - \bar{y})^2 \right)^{1/2}$$

Economic polarisation

Derived axiomatically, the Esteban and Ray measure is given as the following formula:

$$ER = k\sum_{i=1}^{n}\sum_{i=1}^{n} p_i^{1+\alpha} p_j \, |y_i - y_j|$$

Therein, n groups constitute p_i proportion of the total population and have an economic endowment (income, assets, etc.) of y_i. The constant k is a normalising function that can be set to $1/\mu$ (where μ is the overall population mean) to allow for comparability across populations. The other constant, α, is the required degree of 'polarisation sensitivity' (Esteban and Ray 1994: 834) and is bounded by the range $0 \leq \alpha \leq 1.6$. Where $\alpha=0$, the formula is exactly equivalent to the Gini coefficient; as α rises, the measure places more weight on how far the population is polarised into two large economically distant groups. Note also that when the economic aspect $|y_i - y_j|$ is disregarded and α is set to 1, the measure is equivalent to the MRQ demographic polarisation index.

Generalised fractionalisation

Bossert *et al.* (2011) derive the GELF index by defining a similarity matrix S which compares each individual within a society to each other individual and assigns them a similarity rank which ranges from 0 (the two individuals are not similar across any dimension) to 1 (the individuals are exactly similar on every dimension). Hence for example, in a population of three people, the similarity matrix might appear as the following:

$$S = \begin{Bmatrix} 1 & 1/2 & 0 \\ 1/2 & 1 & 0 \\ 0 & 0 & 1 \end{Bmatrix}$$

Obviously, every person is exactly identical to themselves, producing the diagonal series of 1s in the matrix (person 1 compared with person 1; person 2 compared with person 2, etc.). In addition, Bossert *et al.* stipulate reasonably that similarities must be transitive – person

1's similarity to person 2 must be the same as person 2's similarity to person 1. Hence, the matrix is symmetrical along the diagonal. In this example matrix, person 1 and person 2 have a similarity score of ½, while person 3 is completely different from both person 1 and person 2. Bossert *et al.* then define their generalised fractionalisation index:

$$GELF = 1 - \frac{1}{n^2} \sum_{i=1}^{n} \sum_{j=1}^{n} sij$$

In that equation, s_{ij} is the degree of similarity between person i and person j, i.e. the respective value in the similarity matrix S. As defined by Bossert *et al.*, the GELF is calculated on the individual level, but it is easy to see that the index can be modified to take account of groups of different sizes that are internally homogenous. Defining t_{gh} as the similarity index between two internally homogenous groups that constitute proportion p_g and p_h of the total population ($p_g + p_h + \ldots + p_m = 1.00$), the GELF can be rewritten as follows:

$$GELF = 1 - \sum_{g=1}^{m} \sum_{h=1}^{m} p_g p_h t_{gh}$$

Political exclusion (N*)

Algebraically, the N^* measure is defined as:

$$N^*(r,k) = 1 - \prod_{i=1}^{n-1} \frac{\{r(i)/r\}^{-k}}{1 + \{r(i)/r\}^{-k}}$$

where:

- $r(i)$ is the share of the combined population share of each dyadic relationship due to the non-EGIP group. For instance, if the EGIP constitutes 10 per cent of the population, and the remainder is split into three equally sized groups of 30 per cent, then for each of these three groups the dyadic relationship with the EGIP would give a value of $r(i) = 0.1 + 0.3 = 0.4$;
- parameter r is a 'threshold value' which 'stipulates at what demographic balance the odds are even for a [political] challenge [to the EGIP]'. Cederman and Girardin recommend 0.5;

- parameter k controls how fast the risk of conflict increases. Cederman and Girardin recommend 5.

References

Alesina, A., Devleeschauwer, A., Easterly, W., Kurlat, S. and Wacziarg, R. 2003. 'Fractionalization', *Journal of Economic Growth* 8: 155–94.

Anand, S. 1983. *Inequality and Poverty in Malaysia: Measurement and Decomposition.* Oxford University Press.

Anderson, B. 1983. *Imagined Communities: Reflections on the Origin and Spread of Nationalism.* London: Verso.

Bangura, Y. 2001. *Ethnic Structure and Governance: Reforming Africa in the 21st Century.* Geneva: UNRISD.

Bates, R. 2004. 'Ethnicity', *The Elgar Companion to Development Studies.* Harvard University.

Bossert, W., D'Ambrosio, C. and La Ferrara, E. (2011). 'A Generalized Index of Fractionalization', *Economica* 78 (312): 723–50.

Brass, P. 1985. 'Ethnic groups and the state', in *Ethnic Groups and the State*, P. Brass (ed.). London: Croom Helm.

Brown, G. K. and Langer, A. 2011. 'Riding the Ever-rolling Stream: Time and the Ontology of Violent Conflict', *World Development* 39 (2): 188–98.

Brubaker, R. and Cooper, F. 2000. 'Beyond Identity', *Theory and Society* 29: 1–47.

Bruk, S. I. and Apenchenko, V. S. 1964. *Atlas Narodov Mira.* Moscow: Glavnoye Upravleniye Geodezii i Kartografii Gosudarstvennogo Geologicheskogo Komiteta SSSR and Institut Etnografii im N. N. Miklukho-Maklaya Akademii Nauk SSSR.

Cederman, L. -E. and Girardin, L. 2007. 'Beyond Fractionalization: Mapping Ethnicity onto Nationalist Insurgencies', *American Political Science Review* 101: 173–85.

Chandra, K. 2001. 'Cumulative Findings in the Study of Ethnic Politics: Constructivist Findings and Their Non-Interpretation', *APSA–CP* (Winter) 12: 7–11.

Cohen, R. 1999. 'The Making of Ethnicity: a Modest Defence of Primordialism', in *People, Nation and State*, E. Mortimer and R. Fine (eds.). London: I. B. Tauris.

Coleman, J., Hoffer, T. and Kilgore, S. 1982. 'Achievement and Segregation in Secondary Schools: a Further Look at Public and Private School Differences', *Sociology of Education* 55: 162–82.

Collier, P. and Hoeffler, A. 1998. 'On Economic Causes of Civil War', *Oxford Economic Papers* 50 (4): 563–73.

2002. *Greed and Gievance in Civil War*. World Bank, DECRG, http://econ.worldbank.org/programs/conflict.

Doornbos, M. 1991. 'Linking the Future to the Past – Ethnicity and Pluralism', in *Ethnicity and the State in Eastern Africa*, M. M. A. Salih and J. Markasis (eds.). Stockholm: Elanders Gotab.

Duclos, J.-Y., Esteban, J.-M. and Ray, D. 2004. 'Polarization: Concepts, Measurement, Estimation', *Econometrica* 72: 1,737–72.

Easterly, W. 1997. 'Africa's Growth Tragedy: Policies and Ethnic Divisions', *Quarterly Journal of Economics* 112: 1,203–50.

Easterly, W. and Levine, R. 1997. 'Africa's Growth Tragedy: Policies and Ethnic Divisions', *Quarterly Journal of Economics* 112: 1,203–50.

Esteban, J.-M. and Ray, D. 1994. 'On the Measurement of Polarization', *Econometrica* 62: 819–51.

Ezcurra, R. 2009. 'Does Income Polarization Affect Economic Growth? The Case of the European Regions', *Regional Studies* 43: 267–85.

Fearon, J. D. 2003. 'Ethnic and Cultural Diversity by Country', *Journal of Economic Growth* 8: 195–222.

Fearon, J. D. and Laitin, D. D. 1996. 'Explaining Interethnic Cooperation', *American Political Science Review* 90: 715–35.

Geertz, C. 1963. 'The Integrative Revolution – Primordial Sentiments and Civil Politics in the New States', in *Old Societies and New States – The Quest for Modernity in Asia and Africa*, C. Geertz (ed.). London: Collier–Macmillan.

Glazer, N. and Moynihan, D. P. 1976. *Ethnicity: Theory and Experience*. Cambridge, MA: Harvard University Press.

Goertz, G. 2006. *Social Science Concepts: a User's Guide*. Princeton, NJ: Princeton University Press.

Green, E. D. 2004. *The (Mis)use of Ethnicity in the Current Political Economy Literature: Conceptual and Data Issues*. Paper prepared for WIDER Conference on Making Peace Work. Helsinki, Finland, 4–5 June.

Hardin, R. 1995. *One for all – The Logic of Group Conflict*. Princeton, NJ: Princeton University Press.

Horowitz, D. L. 1985. *Ethnic Groups in Conflict*. Berkeley: University of California Press.

Kalyvas, S. N. 2008. 'Promises and Pitfalls of an Emerging Research Program: the Microdynamics of Civil War', in *Order, Conflict, and Violence*, S. N. Kalyvas, I. Shapiro and T. Masoud (eds.). Cambridge University Press.

Kanbur, R. and Zhang, X. 1999. 'Which Regional Inequality? The Evolution of Rural-urban and Inland-coastal Inequality in China from 1983 to 1995', *Journal of Comparative Economics* 27: 686–701.

Kasara, Kimuli 2010. *Local Segregation and Inter-ethnic Violence in Kenya*. Mimeo.

Kertzer, D. I. and Arel, D. 2002. 'Censuses, Identity Formation, and the Struggle for Political Power', in *Census and Identity: The Politics of Race, Ethnicity, and Language in National Censuses*, D. I. Kertzer and D. Arel (eds.). Cambridge University Press.

Laitin, D. and Posner, D. 2001. 'The Implications of Constructivism for Constructing Ethnic Fractionalization Indices', *APSA–CP* (Winter) 12: 13–17.

Maasoumi, E. 1986. 'The Measurement and Decomposition of Multi-dimensional Inequality', *Econometrica* 54: 991–7.

Mancini, L. 2008. 'Horizontal Inequality and Communal Violence: Evidence from Indonesian Districts', in *Horizontal Inequalities and Conflict: Understanding Group Violence in Multiethnic Societies*, F. Stewart (ed.). London: Palgrave.

Montalvo, J. G. and Reynal-Querol, M. 2005. 'Ethnic Diversity and Economic Development', *Journal of Development Economics* 76 (2): 293–323.

Nafziger, W. E. and Auvinen, J. 2002. 'Economic Development, Inequality, War, and State Violence', *World Development* 30: 153–63.

Posner, D. 2004. 'Measuring Ethnic Fractionalization in Africa', *American Journal of Political Science* 48: 849–63.

2005. *The Implications of Constructivism for Studying the Relationship between Ethnic Diversity and Economic Growth*. Department of Political Science, University of California, Los Angeles

Premdas, R. 1995. *Ethnic Conflict and Development: the Case of Guyana*. Avebury: Aldershot.

Rabushka, A. and Shepsle, K. A. 1972. *Politics in Plural Societies: a Theory of Democratic Stability*. Columbus, OH: Charles E. Merrill.

Ranger, T. 1983. 'The Invention of Tradition in Colonial Africa', in *The Invention of Tradition*, E. Hobsbawm and T. Ranger (eds.). Cambridge University Press.

Reardon, S. F. and Firebaugh, G. 2002. 'Measures of Multigroup Segregation', *Sociological Methodology* 32: 33–67.

Reardon, S. F. and Yun, J. T. 2001. 'Suburban Racial Change and Suburban School Segregation, 1987–95', *Sociology of Education* 74: 79–101.

Rodrik, D. 1999. 'Where Did All the Growth Go? External Shocks, Social Conflict and Growth Collapses', *Journal of Economic Growth* 4: 385–412.

Sambanis, N. 1999. 'Partition as a Solution to Ethnic War: an Empirical Critique of the Theoretical Literature', *World Politics* 52: 437–83.

2005. 'What is Civil War? Conceptual and Empirical Complexities of An Operational Definition', *Journal of Conflict Resolution* 48: 814–58.

Shils, E. 1957. 'Primordial, Person, Sacred, and Civil Ties', *The British Journal of Sociology* 8: 130–45.

Ukiwo, U. 2005. 'The Study of Ethnicity in Nigeria', *Oxford Development Studies* 33: 7–24.

2006. Horizontal Inequalities and Violent Ethnic Conflicts: a Comparative Study of Ethnic Relations in Calabar and Warri, Southern Nigeria. Ph.D. thesis, Oxford Department of International Development, University of Oxford.

van den Berg, S. and Louw, M. 2004. 'Changing Patterns of South African Income Distribution: Towards Time Series Estimates of Distribution and Poverty', *South African Journal of Economics* 72: 546–72.

Van den Berghe, P. L. 1978. 'Race and Ethnicity: a Sociological Perspective', *Ethnic and Racial Studies* 1: 401–11.

Varshney, A. 2001. 'Ethnic Conflicts and Ancient Hatreds: Cultural Concerns', *International Encyclopaedia of the Social and Behavioural Sciences* 4: 810–13.

Williamson, J. G. 1965. 'Regional Inequality and the Process of National Development: a Description of the Patterns', *Economic Development and Cultural Change* 13: 1–84.

Young, C. 1985. 'Ethnicity and the Colonial and Post-colonial State in Africa', in *Ethnic Groups and the State*, P. Brass (ed.). London: Croom Helm.

2003. 'Explaining the Conflict Potential of Ethnicity', in *Contemporary Peacemaking: Conflict, Violence and Peace Process*, J. Darby and R. MacGinty (eds.). Basingstoke: Palgrave Macmillan.

3 | Essence of ethnicity: an African perspective

BETHWELL ALLAN OGOT

Introduction

The roots of African ethnicity reach back into the pre-colonial past. They must be recognised and investigated since their history matters today.

Recent African political history, not least its violence, is intimately bound up with popular perceptions of societal and ethnic identities – perceptions that are social constructions, representations rather than realities. Moreover, they not only change over time; they can be distorted and manipulated as part of a 'discourse of domination', employed by those who have held power in successive pre-colonial, colonial and post-colonial regimes. This historian's perspective of changing representations contrasts with those of sociologists and anthropologists who have seen ethnic groups as cultures that develop distinctive features because of their original, and enduring, isolation from each other. Their boundaries are said to be clear-cut and impermeable; members of an ethnic group supposedly speak one language, hold to distinctive social practices and share a common system of belief. Kenya's history reveals the hollowness of such theories.

The Kenya case shows how the essence of ethnicity has been transformed from a malleable cultural identity in the past to an antagonistic political solidarity protective of territory and supposed group interest today. It corroborates the thesis advanced by Lonsdale in Chapter 1, and further highlights the difficulty of quantifying African ethnicity (Chapter 2). It suggests that in Africa democracy may have to take account of the pervasive influence of ethnic allegiance – both vertical and horizontal. Ghai develops this theme in Chapter 4. This chapter also prepares us for Shipton's exposition (Chapter 7) of the reciprocal

This chapter is a shortened version of an essay published as a Japan International Cooperation Agency Research Institute (JICA-RI) working paper.

relationship between ethnic consciousness, 'territorial confinement' and economic instability.

Ethnic fluidity in pre-colonial Kenya

By the end of the nineteenth century the communities of the future Kenya had long been inter-penetrated by each other in a complex, inter-dependent world. There were no watertight ethnicities. Clans and lineages expanded and contracted, gaining and losing members across porous cultural frontiers. New communities and languages emerged. The colonial idea of 'tribe' as an isolated, closed group of inter-related lineages is a myth, and ultimately a racist one. The traditions of the different Kenyan nationalities include no narrow cultural nationalism. To the contrary, they stress integration by an ever-fruitful mingling and migration, and reveal identities both malleable and dependent upon relations with others. The colonial idea that there had formerly been perpetual inter-clan and inter-ethnic rivalry and war is further under-mined by considering the political, economic and cultural situations in different regions of future Kenya.

For the previous two centuries in western Kenya, contact between Bantu- and Kalenjin-speakers produced new societies that were ethni-cally Kalenjin but which today are culturally and linguistically Luyia. But the Kalenjin legacy remains: Luyia have borrowed their custom of circumcision from Kalenjin, and many of their place names are Kalenjin in origin. In Central Kenya, Kikuyu were expanding north-wards into Nyeri and southwards into Kiambu throughout the nine-teenth century. They absorbed indigenous people such as the Gumba and Athi, and forged commercial, cultural and marriage relations with the Maasai to both north and south. Muriuki (1974) estimates that around half the population in Mathira and Tetu in Nyeri County is of Maasai origin. Several of their *mbari* (lineages) are predominantly Maasai. Mathira had almost become a 'sub-tribe' with a distinct dia-lect by 1900.

To the south, many Maasai took refuge among the Kikuyu of Kabete during the time of adversity, 1880–90. One of them, Waiyaki wa Hinga, even became a Kikuyu leader. Today, the story of Kikuyu resist-ance to foreign rule starts with him. He is the most eminent of a pan-theon of Kikuyu rulers who include Kenyatta and Koinange – heroes whose lives offer models of virtue. Kikuyu also borrowed cattle-related vocabulary, core religious concepts, initiation rituals and military tactics from the Maasai. Kamba–Kikuyu relations were similarly fruitful. They inter-married and traded with each other, especially during the famines repeatedly suffered by Kamba. Kikuyu sold foodstuffs, ivory and skins with Kamba, in exchange for coastal wares.

Inter-dependence and cultural fluidity were even more marked on Kenya's Indian Ocean coast. In the Tana River area Pokomo, who settled in their present area towards the end of the sixteenth century, were much influenced by Oromo culture, while many Oromo groups have been assimilated into Pokomo society. Such inter-dependence was even more pronounced among Swahili-speakers. Their towns could trade overseas thanks largely to their commerce with their inland neighbours: Lamu islanders relied for food on Pokomo cultivators, Dahalo and Aweera hunter–gatherers and Oromo and Somali pastoralists. These peoples also gave Lamu military assistance when needed. Cultural and economic integration was further stimulated by rural–urban migration, as inland populations constantly moved to towns, where new ethnic identities were negotiated and defined. This was still more true of Mombasa, with its varied population. Twelve Swahili communities or *mataifa* had peopled it, organised in two groups: the Nine (*Tisa Taifa*) who settled at Mvita on the north side of Mombasa Island and the Three (*Thelatha Taifa*) who chose Kilindini on its southern shore.

In northern Kenya, to take yet another example, there was a symbolic relationship between the Samburu and Rendile, 'nomads in alliance', despite the fact that the former are Maa-speakers and cattle-keepers while the latter are Cushitic-speakers who herd camels. Some Rendile sections adopted Samburu clans, joined their age-sets, married their women and became cattle-keepers.

The evolution of western Kenya's Luo into an ethnic group reveals particularly complex processes of cultural and social integration. By 1300 AD, the earliest Luo polities in their Southern Sudanese cradleland were already plural societies of Luo, Central Sudanic (Moru-Madi) and Eastern Nilotic clans. This absorptive ethnic pluralism became a distinctive – pervasive – feature of Luo societies as they moved south into eastern Africa. Groups merged, amalgamated and developed into new collectivities with newly emergent identities. Around 1500 AD, the first Luo cluster to arrive in western Kenya, the Joka Jok, had already incorporated many non-Luo elements – Central Sudanic, East Nilotic and Bantu (Ogot 2009).

Co-existence between Gusii and Luo led to inter-marriage and the emergence of the Muksero and Abasweta communities who became Luo-ised. The Luo of Kasipul traded their cattle-salt, hides, ghee, milk, fish, baskets and pottery for Gusii grain, vegetables, axes and spears. The markets of Mosocho and Muksero survive as trading centres to this day. Gusii might flee to Kasipul for refuge during inter-clan conflicts, wars with the Maasai or famine, and later return home when conditions improved. In the past, however, some stayed on and assimilated. Famine might similarly force Luo to go to Gusiiland to solicit for food.

Hartwig (1976) has shown that the Victoria Nyanza's east coast was a single trading zone. The lakeside peoples traded salt, iron, grain, dried hippo meat and fish over long distances between what is now northern Tanzania and western Kenya. A colony of hippo hunters from Ukerewe called Wasenge established themselves on Usenge Hill in Yimbo, Siaya County, where they were subsequently assimilated. Baganda and Basoga also traded dried bananas from present-day Uganda to the western Kenya's lakeshore by canoe. Kaksingri salt in southern Luoland was exchanged for Samia's iron in Buluyia. The region also imported wives from Tanzania. This low-lying, dry, eastern lakeshore corridor was a Bantu culture area until Luo invaders from the north became dominant. Many Luo-speakers entered the lakeshore trade; Dholuo gradually supplanted Luganda as the commercial lingua franca of this East African lakeside common market. But Bantu-speaking fishing groups, some with trans-lake connections, continued to move up and down these shores, bringing a complex admixture of peoples and a confused and multifaceted pattern of remembered history.

Inland, the Luo economy was much influenced by its Bantu neighbours. Domestic knowledge was widely shared, shown by similar Dholuo and Luyia terms for homestead, soil, wooden hoe, maize, sweet potatoes, beans and leafy vegetables. Close contact between western Kenya's communities thus led to trade, inter-marriage, cultural interchange and bilingualism or even multilingualism. Famine, drought and disease might also force them to seek assistance from neighbouring communities. These disasters prompted both population movement and trade across the Luo-Luyia, Luo-Gusii and Luo-Maasai frontiers, and help to explain why earlier ethnic borders were not as well-defined as they are today.

In the late 1880s the Siria Maasai, for example, were hard hit when pleuropneumonia and rinderpest almost wiped out their herds and smallpox killed many people. They had already been subdued by the Loitai Maasai, who took stock, women and children. Siria had to seek refuge where they could among Gusii, Kipsigis and Kuria; a majority migrated and settled in Luo Kanyamkago. So, although ethnic frontiers were becoming more clearly defined during the later nineteenth century, one could still cross them in crisis. Communities exploited mutual commercial and other relations in order to survive defeat, disease and loss of livestock, like the Siria Maasai in their Kanyamkago exile. British rule enabled the Siria to return to Maasailand, because frontiers had now to be closed, with each ethnic group occupying a 'homeland'.

This picture can be multiplied across the territory that became Kenya in 1920. It emphasises the complex nature of former frontiers and settlements. There were no pure ethnic groups. Each was a dynamic and living unit whose continuity depended less on its purity or single origin than an ability to accommodate and assimilate diverse elements and ideas. Most of the myths, legends and rituals one meets in stories of origin, migration and settlement serve to foster the integration of peoples with diverse origins. Africa's pre-colonial history teaches useful lessons about nation building.

Ethnicity and colonial administrative boundaries

In pre-colonial Africa, then, mapped boundary lines did not exist; forests, river valleys, plains or deserts served as frontiers of separation or buffer zones, over which no community claimed or exercised authority. Colonialism introduced boundary lines. Since administrative boundaries tended to be based on ethnic or linguistic units, they also froze cultural development and population mobility at a point in time, fossilising previously fluid situations. How then were ethnic identities re-negotiated and re-defined during the colonial period and how did colonial boundary changes transform ethnic identities?

Following the establishment of the East Africa Protectorate (EAP) in 1895 with its headquarters at Mombasa, four provinces were created – Coast, Tanaland, Jubaland and Ukamba – each divided into districts. A European sub-commissioner (later provincial commissioner or PC) headed each province, and European collectors (later district commissioners or DCs) were put in charge of districts.

Coast Province (Seyyidie) was sub-divided into three districts based at Mombasa, Malindi and Vanga. The Sultan of Zanzibar's nominal rule over the coastal peoples was recognised by transforming his administrative agents such as *liwalis, kadhis* and *akidas* into agents of British authority. Coastal society was dominated by an Arab and Swahili ruling class. Hardinge, the EAP's first commissioner, called those Africans who enjoyed close relations with them 'the Nyika *tribe*'. Having a low opinion of Africa's 'barbarous races', he hoped Arab administrative agents and, to a lesser extent, Swahili-speakers would be a civilising influence. The division of Kenyans into primitive 'tribes' and civilised 'non-tribes' had begun (Hardinge 1928).

Tanaland covered the northern coast. Zanzibar's nominal rule applied here too; Arab and Swahili populations, accordingly, enjoyed a privileged status. Old symbiotic relations among local peoples were cut by a system that encouraged racial and 'tribal' segregation. Gradually, Pokomo, Oromo and others were herded into 'native' reserves; many Mijikenda people became squatters. They and ex-slaves were banned from owning land in the province. The 1930s invention of a Mijikenda identity was a response to these colonial oppressions.

The third province, Jubaland (ceded to Italy in 1924), was inhabited mainly by Somali. It is hard to understand how the British could use the term 'tribe' for the Somali, segmented as they were into sections and clans. The new ruler's knowledge of the peoples enclosed within these borders was rudimentary and the latter were unaware of borders and unconcerned about the social effects the borders were likely to have. Oromo were divided between Ethiopia and the EAP, and Somali between Italian and British spheres. The Somali irredentism of the decolonisation era can be traced back to these colonial boundaries.

In the fourth province, Ukamba, of which Nairobi became the capital in 1899, the Taita–Taveta peoples felt they were wrongly placed, since they had more in common with coastal peoples. Their hopes were realised in 1902 when they were transferred to Seyyidie. The Kamba, who thought of themselves as one people, were divided into two districts. When the British pushed north to Mount Kenya they did the reverse, inventing an Embu 'tribe' with its Embu and Mbeere 'sub-tribes' in one district. But the two were distinct, inhabiting contrasting ecological zones.

The EAP's shape was fundamentally altered in 1902 by gaining Uganda's Eastern Province – to become Kisumu and Naivasha Provinces (later Nyanza and Rift Valley). Bounded within their respective districts Luyia, Luo, Gusii and Kuria 'tribes' evolved under colonial rule, while both Nandi and Kipsigis continued to consolidate their pre-existing ethnic consciousness.

The British undertook to define the boundaries of different ethnic groups as part of their 'divide and rule' policy. But there was more. Eliot, who succeeded Hardinge as the EAP's Commissioner in 1901, had an even lower opinion of African 'tribes' and did not expect them to contribute much to the economy. Attracted by the temperate highland climate, he proclaimed that Kenya would become a 'white man's country' similar to Canada, New Zealand, Australia and South Africa (Eliot 1905). British South Africans were the first to arrive, from 1903, with fixed ideas about white supremacy. They settled around Nairobi and along the railway line on land belonging to Kikuyu. This was alienated, without survey, under the Crown Lands Ordinance of 1902. There was soon an urgent need for African 'reserves' protected from alienation. New racial frontiers promoted ethnic and racial consciousness among Africans.

Unlike the South African settlers, the earliest British settlers were aristocrats such as Lord Delamere, who first arrived in Kenya in 1897, and Lords Hindlip and Cranworth and retired officers or gentlemen adventurers such as Ewart Grogan. They brought with them, as did seventeenth-century emigrants to America, their English ways, hopes and plans for a more prosperous life in a new country they would make their own (Cranworth 1912; Sorrenson 1968; Wymer 1959). As Elspeth Huxley (1953), Delamere's biographer, has written, these aristocrats brought 'something of the grand manner of an age already dying, and tried perhaps unconsciously to create … a replica of the feudal system of their fathers'. Karen Blixen (1954) described them as 'outcasts' from England: 'it was not a society that had thrown them out but time had done it, they did not belong to their century. No other nation than the English could have produced them, … [but] theirs was an earlier England, a world which no longer existed'.

Thus the pioneer white settlers – an alien ethnic group – were a strange mixture of Trekboers, South African British 'colonials' and Britain's own 'outcasts'. They dreamt of prosperity based on cheap black labour and compared themselves to earlier settlers in other British dominions. As land around Nairobi was taken up, they turned to the country along the railway line in the Rift Valley, inhabited largely by Maasai. In the later nineteenth century different Maasai sections had fought, separated and dispersed, sometimes as refugees among other communities (Waller 1979). Now the British decided to move some sections from their favourite pastures in the central Rift, fondly called *Entorror*, in order to make way for white settlement. They would go to two reserves, one in Laikipia to the north, the other to the south, on the border with German East Africa (mainland Tanzania) where other Maasai sections already lived. Different Maasai clans would have to live together and see themselves as one people, as Maasai rather than Purko, Uasin Gishu, Laikipiak, etc.

On 10 August 1904, a 'treaty' between the British and Maasai was agreed, intended to provide a permanent solution to the Maasai 'problem'. The two territories were promised to the people for 'so long as the Maasai as a race shall exist' (Hughes 2006; King 1971a and 1971b; Leys 1924; McGregor Ross 1927; Sandford 1919). But even this grave injustice did not satisfy the white appetite for land. Settlers soon demanded that the Laikipia or 'northern' Maasai should be moved again to an extended southern reserve so that the 'tribe' could be united. The northern Maasai were evacuated in 1911, at gunpoint, with heavy loss of life, both human and bovine. Two years later Maasai contested the legality of this second move in the High Court and, equally fruitlessly, sought compensation for their stock losses. So began Maasai resistance to colonial rule under their leader Molonket ole Sempele (1886–1955).

The Maasai fight for their rights and lands continued through the twentieth century. Warrior uprisings in 1918, 1922 and 1935 preceded a major agitation in the 1950s over a British plan to restrict Maasai use of the Mau Forest. The largest political meeting Maasai had ever held sent a petition to the Governor, signed by forty influential figures, Sempele included. Desire for justice simmered for a century, with outbursts both before the 1930s Kenya Land Commission inquiry and during Kenya's independence negotiations in the 1960s. Maasai, like other Kenyan communities, asserted their rights, separate identity and cultural heritage in the face of attempts by colonial and post-colonial governments, backed by mainstream society, to assimilate or marginalise them. Rights to land and natural resources are central to this struggle for ethnic sovereignty. After all, the Maasai lost over 50 per cent of the land they had once inhabited.

The nineteenth-century dispersal of Uasin Gishu Maasai opened the way for Nandi warrior bands to terrorise western Kenya. Raiding endowed Nandi with wealth and wider pastures, fostered military efficiency and, with it, ethnic pride and warrior arrogance. In this precolonial upsurge of ethnic consciousness, Nandi were encouraged by the ministration of *laibons* or prophets they had imported from the Uasin Gishu Maasai. Nandi nationality was an established fact before colonial rule. The British dealt ruthlessly and deviously with the consequent Nandi resistance. From 1895 to 1905, Nandi waged a great patriotic war to defend their land and freedom against British invasion. The British mounted eleven expeditions and patrols in all, looking for a 'final solution' to the Nandi menace. In 1905 they mustered the strongest force employed in Kenya before the 1950s Mau Mau Emergency, comprising 60 European officers, 1,500 Kings African Rifles, 200 Indian soldiers, 1,000 Maasai levies, 500 armed porters, 300 Sudanese volunteers, 10 machine gun sections and 2 armoured trains. Thousands of Nandi were killed, including the *orkoiyot* Koitalel arap Samoei, their spiritual leader, treacherously assassinated by a British officer, Richard Meinertzhagen, a serial psychopath (Matson 1993; Meinertzhagen 1957; Ng'eny 1970). The Nandi were promptly confined to an illegal 'native reserve'; 1,250 square miles of their best land was taken from them and given to white settlers. All Nandi sections were forced to move into the reserve, a confinement that only intensified ethnic pride. Land alienation in the North Rift region was therefore a core factor in the enhancement of ethnic consciousness. Africans reacted to white racism by re-defining themselves along ethnic lines.

By 1914, the Protectorate's European population was about 5,440, of whom fewer than 1,000 were farmers or planters. About 5 million acres had been alienated to this tiny population. The 1915 Crown Land Ordinance lengthened their agricultural leases to 999 years. After the Great War, many ex-servicemen were settled on an additional 2.8 million acres. The Soldier Settlement Scheme focused on Nandi border areas, from which over 2,000 inhabitants were moved, making them homeless and landless. By 1923 it was estimated that one-third of all Nandi were squatters on their ancestral lands, now 'white' farmland. Here was the root of the 1923 Nandi protest, their first organised resistance since the wars of 1905–6. No less important in determining their response to colonial rule was the settler demand for labour. As farm squatters in the Trans Nzoia, Uasin Gishu and Kisumu-Londiani districts, Nandi played a key role in the area's economy, parallel to that of the Kikuyu squatters in the Rift Valley. The *orkoiyot* recovered his role as the focal point of resistance: colonial threat encouraged Nandi ethnic cohesion.

Land was now Kenya's core political issue. In 1932, Britain set up the Kenya Land Commission under Sir Morris Carter to examine boundary disputes between black and white farmers and to decide, finally, who owned what land (Kenya Land Commission 1934). Carter refused to consider any African right to land in the 'White Highlands'. This cleared the way for the notorious Resident Labour Ordinance of 1937, which defined squatters as wage-labourers and no more. The Commission also directed that disaffected Kikuyu be awarded 21,000 acres (8,500 hectares) of land and £2,000 as compensation for their losses (Kanogo 1987). There were other minor adjustments elsewhere but the grievances of Maasai, Kalenjin and Mijikenda, all major victims of land alienation, were never addressed, nor did Kikuyu accept as adequate what little they were given. Agitation for recovery of expropriated land soon began. In Kikuyuland 'popular anger over the land was on the rise' following publication of the Commission's Report. Moreover, the compulsory return of large numbers of squatters to overcrowded 'reserves' caused discontent that would explode into the Mau Mau war of the 1950s (Clough 1990).

After the Second World War, as after the First, demobilised British officers, many from India, came to Kenya. Existing white farmers, alarmed by their isolation among a rising African population, welcomed these and other middle-class settlers, including Italians interned in Kenya as prisoners of war. To assuage their fear of 'wild Africans' they sub-divided their farms to offer newcomers smaller properties of about five hundred acres each. The colonial government encouraged and financed this 'closer settlement'. The European population in Kenya doubled during 1938–51, to about 40,000 (Odingo 1971). Squatter rights to hold stock were curtailed and then eliminated, so destroying the very basis of squatter existence, whether Luo, Kalenjin or Kikuyu. The Carter Report's denial of African property in the 'White Highlands' had authorised this segregation of Kenya into a 'dual' economy and society. Worse still, the settlers who came after 1945 were, according to Blundell (1994), reactionary and racist, with an 'almost

fascist concept of organization and massed emotion'. They were determined that Kenya would for ever be a bastion of white supremacy,
oblivious of the fundamental changes taking place all around them
globally and ignorant of the stirrings of African nationalism.

Administrative boundaries, local authorities and ethnicity

The colonialists assumed that 'tribes' were discrete units that lived
in defined areas and spoke a common language. All 'natives' must
therefore be 'tribally' classified and neatly pigeon-holed within district boundaries. But many classifications were arbitrary. In some cases
they divided groups more sharply than before while in others they
combined those that had been distinct. New 'tribes' emerged, such as
'Embu' and 'Meru', while some supposedly ethnically homogeneous
administrative units could confuse language, ethnicity and culture.

There was a further, more strictly political, process required by colonial administration. Apart from some coastal areas and a few communities such as the Wanga in Western Province, Nandi and some
Luo 'tribes', no 'Kenyan' people had kings, sultans or chiefs and so
lacked any *political* identity before British rule. To introduce executive
rule over them was a daunting problem. But the British had to have
such executive power when they wanted to build roads or hospitals,
to levy taxes and conscript labour. Whereas power had been socially
dispersed, it was now concentrated in a few hands – those of colonial
agents.

The first collectors, later called district commissioners or DCs, were
sent out to govern a 'tribal' area, maintain law and order, administer
justice and collect taxes, backed by small detachments of African soldiers or armed police. To build an executive each had to find people
who could issue orders that would be obeyed, turn out a labour force,
collect taxes and deal with petty crimes. They seized on the institution
of chiefship where it could be found and invented it where it did not
exist. Some individuals, actuated by pride or the hope of gain, pre-
tended to occupy a chief-like status. British officers sometimes built up
these pretenders to the throne, glad to have someone through whom
to get things done. In Kikuyuland, Kinyanjui wa Gathirimo, of no
traditional standing, rose to be a senior chief in Kiambu, while Karuri
Gakure, also of lowly birth, emerged as chief-maker in Murang'a and
Nyeri districts.

The DC and his chiefs acted as unifiers, simplifying, transforming, even creating African political systems. All districts were governed in the same way. As far as possible, Africans were ruled in their own language units; district boundaries seldom cut across 'tribal' frontiers. The effect was profound: modern local government was established on a 'tribal' and linguistic basis, with 'tribal' sentiment as its political glue. So local government institutions strengthened ethnic exclusiveness; even the most loosely organised groups developed a 'tribal' patriotism. Africans themselves began to promote an ethnic consciousness which competed with the authority of the DC and chiefs. A constant struggle emerged, between ethnically conscious cultural nationalists and the agents of imperialism, which helped to define ethnicity still more sharply and rigidly.

In summary, the British aimed to draw district boundaries to coincide with 'tribal' or linguistic units. Their efforts were vitiated by their definition of ethnic groups as 'tribes', a concept both racist and a-historical in the sense that it regarded nationality groups as static, exclusive and internally homogeneous. 'Tribe' was an abstraction, a mental invention intended to portray people without rulers, without government, without culture and without history, in order to justify colonial rule. These imagined, inward-looking, self-regenerating and exclusive units had to be encased within their districts to avoid contamination by culturally and linguistically different neighbours. We can legitimately talk of the colonial invention of 'tribe'.

Administrative boundaries froze historical processes whereby dynamic group interaction had produced ever new cultural syntheses and differentiations. Individuals could no longer move to other areas nor could people form or reform. Inter-marriage was discouraged; bilingualism and multilingualism gradually died out. Yet language purveys values and social knowledge, so cultural and ethnic purists soon emerged to stress each 'tribe's' uniqueness, even accepting 'tribe' as an appropriate appellation. With the support of such African converts it was not difficult to introduce 'tribal' local governments on which the colonial power built its subordinate agencies. Local councils became 'tribal' councils, dealing with the interests of particular ethnic groups; groups that had been ignored demanded 'local native councils' of their own.

The trend continued after independence. New districts were established to give neglected ethnic groups their own districts. Jomo Kenyatta was cautious about this but his successor, Daniel arap Moi,

created twenty-four districts in twenty-four years. While he was opposition leader, Mwai Kibaki opposed this administrative multiplication
as financially unsustainable. But he himself has created more than 130
new districts since coming to power in 2002. That post-colonial governments have retained and multiplied colonial district boundaries
has made it difficult, if not impossible, for Kenyans to live in toler-
ant multicultural, multiethnic societies that happily live with diversity
and protect minorities. Ethnic enclaves, created by colonial boundary-
making and accepted by post-colonial African elites, are hindering the
evolution of a democratic framework within which a culture of peace
could grow.

The construction of ethnicity and tradition:
the struggle for ethnic sovereignty

John Iliffe (1979: 318, 324) wrote of colonial Tanganyika:

The British wrongly believed that Tanganyikans belonged to tribes;
Tanganyikans created tribes to function within the colonial framework.

[The] new political geography ... would have been transient, however, had
it not coincided with similar trends among Africans. They too had to live
amidst bewildering social complexity, which they ordered in kinship terms and
buttressed with invented history. Moreover, Africans wanted effective units
of action just as officials wanted effective units of government ... Europeans
believed Africans belonged to tribes; Africans built tribes to belong to.

In discussing central Kenya's colonial history, Marshall Clough (1990)
argued that Kikuyu avoided inter-ethnic alliances, turned inward and
concentrated on ethnic, regional and district issues. He noticed two
enduring Kikuyu political traditions – moderate conservative and radical. Both camps had strong leadership: Koinange wa Mbiyu and other
chiefs led the conservatives in the Kikuyu Association while Jomo
Kenyatta, with others, championed the radical cause in the Kikuyu
Central Association (KCA). Both sides were motivated by ethnic pride
and Kikuyu nationalism. Each emphasised three requirements: Kikuyu
unity, preservation of identity and self-help, especially in education and
economic development. The ties between Kenyatta and the Koinange
family symbolised this radical-conservative consensus.

In 1928 the KCA newspaper *Muigwithania* ('Unifier' or 'Reconciler')
appeared, with Kenyatta, KCA Secretary, as editor. It promoted the

same three themes: unity, identity and industrious self-help. It constantly reminded Kikuyu that, no matter from which district, they were one people, with the same language, culture and historical roots; they must respect each other if they wanted other people to respect them. If colonial rulers invented ethnicity as a tool of domination, African intellectuals were soon trying to reinvent it in search of cultural pride and freedom. Kenyatta's anthropological tract, *Facing Mount Kenya*, a fascinating, if static and idealised picture of a Kenya society, pioneered this tradition of re-invention (Kenyatta 1938, 1944).

A new revolutionary atmosphere prevailed after 1945, under 'the second colonial occupation'. In Kikuyuland the old KCA, banned in the Second World War with its leaders detained, continued to operate underground. Its leaders were also members of the so-called 'Kiambaa Parliament' which met at ex-Senior Chief Koinange's home. In 1944, after the KCA leaders were released from detention, members revived a loyalty oath that bound the various elements of the Kikuyu people together as one. Kenyatta was oathed on his return from Britain in 1946 and himself promoted the loyalty oath in Central and Rift Valley Provinces (Kyle 1999: 49).

The Mau Mau war followed. After it ended and independence negotiations began Kenyatta was himself released from detention in 1961. He again embraced this Kikuyu nationalism. He was active in creating the Greater Kikuyu society, which now included a diaspora composed not simply of squatters and migrant workers as in earlier years but of people now permanently settled elsewhere. Dispossessed Kikuyu could now inherit land not only within their reserves, but also in the former 'white highlands' and at the coast – an idea appealing to former squatters and some ex-forest fighters. Kikuyu ethnic sovereignty had to be established, and Kenyatta, Founding Father of the Kenya nation, was the chief architect and patron of the Greater Kikuyu community.

Kikuyu were not alone in constructing ethnicity and tradition in colonial times. In Western Kenya the early 1920s saw the rise of a new generation with new ambitions. With grassroots support these elites coordinated the development of ethnic consciousness, stimulated largely by rural grievances and aspirations. The Luo presented the most radical of demands for ethnic sovereignty. In December 1921, 9,000 leaders from all over Luoland assembled at Lundha in the present Gem district, to demand both recognition of the Luo as a nation and a devolved local government subject to an autonomous Luo state headed by an elected president (*Ker*), after the examples of Botswana, Lesotho and Buganda. If this Luo ambition could not be accommodated in Kenya, then Luoland should be transferred back to the Uganda Protectorate, which respected such autonomous kingdoms. A Young Kavirondo Association (YKA), led by Jonathan Okwiri and his colleagues, all products of Maseno School, drafted a Luo constitution, to be discussed with the Governor. The Association adopted a deliberately anonymous name, *Piny Owacho* ('the people's voice'), to protect its officials from prosecution. This first serious attempt to unite all Luo people in Nyanza, irrespective of age, education, experience, religion or location, lasted for three years. After inconclusive meetings with Nyanza's PC, the draft constitution was presented to the Governor, Sir Edward Northey, at Nyahera in the present Kisumu County in July 1922. Northey accepted the request for a devolved political structure but nothing came of it. The Harry Thuku riots in Nairobi in March, a few months earlier, had persuaded the nervous government to nip in the bud what they saw as an impending revolt in Nyanza. YKA was replaced by a conservative, mission and government dominated, Kavirondo Taxpayers' Welfare Association (KTWA) in 1923 (Ogot 2009: 706–24).

Reinvention of the Luo gathered pace in the 1940s and early 1950s. The Luo Union, founded in Nairobi in 1922 to cater for the welfare of urban Luo, developed into a major organisation in both urban and rural areas. Branches opened in all large East African towns and in Kenya's rural locations. In 1953, they came together as the Luo Union (East Africa) with Oginga Odinga as the first elected *Ker*. Its main concerns were cultural identity, unity, self-help and history, real or invented. Luo now called themselves *Joka Nyam* (the river–lake people) or *Nyikwa Ramogi* (Ramogi's descendants), to underpin their common history. They started a newspaper, *Ramogi*, edited by Achieng Oneko. Under Odinga's populist leadership their cultural nationalism responded to modern Kenya's political and economic challenges and, by independence, had achieved a coherent community and ethnic sovereignty that has yet to find a niche in the National Project.

In the present Western Province, the arrival of a second generation of modern political leaders was marked by the creation of the North Kavirondo Central Association (NKCA) modelled on the Kikuyu Central Association, with which it collaborated in the 1930s. The area's first modern political generation had formed the North Kavirondo

Taxpayers and Welfare Association (NKTWA), seceding from the original KTWA. The NKCA responded to fears for land security arising from the discovery of gold in Kakamega. By 1938 it had 800 members; most of its leaders were young men, full-time politicians; most members were Christian. While land was their main preoccupation, a common identity for the twenty or so Luyia sub-groups came next. What to call 'their people' was problematic; names earlier proposed by NKTWA, *Abakwe* (people of the east) and *Abalimi* (farmers) had been rejected. In 1935, the NKCA published a pamphlet on their common identity entitled *Avaluhya*. The present name Abaluyia or Abaluhya owes much to NKCA efforts. It comes from the word *oluhia* (fireplace) at which community elders used to meet each morning to discuss clan issues. While the NKCA espoused cultural nationalism and imagined a greater Luyia community the association ended in 1941 when its leaders accepted a government 'request' to disband voluntarily because of the Second World War – or face detention.

In the northern part of Western province the transition to the nationalist period was different. Land was again the main concern, becoming acute in 1946 when the 'white' Trans Nzoia district placed restrictions on squatters, many of them Bukusu people, to make room for new white settlers on land that Babukusu believed to be their ancestors', now stolen by the British. A religious response came in *Dini ya Misambwa*, which sought to expel Europeans from Kenya and rejected their civilisation, especially its religion. Elija Masinde, the movement's founder and prophet, had worked on a European farm. He opposed the conscription of Africans to fight the Second World War, a white man's war in which Africans had no stake. Convicted of assault, he was imprisoned in 1945. After his release in 1947, Masinde urged the Babukusu to take up arms. He was re-arrested but his followers continued to demand their 'stolen lands' and the expulsion of Europeans. In 1948 Masinde and two other founder members of *Dini ya Misambwa* were convicted of treason. They remained in detention until the end of the State of Emergency in 1960, when they were released with other more famous detainees such as Jomo Kenyatta, Achieng' Oneko and Paul Ngei (Shimanyula 1978; Simiyu 1977; Wipper 1977).

Politically, the Babukusu responded by transforming the Bukusu Union (formed by Pascal Nabwana and others after the banning of the Kitosh Education Society in 1940) into a branch of the Kenya

African Union (KAU). Both society and union had been concerned with education and with uniting Bukusu separately from other Luyia communities. With the new threat to land, the leaders of the Bukusu Union decided to join the KAU and so opted for national solutions to their local problems.

Similar constructions of ethnicity with invented traditions emerged among other Kenya peoples. Economic hardship in the 1920s gave rise to a new religious movement among the Kamba that was designed to re-unite an increasingly divided society in resistance to colonial demands (Forbes Munro 1975). Led by Ndonye wa Kauti, it offered a millenarian, messianic release. In 1938 Kamba took to politics when the Ukamba Members Association (UMA) was founded in Ngelani. It opposed the compulsory destocking intended to prevent soil erosion and provide carcases for a meat canning factory. The Ngelani people demanded to see the Governor. The UMA President Samuel Muindi and his officials, all wealthy stock-owners, led 2,000 men, women and children in a march on Nairobi, the first non-violent resistance movement in Kenya's history. They camped for six weeks until the Governor promised to meet them in Ukambani – where he announced some concessions. Abandoning the destocking campaign he nonetheless deported Muindi to Lamu. The UMA kept up its protests until being proscribed, together with the KCA, in 1940, when more of its leaders were detained (Newman 1974).

In the Taita–Taveta area people were also unjustly dispossessed. After 1918 Ewart Grogan, who already owned large areas around Nairobi, was granted 122,000 acres in Taveta for his war effort. After independence two political families (Kenyatta and Criticos) acquired 26 per cent of Grogan's Taveta land. Only the name of the owners changed. It was a different story in neighbouring Taita. Between the wars the colonial authorities tried to move Taita people from the hills to the plains. The Taita Hills Association (THA) emerged in 1939 to oppose the alienation of the hills to white settlers, forced labour and high taxation. Led by Mengo Woresha Kalonzi, the 4,000-strong THA worked closely with the Kamba UMA and organised a successful strike in 1940, something that could not be tolerated in wartime. THA leaders, together with those of UMA and KCA (twenty-three leaders in all) were arrested and detained at Kapenguria – a place later made famous by the trial of Jomo Kenyatta and his five associates. All three associations were banned but not before THA pressure had forced the government not only to allow the Taita to remain in their hills but also to enlarge their reserve.

It was in the same World War Two period that the so-called Nandi-speaking peoples transformed themselves into the Kalenjin, an imagined ethnic group that included Pokot, Tugen, Keiyo, Marakwet, Nandi, Kipsigis and Terik. 'Kalenjin' means 'I tell you'. These peoples – related to each other by common origin, migration, settlement, language and culture – had come to see that in their geographically separate sections they were of lesser account than larger, more cohesive, groups. Unity and common purpose could give them a power not easily disregarded. An immediate concern was to prevent the infiltration of other 'tribes' into Kalenjin areas. Looking to the future, a united front seemed essential if Kalenjin were not to lose from the Africanisation of power. In 1959 they took the bold step of forming the Kalenjin Political Alliance – an unashamedly ethnic party (Omusule 1989).

Similar processes of consolidation and expansion occurred among Maasai – despite their deliberate isolation from centres of power and, at the coast, among Swahili-speakers and Mijikenda (King 1971a; Spear and Waller 1993: 117–37; Willis 1993). For, as Iliffe observed of Tanganyikans so Kenyans, too, 'had to live amidst bewildering social complexity which they ordered in kinship terms and buttressed with invented history'. They invented larger and more cohesive communities that seemed more effective in the struggle for ethnic sovereignty than the original 'tribes' to which the British assumed they belonged. This invention of larger ethnic communities that grew in self-awareness and assertiveness after 1920 had serious implications for Kenyan nationhood.

From ethnic to national sovereignty

Kenya's colonial state was a British construct, forged and maintained by force. It attempted to provide political and economic security to white settlers by creating a dual economy divided between native reserves and 'white highlands'. This segregation set the stage for the construction of ethnic identities and the ethnicisation of society. Each ethnic group had control over a specified reserve. Africans could neither own land nor organise politically outside their reserve. Political struggle was ethnicised according to the identity of its leaders. Colonial policy emphasised group distinctiveness, the African elite later embraced it.

Then, as Kenya approached independence in the late 1950s, its communities became mutually apprehensive. Who would control the nation-state and take over the apparatus of power and wealth created for the purposes of colonial oppression and exploitation? Who was to inherit the settler economy and to what purpose? Who would own Kenya?

The populist leaders who emerged could reach no consensus because before the 1950s there was no basis for national political organisation. The leaders who sprang to prominence with the formation of district associations in 1955 and the first direct African elections to the Legislative Council in 1957 were ethnic bosses: Daniel T. arap Moi, Masinde Muliro, Ronald Ngala and Oginga Odinga. Each had built a strong base in his respective area; none was subject to any common policy or discipline. Under what ideology could ethnic bosses unite to build a nation? Could Kenyans harness ethnic energy for a common purpose? Above all, how could minority ethnic groups be assured that they would not be dominated and marginalised by larger ones?

On 14 May 1960, African political leaders met to launch the Kenya African National Union (KANU) but failed to agree on policy or leadership. Kikuyu leaders swore they would never be led by a Luo. Muliro boycotted the conference. Ngala refused the treasurership because his coastal supporters feared up-country dictatorship. Moi declined the position of assistant treasurer for the same reason: his Kalenjin would not support a party dominated by a Kikuyu–Luo alliance. Moi attended Kalenjin Political Alliance meetings instead. Over 6,000 people came to one of his rallies. He warned them against any political organisation that started at the top; politics should start from the bottom to avoid dictatorship. On 25 June, at Ngong', KPA representatives met six other ethnic organisations, including the Maasai United Front, the Coast African Political Union and the Somali National Association. Together they formed the Kenya African Democratic Union (KADU) to challenge what they called the danger of Kikuyu–Luo leadership. Kalenjin and coast people were particularly concerned that land lost to white settlers should revert to them (Kyle 1999).

The fundamental question facing the constitution-makers at London's Lancaster House in 1961 and 1962 was: how could a democratic future be ensured? The same question faced delegates to the National Constitutional Conference at Bomas in Nairobi forty years later. KADU's answer was to *devolve* power to Kenya's regions.

Regionalism (*majimbo*) seemed the only way to resist an otherwise inevitable Kikuyu domination, especially dangerous when it came to re-allocating land. Kalenjin and Maasai feared that the White Highlands would be given to 'outsiders', not to those who had earlier occupied the area.

The British appointed five commissions of enquiry into the shape of independence. One of them, a Regional Boundaries Commission, heard from 210 delegations before recommending that Kenya be divided into six regions. Two principles guided their report: to retain existing administrative boundaries where possible and to heed popular wishes. As to the latter, many Kenyans declared a wish to be associated with some groups and not with others. This was the most ambitious attempt in Kenya's history to group people according to their ethnicity. A Kenyan version of apartheid resulted – ethnic enclaves that cut through some colonial district boundaries in order to separate antagonistic 'tribes' and to group together others who wished to be so associated (Regional Boundaries Commission 1962).

The government accepted the Commission's report, with minor variations, and had to modify some district borders to prevent them overlapping a new regional boundary. Three districts were partitioned out of existence and three new ones created. In thirty-five of forty-one districts, one ethnic group constituted an absolute majority of the population and in seventeen districts over 90 per cent were of the same ethnicity. Luyia were settled in large numbers in parts of the northern Rift. Nandi, of whom many were left landless, felt cheated while Kikuyu and Luyia acquired their new smallholder farms. These border conflicts have persisted to date, largely because the report emphasised ethnic exclusiveness.

Ethnicity and power

In *Citizen and Subject* (1996), Mahmood Mamdani attributed the construction of ethnicity in Africa to colonial rule. While using the concept of civil society to mould Africans into good citizens, colonialists also rounded up peasants under native authorities constituted by 'tribe' – a tool for ruling natives. This 'regime of differentiation' kept tribes divided and helped maintain order. *Political* ethnicity resulted. By the time of independence, 'the tribal logic of native authorities easily overwhelmed the democratic logic of civil society'.

Post-colonial Africans therefore possess dual citizenships that bestow on them contradictory and competing identities, rights, allegiances and obligations. On the one hand national citizenship is signified by identity cards, passports and laws that specify citizenship rights and obligations, most of which the state is too weak to enforce. On the other hand ethnic or sub-national citizenship grants the same individual ethnic identity, rights and obligations that are enforced by cultural practice and moral economy. By comparison with the weak post-colonial state, the ethnic community enjoys greater legitimacy and exercises a more pervasive authority or influence over individuals.

In Kenya the 'tribal logic of native authorities' carried colonial 'divide and rule' over into post-independent politics, while protecting perpetrators of negative ethnicity from being answerable to Kenyans. Lonsdale (2004) discusses how political ethnicity allows those in power to manipulate resources in such a way that they can mobilise members of a specific ethnic community (predominantly their own) to rally behind them in their quest for power, and in return, offer these members 'rewards', whether real or symbolic. This patron–client relationship has come to define politics and has ensured that Kenya has remained ethnically divided.

'The ethnicity of the president is the surest clue to the ethnic tinge of the government' (Mamdani 1996: 289). During 1964–78, the Kenyatta regime consolidated its state power to preserve its class and ethnic interests. It did so through coercion and co-option: dissenting voices were jailed, exiled or killed; resource allocation became grossly inequitable; the public sector was increasingly ethnicised; contracts were awarded according to ethnic or political affiliation. State power, previously coloured by colonial racialism, now took an ethnic shape. Crucially, Kenyatta appeased the land hunger of former Mau Mau fighters by settling them on soft loan terms. Kikuyu returned to the Rift Valley in large numbers, and the Kikuyu reserves now reached socially and politically into the central Rift Valley, turning it into a new Kikuyu reserve – and even beyond the Rift into Nandi, Kericho and Uasin Gishu districts. Rift Valley estates were given to the president's closest sycophants such as Njenga Karume (Karume 2009: 122–228). The project of communal land ownership so dear to *majimbo* hopes was jettisoned: nobody in authority listened to the cries of 'lost lands' from such historically aggrieved communities as Maasai and Kalenjin.

Neither the Kenyatta nor the Moi regime repaired the injustice done to the Laikipia Maasai, violently uprooted and with great loss in 1911, to make room for white settlers, as told above. Indeed, Maasai became still more marginalised. Godfrey Kariuki, member of parliament for Laikipia for twenty years and an assistant minister for ten, founded the Laikipia West Farmers' Company, with Kenyatta's encouragement, to buy land from white farmers on which to settle its mostly Kikuyu shareholders. By 1983, and after he had served as a cabinet minister, his company had bought more than 127,000 acres of land and settled more than 20,000 families in Laikipia, almost all of them Kikuyu (Kariuki 2001). Such land purchases created tension between Kikuyu and other communities who had earlier lived there, particularly Maasai, Samburu and Pokot. The inter-ethnic conflicts of the 1990s followed. Worse still, other groups, especially Kikuyu, started to infiltrate into the southern Maasai districts of Narok and Kajiado to grab land there. The Enoosupukia skirmishes of 1993 and the demands by Laikipia Maasai in 2004 for the return of their one million acres stolen, first, by thirty-eight foreign ranchers, and latterly by their Kenyan counterparts, arise from this history. The Kikuyu fought the British to recover their 'stolen lands' but, with former inhabitants excluded from settlement schemes, most of the lands on which Kikuyu have since settled were never theirs.

Moi's home province – the Rift Valley – was a decisive factor in his appointment as vice-president and then as president. The white settler community had vast interests in the Rift Valley and, as noted, Kenyatta settled most of those Kikuyu displaced during the Emergency in the Rift. The need to protect their interests largely determined the decision of who should succeed Kenyatta as president. The Kikuyu–Kalenjin alliance forged with Moi from late 1964 became a categorical imperative for Kenyatta. It enabled Kikuyu to settle in the former White Highlands as freeholders, contrary to the wishes of Kalenjin radicals, whose Nandi Hills Declaration had stated that any newcomers who did not identify with Nandi law and custom would face undying Nandi anger. Two leading radicals were convicted of sedition, on grounds of instigating ethnic ill-will (*Daily Nation*, 6 October 1969).

The Kenyatta regime was involved in similar injustice at the coast. Much of the land there was designated as government, unregistered, or trust land; few of the local Mijikenda community held title deeds.

Less than 10 per cent was categorised as freehold and registered; most of this was owned by Arab and other Asian immigrants, and later by well-connected individuals from up-country. Settlement schemes also deprived local populations of their land. Most of the land allottees in the coastal Jomo Kenyatta (Mpeketoni) Settlement scheme were non-locals. The result of such historical injustice, perpetuated by both Kenyatta and Moi regimes, was an eruption of violence in 1977 against up-country Kenyan settlers. Hundreds were killed or maimed, thousands displaced and made homeless, and many businesses and homes destroyed by fire (Kenya Human Rights Commission 1997).

Kenyatta's ethnicity was defining the state and the direction of Kenyan politics. In 1970, his decision to centralise most power in his own hands increased this tendency, leading to disunity, corruption, a bloated and inefficient civil service and economic marginalisation for some groups. The 1970s saw Kikuyu hegemony or ethnic sovereignty expand over economic and political life. Central Province became the most developed area. The business domination enjoyed by Kikuyu and related groups assisted their aggressive land acquisition in the Rift, at the coast and in major towns beyond their 'homelands'. It could truly be said that they owned Kenya and controlled its state. Kenyatta became an imperial president, owning vast properties and businesses all over the country.

Kikuyu ascendancy caused fear and resentment among other communities who felt marginalised. They took little pride in a Kenyan identity, indeed people's primary loyalty did not lie with the nation called Kenya. Kenyan patriotism meant nothing to those excluded from power. Kikuyu nationalism, one of the oldest anti-colonial movements, was now killing Kenyan nationalism. Who needed Kenya?

Within KANU, Luo nationalism haunted this Kikuyu nationalism by demanding equity between communities. There was also Tom Mboya, secretary general of the party who, although a Luo, rejected identity politics, for his birth and upbringing had 'situated [him] from childhood to be a Kenyan' (Atieno Odhiambo 1992b). Born in Kiambu, Mboya grew up in a multiethnic community of Kikuyu, Kamba and Luo farm squatters and began his political career in Nairobi, a cosmopolitan constituency, to become a national leader before he was a Luo leader. As a quintessential non-tribalist and possible successor to Kenyatta, Mboya threatened Kikuyu ethnic nationalism. When, in 1967, Kenyatta barely survived a heart attack, Mboya was first weakened – with his multiethnic urban constituency invaded and trade union power-base undermined – and then eliminated. In July 1969, aged thirty-nine, he was assassinated by a Kikuyu, Nahashon Njenga Njoroge, on the orders of a 'big man' whose identity has never been disclosed. A brilliant minister, shrewd political strategist, efficient administrator, the ablest official spokesman at home and abroad, Mboya was Kenya's pre-eminent non-tribalist politician. His death caused bitter anti-Kikuyu feelings among Luo and he became what he had never been in life: an ethnic hero.

Luo rioted in Nairobi, Kisumu and elsewhere in western Kenya. Ethnic polarisation became total as Kikuyu, led by Kenyatta, initiated an oathing campaign in which almost every adult Kikuyu male was forced to swear in mass ceremonies at Gatundu, the president's home, and on pain of death, to keep the presidency in the House of Muumbi, the Kikuyu Eve. Oath-takers pledged, ominously, to maintain Kenya 'under Kikuyu leadership … No uncircumcised leaders will be allowed to compete with the Kikuyu. You shall not vote for any party not led by the Kikuyu. If you reveal this oath, may this oath kill you' (Njenga Karume 2009: 205–6; *Daily Nation*, 10 April 2001). One had to strip naked, chew some mucky stuff and pledge loyalty to Kenyatta and his government, and for ever to stand united with the Kikuyu leadership. All this went by the euphemism *cai wa Gatundu* – Gatundu tea, but those who refused to drink faced dire consequences. A Presbyterian clergyman, the Rev. Samuel Githinji Mwai, and his wife were beaten senseless by *jeshi la Mzee* – the Old Man's Army. Githinji died two days later: his wife long nursed physical and psychological wounds. As no cleansing oath has since been taken, one must assume that the oath still binds those who took it.

In April 2011 a public rally crowned Uhuru Kenyatta, son of Jomo Kenyatta, 'King' of the Kikuyu. He urged Kikuyu to unite, speak with one voice and prepare to defend themselves against their enemies. Kikuyu leaders who failed to toe the line would be followed to their homes and exposed as traitors (*The Standard*, 4 April 2011). Forty years after the Gatundu oaths, 'tribal' rituals are still used to consolidate ethnic hegemony. Can such ethnic nationalism co-exist with territorial nationalism?

Oginga Odinga was an influential nationalist and had been Kenyatta's ally. It was he who had first dared to suggest, in Legislative Council, that Kenyatta and his fellow detainees, whom the British hoped were forgotten people, were Kenya's true leaders. The two later politically parted company after disagreeing, not on ethnic but on ideological grounds – whether Kenya should take a socialist or capitalist course. Odinga resigned the vice presidency, quit KANU and formed the Kenya Peoples Union (KPU). Instead of fighting the opposition party ideologically, Kenyatta decided to 'other' it by playing up ethnic difference, so undermining the idea of a nation. In a struggle for power, the 'other' must be seen as inferior to 'us': 'our' culture as superior to theirs.

Ethnic stereotypes must also be normalised. The KPU was demonised and ridiculed as a Luo 'tribal' party and its Kikuyu adherents such as Bildad Kaggia condemned as 'Kibu', similar in sound to the KPU acronym but which in Kikuyu means chameleon. During the Little General Election of 1966, Kenyatta campaigned against Kaggia. He wondered, rather contemptuously, why Kaggia was languishing in poverty while his former fellow detainees were wallowing in wealth. He urged the renegades not to join the 'black necks', code for [Luo] people from around Lake Victoria (Ndegwa 2006: 277). Political stereotypes are a form of control. Kenyatta often publicly dismissed Luo as lazy, unable to lift a *jembe* (hoe) to save their lives, while repeatedly playing up the rhetorical stereotype of the industrious Kikuyu until it became economic and political reality. Images shape competitions for power. The rivalry between Kenyatta and Odinga would for long colour political perceptions of their two ethnic groups.

The scheme to root out the Left from Kenya's political mainstream had begun in early 1965 with the murder of Pio Gama Pinto. It concluded in a bloody encounter when presidential guards gunned down over 100 people in Kisumu in October 1969. The president was to have made an elaborate tour of the region, to show Luo who was boss. When opening the New Nyanza Hospital in Kisumu, he lambasted the KPU as 'locusts' that he would grind into flour. The crowd reacted, demanding that he produce Tom Mboya and shouting *dume, dume* (bull, the KPU symbol). Kenyatta responded with obscenities, admonishing Odinga with 'your mother's cunt, this *dume, dume*' and threatened to detain him as a 'good-for-nothing noisemaker'.

The president's bodyguard and police fired on the crowd, killing at least 100, including women and schoolchildren who had been paraded to salute the president. Nobody has since been held responsible for this Kisumu massacre, a crime against humanity. The KPU was banned and its leaders detained, together with several members of parliament, to join other Luo men and women, especially trade union leaders, already in detention. Luo civil servants and professionals were dismissed. Kenyatta swore never to step foot in Luoland again, a promise kept until his death in 1978. His boycott meant that all planning in the area ceased, causing long-lasting under-development. A strong military and police presence also put the people under siege. Kenyatta had in effect declared war on a section of his citizens; the state's marginalisation of an entire ethnic community was complete. Luo reacted with an enhanced ethnic nationalism that further denied the nation a unified voice. This pervasive Luo opposition mentality intensified in the multiparty politics of the 1990s.

Freed from both contenders for policy and power, Odinga and Mboya, Kenyatta was finally able to pursue his own agenda. Scholars have talked, correctly, of two transfers of power in Kenya: one from the British to nationalists in 1963 and the second from the nationalists to Kenyatta after 1969. The president accumulated power by a succession of constitutional amendments: Parliament approved thirteen of them under Kenyatta's rule, creating a presidency stronger than parliament and judiciary. Kenyatta was able to establish a Kikuyu ethnic sovereignty which permanently destroyed territorial nationalism. Who, then, needed Kenya?

The establishment of Kalenjin ethnic sovereignty

Daniel arap Moi became president in August 1978 on Kenyatta's death. He was confronted by an entrenched Kikuyu elite who had tried to prevent his succession by changing the constitution. Since his Kalenjin supporters believed it was their turn to 'eat', Moi had to replace Kikuyu with Kalenjin hegemony. Kalenjin replaced Kikuyu public servants; the economic foundations of the Kenyatta state were then wrecked by unfair taxation of Kikuyu agricultural associations and businesses while Moi consolidated his executive still further, transforming personality cult into autocracy. Many new constitutional amendments were passed, including the notorious Section 2A, which turned Kenya into a *de jure* one-party state in 1982. By 1991, the Constitution had been amended thirty-two times (Odhiambo-Mbai 2003). Dissenting voices were detained, jailed, tortured and killed. Like Kenyatta, he consolidated power by co-option, patronage, coercion and fear.

By the late 1980s, Kenya had become an artificial state, controlling an unstable amalgam of ethnic enclaves through satellite barons created, sustained and controlled by state patronage. Like Kenyatta, Moi mobilised both class and ethnic interests in order to survive.

Ethnic wars of conquest

By 1990, Moi felt strong enough to embark on a most ambitious and bloody project – the re-colonisation of the Rift Valley Province by forcibly evicting all ethnic groups not indigenous to the area. His tools were state and extra-state violence.

In 1991, pressure from internal pro-democracy movements and financial sanctions from external donors forced Moi to repeal the legislation that had turned Kenya from a *de facto* one-party state in 1969 into a *de jure* one in 1982. For the first time in twenty years, the regime faced the prospect of multiparty elections. Worse still, Moi and the ruling party, KANU, had to contend with new electoral rules: to be elected president, one had to be an elected member of parliament (MP), obtain a majority of votes nation-wide and get more than 25 per cent of the votes in five out of Kenya's eight provinces. Moi had already warned that multipartyism would lead to ethnic violence because the country was not sufficiently cohesive.

At public rallies in the Rift Valley, Kalenjin leaders openly advocated expelling non-native inhabitants from the region if they did not toe the KANU line. They called for a return to *majimboism*, the form of federalism KADU had advocated in the early 1960s. But as Judge Akiwumi, who later conducted an inquiry into the 'tribal clashes' of the 1990s in the Rift and elsewhere, noted, '*majimbo* according to the evidence presented to us was not federalism in the real sense of the word, but an arrangement in which each community would be required to return to its ancestral district or province and if for any reason they would be reluctant or unwilling to do so, they would by all means be forced to do so' (Republic of Kenya 1999).

Majimboism in the Rift was a euphemism for ethnic cleansing. In 1989, Kikuyu constituted 19 per cent of Rift Valley population; another 16 per cent were Luyia, Luo and Kisii 'outsiders' or 'foreigners', totalling 1.8 million people (Kagwanja 1998). To evict such huge and diverse populations necessitated ethnic war. That is what happened, not simply ethnic 'clashes' or 'violence'. War was declared on unarmed and defenceless civilians. Kalenjin and, less often, Maasai communities, who saw themselves as the province's main indigenous ethnicities, attacked members of ethnic groups associated with the opposition: Kikuyu, Luo, Luyia and Kisii. The war started in Nandi District, on Miteitei farm, then spread to other parts of Nandi and Kericho, where hundreds of Luo and Kisii were attacked from early November 1992, their homes being looted before being burnt down. Self-styled Nandi Warriors circulated leaflets warning non-Kalenjin to leave by 12 December (Kenya's independence day) or else. In December the Luyia communities in Uasin Gishu and Trans-Nzoia districts were driven from their homes. Violence spread in the northern Rift and in some border areas of western Kenya. The 'warriors' killed, maimed and raped, burnt homes and killed or raided livestock. Over 1,500 people died in the late-1992 election period, and over 300,000 others, mostly Kikuyu, were displaced.

But in spite of this massive expulsion of so-called non-indigenous peoples from the Rift Valley, tension increased between Kalenjin and the Kikuyu diaspora in 1993, especially in Uasin Gishu district. Violence then spread along a mosaic of ethnic frontier zones west of the Rift, instigated mainly by Kalenjin but occasionally by Maasai. According to the Kiliku Report nearly 40,000 more people were forcibly displaced in 1993. The situation remained tense until the end of 1997. Then, during the 1997 election, the Moi government again used violence to achieve political and economic ends. Moi won – to serve his last term under the new constitution. Some communities who voted for the opposition were forcefully evicted from their farms. In January 1998, Samburu and Pokot warriors raided Kikuyu residents in Laikipia district while Kalenjin warriors attacked Kikuyu settlements in the central Rift. The casualties of the two elections in the 1990s totalled 2,000 killed, 500,000 displaced and others intimidated into not voting. The Rift Valley's political landscape changed permanently. By 2002, 70 per cent of those evicted from their land in the 1990s had not returned (Africa Watch 1992; Boone 2007: 20). In this ethnic war, militias were armed, trained – locally and in Cambodia, Iran, Israel and Tanzania – and coordinated by Kalenjin leaders and army officers, while government trucks and helicopters transported them to their work (Nzeki 2009; Republic of Kenya 1992). Moi had accomplished his mission of re-colonising Rift Valley Province.

The passivity and apparent collusion of state officials implied that the government was involved in organising and fighting the war. Moreover, despite both the death and destruction and the official enquiries that have implicated politicians as the instigators of essentially political violence, no one has been punished. Indeed, youthful warrior militias were paid for a job well done, or offered employment or land. A culture of impunity developed in which those who killed, maimed, raped and pillaged, far from being brought to justice, were rewarded as ethnic heroes.

Following the 2007 disputed or 'stolen' elections, ethnic violence erupted again. Organised gangs patrolled slums and parts of the countryside, exacting retribution, as well as killing, robbing, raping and destroying property. Kikuyu gangs retaliated against both Luo and Kalenjin. The *Report of the Commission of Inquiry into Post Election Violence* (Republic of Kenya 2008), chaired by Justice Philip Waki, established that over 1,100 people were killed in the first three months of 2008 – principally among Luo and Kikuyu, followed by Luyia and Kalenjin; that rape and sexual violence were rampant; that over 110,000 properties were destroyed; and that over 300,000 people were displaced from their homes. The security forces were the chief killers, responsible for over one-third of all deaths.

The Waki Report shows Kenya, ethnically speaking, to be a sick society, with a failed political system. Ethnic sovereignty is entrenched in the Rift Valley; 'foreigners' have to return to their ancestral homes and, as happened under Kenyatta's Kikuyu sovereignty, other communities seek survival in a rising political ethnicity of their own. Only force seems able to alter ethnic borders imposed by force. A history of impunity means that Kenya lacks the political will to reconcile citizens, dispense justice and build a democratic and prosperous future. Ethnic citizenship enjoys greater legitimacy and exercises more persuasive authority over Kenyans than their weak and fragmented nation-state.

Ethnicity and constitutionalism

Since 2008, Kenya's balkanisation into ethnic fiefdoms has gathered pace. Business people, farmers, farm workers, university students and staff and even religious leaders, are retreating to ethnic enclaves where they feel safe. The notion of Kenya as a nation whose citizens can live and work anywhere in the country has fewer supporters today than at independence in 1963. Worse still, skepticism over nationhood is most pronounced among the political elite who see the citizens of various ethnic groups as their property, to be used in bargaining for royalties. Within their respective ethnic areas, leaders see ethnicity as a political interest group that can manipulate peasants, urban workers and intelligentsia, through patronage, neighbourly solidarity, sub-ethnic consciousness and individual 'bossism'. Ethnic barons continue to dismember Kenya, perpetuate disunity and exploit their client masses. How can Kenya free herself from the tyranny of ethnic chieftains?

The answer partly depends on how the over forty Kenya nationalities can both respect cultural diversity and act as a common political community, for the groups to which people belong do represent moral communities that any political theory should respect. This is perhaps what Kwame Antony Appiah meant when he said that social pluralism remains not only 'a fact waiting for some institutions, but also a reality awaiting theorization' (Appiah 1992). Ali Mazrui (2001) dramatised this centrality of ethnicity in Kenya's politics and constitution-making in this manner:

One major characteristic of politics in post-colonial Africa is that politics is ethnic-prone. My favourite illustration from Kenya's post-colonial history was our old friend the late Oginga Odinga and his efforts to convince Kenyans that they had not yet achieved *Uhuru* and were being taken for a ride by a corrupt elite and the elite's foreign backers. Jaramogi Oginga Odinga called upon underprivileged Kenyans to follow him towards a more just society. When Oginga Odinga looked to see who was following him it was not all under-privileged Kenyans regardless of ethnic group but fellow Luos regardless of social class. It was not the song of social justice, which attracted the followers, it was who the singer was. Also it was not the song of social justice that kept away others, it was who the singer was. Not the message but the messenger.

The Constitution of Kenya (2010) constitutes an attempt to respect social pluralism. Its preamble states the national message, and the messengers are the people of Kenya. The message presents a vision of the development of a just society in which big ethnic groups do not push smaller ones to the periphery; and proclaims the possibility of Kenyans living together in harmony while appreciating national diversity. To manage diversity, parliament passed the National Cohesion and Integration Act, 2008. This established the National Commission on Integration and Cohesion (NCIC) with a mandate to work towards the elimination of ethnic, religious and racial discrimination. The Act requires Kenya's diversity to be represented in all public bodies; no more than one-third of each of their staffs may be recruited from any one ethnic community. In its *First Ethnic Audit of the Kenyan Civil Service* (2011), the NCIC made it clear that Kenya still suffers from a crisis of ethnic exclusion. Five of the main ethnic groups: Kikuyu, Kalenjin, Luyia, Kamba and Luo account for 70 per cent of all civil service jobs. Of all government workers, 22.3 per cent are Kikuyu, 16.7 per cent are Kalenjin, followed by Luyia (11.3 per cent), Kamba (9.7 per cent), Luo (9.0 per cent) and Gusii (6.8 per cent). Kikuyu and the Kalenjin are particularly well placed in key strategic areas. Yet Kikuyu constituted only 17.7 per cent of the population in 2009 and Kalenjin 13.3 per cent. These numbers suggest a direct relationship with presidential power; the two communities have alternated in the presidency for all Kenya's independent history. At the other extreme, the NCIC report states that twenty small ethnic groups have produced less than 1 per cent each of the country's civil servants (*Daily Nation*, 7 April 2011).

Since independence in 1963, then, those wielding state power have distributed the national cake disproportionately to their co-ethnics and cronies. Development projects, contracts and public positions have been planned, issued and recruited in a skewed manner. A few ethnic groups have dominated key ministries and professional roles such as finance officers, accountants, internal auditors, economists and engineers. So have the seeds of discord been sown and so also, over time, the belief that each community needs one of their own in State House to get their slice of the national cake. The big ethnic groups have allied to take power, share its spoils and push small communities to the periphery. This is what drives Kenya's ethnic-based politics and the dynamic of 'our turn to eat' (Wrong 2009). The new Constitution has set the country on the right course in terms of representation, just-ice, ethnic relations, equitable wealth distribution, a threefold separation of powers and respect for human rights. As Kenya prepares to devolve power and resources to the forty-seven counties, the country should take care that injustices previously perpetrated nationally are not replicated at the local level.

Conclusion

Citizen Television is currently running a provocative weekly programme on 'who owns Kenya?' This has shown that Kenya is owned
by a small, ethnic, power elite. For all other Kenyans the nation-state
is alien; it lacks shared history, memories and values. Such revelations
merely confirm academic studies which show that in Africa dominant classes or social groups are made by ready access to the state – a
resource, a 'national cake', whose capture wins access to wealth. Most
wealthy Africans are so, not because they are hardworking or creative,
but because they enjoy state power. Kenyans have hitherto accepted
that the state cannot be anything other than the instrument of domination and access to *mali ya umma* (public property). Public property
can be plundered with impunity because the nation-state lacks any
moral anchor or concept of the common good. The economy encourages consumption over production.

The struggle to control state power has led to state-sponsored ethnicity. The Kenyatta and Moi regimes used state institutions to create
both class interests and ethnic domination by a system of reward and
exclusion. They withdrew patronage to punish any community that
showed signs of dissent. Kenyatta denied services to the Luo community for fifteen years. The Moi and Kibaki regimes rewarded people
on the basis of ethnic affiliation by giving them new districts, university colleges, public land and basic infrastructure such as roads,
water and rural electricity. Jobs were distributed along ethnic lines.
Communities seen as hostile to the state and its leaders were denied
employment; loyal ethnic groups were rewarded, irrespective of their
qualifications. Kenyans have come to see the state as a site of eating;
ethnicity feeds you when your kith and kin are in power. Kenyans are
empowered not as citizens but by their ethnicity, dependent on their
group's access to the state. For most of them the Kenyan nation is yet
to be born.

Furthermore, due to inward-looking belief systems and polarised
thinking, Kenyan society has produced an 'us' and 'them' dichotomy.
All Kenyans are seen as belonging to a particular ethnic group, so
one is a non-person, *madoa-doa*, outside his or her enclave. Most
successful farmers, business people and professionals who lived in
so-called 'foreign lands' were ordered by the 'indigenous people' to
return to their 'ancestral homes'. Many had no such ancestral home;

they became refugees, mere statistics, in their own country, living as displaced persons in camps or with relatives.

So we have 'the guiltless native'. Any crime (including crimes against humanity) one may commit against 'foreigners' who live in one's region cannot be a crime, for it is done on behalf, and for the good, of one's ethnic group. Nobody accepts responsibility or apologises; criminals become ethnic heroes. But without confession, there can be neither reconciliation nor social healing. By hiding behind their ethnic groups, individuals are absolved from all their crimes or sins. This is the rhetoric of the 'eating chiefs'.

At independence, political leaders promised citizens material and political progress; they have delivered little more than crushing poverty and repression. The gap between expectation and experience, rhetoric and reality, especially when expressed in ethnic terms, has led to bitter hopelessness. Independent Kenya's history has been characterised by poor governance, corruption, poverty, inequality and impunity and, now, chronic ethnic balkanisation. Ethnic citizenship is still more powerful and more engulfing than national citizenship. So, who needs Kenya?

References

Africa Watch 1992. *Divide and Rule: State-sponsored Ethnic Violence in Kenya*. New York: Human Rights Watch, 70–2, 79–80.

Appiah, Kwame Antony 1992. *In my Father's House: Africa in the Philosophy of Culture*. London: Methuen.

Blixen, K. 1954 [1937]. *Out of Africa*. London: Penguin Books.

Blundell, Michael 1994. *A Love Affair with the Sun: a Memoir of Seventy Years in Kenya*. Nairobi: Kenway Publications.

Boone, C. 2007. 'Winning and Losing Politically Allocated Land Rights', unpublished paper for the African Studies Meetings, New York.

Clough, Marshall S. 1990. *Fighting Two Sides: Kenya Chiefs and Politicians, 1918–1940*. Niwot, CO: The University Press of Colorado.

Cranworth, Lord 1912. *A Colony in the Making: Profit and Sport in British East Africa*. London: Macmillan and Co.

Eliot, Sir Charles 1905. *The East African Protectorate*. London: Edward Arnold.

Forbes Munro, J. 1975. *Colonial Rule and the Akamba: Social Change in the Kenya Highlands 1889–1939*. Oxford: Clarendon Press.

Hardinge, A. H. 1928. *A Diplomatist in the East*. London: Jonathan. Cape.

Hartwig, G. W. 1976. *The Art of Survival in East Africa*. New York: Africana.

Hughes, Lotte 2006. *Moving the Maasai: a Colonial Misadventure*. Houndmills: Palgrave Macmillan.

Huxley, E. 1953. *White Man's Country*, second edn, 2 vols. London: Chatto and Windus.

Iliffe, John 1979. *A Modern History of Tanganyika*. Cambridge University Press.

Kagwanja, Peter Mwangi 1998. *Killing the Vote: State Sponsored Violence and Flawed Elections in Kenya*. Nairobi: Kenya Human Rights Commission.

Kanogo, Tabitha M. J. 1987. *Squatters and the Roots of Mau Mau*. London: James Currey.

Kariuki, G. G. 2001. *Illusion of Power: Fifty Years in Kenya Politics*. Nairobi: Kenway Publications.

Karume, Njenga 2009. *Beyond Expectations: from Charcoal to Gold – An Autobiography*. Nairobi: East African Educational Publishers.

Kenya Human Rights Commission (KHRC) 1997. *Kayas of Deprivation, Kayas of Blood: Violence, Ethnicity and the State of Coastal Kenya*. Nairobi: KHRC.

1934. *The Kenya Land Commission Report 1934* (Cmd. 4556). London: HMSO.

Kenya Regional Boundaries Commission 1962. *Kenya Report of the Regional Boundaries Commission*. London: HMSO.

Kenyatta, Jomo 1938. *Facing Mount Kenya*. London: Martin Secker and Warburg.

1944. *My People of the Kikuyu, and the Life of Chief Wang'ombe*. London: United Society for Christian Literature.

King, K. 1971a. 'The Kenya Maasai and the Protest Phenomenon, 1900–1960', *Journal of African History* 12: 117–37.

1971b. 'A Biography of Molonket ole Sempele', in *Kenya Historical Biographies*, K. King and A. Salim (eds.). Nairobi: East African Publishing House.

Kyle, Keith 1999. *The Politics of the Independence of Kenya*. Houndmills: Palgrave Macmillan.

Leys, Norman 1924. *Kenya*. London: Hogarth Press.

Lonsdale, John 2004. 'Moral and Political Argument in Kenya', in *Ethnicity and Democracy in Africa*, Bruce Berman, Dickson Eyah and Will Kymlicka (eds.). Ohio: James Currey, 73–95.

Mamdani, Mahmood 1996. *Citizen and Subject: Contemporary Africa and the Legacy of Late Colonialism*. Princeton, NJ: Princeton University Press.

Matson, A. T. 1993. *The Nandi Resistance to British Rule*. Cambridge African Monographs.

Mazrui, Ali 2001. 'If African Politics are Ethnic-Prone, Can African Constitutions be Ethnic-Proof?', lecture to the Constitution of Kenya Review Commission, 23 August, Nairobi.

Meinertzhagen, R. 1957. *Kenya Diary, 1902–1906*. London: Oliver and Boyd.

Muriuki, Godfrey 1974. *A History of the Kikuyu, 1500–1800*. Nairobi: Oxford University Press.

National Commission on Integration and Cohesion (NCIC) 2011. *The First Ethnic Audit of the Kenyan Civil Service*. Nairobi: NCIC, published in the *Daily Nation*, April 7.

Ndegwa, Duncan 2006. *Walking in Kenyatta's Struggles – My Story*. Nairobi: Kenya Leadership Institute.

Newman, J. R. 1974. *The Ukamba Members Association*. Nairobi: Transafrica Publishers.

Ng'eny, Samuel K. arap 1970. 'Nandi Resistance to the Establishment of British Administration, 1883–1906', in *Hadith* 2, B. A. Ogot (ed.). Nairobi: East African Publishing House, 104–26.

Nzeki, Ndingi Mwana 2009. *A Voice Unstilled*. Nairobi: Longhorn, 104–34.

Odhiambo, Atieno 1992a. 'From Warriors to *Jonanga*: the Struggle over Nakedness of the Luo of Kenya', in *Solomaka: Popular Culture in East Africa*, Werner Graebner (ed.). Amsterdam: Radopi.

1992b. '*Tom Mboya*' in *Political Leaders of Contemporary Africa*, Harvey Glickman (ed.). Boulder, CO: Greenwood Press, 151.

Odhiambo-Mbai, C. 2003. 'The Rise and Fall of the Autocratic State in Kenya', in *The Politics of Transition in Kenya: from KANU to NARC*, W. Oyugi, P. Wanyande and C. Odhiambo-Mbai (eds.). Nairobi: Heinrich Boll Foundation, 69.

Odingo, R. S. 1971. *The Kenya Highlands*. Nairobi: Hutchinson.

Ogot, B. A. 2009. *A History of the Luo-Speaking Peoples of Eastern Africa*. Kisumu: Anyange Press.

Omusule, M. 1989. 'Kalenjin: the Emergence of a Corporate Name for the Nandi-speaking Tribes of East Africa', *Afrique* 27: 73–88.

Republic of Kenya 1992. *Report of the Parliamentary Select Committee to Investigate Ethnic Clashes in Western and other Parts of Kenya*. Nairobi: Government Printer.

1999. *Report of the Judicial Commission Appointed to Inquiry into Tribal Clashes in Kenya* (Akiwumi Report). Nairobi: Government Printer.

2008. *Report of the Commission of Inquiry into Post Election Violence*. Nairobi: Government Printer.

Ross, W. McGregor 1927. *Kenya From Within: a Short Political History*. London: George Allen and Unwin.

Sandford, F. R. 1919. *An Administrative and Political History of the Maasai Reserve*. London: Waterlow and Sons.

Shimanyula, James B. 1978. *Elija Masinde and the Dini ya Musambwa*. Nairobi: Transafrica Publishers.

Simiyu, V. G. 1977. *Elijah Masinde: a Biography*. Nairobi: East African Educational Publishers.

Sorrenson, M. P. K. 1968. *Origins of European Settlement in Kenya*. Nairobi: Oxford University Press.

Spear, Thomas and Waller, R. (eds.) 1993. *Being Maasai: Ethnicity and Identity in East Africa*. London: James Currey.

Waller, Richard A. 1979. '"The Lords of East Africa": the Maasai in the mid-Nineteenth Century (c. 1840–1885)', Ph.D. thesis, Cambridge University.

Willis, Justin 1993. *Mombasa, the Swahili and the Making of the Mijikenda*. Oxford: Clarendon Press.

Wipper, Audrey 1977. *Rural Rebels: a Study of Two Protest Movements in Kenya*. Nairobi: Oxford University Press.

Wrong, Michela 2009. *It's Our Turn to Eat: the Story of a Kenya Whistle Blower*. London: Fourth Estate.

Wymer, N. 1959. *The Man from the Cape*. London: Evans Brothers.

PART II

Does ethnic diversity hinder economic development?

4

State, ethnicity and economy in Africa

YASH PAL GHAI

Introduction

This chapter examines the role, and impact, of the state and law in economic change, with particular reference to the market. I focus on the constitution as the political framework for economic activity, on which there is a large literature.[1] But I introduce an additional element: ethnicity – by which I mean ethnic affiliations, loyalties and preferences. Ethnicity impinges on access to the state and on its working, so influencing patterns of resource allocation; ethnicity therefore affects economic change. On this there is a more limited literature.[2] Ethnicity mediates between state and economy, since control over the state is a critical factor in access to economic opportunity. Ethnicity is sometimes an explicit element of the constitution, in defining the rights of ethnic groups, including those relating to representation and property, but often it expresses itself informally in political practices such as political parties and electoral mobilisation. This chapter offers

---

[1] Legal sociologists have written much about the relations between law and economy. Max Weber's views can conveniently be consulted in Rheinstein (1954). Relevant writings by Marx and Engels are collected in Cain and Hunt (1979). Their views on law and economy are hard to understand except within their magisterial theories of society and state. While Weber focused on legal institutions and doctrines, law was of less interest to Marx and Engels as 'superstructure', reflecting rather than determining the foundations of society.

[2] Among studies on ethnic policies and the economy, and the political consequences of uneven ethnic policies, see Faaland et al. (1990) and Jesudason (1989). J. S. Furnivall (1958) offered important insights on the nature of colonial polities, which he called plural societies: 'In Burma, as in Java, probably the first thing that strikes the visitor is the medley of peoples – European, Chinese, Indian and native. It is in the strictest sense a medley, for they mix but do not combine ... As individuals they meet, but only in the market place, in buying and selling. There is the plural society, with different sections of the community living side by side, but separately, within the same political unit ... There is, as it were, a caste system, but without the religious basis that incorporates caste in social life in India.'

an institutional perspective on the socio-economic dynamics that may underlie any negative relationship between ethnic diversity and macroeconomic performance in Africa, as highlighted in the Introduction (Ranis) and elsewhere in this volume.

Regardless of the preferred type of economy, a good constitution establishes the conditions in which an economic system can operate and flourish. The constitution establishes a government that ensures law and order. It provides procedures for the succession to power, thereby promoting political stability. It creates institutions and mechanisms broadly acceptable to the people, enabling them to develop a national consensus on laws and policies and to settle disputes. It establishes a legal infrastructure that facilitates economic transactions, such as defining property and procedures to create rights and obligations. Within these broad parameters, constitutions reflect different economic ideologies, predominantly in favour of the market or of state ownership and planning.

Contemporary constitutions, especially since the fall of the Berlin Wall, have aimed to establish democratic states and, for the most part, liberal economies. This trend is most marked in Eastern Europe. Elsewhere too, especially in Africa, most constitutions assume a liberal state and market economy. Western scholars such as Max Weber and, in more contemporary times, Douglass North, have developed theories that explore the relationship between market economy, the state and law (Buchanan 1990; North 1990).[3] It is not surprising that African constitutions, with their origin and inspiration from Western democratic, market states, incorporate many 'Western' characteristics. These are seldom explicitly presented as features of a market economy, since the market's overriding influence on African constitutions is mediated by legal and constitutional concepts that can obscure such close connections. Relations between citizens and the state and between citizens themselves are mediated through these concepts, rather than directly. The influence of market economy is therefore indirect (Ghai 1993, 1999).[4]

---

[3] For Weber, see above. For North, see North (1990) and Buchanan (1990).

[4] The link between Marxist socialist economy and the constitution is more explicit. Communist constitutions used to describe the economy as state-owned, vested the means of production in the state, required the state to plan development and restricted the uses of private property, the scope of private enterprise and the right to employ others. The Chinese constitution is still of this type. Ironically, across

But many new constitutions have another function: that of nation building, a response to the ethnic heterogeneity of the people, who are seen to owe their primary loyalty to tribe or clan, hindering national integration and solidarity. In older states, their constitutions played a rather limited role in nation building. They were mainly concerned with state structures; nation building came from coercive, often assimilatory, government policies, from the market or from the influence of dominant social forces. New constitutions, despite their liberal orientation, can contain provisions intended to promote national identity and solidarity. Some of these may not be consistent with traditional understandings of liberalism, since they require state intervention in economic and social affairs to redress past injustices, and to protect group and communal entitlements, at the expense of individual citizens (Ghai 2010a). If, however, these measures do produce social stability and consensus, they are likely to promote rather than hinder market economy.

My interest in this chapter is on how the state affects the emergence and regulation of the economy, and on tensions between political authority and market, as mediated by ethnicity. My focus is on post-colonial states, which still carry a heavy burden of past imperial rule. Despite any legal thrust towards a liberal, rule-of-law driven state and market principles, a constitution will fail to achieve either, at least in the short or medium term, until the economy and business transactions establish their own autonomy. Nor have many constitutions succeeded in nation building; to the contrary, a constitution can deepen divisions in multiethnic states. This divergence between constitutional aspiration and outcome is due to the nature of the post-colonial state and its relationship to, and the nature of, its civil society, shaped by social forces emerging in both the colonial and post-colonial periods. This chapter reinforces the historical perspectives on post-colonial political economy discussed in Chapter 3 (Ogot).

My method is to examine the emergence of state forms and the economy in Kenya by comparison with the development of the state, society and economy in the West. In a stimulating exchange Lonsdale has queried whether one should measure the African experience against the European (in fact British) experience when the historical context is so

its border, Hong Kong's constitution is as complete a codification of a free market as has ever been devised.

very different. He says, 'The constituent processes of making the state more accountable, and the rule of law more effective etc., are surely bound to be different too. We may agree on the current shortcomings of African states but why should we expect that they will be remedied by the same processes as occurred in Britain? Kenya will never have an industrial revolution, the key democratising shock in Britain, I think. Of course, if one agrees with that observation, then it is still more difficult to identify the sources of [Kenyan] societal energy that might act to reform the state.'

What I have tried to do is to identify what I consider to be the features and institutions that the West and Africa have both experienced: state, society and market. Their relative salience differs, as do their consequences. I show that similar rules and institutions have worked differently, to some extent because ethnic consciousness has been stronger in Africa than in the West. Insofar as there is some logic in the state and in market economy, an examination of the way they operate in the West and Africa may help towards understanding African realities, and perhaps even to make predictions. I assume that the social, political and economic forces emerging under the auspices of the state and economy are going to be critical to development.

I also recognise that in the West it was society that shaped the state, while in colonial and post-colonial Africa, the state has so far shaped society. The question is whether the dominant social classes will be able to subordinate the state to their purposes. Our challenge is to identify, as Lonsdale points out, precisely what changes in society would trigger a fundamental change in state and economy. I do not assume that these must be the same as in Europe, but I do consider that the European experience can throw light on what should be done in Africa. And insofar as the state *is* as central in Africa as I argue below, to humanise the state and bring it under the sovereignty of the people must be a critical aim.

Constitution and market

Modern liberal constitutions arose in the West with the emergence of capitalism. Their fundamental concepts and institutions reflect market economy. Constitutions served to redefine state powers and structures, to register the victory of the bourgeoisie over feudal lords and, later, over monarchies. Since market economy is a private economy, dependent on the initiatives, decisions and organisations of private individuals or groups, the constitutional task is to create conditions which impose minimal restraints on these private activities, while resources and the means of production are released from state or communal constraints. Also, because market economy is a form of class rule, the role and status of the state is crucial. Direct control of the state may suit the bourgeoisie, and was indeed the practice in the early days of European capitalism as well as in the Americas, but it lays bare the exploitation inherent in the system. It was therefore difficult to sustain for long, especially as it clashed with market ideology itself. So concern shifted to the less explicit subordination of the state to the bourgeoisie.[5]

Market economy requires certain instruments such as contracts to facilitate exchange and planning for the future, currency, weights and measures and exclusive rights, particularly over property. The ability to predict and plan for future outcomes is crucial. General rules are therefore needed that, for example, limit the state's functions and regulate its power to intervene. Mechanisms for settling disputes must be faithful to these rules and to agreements between parties reached in accordance with them. Market economy is extraordinarily productive of disputes and quarrels, and the legal system sometimes allows parties to resile from their obligations – in return for penalties.

Some of the standard devices of liberal constitutions are responses to the needs of market economy. Foremost among them are fundamental rights and freedoms, which are oriented towards the individual and seek to free him or her from communal constraints. In their origin in the West's bourgeois revolutions, rights celebrated individual autonomy, marking humans as entrepreneurs. He (I use the masculine form advisedly) was equipped with rights to property, contract, association and mobility without which capitalism could not have flourished. The political analogue of man as entrepreneur was man as citizen, his citizenship based on equal rights and obligations, with the state, in turn, obliged to foster a national economy.

[5] One is reminded of Marx's statement in *German Ideology* (1845), 'For each new class which puts itself in the place of one ruling before it, is compelled, merely in order to carry through its aim, to represent its interest as the common interest of all the members of society, that is, expressed in ideal form: it has to give its ideas the form of universality, and represent them as the only rational, universally valid ones.'

Another set of concepts aimed to limit the power of the state – concepts such as the separation of powers, checks and balances and the rule of law, the last of which restricted the discretion of state officials. Independence of the judiciary was necessary to hold the predetermined balance between state and economy, between the government and the citizen and to uphold the legal framework within which individuals and corporations dealt with other individuals and corporations, especially in economic transactions. Through the constitution, laws and other means the state legitimised the economic system. However, the market requires a particular form of social and political order. This cannot be generated by the state, but by the reverse: by restrictions on state powers and functions, with effective mechanisms to enforce those restrictions. Every economy is a political construct. The relationship between state and market is always problematic for, paradoxically, the greater the burden on the state to sustain capitalism, the more likely it is that the state will be forced into regulating the market.

Relations between state and market can therefore be neither static nor uniform; they are shaped by specific histories and traditions. Relationships have changed over time – from *mercantilism* when the bourgeoisie needed the state to subdue feudalism and open the path to expansion overseas, to *laissez faire* when the bourgeoisie felt confident in the self-sustaining capacity of the market. They have also reflected the changing balance between agriculture and industry, as argued in Charles Beard's brilliant study of the economic origins of US constitutionalism (Beard 1965). Economic tension can also generate change, as when the rise of trade unions and pressure for the extension of the franchise led to the growth of the welfare state (Hurst 1982). The rise of democracy introduced a new dialectic between market and state, while justifications for the market shifted from the purely economic to the political.

Nor has the saga ended for, under globalisation, there is significant shift of power from the state to international economic institutions, public and private. Economic power is once again being stripped of its political clothes, and market rationality is again advanced largely in economic terms, with political considerations diminished. 'Governance' is now primarily an economic concept, edging out democracy and participation as primary values. One can see this in the way the new constitutions of Eastern Europe, influenced by the American Bar

Association, entrench the mechanisms of a 'self-sustaining' market (Howard 1993).

More important are constitutional responses to supra-state markets, of which the outstanding example is the economic and political union of European states. This holds profound consequences for the political order of these states, stripping away layer after layer of their sovereignty. Small states such as Kenya, heavily indebted to outsiders, with economies nurtured by various forms of protectionism and state intervention, are even more vulnerable to globalisation. They can neither defend their sovereignty nor their economy. What can be the basis of such a state's constitution?

When we turn to the ethnic dimension in the equation between state and market, it is important to distinguish between constitutions that build primarily on citizenship, ensuring equal rights for all, and those which incorporate communal entitlements, often on a differential or discriminatory basis. Fiji and Malaysia are examples of the latter: there, 'indigenous' people have special rights to land and education and, in Malaysia, with respect to religion, too ([Malaysia] Faaland *et al.* 1990; Sundaram 1998, 1999; [Fiji] Ghai and Cottrell 2007a: 639–69). In Bosnia–Herzegovina some rights, particularly to representation in various political institutions, depend on ethnic affiliation, so that control of each institution is vested in one community (Ghai 2004). Several recent Latin American constitutions recognise the rights of indigenous peoples to their traditional habitats, and give them some measure of control over their land (Yrigoyen Fajardo 2000: 197–222; Roldán Ortiga 2004). The South African apartheid system built a more extensive regulation of land ownership, right of residence and qualification for employment, based on ethnic affiliation, all privileging the white community (for an introduction, see Sachs 1973). Constitutions that aim ultimately at equal rights for all citizens sometimes provide for group entitlements, theoretically as a temporary measure; India is a well known example (Horowitz 1985).

Arrangements of these kinds require administrative institutions which intrude increasingly on individual choice and the autonomy of the market. To work, they depend on a particular ethnic group's control of the state, and on state intervention in the economy. Economic globalisation poses a major challenge to these arrangements, since their supposed inefficiencies reduce global competitiveness – and could therefore reverse local ethnic differentiations. Such reversal might cause injustice to communities whose weaknesses it exposes. Since global economic transactions are still largely conducted through states, their elites can do much to preserve their own interests, regardless of the effect on the rest of the population.

Many new constitutions are based on liberal political principles: individual and corporate rights, protection of property, including contracts and intellectual property, industrial relations, an independent judiciary and so on. But they do not necessarily reflect political or economic realities; actual practice can be contrary to the constitution and its values. Rulers and dominant social powers have vested interests in such practices, and so disregard the constitution, especially in Africa. To understand economic dynamics in Africa and their relationship with ethnicity, one must understand the obstacles facing liberal constitutions. For this purpose I turn to a case history, Kenya's, before returning to the broader, theoretical issues central to this chapter.

Kenya: a case study

Contributions to this volume by Lonsdale (Chapter 1), Ogot (Chapter 3) and Berman (Chapter 5) provide a useful background to colonialism and its socio-economic impact (Berman 1990). So I restrict myself to a brief history, told from the perspectives of state and ethnicity.

When the British came to what is now Kenya, Africans lived in largely self-contained and self-regulating communities or tribes – as anthropologists called them – with their own organisations and rules, occupying relatively well-defined territory. Community fortunes depended on natural resources, rains, disease, the ebb and flow of trade and on internal conflicts as well. Most communities had contacts with neighbouring tribes, trading as well as raiding. Among cultivators, abundant resources meant that there was little conflict over them; resource conflict was more common among pastoralists. But no organisation or rule extended beyond a tribe. Differences between tribes were settled by negotiation, perhaps leading to reparations, or by force. Tribal boundaries were porous.

All this changed under the impact of external traders, Swahili and Arabs, who came in search of ivory and other goods, but most critically with the arrival of the Imperial British East African Company (IBEAC), chartered by the British government, whose objectives went beyond trade. The IBEAC was given responsibility for administering the territory over which the British claimed jurisdiction – a claim more relevant *vis-à-vis* other European powers competing for territory in Africa than for the Africans over whom they assumed powers of administration. Later, the British government took over the territory's administration, to facilitate its broader objectives, including control of the Nile and exploitation of local resources, especially land.

For our purpose, the British arrival created the concept of a colony, with defined boundaries within which were included the many tribes who had long lived there. The British brought the concept, institutions, and constitution of a state. By virtue of their administrative and legislative acts there emerged the beginnings of a common rule over both indigenous tribes and immigrants who entered the colony for trade or other purposes. Local ways of organising and regulating communities were gradually displaced. One system of governance began to be superseded by another, alien and powerful, which has become the basis of modern Kenya. The legal system showed a curious dichotomy: that part which applied to Europeans and to lesser extent to Indians, bore some resemblance to the law as administered in England; but so far as Africans were concerned, the system was arbitrary, dependent more on the whim of individual officials than the imperatives of the law.

Colonial rule was administered through institutions established by the British but was also reliant on alliances with members of friendly tribes. Armed force played its most critical role at the start of British rule. A police force was established early, not to protect the people, but to coerce them into submission. The aggressive force of the police played a key role in building the structures of British administration – a role that has continued to this day. The colonisers expropriated vast areas of land, in disregard of local rules but justified by alien concepts of ownership; some peoples were moved from their traditional habitations (Leo 1984, chs. 1–3; Okoth-Ogendo 1991).

The states the British established in Africa were rooted in violence and the exploitation of African peoples, for three main reasons. Firstly, such regulations as bound the European powers in acquiring territory were, after all, made by European statesmen ignorant of Africa and Africans. In the scramble for Africa, European force counted for more than the integrity of their colonised subjects; diverse tribes were brought within any one colony; some territories lacked any geographic rationality. Secondly, the states they established were of an alien people, based on organisational principles very different from

African community institutions. Thirdly, they were founded on violence and the violation of human rights. But no state can long survive by force alone, and in time the British set up civilian administrations, built on district officers and a provincial administration, another foundation of the modern Kenyan state.

The colonial state required legal foundations – a constitution. On what basis was British sovereignty established in Kenya? Did it conform to the rules Europeans adopted for the scramble for Africa? Did it satisfy British rules for the acquisition and governance of overseas possessions? Legislation and regulations issued in Kenya at the end the nineteenth and beginning of the twentieth century had to answer these questions.

There is no need to go into these laws except to make the following points (Ghai and McAuslan 1970, chs. 1 and 2). It is clear that the early constitutions the British drafted for Kenya had less to do with Kenya's people than with how the British would rule them. Nor did the British seek Kenyans' consent, either to the fact of alien rule or to how it was carried out. If British rule met any legal obstacle, London legislated to 'regularise' the situation. The nature of this state power, existing outside its subject communities, was new to African communities, and more or less disempowered them. The courts, whether in Kenya or Britain, refused to exercise any real control over Kenya's British administration, the famous Lord Denning once saying, as late as 1956, 'The courts rely on the representatives of the Crown to know the limits of its jurisdiction and to keep within it. Once jurisdiction is exercised by the Crown the courts will not permit it to be challenged' (*Nyali Bridge Ltd. v Attorney-General* [1956] KB1 at p.15). Courts thus largely abandoned any attempt to ensure the legality of government actions – something else that has marked the post-independence period.

The state was the source of patronage, favours and wealth, which facilitated the co-option of local collaborators. British rule also affected African social and economic structures. The rhythms of life were seriously disrupted. Self-sufficiency gave way to new forms of political economy, and although part of the colonial strategy was to preserve a measure of traditional society and to restrict African mobility, many political, social and economic forces drove society in new directions. It led to uneven development, horizontal inequality, between groups and regions – with great significance for post-colonial ethnic relations.[6] It brought greater contact among communities and competition between them for access to the newly developing economy and state largess. Market forces and administrative practice undermined the basis of egalitarianism, leading to differentiation between and within communities. These tendencies accelerated with the approach of independence, destroying trust within communities as well as between them – not without the connivance of the colonial power (Branch 2011).

This was the context in which the independence constitution was negotiated. That it was negotiated distinguished it from the previous colonial constitutions, externally imposed. But, far from independence solving the problems generated by colonialism, it made many of them more acute and produced several more, arising from the transfer of power to Kenyans. Land problems, with their layers of injustice, were not resolved, and the independence settlement created new ones (Cowen 1982; Kanyinga 2000; Okoth-Ogendo 1981). Differential regional development led to political fragmentation and anxiety lest power pass to a few privileged tribes. The bureaucracy and armed forces remained entrenched, with State House able to exercise power across the country through its network of provincial commissioners, district officers and chiefs.

The independence constitution made some attempt to re-distribute state power and inserted a bill of rights aimed at strengthening the independence of the judiciary, while making the police more autonomous and more accountable. The question was whether these embellishments would do anything to change the logic and dynamics of the state, an artefact of colonial exploitation and oppression, divorced from the ethos of Kenya's communities, and now ready to be captured by factions, resistant to change. What Britain bequeathed to Kenyans was a country with its many communities tied together by political structures and with an economy devised for their subordination, but with the additional problem of finding and creating a common identity and destiny: a state without a nation.

The independence constitutional settlement was short-lived. The logic of a state governed by constitutionalism – such a radical departure from the colonial scheme of things – did not suit the new rulers. The president, Jomo Kenyatta, began dismantling it immediately,

[6] For which see Chapter 8 in this volume, by Brown and Stewart.

particularly its provisions for democracy, power-sharing and human rights. Along with the amendments made by his successor, Daniel arap Moi, governance reverted, in effect, to the colonial system, with vast executive powers, decreasing political accountability and exploitation of ethnic distinctions. Checks and balances were removed, as were regional governments. The land chapter was reduced to a few provisions on trust land, giving the national government almost complete control over land. Appeals to the Privy Council from Kenyan court decisions were abolished, enabling the executive to destroy the independence of the judiciary by constitutional amendment and threats or bribes.[7]

So ended any careful sharing and balancing of power, and safeguards for citizen's rights and freedoms; so, too, were sown the seeds of disunity and destructive ethnic politics (Human Rights Watch 1991).[8]

These amendments centralised the state and vested executive power in the hands of the president. This encouraged patronage and ethnic politics as each community focused on this one vital political prize. The centrality of the capture of the state is demonstrated by the intense anxieties and intrigues, and shifting alliances, that attend each succession. Since the dominance of only one tribe is difficult to achieve without extreme violence and repression – and this did happen – it is more expedient to have allies among other tribes, secured by patronage. These allies do not necessarily command support among their own tribes; all three presidencies experienced this problem. A president has to plan resource distribution with care, so that to buy the support of other communities does not alienate one's own – whose leaders remain the main beneficiaries of state largess.

Combined with the lack of accountability, the system led to massive corruption, the principal beneficiaries of which were the president's tribal cronies. The control of land by the government and county councils, and in particular the president's power to grant land without

---

[7] The centrality of the state and the growing importance of ethnicity often leads to another curious result: the removal of constitutional provisions recognising diversity/minorities – Eritrean autonomy in Imperial Ethiopia; Buganda's status and that of other kingdoms in Uganda; *majimbo* and land protection in Kenya; shrinkage of Zanzibar's autonomy and constitutional status – not in the cause of national integrity and unity, but in the interests of a highly ethnicised community seeking control of the entire state. See Ghai and McAuslan (1970: ch. 5).

[8] The massive violations of human rights were carefully recorded by Human Rights Watch (1991) and various issues of the *Nairobi Law Monthly*.

any legal process or consultation, led to massive abuse, illegal land transfers and the dispossession of many, widening the gulf between rich and poor.[9] Pervasive corruption undermined state resources, distracted the president, ministers and senior bureaucrats from their ministerial and official responsibilities and led to declining levels of social services, the emergence of slums, acute poverty for many and obscene affluence for a few. State policies and practices became exclusionary, intensifying ethnic discrimination and conflict, encouraging the militia-isation of politics and armed tribal conflict, causing many deaths and still more displacements, together with the assassination of a few politicians committed to reform and social justice.

The rule of law could not survive the huge powers of the president, some under the law but many with no legal foundation. The impunity of the president and his associates became the licence for many acts of violence, corruption and theft of state resources. All this made people distrust government and caused suspicion and conflict between ethnic communities, as politicians played on ethnic fears and promoted ethnic animosities, weakening national solidarity and threatening the very integrity of the country.

These developments damaged the economy. Britain had already instituted policies to promote the emergence of an African middle class with vested interests in the status quo. The colonial government had laid the legal foundation of commercial farming, by taking land out of communal ownership and giving titles to individuals or corporations and, by using its wide discretionary powers to issue loans and licences, had encouraged participation in commerce (Leo 1984). Several state corporations in the financial, industrial and commercial fields were established in the name of development – a source of enormous patronage. After independence, these instruments were used to favour the president's ethnic colleagues, together with a few from other tribes to widen the president's support. A new bourgeoisie emerged accordingly, among communities allied to the president. Horizontal as well as

[9] These illegal transfers were investigated by a commission chaired by Paul Ndiritu Ndungu (Commission of Inquiry into the Illegal/Irregular Allocation of Public Land 2004). The commission was wound up before its work was concluded; no action was taken on its recommendations. This seems to have been due to an agreement between Mwai Kibaki and Moi, under which the latter promised to support the former in exchange for the termination of the enquiry.

vertical inequalities emerged. The distribution of state jobs illustrates the dominance of the 'ruling tribe' and its close associates (Kanyinga 2006). Key economic decisions were made, not by the logic and mechanisms of the market but by political connections and corrupt means.

This trend was reinforced by the Kenyatta government's decision to remove the restrictions on civil servants taking part in private business.[10] Initially this largely benefited only members of his own tribe and contributed to growing economic disparities between ethnic groups, although the main beneficiaries were a handful of politicians and bureaucrats and, later, business people. Measures of Africanisation were undertaken, to the detriment of Kenya's Asians whose trading licences were cancelled and whose recruitment to the civil service had been stopped. The fundamental principles of the market – equality, competitiveness, security – were compromised; moreover, the colonial model of an administered economy was strengthened. As in colonial days, so now, state policies created both regional differentiation and a division of labour driven by political considerations rather than individual skills or market processes.

In the 1990s, with the end of the Cold War and the West's loss of interest in supporting Moi's regime, some of the constitutional amendments that had increased presidential power were repealed, and some laws which had been used to harass and penalise the regime's political opponents, such as detention without trial, were amended or abolished. But by now people had lost both respect for the constitution and confidence in the political system. People struggled for constitutional reform because they believed that only in this way could the negative consequences of Kenyatta and Moi's changes be removed. They wanted to restore the country to constitutional rule, based on national unity, integrity, democracy, human rights and social justice (Mutunga 1999).[11] Under acute internal and external pressures, in late 2000 Moi agreed to a wide-ranging review of the constitution. A draft was prepared by an independent commission and adopted by the National

---

[10] The *Report of the Commission of Enquiry 1970–71*, by the former head of the public service, Duncan Ndegwa (1971), had a major impact in increasing the economic role of Africans, since it recommended that civil servants be permitted to maintain business interests while holding posts in the government and the public sector. This led to massive engagement in the private sector by civil servants, usually with a partner from the private sector. The principal beneficiaries were members of the Kikuyu, Embu and Meru communities.

[11] The best account of the struggle for reform in this period is Mutunga (1999).

Constitutional Conference in March 2004, but its implementation was sabotaged by the newly elected president, Kibaki, who opposed any diminution in the presidential powers which he had himself criticised when in opposition (Ghai and Cottrell 2007b: 1–25).

It was only with the fraudulent 2007 elections, and the terrible atrocities of the ethnic killings which followed, that the issue of constitutional reform re-appeared on the agenda of reconciliation and a new start, as negotiated by Kofi Annan and other eminent Africans. The underlying reform principles were the same as they had been in 2000.

The objectives of the new constitution are nation building and state building; these are interconnected (Ghai and Cottrell 2011). As to nation building, the emphasis is on unity, patriotism, equal rights, inclusiveness and social justice, described as national values and principles that should suffuse all state institutions. There is much stress on redress of past injustice, help for marginalised and vulnerable communities, respect for diversity of culture and religion and the promotion of local languages. By implication, ethnic politics are incompatible with these national values; political parties must have a national character. As regards state building, integrity in public life and official conduct, transparency, accountability, popular participation, an end to impunity, a greatly strengthened judiciary, several independent institutions and reform of political parties are the dominant principles and objectives. Devolved government as a form of power sharing, self-government and public participation, have elements of both nation and state building.

The constitution also emphasises public welfare. It addresses the question of poverty mainly by introducing social and economic rights – to health, education, housing, sanitation, food and social security – and measures against corruption. It acknowledges that land issues are central to equitable economic development, that the administration of the current land law is riddled with corruption and, therefore, that its application is deliberately confusing, obscure and secretive. Illegally acquired land will be excluded from the constitution's protection of property rights.[12] A strong bill of rights defends

---

[12] The principles underlying land policy, use and management are equity, efficiency, productivity and sustainability. Security of land rights is subject to the legality of their acquisition. In order to attract investment, freehold or long-term leases, if held by non-citizens, are converted into leaseholds with a maximum duration of

privacy and protects people against undue government interference and unfair administrative practices. The constitution, further, guarantees various rights to the media, increases the transparency of the financial and budgetary process, strengthens the judiciary and, with other judicial reforms, should secure a more efficient and impartial machinery for dispute settlement. Business and professional people, who have long criticised a corrupt and incompetent judiciary, have welcomed the new constitution.

The new constitution promises many reforms: economic, political and social – particularly related to gender. But will they be fulfilled? It is important to note that the people imposed this constitution on the politicians and bureaucrats, unlike previous ones that politicians imposed on the people. The people made the final decision in a referendum after the politicians, although anxious to enact many amendments, had failed to agree on them. The new constitution does not reflect the values and interests of the politico-bureaucratic class. They will surely resist it and their grip on power is strong. But will they succeed? In search of an answer, I will sketch the historical connection between constitutionalism and the rise of market economy – and its relevance to new states. I also look for the social and economic forces that might welcome, or resist, this type of constitution.

Absence of constitutional order

The main idea behind constitutionalism is the limitation of state power. A constitutional regime is governed by a constitution which is supreme and represents the highest ideals of the nation; where state authority is subject to limits which arise from the rights of the people and the principles of good government, in which there is separation of powers, horizontally and frequently vertically, to provide checks and balances; where the judiciary is competent, honest and independent; and where people elect and remove governments, holding them responsible and accountable with the help of independent institutions. A central feature of constitutionalism is the impersonalisation of power. Power belongs to state offices, not to their individual office-holders, however

ninety-nine years. Rules of land tenure and succession are gender-neutral. Clearly, the constitution tries to balance the many different interests in land – as economic resource, and as a basis of both justice and communal security (Art. 60).

exalted, and exists for the welfare of the people.[13] The purposes of power and how it should be used are set out in law. The rule of law is crucial. It requires state authorities and private persons to be bound by the law; policies to be based on law; and administrative discretion to be exercised in accordance with the law.

The idea of constitutionalism sketched out above is based on the experience of Western states. In Africa constitutions have been regarded as the means for creating state structures and powers, together with their limits. They seldom represent any continuity in the development of public power. Nor do they have much connection with the reality of power's reach, or its public accountability. For Africa, the dilemma is that its constitutions follow colonial precedent in creating and sanctioning an extraordinary aggregation of power which only then do they try to regulate, modulate and control. In most African countries, even where civilian regimes have prevailed since independence, their constitution has failed in this latter task.

Kenya's experience, outlined above, is therefore typical of most African countries – in starting with a constitution that embodied high ideals of democracy and rights, to be followed by a period of *de jure* or *de facto* one-party, authoritarian rule and then a reversion to democratic constitutions. While African governance has varied to some extent in its degree of democracy and accountability, in most cases power has been used and abused with little regard to the constitution. At the end of the Cold War many countries searched for a political order governed by the rule of law and constitutionalism. The record of these new constitutions is uneven but, on the whole, not encouraging.

In general, one ought not to expect the state to make much of an effort to implement a constitution. The task of establishing constitutionalism lies in other spheres: in political conduct as a construction of values and policies, in a judiciary entrusted with the authoritative interpretation of the constitution, in the rise of professional and civic associations to suffuse the public sphere with appropriate economic and social values and practices, enlightened leadership – and an

---

[13] The Kenya constitution makes this point in several places: 'Executive authority shall be exercised in a manner compatible with the principles of service to the people, and for their well-being and benefit' (Art. 129 [2]); and 'Authority assigned to a State officer ... vests in the State officer the responsibility to serve the people, rather than the power to rule them' (Art. 73[1] [b]).

actively vigilant public. Only society can ultimately control the state; if the state has subordinated society, that control becomes impossible.

I now turn to examine the three elements, state, economy and society, which determine the fortunes of a constitution. In particular, one must ask what happens to a liberal constitution when it is turned to tasks that are alien to its values and institutions. To some degree Kenya's changed political and economic trajectory was accommodated within the constitution simply by amending it – especially in permitting the political opposition to be emasculated and then destroyed. Still more important for our purposes is to examine what happens to liberal institutions under the weight of patrimonialism, ethnicity and corruption. The first consequence is that the economy is subordinated to politics. The second is a constant violation of the rule of law, for only by departing from general rules and their impersonal application can public goods be appropriated for private accumulation or to provide the resources of patronage.[14] The third is a huge increase in corruption, for that is how officials and their associates benefit from their disregard of general rules and procedures. Fourthly, the powers and functions of public institutions are seriously distorted, even effectively negated. Finally, institutions of accountability such as the judiciary suffer the most. They are co-opted or subordinated, with their supposed independence used to benefit corrupt officials by, for example, judicial decisions which uphold breaches of the law.

The market economy can scarcely function in a system so distorted by practices that are alien to it. Economic decline is frequently due to political risks, to the lack of commercial security, the unpredictability of judicial decisions, the prevalence of corruption and the distortion and failure of institutions. The whole system runs into a series of crises, and its legitimacy is compromised, at least in terms of its stated constitutional values. Alternative ideologies may be sought in ethnicity, communalism or fundamentalism, theorised by court intellectuals. But they are seldom satisfactory, and can generate even more intractable problems.

Social scientists who have discussed the state have seldom examined the significance of the constitution, and often assume that it is of

---

[14] Jean-Francois Bayart calls this process the criminalization of politics and the state, defined as 'the routinization, at the very heart of political and governmental institutions and circuits, of practices whose criminal nature is patent' in Bayart *et al.* (1999). For his searching scrutiny of the African state, see Bayart (1993).

no great moment. They tend to explain the failure of constitutions to promote social solidarity or mould state practices by a series of social absences: of a democratic culture, of education, of a middle class and, conversely, the persistence of pre-democratic social structures. Legal scholarship is more formalistic and normative – focusing on the role of individuals as presidents, etc., rather than on the broader context.

While there is some truth in these observations, I want to offer a more structured explanation. I trace a constitution's links with three critical factors that are integral to it in different ways: state, economy and society. The state and its structures are a constitution's principal object, while the economy is its underlying, sometimes overt, concern, theme and, often, its ideology. A constitution's basis is society, both its maker and recipient. There is a complex relationship between these two, with the constitution sometimes reinforcing and at other times aimed at transforming social norms and practices. A constitution tries to shape each of these three factors rather than take them for granted; but each in turn reacts on it, supporting or subverting its values and objectives. I argue that this interaction may be the key to understanding the potential of any constitution and to explaining its success or failure. I draw my perspectives on this interaction from experiences in the West, particularly Britain.

State: hindrance to observance of constitution and consequent instability

It may seem strange to argue that the state may hinder the implementation and observance of its constitution since the state itself is structured, and given authority, responsibility and powers, by the constitution. Why cannot the framers of a constitution, knowing the sins committed through, and in the name of, the state rectify its structure, impose accountability on its institutions, and require it to adhere to fair and transparent procedures? Well, the framers have done precisely this in many cases – Uganda, South Africa, Ethiopia, Rwanda, Mozambique and Kenya for example – but not always, as I have demonstrated above, with any significant improvement in the ways of the state. There is, I realise, a risk of reifying the state; I want to make it clear that I do not mean the state as an abstract entity. A state is always the agency of particular groups, although its structures and procedures may, and often do, have their own dynamics. My focus is on the aggregation of the powers and resources secured through the state, and its relationship to society as a whole and to particular groups within it.

We may get some purchase on my argument if we look briefly at the relationship between state and society in Europe, where the modern state originated (Poggi 1990). This relationship has changed over the centuries since states began to be separated from civil society, that is, when the autonomous self-management of a community's affairs were replaced by an authority outside the community. When this happens, the relationship of that authority to the community becomes a matter of great importance – and has been the object of great political and social speculation and analysis. At one period power was dispersed between a king and a number of barons, in relationships based on land holding (feudalism), and then more widely shared between a king and social and territorial groups such as emerging urban centres with their own corporate structures. Later still the consolidation of royal power initiated an age of monarchical absolutism. With the rise of new classes (the bourgeoisie) associated with the growth of urban organisations and the industrial revolution, the king was compelled to share power with them, leading in due course to democratic systems in which royal powers were gradually reduced, until they have become nominal.

These changes were slow and organic, reflected in the gradual trans-formation of the state. In England the changes were based on the common law and remained unwritten, except when the widening of the franchise required statutory amendments. In continental Europe, however, the idea emerged of the constitution as a social compact between key social classes. To be politically effective, such a compact had to recognise and consolidate any major shifts in power and prin-ciple, including notions of human rights – a practice initiated by the French revolution whose legal contours were delineated in a constitu-tion negotiated between key social forces and then imposed on the king. This democratisation was accompanied by the notion of territo-rial organisation of the 'nation-state', emphasising the cultural homo-geneity and distinctiveness of its people. These changes, even 'nation building', were not achieved without considerable violence. However, coercion was gradually replaced by consent and the formal sharing of state power between key social forces.

The growth of the state and its constitutional ordering responded to changing social power and relations. The industrial revolution produced powerful social classes, to some extent but never fully, balanced later by the organised working class. The power of the bourgeoisie shaped the purposes and operation of the state, just as earlier social forces had done. But direct and exclusive control of the state ceased to be necessary as society developed and diversified. Economy rather than force became the source of power as market relations transformed social relations.

In Africa, however, the growth of the colonial state was neither gradual nor organic. It was not rooted in local developments but imposed from outside, to suit colonialism. It was exclusionary, built on racial and ethnic distinctions. Its bureaucracy was rooted in the imperative of domination over the colony's various societies, in a close relationship with the foreign business community, and in a resistance to democracy that was buttressed by repressive laws, a repressive legal system and the control of armed force.

The state in developing countries, however vulnerable to global forces, is dominant locally – and scarcely rooted in society. The postcolonial state, it used to be said, was 'overdeveloped' in relation to local social forces, going beyond what Marxists argued was its necessary superstructure (Alavi 1972; Leys 1976).[15] In fact it is both powerful and weak. It is weak internationally, dependent on handouts from Western governments and with some of its essential tasks performed by international organisations or civil society groups. But it is strong internally in the sense that it represents a far greater concentration of financial, bureaucratic and, above all, coercive power than other groups. It has become the principal source of accumulation or what Marxists call primitive accumulation. By capturing the state, which is the principal pre-occupation of politicians and the business community, paupers can become millionaires within a year. Their accumulation grows through illegality, it breeds impunity and gives elites a vested interest in criminality.

The more a state is reformed, with new regulations enacted to curb predatory practice, the more predatory practices flourish through systematic violations of the law, backed by a culture of impunity. The independence of judges and prosecutors is subverted by bribe and threat. The tendering process is manipulated; fictitious companies are

---

[15] The concept of the 'overdeveloped' state was advanced by Alavi (1972). For a critique, see Leys (1976).

set up by ministers to receive huge payments for services that were never going to be delivered – in Uganda called 'paying for air'. Those who have the audacity to protest are physically eliminated, generally with the help of the police; illegality and violence are woven into the very fabric of the state. The state depends on neither consent nor legitimacy but on coercion. For this last the state will have a disproportionate capacity, thanks to foreign governments who are only too keen to arm it in the interests of law and order – and against terrorism. Nor does the need to raise revenue lead to negotiation with citizens, as it did in Europe, since public welfare is not a high priority and obliging foreign governments provide the funds.

African constitutions not only fail to mould civic values and the behaviour of key political actors, they also fail to generate a state capable of sound social policies and fair and honest administration; the inherited, pre-constitution bias of the state apparatus places obstacles in the way of progress. Less attention has been paid to these institutional obstacles than to societal obstacles, because it is assumed that the constitution, par excellence, designs and structures the state. A constitution may indeed structure institutions, but often fails to infuse them with appropriate values and principles. A constitution tends to structure macro institutions but often says little about values and procedures, and the culture of a state's administration may well persist from one constitution to another. Two factors at least have characterised the African state. The first is the legacy of the colonial state, already described, designed to dominate, to discriminate between races and ethnic groups, to favour foreign business at the cost of widening economic disparities and to resist democracy. It is this administrative tradition rather than any adaptation to independence or democracy that marks the present reality – through the office of the president, supported by the provincial administration, administrative police and civil service habits.[16] These continuities ensured that independence would not bring about social transformation, merely the partial replacement of the alien rulers by a local elite who found the colonial repressive apparatus highly functional. Bayart identifies three factors

---

[16] It is pertinent that both Moi and Kibaki (and most senior civil servants) fiercely resisted the elimination of the provincial administration during Kenya's constitutional reform debates and proposals, despite its inconsistency with the new values of democracy, accountability, participation and, especially, devolved democratic government.

that have sustained the authoritarian tradition, despite democratic appearances: control over the security forces, which permits a covert harassment of opposition forces; control over economic rents, with which to buy off dissident politicians and weaken the opposition; and the support of Western powers obsessed with 'order and stability'. The predatory colonial state remains, but cruder and criminalised, reliant on impunities and without the colonialist's sophistication.

The second factor is what Bayart has called the 'politics of the belly'. For the state just described nurtures, and is sustained by, a particular political class, now common to most African countries, with a vested interest against reform. It is a class such as that of Max Weber's politicians who live *by* politics, as opposed to those who live *for* politics.[17] Those in charge of the state apparatus have endless opportunities for personal aggrandisement, amassing corrupt fortunes. They have little interest in or incentive for limiting the state's powers. Other groups in society lack the capacity – or think that they lack the capacity – to control the government and less still to hold it to account. It is significant that in a number of recent African constitutional reviews, while civil societies have emphasised values, democracy, rights and integrity, their politicians have focused almost exclusively on institutions and access to state power. It is as if there are two views of the constitution: one seeing an instrument for societal values and nation building, the other seeing an instrument for power, domination and 'eating'.

Subordination of society

The relationship between constitution and society is complex and contradictory. The constitutions of European countries have adapted to social and economic changes over a long period, giving a significant congruence between the purposes and institutions of state and society. Despite some ruptures, the growth has been organic, generating a broad acceptance of state powers and procedures.

In Africa, states did not reflect the values and structure of local society, and so had to rely on considerable force. States have had much more impact on society than vice versa. This may explain why constitutionalism faces such difficulties in Africa; society is weak, unstable and amenable to ethnic mobilisation, as convincingly explained by

[17] Max Weber (1919) 'Vocation of Politics'.

Lonsdale (Chapter 1) and Berman (Chapter 5) in this volume. I will now examine three aspects of the relationship between constitution and society. The first is the impact of societal forces on constitutional reform and practice, the second is the constitutional agenda of societal reform itself and the third is the passivity of much of society when confronted by the state.

At first, in some African countries, civil society was relatively undifferentiated. Where there were social hierarchies, one colonial strategy was to co-opt local rulers, such as sultans and chiefs. Since then there have been major social changes, influenced largely by the changing relationship of different communities or groups to the state. Society has become more differentiated, in diverse ways; competing and sometimes contradictory interests have emerged; but the centrality of the state to political, economic and even social management has remained. The question is whether new societal forces are likely to influence the shape of the constitution, and thus the distribution of power. I have already discussed the logic of the post-colonial state and its economic organisation, which suggests that, for the time being, important elites are content with the post-colonial constitutional order. To decide whether this is a transitional period, with new forces compelling significant change, one must first outline the degree of cohesion in society.

Subjectively, the important divisions are not social or class but ethnic; ethnicity dominates political strategies, alliances, allegiances and discourse. Elites depend on the state for largess since society is still at the stage of primitive accumulation. They find it easy to mobilise ethnic support, and so to exclude other groups from state power. The persistence and mobilisation of ethnicity are facilitated by vulnerabilities produced by both economy and state, thanks to the disruption of the rhythms of traditional life and the growth of clientelistic politics, grounded in access to the state. Politicians have no interest in reforms that might jeopardise their favoured access to power. Most of the political class support this exclusionary approach – with a profound impact on social cohesion and popular perceptions of the state.

Here again it is helpful to draw on Western experience. From the eighteenth century on, as Europe's political map was re-drawn, the homogeneity of a people – defined by cultural and linguistic affiliation – became the basis for creating new states. Congruence between cultural community and state boundaries became the major principle in re-shaping states as 'nation-states'. This nationalist approach was justified on the grounds that a common culture made for democracy and, much later, that only the social solidarity inherent in a common history and culture would consent to the resource re-distribution implicit in social welfare provision. In Africa, the rise of ethnic consciousness and its political mobilisation, namely 'ethnicity', has challenged such assumptions, starting with the concept of a homogeneous people.

Heterogeneity renders difficult the emergence of a nationalism shared by the whole country. There are often stronger allegiances to a community or region, and various, often conflicting, world views. Competing ethnic claims deny social solidarity. In states where society provides cohesion, stability and common values, the role of a constitution is secondary, concerned more with law-making and administration than promoting a national unity that is taken for granted. In post-colonial multiethnic states, on the other hand, 'nation building' is an essential task of the constitution. Almost everywhere this has proved extraordinarily difficult, because the pursuit of ethnic advantage diminishes the value of citizenship, human rights and the rule of law.

A combination of the dominance of ethnicity and the state's role in accumulation leads to intense competition for the capture of the state. This leads to the abuse or subversion of the democratic aspects of a constitution, such as publicly financed political parties, an independent electoral system, the operational independence of the police, freedoms of expression and association and judicial impartiality. In many former colonies, the rise of a commercial class is built on ethnic foundations. It relies on favours from a still exclusionary state, now dominated by clan or tribe. Thanks to its client status, the new commercial elite does not want what capitalists are supposed to want, some respectable distance between itself and the state. Close connections and alliances between class and state continue to be critical, despite accumulation and business growth, for primitive accumulation is followed by an alliance of capital and state, a post-colonial mercantilism. As the business class rises on the back of an 'ethnic' state it finances, in return, its political sponsors' electoral campaigns. Both the state's ethnic favours and the state-and-capital alliance militate against any generalised rule defining relations between state and market economy, or at least the even-handed application of such a rule. Ethnicised politics also weaken any commitment to human rights and encourage the evasion or distortion of any of the democratic procedures listed above.

The second aspect of civil society to discuss arises from the social reform agenda of many new constitutions. The violations of the rights of various groups arise not only from oppression by the state but also and often more vigorously, by society. Typical forms of oppression are the lowly position of women (including widows), exploitation of low caste groups, child labour and the marginalisation of occupational groups such as forest people or pastoral communities. Poverty is now widespread in Africa, with the appropriation of property by a few and the landlessness of many. Some constitutions seek to redress this imbalance or provide for affirmative action for past injustices. African problems of societal discrimination, exploitation or exclusion are less pervasive than in India or Nepal, but they exist nonetheless. The solutions are harder because the groups who benefit from discrimination are allied to the state. But my concern here is with the prejudices of and resistance by societal forces. A common form of resistance appeals to cultural relativism by arguing that pressure for constitutional reform is derived from Western values that undermine indigenous ones. A second argument, supportive of a discriminatory state, relies on the politics of identity, claiming that differences of culture and history justify the status quo. This can lead to wide-scale disregard or violation of the provisions of the constitution.

A constitution operates within *society* and seeks to influence its development. The distinguished Indian sociologist, André Beteille, believes that while a constitution can provide directions for national development, whether that path will be taken and at what pace are matters that depend on society (Beteille 1991). The constitution may set out guidelines for the exercise of power and aspirations for the state to meet. But the social reform agenda characteristic of contemporary constitutions challenges existing societal values and prejudices that for the most part favour elites. Constitutional reformers cannot assume that society is uniformly supportive of their proposals. Different sectors have different, often clashing, interests. The constitution's design of a political order competes with other political models and realities. The common constitutional value of impersonal power, for example, contradicts older ideas of how a 'chief' can and should act, ideas that may underlie the 'strong man' syndrome often found in presidential government and equally supportive of politicised ethnicity.

While the state is strong in its subjugation of civil society, it is weak in its capacity to direct social change, as Lonsdale argues elsewhere in this volume (Chapter 1). Most politicians have little desire for social progress, concentrating as they do on their predatory practices, protected by political fragmentation and the ethnicisation of society. In this vortex of constitutional values and mandates in competition with the ambitions and predations of politicians and bureaucrats, there seems no room for moral values, equality under law, or settled legal principle and practice. Both this type of 'strength' and weakness/incapacity are harmful for the growth of constitutionalism. 'Strength' can lead to the disregard of values and 'weakness' to a failure to implement them.

The final point I want to make is that despite the post-colonial rise of an incipient bourgeoisie and other social forces, the overwhelming political factor is the passivity of the majority of the people. By passivity I do not mean that they do not care – they do care, because they are at the receiving end of the predatory and violent practices of the state. Although peasants and workers constitute a majority, they cannot translate their grievance into political clout or pressure, since they have allowed themselves to be divided by the politicisation of ethnicity. Thus to prevent the growth of their class consciousness is a critical strategy of the political class, the one class united by its many common interests. The most active popular political actions take ethnic forms and occur most patently at election times. There are few political parties in the classical sense of aggregating, articulating and protecting the interests of key sectors of the public – despite legislation that requires these objectives, on pain of a party's dissolution.

Massive unemployment heightens worker vulnerability. Trade unions, once of some political significance, now wield little power, in part because of the globalisation that tilts the balance in favour of capital. Peasants once organised themselves into co-operatives but now have little means to express their concerns and demands. The youth also find themselves powerless despite their education, and are easily recruited into militias by gangsters or politicians. Non-governmental organisations (NGOs), particularly those concerned with human rights, funded exclusively by Western governments, are largely urban based and do little to raise the consciousness of the marginalised and dispossessed. But Western governments also act as censors, insisting that NGOs stay away from politics, thus denying the close link between rights and politics that is crucial to the effectiveness of a rights strategy.

These weaknesses in civil society make it difficult to put any effect-ive pressure on the state. Politics then becomes the occupation of a few professional politicians, and results in fluid parties, few of which are based on membership. Few other voices are given expression by a media that has fallen increasingly into corrupt political hands.

Obstacles to the functioning of market economy

A degree of autonomy for civil society from the state is a necessary condition for a functioning market economy. In post-colonial con-texts the rise of that autonomy often requires the state's permis-sion. Relations between state and economy vary – and are complex. Emerging principles of market economy exercised a dominant influ-ence on the changing structures of European states, particularly on the importance of the rule of law. The case in which an English court questioned the monarch's authority to grant commercial monopolies and thus restrain competition was one of the first decisions to limit royal power in England. In the typical English manner, the monarch, without conceding the restriction, promised not to grant monopolies by prerogative, that is, outside the law. The market requires much more than restriction on monopolies – it requires clear rules defining the nature and uses of, and transactions in, property, the framework for, and the sanctity of, contracts and guarantees of state enforcement of agreements made by private parties while also limiting the state's direct economic role. The market needs and to some extent produces constitutionalism – keeping the state at bay and yet needing its legally coercive power to ensure protection for the lawful expectations of individuals and corporations, based on contract or ownership of prop-erty. Such predictability is critical to market economy, based as it must be on promises of future performance.

As already discussed, although the rule of law is an important component of Western ideology, it played little role in the colonies. The discretion of colonial officials was more critical than the predict-ability or protection of law, certainly more flexible and less prone to legal challenge. Post-colonial economies have a more elaborate legal framework and are more integrated globally, but are by no means free economies. Many are based on minerals (including oil) with the state playing a central role in decision and management. Most post-colonial economies are 'administered economies', partly dependent on market mechanisms but still more on state regulation or monopolies. Despite some degree of liberalisation and privatisation they are dominated by permits and licences, exemptions from tax or other impositions, price controls, state contracts, state ownership and management of sectors or industries and external aid conditions.

As with a planned economy, the administered economy requires a state subject to its directly ruling class. The discretion vested in ministers and bureaucrats requires businesses to cultivate the political and bureaucratic elite, with their mutually beneficial relations lubricated by money. State and economy are linked by corruption. In our context the ruling class often assumes an ethnic bias; its ethnicity is its guarantee of impunity. At first the political elite requires payment by economic actors, a species of feudal dues, in return for some concession or protection. Later it insists on a share of the equity and profits from foreign enterprises, content with the role of sleeping partner. Later still, it insists on deciding investment policy and a share in management. The political elite's relationship, especially with the expatriate business class, has become complex. With both collaboration as well as competition there is tension. Collusion with some business interests sustains a mutually profitable relationship, but increasing corruption will threaten that alliance, as will the political class's direct entry into the market.

The ability of the political class to make such an economic transition depends on its hold on the state. Massive evasion of the law is the sole guarantee of that, especially as the regulatory framework is tightened and political discretion narrowed, under pressure from international economic institutions. And evasion demands the collaboration of state officials and institutions. The state becomes a secretive network, not only dedicated to corruption and theft, but also to suppressing knowledge of its irregularities. This is not straightforward mercantilism as in eighteenth-century Europe when state and capital joined in close partnership, although even there, in some cases, ethnicity played a role.

Much business is, therefore, criminalised. Trade unions, which often played a critical role in the independence struggle, have been marginalised or co-opted by the state. And as political alliances shift according to temporary convenience, there is honour among thieves. Politicians can be torn by serious conflict, as in Kenya's post-election violence in 2008, but are nonetheless united by a common interest in plunder, of or through the state, and in the suppression of information about their devious ways. The recent emergence of an alliance between Uhuru Kenyatta, Kikuyu and William Ruto, Kalenjin, shows not only the underlying common interests of the political class but also its foundation in ethnicity. These politicians were ethnically opposed to each other during the terrible atrocities that following the contested and rigged December 2007 elections; both are on the International Criminal Court's list of suspects. What unites them is their opposition to Raila Odinga, a Luo. So is the political class formed, making the adoption of a liberal constitution, or at least its implementation, extremely unlikely.

Conclusion

It is time to draw together the strands that highlight the impact of ethnicity on state and economy. Many aspects of the reciprocal relationship between economy and state discussed here would be true of other developing states, regardless of their people's composition. If ethnicity is important to a country's political and economic system, what specific effects may it have? My examples may be taken from Kenya but the conclusions I draw are applicable to many other multiethnic states.

In the colonial era the economy was seldom, if ever, determined by the market. Colonialism was a device to exploit a country's resources for imperial benefit, with a government that regulated an administered economy. Kenya's colonial rule had a particular ethnic character, privileging some ethnic groups over others in land, agriculture, commerce and bureaucracy; state power and racial privilege distorted market disciplines.

Kenya's experience suggests that the politicisation of ethnicity is usually due to the policies and practices of the state's political elites. In Kenya, ethnic consciousness or demands did not emanate from below, from the people. Different cultural, religious, tribal and racial communities certainly exist but people accept them without much fuss. Language presents no great problem; people happily use Swahili for mass communication and English for official purposes. Religion has seldom been a source of friction, except in a few politically determined contexts. Cultures differ but Kenyans are happy to share their diversity.

People from different categories get on well enough at the workplace and elsewhere, even in informal settlements. There is little evidence of identity crises; if they exist, they are to do with class, gender and age rather than ethnicity.

Ample evidence suggests that ethnic difference and conflict – land grabbing, displacement, assault, rape, murder – are almost always politically engineered.[18] Violence often occurs at election time – an art perfected by Moi, aided by impunity. Ethnic political differences tend not to be reflected in other social spheres; where these more general suspicions or hostility exist, they reflect politically promoted inter-ethnic violence. State policies since the days of British rule have stimulated ethnic tension by moving people around, by settling groups into what another group regards as its ancestral territory, marginalising a community by favouring others, and so on.

Politicians promote ethnic difference and animosity to advance their careers, to win state power or achieve senior office, all for personal material gain – the reward of power or influence. Political ethnicity therefore comes not, as in some countries, from below, but from above. Politics and state do not so much reflect society as create conditions in which society accepts the state as the agent of ethnic politics.

Manipulation from above is easier to achieve if there is no prior or existing sense of social solidarity, shared history, or a sense of common destiny. People who are disadvantaged, poor, insecure and vulnerable are susceptible to demagogic incitement to the hatred of others, and are inclined to believe that members of other communities are responsible for their misery. And in times of tension and crisis, many seek security in association with, and proximity to, members of their own ethnic group, especially but not only in urban areas.

Kenya's experience suggests that violence motivated by inequality is more likely to occur in multiethnic states than in homogeneous ones. Underlying solidarities in homogeneous societies prevent them from easily dividing into opposing sides. In heterogeneous societies, ethnic difference can be invoked to argue the case for a basic lack of common interest; indeed for fundamentally competing interests.

---

[18] Among several accounts of this politically inspired violence an authoritative source is the *Report of the Commission of Inquiry into Post Election Violence (CIPEV)* chaired by Justice Philip Waki (2008, often referred to as the Waki Report).

The state's constitutional structure can also effect inter-ethnic relations (Ghai 2002; Choudhry 2008).[19] Moi was fond of saying that the one-party state he had engineered was better than a multiparty state in promoting ethnic harmony. He overlooked a more critical point: that a political system that vests all state power in one office without checks and balances is more likely to produce an exclusionary and arbitrary state, more likely to lead to violence, than a more participatory system such as a parliamentary, cabinet or federal sharing of power. Where there is competition for scarce resources, and fear of others' intentions, an all-powerful presidency becomes the only worthwhile prize, to be seized at all costs. It is then easy for a candidate to persuade members of his ethnic group to vote for him or her, and for the candidate to be confident of their support – what Indians call a 'vote bank'.[20] The key electoral issue then is tribal, not social policy or justice.

A presidential system does not of course foreclose other options. In which political direction it leads depends on several factors, one of which is the number and size of ethnic groups. Kenya has many ethnic groups, none of them numerically dominant. This encourages negotiation in order to build a winning coalition – but negotiation based on ethnic arithmetic only reinforces the political centrality of ethnicity. Another option is to break away from the straitjacket of ethnicity, to adopt a broad, nationally integrative approach – the nation building project. The only senior East African politician to adopt this policy was Tanzania's Julius Nyerere; he had considerable success. Kenya's leaders have been less visionary – each president, starting with Jomo Kenyatta, has been a tribalist. By virtue of presidential bounty, their cronies have built considerable economic power. This gives them great influence, narrowing presidential options and underlining the force of ethnic calculation.

[19] There is a large literature on which constitutional systems suit multiethnic states (Ghai 2002). For a useful summary, see Choudhry (2008).
[20] Throup and Hornsby (1998) noted the dominance of 'ethnic nationalism' in Kenya's elections, and the primacy of ethnicity over ideology. Of the 1992 elections they say (but it could be said of all): 'Communal solidarity did not have to be enforced but was clearly voluntary in the homelands of the four major presidential candidates.' A book on the 1997 elections showed how much ethnicity influenced electoral politics, with disastrous results. Multiparty elections take place in a context where ethnicity has either been exploited for political gain or is a manifestation of underlying competition between communities for the resources necessary for collective survival (Rutten *et al.* 2001).

The independence constitution formally structured a state based on democracy and the market. It had an independent judiciary among its separated powers; its common law rules regulated administrative decisions; it protected human rights, including property rights and commercial contracts. But the logic of the constitution was contradicted by various factors: especially the new African political class's resentment of the economic dominance of other races, Europeans and, still more, Asians. As the indigenous population won power, so the divide between political and economic power was heightened. African communities, too, were differentiated in their political access and economic opportunity, giving personal greed and political ambition a communal dimension. These differences have been more enduring. The post-colonial state has played just as great if not a greater role in accumulation than before, with many more devices and institutions for patronage and other illegal ways of siphoning off state resources for private gain. The difference between the colonial and post-colonial state is that, in the former, the primary exploitation was for imperial or corporate purposes, which law and official practice accurately reflected; since independence economic processes have relied on a systematic and persistent violation of the law in the personal pursuit of wealth.

A key element in securing access to the state is the electoral system, especially the conduct of elections. The constitution that was replaced in 2010 gave the sitting president great influence over the process, including appointments to the supposedly independent electoral commission. Moi abolished the secret ballot when he feared it would work against him; in 2007 Kibaki violated the convention whereby the party allegiance of individual members of the electoral commission should reflect the relative size of their party's parliamentary representation. All elections since independence have been marked by bribery, violence and rigging, and the courts have resisted challenges to the winning candidates, especially presidential candidates, by demanding strict adherence to conditions pertaining to the delivery of court summonses.[21]

Moreover, ministries and state agencies are packed with fellow tribals, particularly in strategic institutions such as the Treasury, Ministry

---

[21] Details of faulty elections have been documented in a number of scholarly studies, including Marcel Rutten *et al.* (2001); Kanyinga and Okello (2010); the Waki Report Part II (2008) and the *Report of the Independent Review Commission on the General Elections held in Kenya on 27 December 2007* (2008).

of Security, Ministry of Land, provincial administration, security agencies and state corporations. This enables the manipulation or evasion of most rules, including tendering procedures. Wide presidential powers to allocate land have been a major source of corruption. A plethora of state corporations in commerce and industry have provided the cash. And when privatisation became fashionable, ministers and their friends made huge fortunes by giving away state enterprises at low prices, in response to bribes.[22]

These illegal transactions would be difficult without the support or connivance of the attorney-general, public prosecutor and judiciary. A combination of the repression that the president and his cronies can deploy and the bribes they can offer have bought the co-operation of these legal officers. Corruption thrives in this land of impunity. The legal system has become grossly dysfunctional for the public, including investors. And the legislature too is falling prey to corruption – votes of parliamentarians are regularly bought, sometimes at great cost. Since politicians constitute a class, they shield each other, even their current opponents – knowing that alliances can always be re-negotiated.

Some legal forms reflecting diversity and ethnicity persist (e.g. varying degrees of customary law, which may have a significant effect on the economy). Where ethnicity among a diverse people is politically significant, it is bound to distort market mechanisms even if there is a commitment to market economy; the state may intervene, and past advantage will nullify assumptions of equal opportunity. The dominance of ethnicity as a political mobiliser limits and impoverishes economic or social policy discourse and, in so far as such discourse occurs, it concentrates on ethnically related issues: quotas, inequality, proportionality and so on. When ethnicity is politicised, there will likely be both competition for and the use of the state in ways that are inconsistent with market logic. Moreover, conflict is likely whenever a community is marginalised. Given Kenya's ethnic configuration, violence is more liable to occur, and with a particular ferocity, if the group which feels marginalised or cheated is of significant size.

Its capture by an ethnic group or inter-ethnic coalition changes, fundamentally, a state's purpose and nature. It becomes exclusionary, fails to resolve differences or to mediate between competing groups, loses

---

[22] See a study of the privatization of Telkom and Safaricom, two of the biggest firms in telecommunications, African Centre for Open Governance (2011).

its people's trust and therefore its legitimacy, invites corrupt business deals and replaces the predictability and protection of the law with personal patronage – generally to the disadvantage of smaller businesses. At the same time, criticism of economic policy from the one community with the confidence and knowledge to make an informed assessment is disabled by the fear of victimisation.

These and other factors outlined above suggest that Kenya's economy must suffer. The periodic bouts of horrible tribal violence sponsored by government or its allies are not only materially damaging but also destroy the confidence of the people and of the business and professional classes who are vital for economic and social development. The many measures agreed in 2008 to end ethnic and political conflict – grand coalition; police reform; greater independence of judiciary and prosecution; prohibition of hate speech; rehabilitation of internally displaced persons; reconciliation procedures – have largely failed because of the heady mix of ethnicity, power and profit.

Some people may say that these are temporary problems, that state and people are finding their way to a more just, stable and enduring social and economic system. It may be that with the development of a bourgeoisie, even on corrupt foundations, a new relationship between the state and economy will emerge, which will permit a more autonomous economic sphere to emerge in which the business class prospers without state favour. But if the present is any guide, the capitalist class will continue to be defined in ethnic terms, dominated by a few big tribes. The exclusion of others reinforces the risk of social conflict.

Colonial patterns of unequal development, the capture of the postcolonial state, an administered economy and ethnic politics are not unique to Kenya. This does not mean that other countries are bound to follow the same trajectory as Kenya. Kenya's outcomes result from a specific conjuncture: a mixed population in which no one group dominates others numerically; the dispersal of ethnic groups in distinct and, mostly, compact regions; the country's geopolitical importance and external support for the regime; and a recklessly greedy political leadership. Other countries with similar histories have been able to reach a broad consensus on national goals, with explicit or implicit agreements on communal entitlements and roles. Some have had enlightened leaders who have fostered inter-communal solidarity and a modicum of justice. Some have a reasonably functioning democracy which, while generating tensions, also resolves them. But in others the outcomes are not so different from Kenya's – intense conflicts that the political system cannot handle, innocent people killed and the economy ruined.

According to Lonsdale, 'the English commercial and industrial bourgeoisie first demanded an end to the royal commercial prerogative – but then went much further, in the nineteenth century, in demanding not only the end of the gentry-protecting corn-laws (the gentry being then the political class) but also, not only the extension of the franchise but the wholesale reform of access to state and military office, from "influence" to exam-determined merit'. The incipient African bourgeoisie, preoccupied by its own self-interest in unsettled political circumstances, has little interest in this scale of reform – which may be seen as ending its own privileged status.

In asking if fundamental change might be triggered by workers and marginalised groups, one confronts the dialectics of class and ethnicity. Deprived groups with the most to gain from class politics and action are driven more by ethnic division than by shared misery. Slum-dwellers suffering deprivation, poverty and insecurity have many common interests, not least in fundamental social change – yet at critical moments they take ethnic positions, willing to kill their neighbours. In any conflict between class and ethnicity, ethnicity seems to win. Those who play the ethnic card have the resources to bribe people, while also inspiring fear of other tribes. Kenya's proletariat resembles the French peasants whom Marx in his *Eighteenth Brumaire of Louis Bonaparte* (1852), compared to a sack of potatoes: 'the great mass of the French nation is formed by the simple addition of homologous magnitudes, much as potatoes in a sack form a sack of potatoes'. In other words, Kenya's poor have no common consciousness of their interests, no sense of solidarity, although they share the same disadvantages and the same space.

With millions of its people labouring under the growing hardships of daily life, will Kenya's constitution alert them not only to the mechanisms of domination and oppression, but also to the possibility that new political values and a restructured state might deliver a better future? Despite my earlier pessimism about a constitution's potential, it is just possible that the new constitution will initiate such a process of progressive change. It is quite likely, as intended, that the constitution will weaken the political-cum-business class while strengthening social groups. The political class is both united and fragmented, united in pursuit of the profitable exploitation of state and society, but often bitterly divided by ethnicity in the competition for state power. One political group succeeding to state power after another does not portend real change. For the moment, it is perhaps the dialectics of ethnicity and class that holds the key to that.

References

African Centre for Open Governance 2011. *Deliberate Loopholes: Transparency Lessons from the Privatisation of Telkcom and Safaricom.* Nairobi: African Centre for Open Governance.

Alavi, Hamza 1972. 'The State in Post-Colonial Societies', *New Left Review* 74 (Jul/Aug).

Bayart, Jean-François 1993. *The State in Africa: the Politics of the Belly.* London: Longman.

Bayart, Jean-François, Ellis, Stephen and Hibou, Beatrice 1999. *The Criminalisation of the State in Africa.* Oxford: James Currey.

Beard, Charles 1965 [1913]. *An Economic Interpretation of the Constitution of the United States.* New York: The Free Press.

Berman, Bruce 1990. *Control and Crisis in Colonial Kenya: the Dialectics of Domination.* London: James Currey.

Beteille, André 1991. *Society and Politics in India: Essays in Comparative Perspective.* London: Athlone Press.

Branch, Daniel 2011. *Kenya: Between Hope and Despair, 1963–2011.* Newhaven, CT: Yale University Press.

Buchanan, James M. 1990. *Constitutional Economics.* Oxford: Blackwell.

Cain, Maureen and Hunt, Alan 1979. *Marx and Engels on Law.* London: Academic Press.

Choudhry, Sujit 2008. 'Bridging Comparative Politics and Comparative Constitutional Law: Constitutional Design in Divided Societies', in *Constitutional Design for Divided Societies*, Sujit Choudhry (ed.). Oxford University Press.

Commission of Inquiry into the Illegal/Irregular Allocation of Public Land 2004. *Report of the Commission of Inquiry into the Illegal/Irregular Allocation of Public Land.* Nairobi: Government Printer.

Commission of Inquiry into Post Election Violence 2008. *Report of the Commission of Inquiry into Post Election Violence (CIPEV, also known as the Waki Report).* Nairobi: Government Printer.

Cowen, Michael 1982. 'The British State and Agrarian Accumulation in Kenya', in *Industry and Accumulation in Africa*, Martin Fransman (ed.). Nairobi: Heinemann Denning, Lord, Nyali Bridge Ltd. v Attorney-General [1956] KB1.

Faaland, Just, Parkinson, J. R. and Saniman, Rais 1990. *Growth and Ethnic Inequality: Malaysia's New Economy Policy.* Kuala Lumpur: Dewan Bahasa Dan Pustaka.

Furnivall, John S. 1958 [1948]. *Colonial Policy and Practice: a Comparative Study of Burma and Netherlands India.* New York University Press.

Ghai, Yash 1993. 'The Rule of Law and Capitalism: Reflections on the Basic Law', in *China, Hong Kong and 1997: Essays in Legal Theory,* Raymond Wacks (ed.). Hong Kong University Press.

  1999. *Hong Kong's New Constitutional Order: the Resumption of Chinese Sovereignty and the Basic Law* (2nd edn). Hong Kong University Press.

  2002. 'Constitutional Asymmetries: Communal Representation, Federalism and Cultural Autonomy', in *The Architecture of Democracy,* Andrew Reynolds (ed.). Oxford University Press.

  2004. 'Relationship between the States and Minorities', in *Protection of Minority Rights and Diversity,* Nanda Wanasundera (ed.). Colombo: International Centre for Ethnic Studies.

  2010. 'Constitutionalism and the challenge of ethnic diversity', in *Global Perspectives on the Rule of Law,* James J. Heckman, Robert L. Nelson and Lee Cabatingan (eds.). London: Routledge.

Ghai, Yash and Cottrell, Jill. 2007a. 'A Tale of Three Constitutions: Ethnicity and Politics in Fiji', *International Journal of Constitutional Law* 5: 638–69.

  2007b. 'Constitution Making and Democratisation in Kenya (2000–2005)', *Democratisation* 14 (1): 1–25.

  2011. *Kenya's Constitution: an Instrument for Change.* Nairobi: Katiba Institute.

Ghai, Yash and McAuslan, Patrick 1970. *Public Law and Political Change in Kenya.* Nairobi: Oxford University Press.

Horowitz, Donald L. 1985. *Ethnic Groups in Conflict.* Berkeley, CA: University of California Press.

Howard, Dick A. E. 1993. *Constitution Making in Eastern Europe.* Washington, DC: Woodrow Wilson Centre Press.

Human Rights Watch 1991. *Kenya: Taking Liberties.* New York: Human Rights Watch.

Hurst, James W. 1982. *Law and Markets in United States History: Different Modes of Bargaining among Interests.* Madison, WI: University of Wisconsin Press.

Independent Review Commission on the General Elections held in Kenya on 27 December 2007. 2008. *Report of the Independent Review Commission on the General Elections held in Kenya on 27 December 2007.* Nairobi: Government Printer.

Jesudason, James V. 1989. *Ethnicity and the Economy: the State, Chinese Business, and Multinationals in Malaysia.* Singapore: Oxford University Press.

Kanyinga, Karuti 2000. *Redistribution from Above: the Politics of Land Rights and Squatting in Coastal Kenya.* Uppsala: Nordiska Africainstitutet.

2006. 'Governance Institutions and Inequality in Kenya', in *Readings on Inequality in Kenya: Sectoral Dynamics and Perspectives.* Nairobi: Society for International Development.

Kanyinga, Karuti and Okello, Duncan 2010. *Tensions and Reversals in Democratic Transitions: the Kenya 2007 General Elections.* Nairobi: Society for International Development and Institute of Development Studies, University of Nairobi.

Leo, Christopher 1984. *Land and Class in Kenya.* University of Toronto Press.

Leys, Colin 1976. 'The "Overdeveloped" Post-colonial State: a Re-evaluation', *Review of African Political Economy 5.*

Mutunga, Willy 1999. *Constitution-making from the Middle: Civil Society and Transition Politics in Kenya, 1992–1997.* Harare: Sareat/Mwengo.

Ndegwa, Duncan N. 1971. *Report of the Commission of Enquiry 1970–71.* Nairobi: Government Printer.

North, Douglass C. 1990. *Institutions, Institutional Change, and Economic Performance.* Cambridge University Press.

Okoth-Ogendo, H. W. O. 1981. 'Land Ownership and Land Distribution in Kenya's Large-Farm Areas', in *Papers on Kenya Economy: Performance, Problems and Policies,* T. Killick (ed.). Nairobi: Heinemann.

1991. *Tenants of the Crown: Evolution of Agrarian Law and Institutions in Kenya.* Nairobi: African Centre for Technology Studies.

Poggi, Gianfranco. 1990. *The State: its Nature, Development and Prospects.* Cambridge: Polity Press.

Rheinstein, Max 1954. *Max Weber on Law in Economy and Society.* New York: Simon and Shuster.

Roldán Ortiga, Roque 2004. *Models for Recognizing Indigenous Land Rights in Latin America.* Washington, DC: World Bank, Environment Department.

Rutten, Marcel, Mazrui, Alamin and Grignon, François 2001. *Out for the Count: the 1997 General Elections and Prospects for Democracy in Kenya.* Kampala: Fountain Publishers.

Sachs, Albie. 1973. *Justice in South Africa,* London: Heinemann.

Sundaram, Jomo K. 1998. *Economic Considerations for a Renewed Nationalism.* Seplis-Codesira Lecture No 2, Dakar, Codesira.

1999. *Malaysia's Political Economy: Politics, Patronage and Profits.* Cambridge University Press.

Throup, David and Hornsby, Charles 1998. *Multi-party Politics in Kenya.* Oxford: James Currey.

Weber, Max 1919. 'Vocation of Politics', available at: www.ne.jp/asahi/moriyuki/abukuma/weber/lecture/politics_vocation.html.

Yrigoyen Fajardo, Raquel 2000. 'The Constitutional Recognition of Indigenous Rights in Andean Countries', in *The Challenge of Diversity*, Willem Assies, Gemma van der Haar and André J. Hoekema (eds.). The Netherlands: Thela Theses.

5 | *Ethnic politics, economic reform and democratisation in Africa*

BRUCE J. BERMAN

Introduction

In the earlier chapters John Lonsdale traced the development of ethnic patriotism and the political mobilisation of ethnic communities, while Yash Pal Ghai attributed the failure of constitutionalism and of political reform in African states to the dominance of a political class based on ethnic patronage networks that compete for control of the resources of the state and market and corrupt both institutions. This chapter looks further at the historical development of the state and market in colonial and post-colonial Africa and how this shaped the internal and external politics of the construction of ethnic communities and the dominance of 'big man' patron–client politics, as well as the failure to develop widespread civic trust in the disinterested competence and probity of public institutions. It argues that in that context, thirty years of neo-liberal reforms have weakened states and increased economic inequalities, particularly the horizontal cleavages that are the material basis of ethnic conflict, leading to growing poverty and social decay.

At the centre of this chapter is the paradox that efforts over the past twenty years to reinvent democracy in Africa have, rather than dampening the fires of ethnic conflict, often made them more intense and in the past decade have been accompanied by the explosion of violent conflicts of autochthony, confrontations of 'sons of the soil'. The latter threaten the very bases of social order and cohesion in multiethnic societies, and hence economic stability. I explain this relationship by outlining an argument in five parts. Firstly, I will briefly examine the social construction of African ethnicities since the imposition of European colonial rule, with particular focus on both the role of the state and the market, as well as the internal response in African societies. Secondly, I will discuss the particular relationship between the state, colonial and post-colonial, with effective institutionalisation of 'big man' politics and patronage as the essential link between ethnic communities and the state and of access to the resources of modernity. Thirdly, we will see that both nationalism and ethnicity in Africa share a common origin and focus on grasping control of the state apparatus that reinforces rather than undermines the salience of the nation-state. Fourthly, I will argue that neo-liberal 'reforms' of the state and market have led to significant political, social and economic decay that can reinforce ethnic cleavages and undermine democratisation in multi-party regimes, even where there have been serious efforts at constitutional reforms to contain and limit its political expression. Finally, I will look at the conflicts of autochthony that have exploded in four very different national contexts that share a common relationship to economic crisis, growing social decay and increasing inequality in supposedly democratising nations.

The social construction of African ethnicities

Rather than atavistic survivals of stagnant primordial 'tribal' identities and communities, African ethnicities are new not old, part of complex responses to colonial modernity. As explained more fully in Chapters 1 and 3, in the pre-colonial world the most striking features of African identities and communities was their fluidity, heterogeneity and hybridity; a social world of multiple, overlapping and alternate identities with significant movement of peoples, intermingling of communities and cultural and linguistic borrowing.

Three methodological caveats must be stressed at this point. Firstly, studying ethnicity in Africa involves the analysis of complex causality in which no single set of factors is determinant or can be analysed in isolation from others. The role of theory in this context cannot be to define universal relationships at so high a level of abstraction that they are devoid of empirical content, but rather to provide a conceptual toolkit that can identify common factors and the relationships between them to explain not only the similarities of cases, but also their contingent and idiosyncratic differences (Tilly 1975: 15–17). Theory in such circumstances must understand complexity and the uniqueness of each empirical experience. Indeed, from a political and policy perspective, the idiosyncrasies of each case may be the most important thing to understand.

Secondly, within these varied historical experiences, we must recognise that African societies in the colonial period were never simply passive victims of external domination, but active participants in the process. And this active interaction, and the varied uses of colonialism by Africans, can be traced on ideological, institutional and cultural levels in the construction of ethnicity and nationalism (Bayart 2000). And this, of course, is the methodological and theoretical basis of the importance of context and complex causality.

Thirdly, as argued in the Introduction and earlier chapters, assuming that the number of ethnic groups in a particular nation-state in itself explains anything about its political or economic performance is highly problematic, to say the least. The relationship between ethnicity, political stability and economic performance is grounded in the specifics of context.[1] African ethnicities are open-ended and dynamic processes of social and political creation, rather than static categories before, during and after colonial rule (Berman 1998). One of the key findings of the ethnicity and democratic governance (EDG) programme is that the single most important factor in the social construction and political mobilisation of ethnic communities in Africa and elsewhere is their 'recognition' by public institutions and the forms of access to resources of the state and market it confers (Eisenberg and Kymlicka 2011). The categorising and counting of ethnic groups by state institutions is not an objective recording of a stable reality, but rather in itself an active intervention into the process of ethnic social and political creation (Berman 2011). As a result, the first 'fact' about ethnicity in Africa is that there is no universal agreement about the number of ethnic groups in most countries, their social and spatial boundaries, or their membership, because such designations are contested political acts.

To understand the impact of the colonial intrusion of state and market and the African response, as discussed in Chapter 1, the concept of 'moral economy' is necessary. This concept of moral economy is also crucial to understanding the process of hegemony of which it is the central subject of contestation, and also the political dynamic of change

---

[1] At the turn of the twentieth century, the US was the most ethnically diverse of Western societies and one of the most economically dynamic, although with high levels of labour conflict involving both 'native' and immigrant workers. In April 2010 Statistics Canada announced for the first time that Canada contained 200 ethnic communities, which in the context of its liberal multiculturalism, was regarded as a positive contribution to economic growth and social development. Its two most multicultural cities, Toronto and Vancouver, were also its most culturally and economically dynamic.

from one form of social order to another (Berman, forthcoming-a, forthcoming-b; Crehan 2002). In pre-capitalist societies, like those of pre-colonial Africa, the distribution of values, particularly the allocation of labour, resources and the social product was embedded in hierarchical social relations of authority and subordination, and of social honour and status. The legitimacy of such inequalities was based on the recognised rights of subordinate groups or classes to subsistence from the social product created by their labour, access to land and the means of production, membership and marriage within the community and protection from the ravages of natural disaster or external attack. For acquiescence to relations of inequality by their subordinates, ruling groups had reciprocal obligations to honour these rights and redistribute their wealth to insure the survival and reproduction of the community. At the same time, in an active internal politics both superiors and subordinates constantly sought to evade, violate or renegotiate their reciprocal obligations and rights in establishing the complex mixture of force and consent that is hegemony (Scott 1985).

The politics of moral economy ranged across a wide variety of social forms in Africa from small-scale societies lacking institutions beyond extended corporate lineages, where dependents 'flourished in a big man's shade', to small chiefly states and larger kingdoms where the chief's or king's herds and granaries provided the communities' strategic reserves, and positions of authority from lineage elders to kings controlled access to land, livestock, trade and marriage. Underlying all of them were patriarchal family structures and familial metaphors of social power that infused wider political institutions, paternal and, more rarely, maternal ties of superior and subordinates and fraternal ties of social equals. The most striking fact of these relations is that they were all personal ties or bonds between individuals in positions of power and wealth and individuals in subaltern groups, genders and generations. These relations typically took the form of patron and client, the 'lopsided friendship' of anthropologists, linking unequal individuals in mutual ties of loyalty and support. While such relations were often far more disorderly and coercive in practice than their idealised reconstructions might suggest, the key characteristic is that they were personal, generally face-to-face, ties of supposed mutual benefit between individuals of unequal rank. Positions of authority combined power, wealth and social honour in a single individual; a leader of rank was expected to use the material resources he accumulated to reward his network of client subjects to meet his obligations and sustain their loyalty (Berman 1998, 2004a).

Patron–client relations have been, and probably remain, the most universal and widespread of human power relations from the lineages of small agrarian communities to the highly formalised and ceremonially sanctioned orders of rank and ties of loyalty of historical empires. I emphasise them here because they are important to understanding the impact of the colonial state and market in Africa, which challenged them and shaped the internal politics of developing ethnic communities. Patron–client relations do not involve 'policies' in the sense of impersonal distribution of public goods or services to social classes or geographical regions, or the distributions of commodities through the impersonal exchanges of the market. The development of the collective, impersonal authority relations of the nation-state and universal allocations of resources through the market are among the most dramatic discontinuities of modernity, and both define patron–client ties as 'corruption' within the framework of contemporary moral economies (Berman 1998, 2004b).

The social construction of African ethnicity was and is the outcome of contributions from many hands, European and African, rather than the deliberate creation of any single individual or group and, for that reason, is always incomplete and a matter of controversy. The key actor in the process was the colonial state, acutely conscious that Africans lived in 'tribes', which used the instruments of modern state power to define and classify them through maps and censuses that assigned individuals and communities to what were often erroneously believed to be ancient primordial identities (Kertzer and Arel 2002). This does not mean that Europeans 'created' African ethnic groups to fit their preconceptions or that Africans created 'tribes' on their prompting, but rather that they provided cultural resources and political contexts that Africans, particularly the class of collaborators and educated intelligentsia, could deploy in the internal conflicts that resulted from the unequal and divisive impact of colonial modernity (Berman 1998).

Such categorisation, numbering and mapping of African peoples provided the basis for the creation of administrative units to facilitate political control and institutional integration into the colonial state. Equally important, the state was the central institution, within the broader context of the intrusion of capitalist modernity, in the organisation, production and distribution of social resources, shaping

also the social criteria of access to those resources and the resulting social differentiation between individuals and communities. The
colonial state brokered the articulation of 'tribes' to the capitalist
market as cash-crop farmers, traders and wage labourers, not only
through the imposition of taxes and coercive labour laws, but also
through more positive incentives and resources channelled through
networks of local African collaborators and their supporters, and the
growing employment of a Western-educated intelligentsia in the state
apparatus (Berman 1990). The most important consequence of the
colonial political economy was the creation of horizontal inequalities
(see Chapter 8 below) between ethnic communities in the manner and
degree of their involvement in cash crop and labour markets, access to
education and to higher levels of employment in public institutions;
and growing internal inequalities between the local collaborators and
intelligentsia and their poor clients and dependents.

At the same time, the neo-traditional ideology characteristic of colonial regimes was fearful of the effect on 'tribal discipline' and political
control of the full-scale development of capitalist forms of property
and commodity markets that would create landless peasants and
rootless proletarians (Berman 1990). Instead they implemented in an
often haphazard fashion a partial, fragmented and often contradictory development of a market economy while attempting to sustain
'traditional' culture and authority through their collaborators. In so
doing, the colonial state also delineated the strategic contexts in which
ethnicity was or was not salient and moulded the choices of political
actors with regards to both the ascriptive markers of ethnicity and the
organisational forms in which it was expressed. This shaped, in turn,
the scope of ethnic politics, its relationship with other social cleavages
and the complex interaction of ethnic identities and interests.

Colonial rule rested on complex systems of collaboration with
indigenous local elites linked directly to the colonial state through
patron–client ties with the European field agents of the state. Colonial
power incorporated and built on the power of 'big men' who presided
over intricate networks of clientage involving reciprocal but unequal
relations with 'small boys', as well as power over women and children, and those held in diverse forms of dependence. Colonial power
created the hierarchies of 'decentralised despotism' (Mamdani 1996)
of headmen, chiefs and even kings, ruling through 'native authorities' in various forms of indirect rule involving cadres of African

collaborators, whether directly appointed by the regime or holding indigenous offices incorporated into the state apparatus. European officials rewarded their loyalty through access to resources controlled by the state, including preferential access to trade and commodity production, which became key to the accumulation of wealth and which was controlled by local African officials in the interests of their kinsmen and extensive clientages. Linked to them were the members of the growing literate intelligentsia occupying other positions in the state and small groups of wealthy farmers, cattle owners and traders who also played patron–client politics, using their wealth to invest in social networks to build their own clientage and position themselves for access to the wider patronage networks of the state (Berry 1993). These new sources of wealth and power, however, were distributed increasingly unevenly both within and between developing communities, providing the material basis for the internal and external politics of ethnic formation.

The networks of collaboration and patronage shaped the colonial state's involvement in the process of ethnic construction. Each local administrative unit ideally contained a single culturally and linguistically homogeneous 'tribe' in which people continued to live within indigenous institutions and were subject to 'tribal discipline' through local structures of authority. This made what the colonial state understood to be local institutions of tribe and kinship into the grassroots foundations of colonial domination, as well as means of deriving a degree of legitimacy from association with 'tradition'. Moreover, their knowledge of that 'native law and custom' largely came from the distinctly self-interested accounts of their own local collaborators and agents. The colonial state was, however, engaged in the development of ethnicities that often bore little correspondence to pre-colonial identities and communities, defining the culture and customs of tribes with a degree of clarity, consistency and rigidity that produced an increasingly sharp definition and enclosing of ethnicity and a significant expansion of the scale of ethnic communities. This shaped diverse stories of ethnic development in a process of reformulation involving both the creation of new groups and the disappearance of older ones. Colonial officials, missionaries and anthropologists combined in an 'invention of tradition' through efforts to define clearly bounded tribal societies and identities that would preserve social stability and facilitate political control (Ranger 1983). Africans, for their part, responded through a process of cultural imagining based on real cultural experiences and resources, created and re-fashioned out of both old and new elements (Berman 1998; Ranger 1994).

The impact of colonialism on African agrarian communities generated new cleavages of class as well as exacerbating existing internal differences of gender, generation and clientage. These were argued out in the context of indigenous cultures over issues of 'authenticity', defining the proper boundaries of the community and its culture, and of recognised membership within it that allocated legitimate access to family and property. Ethnicity and class were thus intertwined products of the colonial experience, rather than negating opposites. Africans did not and do not have either class or ethnic identity, but both; this was reflected in the cultural politics of their communities (Berman 2004a). It focused on increasing conflict between rich and poor over their reciprocal obligations, particularly of the former to redistribute their wealth so that their dependants and clients could flourish (Chabal and Daloz 1999; Eyoh 1996).

The issues in dispute were so clearly related to those of 'moral economy' that John Lonsdale and I developed the concept of *moral ethnicity*, as discussed in Chapter 1. Moral ethnicity defines the discursive and political arena within which ethnic identities emerged out of renegotiation of the bounds of communal membership and authority, the social rights and obligations of moral economy and access to land and property (Berman 2004a; Lonsdale 1994). Patronage politics became increasingly unstable, with the obligations of 'big men' focused more and more on distributing the resources of state and market to their clients and communities, while a growing number of excluded poor clamoured to be included. The struggle of the ethnic elites to gain such resources took the form of *political tribalism*, mobilised communal solidarity and political organisation of the community defined by moral ethnicity, first against the alien power of the colonial state and then, increasingly, against the competing interests of rival ethnicities for access to the state and its patronage resources, driven by the horizontal inequalities of the colonial political economy.

The state, nationalism and the politics of patronage

The particular pattern of state–society linkages of colonial Africa – patron–client networks centred on local African agents of colonial power and largely contained within the internal and external politics of ethnic communities – defined a fragmented plurality of communities of trust, within each of which individual probity, rights and responsibilities were the foci of an active political process, while between them an amoral competition for access to the material resources of the state became increasingly intense. Social trust was largely contained within ethnic communities and embedded in the personalistic ties of the patron–client networks that were opportunistically focused on access to material benefits. There was little basis for the development of impersonal systemic trust in the state as the neutral arbiter of conflict or as an honest and disinterested distributor of public resources that supposedly characterised the development of the Western nation-state (Berman 2004b; Ekeh 1990, 2004).

Moreover, while the colonial state was the principal source of wealth and power, it was simultaneously an agency of arbitrary power and oppressive force. For both masses and elites dealing with the state was a mixture of opportunity and danger – an opportunity to gain access to the diverse resources at the disposal of state and its agents, and the danger of running afoul of its apparently arbitrary and capricious actions and its coercive taxes and punishments. The constant resort to metaphors of eating and consuming in the discourse of politics in sub-Saharan Africa, to politics as 'eating' or 'devouring' and repeated references to getting one's share of state resources or 'slice of the cake' vividly expresses the personal, material and opportunistic character of politics, and its dual character: those who aspire to eat can also be eaten in the amoral food chain of politics. The 'politics of the belly' originated in the institutional structures and social relations of the colonial state (Bayart 1993). To survive in such a dangerous world requires support and protection: exactly what patrons and clients are supposed to provide for each other. At the same time, the ethnic community provides security and protection against the state in a social arena in which issues of moral economy could be argued out.

The colonial legacy of African societies – bureaucratic authoritarianism, neo-traditional ideology, patron–client relations, the partial and contradictory development of capitalism, and an ethnic dialectic of assimilation, internal conflict and external competition – produced diverse local variations and provided the context for the development of African nationalism. The end of World War Two brought the 'second colonial occupation' by highly stressed French and British states attempting to use the development of their colonies as part of their efforts at economic recovery and regaining legitimacy in both the metropole and the colonial dependencies (Lonsdale and Low 1976). It involved an unprecedented expansion of the colonial state's apparatus beyond the personalised structures of patriarchal patron–client linkages into a broader and deeper intervention into indigenous societies and a huge expansion of the social and economic resources it had to distribute. It led, much to the consternation of colonial regimes, to growing political conflicts on three levels: within African communities over the unequal distribution of the benefits of 'development'; between ethnic communities over the distribution of access to the resources of 'development' that brought 'tribal' conflicts to the fore; and between farmers and wage labourers and the state over the latter's efforts to extend its control over markets and wages. At all three levels, protest merged into a growing, mass-based, anti-colonial opposition led by the literate intelligentsia – often employees of the state itself – that challenged both the collaborating elites and the European regime (Cooper 1996).

The institutions of the colonial state and European ideologies of nationalism powerfully influenced the development of these nationalist movements. The state was not only the focus of the material opportunities of development, but also French and British conceptions of colonial development precluded any political future except that of turning colonies into nation-states. Both pan-African federation and the 'balkanisation' into ethnic states were rejected by the imperial powers, forcing the liberation struggles to focus on the national territorial framework and the capture of the state (Davidson 1992; Young 2007: 248). African nationalism was primarily an attempt to gain state power and control its collaborative networks and sources of patronage. In Kwame Nkrumah's celebrated dictum: 'Seek ye first the political kingdom.' It was both a discourse of legitimacy for state power and an embodiment of a doctrine of popular sovereignty blending nationalist and universalist claims for the nation as a project tying demands for universal rights and self-determination to diverse ethno-nationalist themes of cultural renewal and identity. A confusing and contradictory blend of civic and ethnic elements in hybrid and internally conflicted movements took control of states that were largely authoritarian bureaucracies with spare and unpractised parliamentary and electoral institutions of European liberal democracies added by hastily written independence constitutions (Berman, forthcoming-a, forthcoming-b).

At independence, African states and nations, ethnic groups and classes were all in flux, processes of active social construction and political contest rather than stable social entities, and they continue to be so up to the present. In the first decades of independence up to the end of the 1970s, nation building as a conscious strategy and objective was dominant in most African states by governments preoccupied with the linkage of national unity and socio-economic development, and under pressure from international and bilateral aid organisations that focused on the paradigm of a secular industrial nation-state as the sole embodiment of modernity and development, and communicated their fear of weak 'new nations' in Africa being torn apart by 'atavistic' tribalism. Even before independence, tenuous ethnic and class coalitions had begun to unravel into competing factions struggling for control over the material rewards of state power. Minority, ethnically based parties challenged dominant nationalist movements in several states (Allman 1993). At independence, competitive elections and the Africanisation of the state apparatus began to make ethnicity increasingly important as the basis of political support and access to the higher levels of the state apparatus (Young 1986).

In the international environment of the Cold War, state-focused development strategies and national development plans were the order of the day. In particular, the Keynesian/social-democratic moral economy of the post-war West was the hegemonic paradigm for state-regulated capitalist national development. Ideologically, nationalism guided and promoted economic development by appeal to national rather than class or regional ethnic interests. This was expressed through a wide variety of nationalist discourses in particular countries that were all, ostensibly, broadly inclusive nation building strategies. In addition to promoting economic development and fighting 'poverty, ignorance and disease', nationalist ideologies focused on education for the masses, including the propagation of a national historical epic of the great struggle for liberation from colonial oppression as a legitimating charter for the 'nation'. The new regimes also pursued the cultural and symbolic dimensions of a national project, from newly created flags and anthems to popular culture and sport, making heroes out of performers and national teams (Young 2007: 248–50).

However, nationalism as a development ideology and nation building through cultural engineering actually proved of only limited effectiveness. All of the nationalist ideologies of post-colonial Africa ultimately failed to reconstruct an effectively hegemonic 'national' moral economy attached to a legitimate, widely trusted arena of civic politics in the state. Nor did there develop a unified and self-conscious dominant class capable of pursuing a project of national development. Instead, behind the façade of ostensibly modern state institutions, the politics of the belly reigned through the pervasive spread of ethnic patronage networks to the very centre of the state apparatus, with ramifying linkages reaching from cabinet to village to produce what J-F Bayart graphically described as the 'rhizome state' (1993). What came to be called 'neo-patrimonialism' was grounded in ethnic patronage networks. At the grassroots, ethnic identity and communal membership was reinforced as the basis for access to the state and its resources. Moreover, in state after state, the political and cultural construction of the 'nation' turned into a cult of personality around the president or leader as the embodiment of the nation and the father of his people. Such a preoccupation with the leader undermined nationalism and reinforced the political culture of traditional personal leadership and patronage, including the taking of traditional – or at least traditional-sounding – titles such as Mobutu Sese Seko or Osagyefo Kwame Nkrumah.

The growth of personal rule by Africa's 'big men' was linked to the growing suppression of political expression and competition and an increasingly authoritarian cast to the state and ruling parties (Jackson 1982). *De facto* and *de jure* 'one party democracies' declared the ruling party to be the essential carapace of national unity, and competing parties, especially those based on particular ethnic communities, were suppressed and their leaders incorporated into the single party led by the great national leader. Increasingly authoritarian rule eliminated the political meaning of citizenship and offered instead an implicit, tenuous moral contract of material benefits in return for political quiescence. The single-party state, meanwhile, offered a 'national' arena within which the distribution of material resources among ethnic communities could be negotiated between the leaders of various groups, without having to resort to the public mobilisation of their supporters. The politics of political tribalism and moral ethnicity thus became linked to the ability of 'big men' holding positions in the state to obtain for their communities a significant share of the large-scale collective benefits of 'development', as well as the more individual rewards apportioned to their personal clients.

The wave of military coups in Africa that began in December 1963 with Togo's 250-man army killing the president, Sylvanus Olympio, brought to power military regimes whose significance as a distinctive political development now seems far less than it seemed at the time. In spite of their extravagant claims of being the real agents of national unity and their suppression of all 'divisive' political parties and organisations, military regimes have represented little change in the state-focused patronage system. Instead, the military magnates incorporated themselves into a dominant position within the patrimonial networks of patronage and appropriation of state resources. Africa's ramshackle and meagrely equipped armies were extravagantly re-armed, claiming larger and larger portions of national budgets, and military 'big men' were among the most enduring and profligately corrupt of its rulers.

Neo-liberal reform and social decay

The rise of neo-liberal hegemony in the dominant capitalist nations and international financial institutions in the 1980s brought a stunning reversal of the conception of 'development' with a rejection of the state-centred strategies of economic development and nation building of the first decades of independence. Instead, the focus was radically narrowed to the market alone, and the supposedly irremediably corrupt and 'predatory' states of Africa were rejected as the enemy of 'development'. Neo-liberal doctrine cast off the legitimacy of politics and sought to remove the state's 'interventions' that distorted the free play of market forces and, it was asserted, retarded growth. For country after country, access to aid and finance was conditional on the implementation of 'reforms' contained in structural adjustment programmes, uniform for each country that imposed the conditions for receiving assistance: currency devaluation, fees for basic public services such as health and education, removal of price subsidies for food, elimination of budget deficits, removal of trade barriers and privatisation of public corporations and other state-owned assets. The painfully won gains of national development of the 1960s and 1970s were dismissed as restraints on market-driven growth. Instead, market-driven reforms were economically and scientifically 'correct' in a way that tolerated no dissent. Efforts at state-led industrialisation and economic diversification had to be abandoned and African countries had to concentrate on their areas of 'comparative advantage' in the production of cash crops, pushing them back into the structural niche of the colonial political economy. Politics could only be a corrupt intrusion into the pursuit of a scientifically determined result.

Neo-liberal structural adjustment programmes, part of conscious efforts at 'globalisation' of the capitalist system, represent the most rigorous and coercive effort to impose the self-regulating market since the early nineteenth century. The result, while producing periods of growth in some countries, has been a general experience of economic decline, growing poverty, inequality, social decay and disorder. Africa has been integrated into the global economy in a socially and spatially asymmetrical fashion that has marginalised large portions of the territory and population of each nation and the continent as a whole and which has generated a general socio-economic decline (Ferguson 2006). In 1976 the per capita gross national product (GNP) of Sub-Saharan Africa was 17.6 per cent of the world average, but had dropped to 10.5 per cent by 1999. The average GNP per capita in African states dropped by almost 10 per cent during 1970–98, while the continent's share of global economic activity was only 1.1 per cent, despite having 10 per cent of world population. Rather than neo-liberal reform bringing predicted increases in foreign investment, Africa received only 0.6 per cent of the world total (Arrighi 2002: 17; van de Walle 2001). By the end of the 1980s, even the economic 'miracle' in the Côte d'Ivoire was in radical decline, while in Ghana the World Bank implemented its Programme of Assistance to Mitigate the Social Costs of Adjustment (PAMSCAD), a tacit admission of the failures of market reform (Brydon and Legge 1996; Hutchful 2002; Marshall-Fratani 2007). Rather than development, neo-liberalism brought what James Ferguson (2006: 48) called the 'steepest economic inequalities seen in human history', with corresponding declines in literacy and life-expectancy and unprecedented growth in the proportion of African populations living in absolute poverty. This was correlated with rural decline, runaway urbanisation with metastasising slums and the 'shadow economy' of the informal sector. The impact of adjustment has been documented in the Human Development Index (HDI) of the United Nations Development Programme (UNDP), developed in 1990 under the leadership of Mahbub ul Haq and Amartya Sen in order to counter the 'preoccupation with the growth of real income per capita as a measure of the well-being of a nation'

(Cleveland 2007) and in detailed empirical studies by the UN Habitat Program (2003; Davis 2006).[2]

The impact of structural adjustment and globalisation on African states has been severe. Cuts of personnel and services 'hollowed out' most states, reducing their administrative capacity and limiting the effective authority of smaller and weaker states to a radius of a few miles around the capital city and other major towns. The undermining of state capacity and loss of direct developmental functions and services did not make space for markets to produce rapid growth, but led to a significant increase in corruption. Equally important was the effective loss of sovereignty to international political and economic forces, both in the loss of control over macro-economic policy to the international financial institutions and of vast tracts of territory and resources to private corporations and non-governmental organisations (NGOs). The particular African experience of globalisation combining integration and marginalisation is found in the development of highly capitalised enclaves, particularly for natural resource extraction, with little connection to the marginalised regions around them. The growth of such enclaves with their private security of hired mercenaries also represents the loss for many states of the key monopoly of legal organised force (Ferguson 2006: 39–40). In addition, the taking over of public services and development programmes by a wide range of NGOs – local, national and transnational – gives them state-like functions to pursue their own political, economic and religious agendas.

Such undermining of the state threatened the established structures of political and economic power, and the politics of patronage. Political elites dependent on state patronage periodically clashed with the international financial institutions over the terms of adjustment programmes, including the civilian Moi regime in Kenya and the military magnates in Nigeria in the early 1990s (Forrest 1995: 242–8; Ndulu and Mwega 1994: 102–17). State deregulation and divestment did not so much free markets as extend political struggles for control of key sectors of the national economy from the state into the private sector. This also includes political elites' deployment of even declining state

---

[2] In the 2011 HDI for 169 countries, the highest ranked for Sub-Saharan Africa were Gabon (93) Namibia (105) and South Africa (110) while 35 of the 42 lowest in human development were from the region. Canada and Japan were ranked eighth and eleventh respectively (UNDP 2011).

power to gain a hold over parts of the rapidly growing international criminal economy, especially those of drugs and arms-trafficking, that has accompanied globalisation (Bayart *et al.* 1999).

The decay of the state and resulting intensified struggle for control of resources and accumulation of wealth in circumstances of growing poverty and uncertainty for the mass of the population has increased both the horizontal and vertical inequalities between and within ethnic communities and the conflicts of moral ethnicity and political tribalism. Contracting states are incapable of creating new programmes and positions or even paying the salaries of existing officials, while patrons with declining or threatened resources are unwilling and unable to sustain distributions to their clients. An increasingly materialistic and opportunistic appropriation of state resources for purely private personal gain undermines the relations of trust underpinning patronage networks with growing cynicism over the failure of 'big men' to meet their obligations of reciprocity and redistribution (Chabal and Daloz 1999). From aiding their followers to a share of the 'national cake', elites are seen as 'eating' the people and failing to protect them from the ravages of neo-liberal 'adjustment'. 'Big men' are seen as agents of sorcery and witchcraft, using their occult powers to suck the life from the poor (Geschiere 1997). Where countries such as Ghana and Kenya are under pressure from both indigenous elites and international financial institutions to develop land markets, control of rural land has become the most important source of conflict within and between ethnic communities (Lonsdale 2008; Tettey *et al.* 2008). While the poor placed greater demands on wealthier kin for aid and families bitterly divide over the inheritance of land and property, the broader conflict between rich and poor is expressed in acts of resistance and escape, as in the growth of parallel economies beyond the grasp of decayed states.

The erosion of state capacity and the declining legitimacy of both civil and military regimes in Africa were accompanied by a widespread increase of social violence. With the withdrawal of social services and decline of patronage networks, social disorder, crime and insecurity became an increasing feature of daily life in African societies. More disturbing was the increasingly savage nature of violence by organised groups, whether national armies and police, criminal gangs, insurgent movements or private 'war-lord' armies. Such violence, typically characterised in the Western news media (which covers little else about Africa) as 'senseless', 'irrational' and an 'end in itself' served as the basis for the construction of African 'difference' and 'darkness' and a reversion to primordial savagery. The problem with this simplistic and inaccurate stereotype is that it obscures a complex reality and renders incomprehensible the relationship between the state and social violence. Compared to the rest of the world in the sanguinary history of the twentieth century, Africa has been no more prone to violent conflicts than other regions, nor have the conflicts been more lethal (Zeleza 2008). The horrific genocides of Rwanda and Darfur do not place Africa outside of 'civilisation', but as part of the grim global record of state-sponsored and organised slaughter that constitutes the evil legacy of modernity (Bauman 1989), including the vicious contemporary ethnic confrontations in the Balkans and Caucasus occasioned by the collapse of Yugoslavia and the Soviet Union. Moreover, most serious civil conflicts in Africa are grounded in the political and economic legacies of the colonial experience and its characteristic harsh and routine use of coercion against the subject population. Up to today, the violence of the state's agents is an ever-present threat in any encounter with its security forces. The level of social violence in Africa has risen from an already violent historical base, whether carried out by state or non-state actors, organised groups or in interpersonal assaults, with the line between political and criminal agents increasingly porous, and all facilitated by the ready availability of small arms, especially automatic weapons, in the post-Cold War arms bazaar.

The most influential explanation of African 'civil wars' by Paul Collier and his colleagues, sponsored by the World Bank, depicted them as driven by greed rather than political grievances or ideology and based solely on rational calculation of the economic returns to violence by predatory insurgent groups and warlords who fought for the control over natural resources ('conflict diamonds'), drug trafficking and ruthless exploitation of local populations (Collier and Hoeffler 2001). What is missing is any conception of the interplay of economic, social, cultural and political factors that shape the context of conflicts and the motivation and meaning of both individual actors and insurgent movements ('grievance'). Based on rational choice models of individual actors motivated solely by maximisation of material rewards ('looting'), for which no empirical evidence in any African context is offered, it offers correlations rather than explanation of the violence based on dubious evidence of poorly understood and mischaracterised cases (Kaarsholm 2006: 14–19; Mkandawire 2008: 103–19).

Here we actually confront the intersection of both common and locally idiosyncratic factors that shape each conflict and in which, as noted earlier, the latter may be the most important in particular cases. The interaction of economic factors with ethnicity and ethnic conflict operates on two key dimensions. Firstly, on the level of structural political economy, the structural adjustment reforms exacerbate the horizontal and vertical inequalities between and within ethnic communities that constitute the material basis for both greed and grievance and violent conflicts (Stewart 2008). However, whether such structural inequalities are translated into different forms of conflict including the most extreme forms of violence depends on political factors unique to each case. For example, the hollowing out of state capabilities and resources, noted above, reduced the patronage resources available to political elites to mitigate the inequalities between communities and for 'big men' to redistribute to their clientage. Moreover, the decline of state administrative capabilities and resources led by the late 1980s to the crisis of 'governance' that prompted ethnically based movements to attack weakened regimes or move out of their shrinking orbit of effective control. On the second level, of economic behaviour, ethnic cleavages can have a significant impact on market behaviour of both individuals and firms, as well as on the behaviour of banks, government services, aid programmes and NGOs assisting local business development. The failure of trust in market exchange can have serious effects on economic growth, but also involves the role of the state and the rule of law in providing and maintaining the essential normative basis of exchange transactions. The impact of ethnicity on actual economic behaviour and its wider structural consequences is a topic that calls for much further detailed research in different national contexts.[3]

Given the conventional wisdom about the artificiality and fragility of African nation-states, they have actually proven remarkably durable during the first half-century of independence, and especially during the

---

[3] While studying indigenous industrial development in Ghana I was told repeatedly by both businessmen and government officials that partnerships between individuals from different ethnic groups rarely worked (Berman 2003). I also observed during numerous interviews at small manufacturing firms that the employees tended to come from the same ethnic group as the owner, if not the same extended family. The extent to which both can be found in Ghana and other countries and their wider significance for economic performance is a provocative hypothesis that requires further research.

past quarter-century of escalating violence. The internal wars of Africa have largely focused on controlling the state within the established territorial boundaries or gaining some degree of regional autonomy or more equitable distribution of resources within it. In only eight cases (Ethiopia, Somalia, Uganda, both Congos, Rwanda, Sierra Leone and Liberia) have insurgents from the periphery destroyed an incumbent regime and its security forces, rather than the switch of loyalty to the new rulers that occurred under earlier coups (Young 2007: 260). In only two instances – the separation of Eritrea from Ethiopia and of South Sudan from Sudan – has the division of an existing state occurred and been internationally recognised. Indeed, the issue of 'state collapse', which has been a major focus of much recent political research in Africa, has, I think, been quite exaggerated. Even where there has been a dramatic recession of state authority and control over wide parts of its national territory, as in Somalia, Zaire, Sierra Leone and Liberia, their national boundaries have remained largely intact and internationally recognised. Indeed, the reconstitution of a functioning state in the portion of Somalia that was the British colony of Somaliland has thus far failed to gain international recognition.

In states weakened by globalisation and neo-liberal reforms the focus of conflict has been of contested nationalisms and battles about state formation and the socio-cultural dimensions of the nation. Much of the violence has been about the reassertion of central state control. Even where the civil administration has temporarily receded in the countryside, the military and police have remained to contest insurgent movements for control of the national territory. And the criminalisation of the state may actually indicate attempts at consolidation and expansion of state resources in ways similar to how wars, piracy and organised crime contributed to state building in early modern Europe (Bayart 2000; Kaarsholm 2006; Tilly 1990). The contests of nationalism suggest not only the degree to which nationhood has become powerfully rooted in the political and cultural imaginary of even small and weak African states (Kaarsholm 2006; Milliken and Krause 2002), but also the increasing intertwining of nationalism and mobilised ethnicity in the complex motives underlying political violence. Indeed, rather than an artificially imposed concept by earlier efforts at 'nation building', the nation has become part of popular consciousness, a 'taken as given' part of social reality (Young 2007: 262). Equally importantly, the socio-cultural boundaries of the nation and citizenship have become increasingly ethnicised and link together the efforts at democratisation and the intense civil conflicts of autochthony.

Democracy and disorder: African nations and the conflicts of autochthony

Of the forty-seven states of Sub-Saharan Africa in 1989, only five possessed competitive multiparty systems, eleven were military oligarchies, twenty-nine were civilian one-party states with varying degrees of permitted competition, and two (Namibia and South Africa) were white settler regimes (Bratton and van de Walle 1997: 79). The 1990s came with a wave of 'democratisation' as popular protests and foreign pressures pressed authoritarian regimes for political reforms and multiparty elections. By the middle of the decade, sixteen countries had newly elected governments, although in twenty-four others incumbent regimes had successfully blocked reforms or were able to manipulate them to win an electoral mandate, often through deeply flawed elections. The decade ended with the outbreak of particularly vicious civil conflicts – extending into the new century – in several of the most important democratised states. 'Democracy' itself appeared to be a source of social disorder.

External pressures for democratisation came from the international financial institutions and major Western powers, especially the US, alarmed at the decay of African states, their obvious loss of legitimacy with their populations and the resulting crisis of governance from efforts to implement neo-liberal reforms. They pushed for the restoration of multiparty politics, free elections and the open development of 'civil society'. The end of the Cold War removed any strategic reasons for the support of authoritarian regimes such as that of Mobutu in Zaire. The sort of democracy promoted by the Western powers was, however, highly elitist and narrowly procedural. The intent was to provide a process that would legitimate ruling groups and entrench neo-liberal reforms and the 'free market' as the untouchable bases of 'democracy'. The version of liberal democracy pressed on African states was a disciplined one in which capitalism and the 'free market' was sacrosanct and there was not 'too much' democracy attending to issues of distribution and inequality (Abrahamsen 2000).

Internal pressures, by contrast, emerged from the growing wave of popular protest between 1988 and 1992 challenging, in circumstances of increasing poverty and insecurity, patrimonial autocracies, both civilian and military. These protests were led by trade unions, students, civil servants, professional organisations and, in some instances, religious institutions. From economic grievances they quickly moved to demands for political reform and civil liberties. In eleven francophone countries, reform movements led to national conferences and new constitutions, while constitutional reform also marked reforms in other countries. Common elements included legalisation of political parties, constitutional separation of powers and multiparty legislative and presidential elections. Space was also provided for the press outside of government control and a new range of civil society organisations. The reform movements were also testimony to the importance of the nation in popular consciousness and the focus on the state as its political expression (Bratton and van de Walle 1997; Young 2007).

In three important cases – Ethiopia, Nigeria and South Africa – democratisation and constitutional reform involved efforts to employ varying forms of federalism to accommodate and manage ethnic diversity. Ethiopia instituted an explicitly ethnic form of federalism, with ethnicity as the basis for the organisation of states and the exercise of significant political and cultural autonomy. In a situation of great ethnic diversity of some eighty groups of widely varying sizes from several million to mere thousands, six states focused on the largest communities with recognisable territorial foci, while three others combined numerous small communities. In Nigeria, in the fourth constitutional iteration since independence, deliberate efforts were made to fragment and sublimate the identities and politicisation of the three main ethnic groups into some twenty-two states, while fourteen are ethnically heterogeneous under the control of smaller minority communities. In both instances, federalism functions as a way of incorporating and rewarding ethnic elites by providing access to state institutions and resources and thereby institutionalising ethnic patronage as the basis of politics. In states without a dominant group, elite competition among minority communities replicates the ethnic politics of centralised states; in Ethiopia the three ethnically fragmented states have been the site of the most violent ethnic confrontations. In both Ethiopia and Nigeria the reality is actually increasing centralisation of control by the federal state. In Nigeria this is linked to the 'federal principle' in the distribution of oil revenues to the states, which has created exceptional state dependence on the centre, as well as generating smouldering conflict with the ethnic communities of the oil-producing states of the Niger Delta (Ejobowah 2008; Turton 2006).

In South Africa the nine provinces were deliberately designed to contain no majority ethno-racial community in the system officially described as 'devolved union' rather than federation, with strong central government powers. In all three states, domination of the central government by a single party has effectively increased the centralised power of the state over the federal units. Federalism, finally, can do little to deal with the internal movement of peoples and loss of territorial focus of increasingly hybrid and intermarried populations, especially in urban areas (Murray and Simeon 2008).

By the end of the 1990s, however, the tide of democratisation was ebbing and many governments were receding back into 'semi-democracies' and a re-assertion of elite control revealed serious limits to the process. Newly elected regimes were unable, under heavy international pressure, to make any departure from neo-liberal policy prescriptions, which compromised their ability to address local issues of poverty and redistribution. Moreover, the shallow and narrowly restricted 'democracy' implemented in most countries actually exacerbated ethnic conflicts and the political mobilisation of ethnic communities. Firstly, the competition between ethnically based patronage networks for access to state resources was intensified by open electoral competition. Despite efforts in some countries to limit the expression of ethnic conflict by banning explicitly ethnic parties and/or requiring candidates to achieve a minimal level of support in all regions of the country, militant ethnic politics has been increasing in many countries. Rather than patronage resources being discreetly sorted out by bargaining among elites within a single ruling party or behind the opaque shield of a military autocracy, elites have to compete publicly for electoral support to gain access to the state. The hegemony of neo-liberal ideology among the parties allows for little variation in ideology or programme between parties and leaves little but their ethnic base for politicians to appeal to. In Ghana, where ethnic cleavages had not been a predominant factor in politics, the series of increasingly successful national elections since 1992 have been marked by the emergence of ethnic bloc voting (Jockers *et al.* 2009). And patron–client politics works very effectively within the electoral process, as it does in so many countries outside of Africa, exchanging client votes for patron/ leaders in return for expected redistribution of material benefits.

At the same time, the winner-takes-all outcome of elections in systems without proportional representation in most states, increased smaller communities' fear of domination by larger groups, the increasingly inequitable distribution of wealth and their ultimate exclusion from access to the state. Instead of reducing corruption, democratisation allowed it to reach new heights as newly elected politicians sought 'our turn to eat', and the politics of the belly revealed the personal, materialistic and opportunistic character of politics and the relative unimportance of ideology, principal or policy in the tightly circumscribed political arena. Western expectations, meanwhile, that the growth of civil society would serve as a force for social and political renewal, have proven illusory. The focus on socio-cultural forms borrowed from the West – churches, professional organisations, trade unions, universities, etc. – has ignored the dense networks of indigenous institutions that surround and pervade them, features of historical experience and the social landscape that are idiosyncratically African and usually ethnically or religiously specific. Such organisations mean that civil society is neither a democratic *deus ex machina* nor a movement of popular empowerment, but traversed by inequalities and antidemocratic and authoritarian politics revealing clashing interests of ethnicity, class and gender and deep and potentially violent conflicts (Fatton 1995).

The most intense of these conflicts have focused on the meaning of citizenship and national belonging. Citizenship has been increasingly ethnicised to mean derivation solely from birth into one of the original ethnic communities of the nation. The socio-cultural boundaries of ethnic groups and their claims to being the native inhabitants of national territory became objects of growing conflict with regards to both political participation and access to material benefits. The issues of 'who can vote?' or 'who can be a candidate where?' show the growing fear of local populations of being outvoted by more numerous 'strangers'; while the decentralisation of development programmes and the increasing involvement of NGOs has triggered confrontations over who could participate in projects (Cueppens and Geschiere 2005). Conflicts over ethnic definitions of citizenship bring new intensity to the politics of authenticity by combining the internal conflicts of moral ethnicity and the external confrontations of political tribalism. These have found expression in conflicts over 'autochthony', of literally being 'sons of the soil' that began in francophone countries and have emerged in varying, but no less violent circumstances, in countries of anglophone Africa as well. These involve struggles over recognition of the authenticity of communal and individual membership in the nation in circumstances of economic distress and uncertainty over the real material issue of access to land and work.

Conflicts of autochthony, however, involve attempts to define fixed criteria of identity and discourses of exclusion to assert group boundaries in real world circumstances of mobility, immigration, urbanisation and mixed ancestry of increasingly diverse populations. They involve efforts to rehabilitate 'authentic' origins and a 're-enchantment' if not actual invention or appropriation of 'tradition'. It is linked to a xenophobia and sense of victimisation that defines the enemy as an interloping stranger and his innocent autochthonous victim (Marshall-Fratani 2007; Mbembe 2000). The righteous imagery of the victim amid the reality of ambiguous and contested identities, as Appadurai notes, gives the violence of the conflicts a particularly vicious quality, as the other can only be definitively eliminated by murder and atrocity (Appadurai 1999).

In the context of democratisation and economic crisis, the violent conflicts that exploded in the Côte d'Ivoire in 2002 pitted 'autochthonous' communities in the south against 'allogenes', including both foreign immigrants from Burkina Faso and Mali and internal immigrants from the north of the country. It was both a struggle over land and of the definition of citizenship of true Ivoirians defined by 'ivoirité' as opposed to foreigners and strangers. Ethnicity as self-identification was linked to autochthony as the basis of national belonging. Demands for group-based citizenship focused on special recognition and precedence for 'true' sons of the soil (Geschiere 2009: 18, 24–5). In the Ivory Coast this was expressed in a 'National Operation of Identification' in 2001–2 requiring every Ivorian to return to his or her village of origin and be identified by a committee of local notables and registered as full citizens with rights to land and to the vote (Geschiere 2009: 98–117; Marshall-Fratani 2007). It was to the participants a 'war of who is who' in circumstances of ambiguity and hybridity that focused on grasping control of the state and its historic role in the definition of group identities. Rather than undermining the nation-state, the conflict reinforced its vitality and importance (Marshall-Fratani 2007: 31–2, 45).

In the north-east corner of the Democratic Republic of the Congo, bordering on Rwanda and Burundi, the outbreak of ethnic violence in 1997–8 centred on issues of autochthony and national citizenship and the role of the state in defining both in a region of remarkable complexity of ethnic identities and communities with constantly changing names and historical claims (Cueppens and Geschiere 2005: 395). The issue was the authenticity of the citizenship of the 'banyarwanda', a composite group of the Banyamulenge or 'Congolese Tutsi' who had settled in the area shortly before the territorial divisions of 1885 placed them under Belgian rule, and later Tutsi and Hutu immigrants, including Tutsi refugees from the first pogroms in Rwanda in 1959 and Hutu refugees fleeing the victorious Tutsi army at the end of the Rwandan genocide of 1994. Mobutu first granted citizenship to the Banyamulenge when he depended on their support and reneged when he needed support from other groups. During 1992–6 he used the citizenship issue to destabilise the democracy movement and made people of Rwandan origin the first target. When the Banyamulenge resisted, it provided the pretext for the organisation of several ethnic militias in the region and the intervention of Rwanda and Uganda ostensibly to prevent another genocide (Nzongola-Ntalaja 2007: 70–6).

While the concept of 'autochthony' is rarely invoked in anglophone Africa, clashes over conflicting claims to land and citizenship are becoming more frequent. Two outbreaks of efforts to exclude strangers or foreigners in early 2008 are particularly striking. Ogot argues in Chapter 3 a major element of the violence following on the contested outcome of the Kenya election of December 2007, as in the outbreaks following the earlier multiparty elections of 1992 and 1997, were attacks by Kalenjin 'warriors' on Kikuyu farmers in the western Rift Valley. An act of blunt ethnic cleansing, later found to have been organised and paid for by senior political figures from the area, it was an attempt by earlier migrants to the area to rid it of late-coming 'strangers', with the likely actual autochthonous inhabitants, the Okiek, too small in number or power to be an issue. The Kikuyu were descendants of landless peasants settled on former white settler estates at the end of the colonial period, but on land the local Kalenjin believed should have once again become their own. For the British, who believed Kikuyu landlessness was a cause of the Mau Mau uprising in the 1950s, it was the solution to a problem (and the first development project in Kenya to be funded by the World Bank), but it turned out to create another in its stead. The Kikuyu established their claim by their productive labour and creation of wealth, while the Kalenjin rejected not their citizenship but their presence in the wrong place and what they perceived as Kikuyu arrogance and dominance (Anderson and Lochery 2008; Lonsale 2008; Mueller 2008).

In multiethnic and multiracial South Africa, in May 2008 violence broke out in the townships surrounding Johannesburg as black South Africans attacked immigrants and refugees, especially those from Mozambique and increasing numbers fleeing the political and social collapse in Zimbabwe. The 'rainbow nation' that prides itself as being a beacon of democracy and human rights revealed a powerful popular undercurrent of xenophobia among all South African racial and ethnic communities, directed in particular at the *makwere-kwere* of African immigrants from across the Limpopo River. Stigmatised as sources of crime and disease and stealers of jobs from real citizens, a majority of South Africans thought they were undeserving of basic human rights, let alone those of citizenship. Xenophobia, as Jonathan Crush noted, turns out to be the underside of democratic nationalism (Crush 2001).

Underlying the conflicts of autochthony and efforts to purify the authentic group is the link of belonging and access to the new resources of wealth and power that can accompany globalisation (Geschiere and Nyamnjoh 2000). For example, at the most local level, this is clear in attempts to decentralise control over development programmes and local resources to indigenous communities and 'traditional' leaders. In the case of conflicts over development programmes for local forest resources in Cameroon, Geschiere has shown the contradiction between combining neo-liberal reform and belief in the market as the solution to all problems with trust in the 'community' or 'customary chiefs' as a source of stability and local control. Instead, the result is that communities limit access to resources and income by closing themselves to 'outsiders' and excluding people previously accepted as part of the community (Geschiere 2009).

Finally, the claims of autochthony are inseparable from 'recognition' by the state that allocates access to political and economic resources. The various political dimensions of the construction of ethnic communities since the colonial period – moral ethnicity, authenticity, representation and recognition – have not so much undermined post-colonial African states, as the older conventional wisdom held, but reinforced them as the most important source of wealth and power, even in times of social decay and global crisis (Berman forthcoming-b). Ironically, given that global development institutions, both international and bilateral, do not understand the relationship between processes of ethnic construction and colonial and post-colonial states in Africa, or that the forms of expert knowledge they apply are also political interventions into the processes they seek to control 'scientifically', the result is that policies such as democratisation and decentralisation can actually promote, unintentionally and unexpectedly, increasingly intense, divisive and violent conflicts.

African ethnicity and nationalism as shadow and portent

The nation-states of Africa, as those elsewhere, are continuously unfinished projects, contingent outcomes of the universalised social forces of globalised modernity and their own distinctive cultural diversity, mediated by the idiosyncrasies of the colonial experience. African nations are both reflected shadows of the development of Western nation-states, the real historical nation-states, rather than the idealised forms too often used to assess the failures of non-Western nations; and are a portent of the challenges posed to all nations by contemporary globalisation and the current world crisis.

The ethnic conflicts of Sub-Saharan Africa of the late twentieth and early twenty-first centuries have been as violent and vicious as those in other parts of the world, but are not unique examples of atavistic savagery. Most of the violence has been focused on defending or gaining control of the state within a nation and redolent of the earlier struggles in the construction of European nation-states, although in a strikingly different global context (Bayart 2000; Connor 1972). The movements of democratisation attest to the continuing reality of African nations and nationalism, both internally for citizens struggling to reconstruct the state and externally for the international community. The repeated efforts to rewrite national constitutions attest to the continuing political energy of nationalism in the popular consciousness (Berman 2009). At the same time, the disturbing connection between democratisation and civil violence, increasingly expressed in the bitter conflicts of autochthony, reveals the growing ethnicisation of nationalism and more narrowly bounded notions of citizenship in Africa.

While aspects of African nationalism, ethnicity and democratisation may reflect at some historical distance the experience of Western states, the context in which they occur makes contemporary Africa an embodiment of the challenges increasingly facing all nation-states in a globalised world. Social and ethnic diversity and the challenges of multiculturalism are increasingly global phenomena through the unprecedented movements of people from the southern hemisphere to the north, many of them from Sub-Saharan Africa to Western Europe and North America, to escape the combination of economic decay and civil conflict. Ethnicised nationalism and conflicts over citizenship have taken on new urgency in a strikingly diverse world embracing local sons of the soil and alien others. At the same time, Western nation-states have been challenged from within by the political mobilisation of minority ethnic communities submerged beneath the juggernaut of earlier nation building, while North America and other former colonies of settlement face the rising demands of suppressed and dispossessed indigenous peoples. Conflicts of autochthony and anti-immigrant politics are growing in 'developed' nations of Europe (Geschiere 2009), as the 2009 elections to the European Parliament strikingly demonstrated. All nations now confront the issues of the meaning of nation and identity, democratic development and accountability, citizen and communal rights, the balancing of multiethnic mosaics versus integrationist melting pots amid intensifying conflicts of cultures, classes and genders. In this setting, the impact of ethnicity on economic development in African states derives not from the diversity of ethnic groups but from the impact of thirty years of neo-liberal reforms on the horizontal cleavages that are the material basis of ethnic conflict and on the access of ethnic communities to the sources of wealth and power in the state and market. This shapes in turn the behaviour of both individuals and institutions, public and private, in the marketplace. And they must do so in the context of a global crisis of capitalism that challenges the ideological hegemony of neo-liberalism and brings the issues of moral economy to the world stage as well as to the domestic politics of every nation.

References

Abrahamsen, Rita 2000. *Disciplining Democracy: Development Discourse and Good Governance in Africa*. London: Zed Press.
Allman, Jean Marie 1993. *The Quills of the Porcupine: Asante Nationalism in an Emergent Ghana*. Madison, WI: University of Wisconsin Press.
Anderson, David and Lochery, Emma 2008. 'Violence and Exodus in Kenya's Rift Valley, 2008: Predictable and Preventable?', *Journal of Eastern African Studies* 2: 328–43.

Appadurai, Arjun 1999. 'Dead Certainty: Ethnic Violence in the Era of Globalization', in *Globalization and Identity – Dialectics of Flow and Closure*, Birgit Meyer and Peter Geschiere (eds.). Malden, MA: Blackwell Publishers.

Arrighi, Giovanni 2002. 'The African Crisis: World Systemic and Regional Aspects', *New Left Review* 15: 5–36.

Bauman, Zygmunt 1989. *Modernity and the Holocaust.* Cambridge: Polity Press.

Bayart, Jean-François 1993. *The State in Africa: the Politics of the Belly.* London: Longman.

2000. 'Africa in the World: a History of Extraversion', *African Affairs* 99: 217–67.

Bayart, Jean-François, Ellis, Stephen and Hibou, Beatrice (eds.) 1999. *The Criminalization of the State in Africa.* Oxford: James Currey.

Berman, Bruce J. 1990. *Control and Crisis in Colonial Kenya: the Dialectic of Domination.* London: James Currey and Athens, Ohio: Ohio University Press.

1998. 'Ethnicity, Patronage and the African State: the Politics of Uncivil Nationalism', *African Affairs* 97: 305–41.

2003. 'Capitalism Incomplete: State, Culture and the Politics of Industrialization', in *Critical Perspectives in Politics and Socio-economic Development in Ghana.* Wisdom Tettey, Korbla Puplampu and Bruce Berman (eds.). Leiden and Boston: Brill.

2004a. 'A Palimpsest of Contradictions: the Study of Politics, Ethnicity and the State in Africa', *International Journal of African Historical Studies* 37: 13–31.

2004b. 'Ethnicity, Bureaucracy and Democracy: the Politics of Trust', in *Ethnicity and Democracy in Africa*, Bruce Berman, Dickson Eyoh and Will Kymlicka (eds.). Oxford: James Currey and Athens, OH: Ohio University Press.

2009. 'Ethnic Politics and the Making and Unmaking of Constitutions in Africa', *Ethnic Politics and the Making of Constitutions in Africa, Special Issue of the Canadian Journal of African Studies* 43: 461–506.

2011. 'Knowledge and the Politics of Ethnic Identity and Belonging in Colonial and Post-Colonial States', in *Public Institutions and Recognition*, Avigail Eisenberg and Will Kymlicka (eds.). Vancouver, BC: University of British Columbia Press.

forthcoming-a. 'Moral Economy, Hegemony, Moral Ethnicity: the Cultural Politics of Modernity', in *Ethnic Claims and Moral Economies*, Bruce Berman, Andre Laliberte and Stephen Larin (eds.). Vancouver, BC: University of British Columbia Press.

forthcoming-b. 'Post-Colonial Nationalism in Africa', in *Oxford Handbook of the History of Nationalism*, John Breuilly (ed.). Oxford University Press.

Berry, Sarah 1993. *No Condition is Permanent: the Social Dynamics of Agrarian Change.* Madison, WI: University of Wisconsin Press.

Bratton, Michael and van de Walle, Nicholas 1997. *Democratic Experiments in Africa.* Cambridge University Press.

Brydon, Lynn and Legge, Karen 1996. *Adjusting Society: the World Bank, the IMF and Ghana.* London: I. B. Tauris.

Cueppens, Bambi and Geschiere, Peter 2005. 'Autochthony: Local or Global? New Modes in the Struggle over Citizenship and Belonging in Africa and Europe', *Annual Review of Anthropology* 34: 385–407.

Chabal, Patrick and Daloz, Jean-Pascal 1999. *Africa Works: Disorder as Political Instrument.* London: James Currey and Bloomington, IN: Indiana University Press, for the International African Institute.

Cleveland, Cutler J. 2007. 'Human Development Index', *Encyclopedia of Earth.* Washington, DC: Environmental Information Coalition, National Council for Science and the Environment (www.eoearth.org/article/Human_Development_Index).

Collier, Paul and Hoeffler, Anke 2001. *Greed and Grievance in Civil War.* Washington, DC: World Bank, Development Research Group.

Connor, Walker 1972. 'Nation Building or Nation Destroying?', *World Politics* 24.

Cooper, Frederick 1996. *Decolonization in African Society: the Labour Question in French and British Africa.* Cambridge University Press.

Crehan, Kate 2002. *Gramsci, Culture and Anthropology.* Berkeley and Los Angeles, CA: University of California Press.

Crush, Jonathan 2001. 'The Dark Side of Democracy: Migration, Xenophobia and Human Rights in South Africa', *International Migration* 38 (special issue 2): 103–33.

Davidson, Basil 1992. *The Black Man's Burden: Africa and the Curse of the Nation-State.* London: James Currey.

Davis, Mike 2006. *Planet of Slums.* London: Verso Books.

Eisenberg, Avigail and Kymlicka, Will 2011. *Public Institutions and Recognition.* Vancouver, BC: University of British Columbia Press.

Ejobowah, John Boye 2008. 'Integrationist and Accommodationist Measures in Nigeria's Constitutional Engineering: Successes and Failures', in *Constitutional Design in Divided Societies: Integration or Accommodation?*, Sujit Choudhry (ed.). Oxford University Press.

Ekeh, Peter P. 1990. 'Social Anthropology and Two Contrasting Uses of Tribalism in Africa', *Comparative Studies in Society and History* 32: 660–700.

2004.'Individuals' Basic Security Needs and the Limits of Democratization in Africa', in *Ethnicity and Democracy in Africa*, Bruce Berman, Dickson Eyoh and Will Kymlicka (eds.). Oxford: James Currey and Athens, OH: Ohio University Press.

Eyoh, Dickson 1996. 'From Economic Crisis to Political Liberalization: Pitfalls of the New Political Sociology for Africa', *African Studies Review* 39: 43–80.

Fatton, Robert 1995. 'Africa in the Age of Democratization: the Civic Limitations of Civil Society', *African Studies Review* 38: 67–99.

Ferguson, James 2006. *Global Shadows: Africa in the Neo-Liberal World Order*. Durham, NC and London: Duke University Press.

Forrest, Tom 1995. *Politics and Economic Development in Nigeria*. Boulder, CO: Westview Press.

Geschiere, Peter 1997. *The Modernity of Witchcraft: Politics and the Occult in Post-colonial Africa*. Charlottesville, VA: University Press of Virginia.

2009. *The Perils of Belonging: Autochthony, Citizenship and Exclusion in Africa and Europe*. Chicago and London: University of Chicago Press.

Geschiere, Peter and Nyamnjoh, Francis 2000.'Capitalism and Autochthony: the Seesaw of Mobility and Belonging', *Public Culture* 12: 423–52.

Hutchful, Eboe 2002. *Ghana's Adjustment Experience: the Paradox of Reform*. United Nations Research Institute on Social Development (UNRISD) and Oxford: James Currey.

Jackson, Robert H. 1982. *Personal Rule in Black Africa: Prince, Autocrat, Prophet, Tyrant*. Berkeley and Los Angeles: University of California Press.

Jockers, Heinz, Kohnert, Dirk and Nugent, Paul 2009. 'The Successful Ghana Election of 2008: a Convenient Myth? Ethnicity in Ghana's Elections Revisited', *German Institute of Global and Area Studies, Working Papers no. 109*.

Kaarsholm, Preben 2006. 'States of Failure, Societies in Collapse? Understandings of Violent Conflict in Africa', in *Violence, Political Culture and Development in Africa*, Preben Kaarsholm (ed.). Oxford: James Currey; Athens, OH: Ohio University Press; Pietermaritzburg: University of KwaZulu-Natal Press.

Kertzer, David and Arel, Dominique 2002. *Census and Identity: the Politics of Race, Ethnicity and Language in National Censuses*. Cambridge University Press.

Lonsdale, John 1994. 'Moral Ethnicity and Political Tribalism', in *Inventions and Boundaries: Historical and Anthropological Approaches to the Study of Ethnicity and Nationalism, Occasional Paper 11*, Preben Kaarsholm and Jan Hultin (eds.). Roskilde, Denmark: Institute for Development Studies, Roskilde University.

2008. 'Soil, Work, Civilization and Citizenship in Kenya', *Journal of Eastern African Studies* 2: 305–14.

Lonsdale, John and Low, Anthony 1976. 'Introduction: the Second Colonial Occupation', in *History of East Africa, Vol. III*, Anthony Low and Alison Smith (eds.). Oxford: The Clarendon Press.

Mamdani, Mahmood 1996. *Citizen and Subject: Contemporary Africa and the Legacy of Late Colonialism*. Princeton University Press.

Marshall-Fratani, Ruth 2007. 'The War of "Who is Who": Autochthony, Nationalism and Citizenship in the Ivoirian Crisis', in *Making Nations, Creating Strangers: States and Citizenship in Africa*, Sara Dorman, Daniel Hammett and Paul Nugent (eds.). Leiden and Boston: Brill.

Mbembe, Achile 2000. 'A Propos Des Écritures Africaines de Soi', *Politique Africaine* 77: 16–43.

Milliken, Jennifer and Krause, Keith 2002. 'State Failure, State Collapse and State Reconstruction', *Development and Change* 33: 5.

Mkandawire, Thandika 2006. 'The Terrible Toll of Post-colonial Rebel Movements: Towards Explanation of Violence Against the Peasantry', in *The Roots of African Conflicts: the Causes and Costs*, Alfred Nhema and Paul Tiyambe Zeleza (eds.). Addis Ababa: OSSREA; Oxford: James Currey.

Mueller, Susanne 2008. 'The Political Economy of Kenya's Crisis', *Journal of Eastern African Studies* 2: 185–210.

Murray, Christina and Simeon, Richard 2008. 'Recognition without Empowerment: Minorities in a Democratic South Africa', in *Constitutional Design for Divided Societies: Integration or Accommodation*, Sujit Choudhry (ed.). New York: Oxford University Press.

Ndulu, Benno and Mwega, Francis 1994. 'Economic Adjustment Policies', in *Beyond Capitalism and Socialism in Kenya and Tanzania*, Joel Barkan (ed.). Boulder, CO: Lynne Rienner.

Nzongola-Ntalaja, Georges 2007. 'The Politics of Citizenship in the Democratic Republic of the Congo', in *Making Nations, Creating Strangers: States and Citizenship in Africa*, Sara Dorman, Daniel Hammett and Paul Nugent (eds.). Leiden and Boston: Brill.

Ranger, Terence 1983. 'The Invention of Tradition in Colonial Africa', in *The Invention of Tradition*, Eric Hobsbawm and Terence Ranger (eds.). Cambridge University Press.

1994. 'The Invention of Tradition Revisited', in *Inventions and Boundaries: Historical and Anthropological Approaches to the Study of Ethnicity and Nationalism*, Preben Kaarsholm and Jan Hultin (eds.). Roskilde, Denmark: Institute for Development Studies, Roskilde University.

Scott, James 1985. *Weapons of the Weak: Everyday Forms of Peasant Resistance*. New Haven, CT: Yale University Press.

Stewart, Frances 2008. *Horizontal Inequalities and Conflict: Understanding Group Violence in Multi-ethnic Societies*. Basingstoke and New York: Palgrave Macmillan.

Tettey, Wisdom, Gebe, Boni Yao and Ansah-Koi, Kumi 2008. *The Politics of Land and Land-related Conflicts*. Accra: Institute of Statistical, Social and Economic Research, University of Ghana.

Tilly, Charles (ed.) 1975. *The Formation of National States in Western Europe*. Princeton University Press.

Tilly, Charles 1990. *Coercion, Capital and European States, 1990–1990*. Oxford: Basil Blackwell.

Turton, David 2006. 'Introduction', in *Ethnic Federalism: the Ethiopian Experience in Comparative Perspective*, David Turton (ed.). Oxford: James Currey; Athens, OH: Ohio University Press; Addis Ababa University Press.

United Nations Habitat Program 2003. *The Challenge of Slums: Global Report on Human Settlements*. Nairobi: UN Human Settlements Program.

United Nations Development Program 2011. *Human Development Report*. New York: UNDP Publications.

van de Walle, Nicholas 2001. *African Economies and the Politics of Permanent Crisis, 1979–99*. New York: Cambridge University Press.

Young, Crawford 1986. 'Nationalism, Ethnicity and Class in Africa: a Retrospective', *Cahiers d'Etudes Africaines* 103: 421–95.

　2007. 'Nation, Ethnicity and Citizenship: Dilemmas of Democracy and Civil Order in Africa', in *Making Nations, Creating Strangers: States and Citizenship in Africa*, Sara Dorman, Daniel Hammett and Paul Nugent (eds.). Leiden and Boston: Brill.

Zeleza, Paul Tiyambe 2008. 'Introduction: the Causes and Costs of War in Africa', in *The Roots of African Conflicts: the Causes and Costs*, Alfred Nhema and Paul Tiyambe Zeleza (eds.). Addis Ababa: Organization for Social Science Research in Eastern and Southern Africa (OSSREA); Oxford: James Currey.

6 | Evidence from spatial correlation of poverty and income in Kenya

NOBUAKI HAMAGUCHI

Introduction

In this chapter, I employ a spatial autoregressive model to analyse the relationship between ethnic diversity and economic development at the district level in Kenya. This approach enables us to assess this relationship on two levels: firstly, the impact of ethnic diversity on poverty and income *within* individual districts and secondly, the impact of ethnic differences *between* neighbouring districts. Our findings in the individual district analysis suggest that districts with higher levels of ethnic diversity have higher levels of income and lower levels of poverty, a departure from the conventional wisdom that associates ethnic diversity with poor economic outcomes (e.g. Easterly and Levine 1997). Next, we extend the model to capture effects of ethnic differences between districts. These differences are conceptualised much like physical distance in the economic geography literature. As such we conjecture, in agreement with Shipton (Chapter 7), that lack of trust between neighbouring areas with different ethnicities creates 'distance' between ethnic communities, and thus works as a deterrent to trade between them. Hence, per capita income of a district would be lower than otherwise if it is surrounded by districts whose ethnic compositions are quite different from its own.

In other chapters of this book, Lonsdale, Berman and Shipton (Chapters 1, 5 and 7) employed qualitative strategies to understand the relationship between ethnic diversity and economic volatility in Africa. Drawing on historical evidence and inferences, these authors argued that quantitative approaches to ethnicity are inherently problematic because: (1) ethnicity is specific to time, location and occasion, and is hence difficult to measure; and (2) the relationship between ethnicity and economy is too complex to be captured through simple mathematical equations. However, I believe that regression analyses provide valuable insights into this relationship if we carefully consider and address the potential shortcomings of quantitative strategies.

How is our approach free of some of the weaknesses identified by Lonsdale, Berman and Shipton? Firstly, we employ data from Kenya's national census to determine the ethnic configurations of each district. For the census, recipients are asked to identify their own ethnicity out of the full list of ethnicities provided in the questionnaire. Therefore, the census not only provides a direct measure of geographic ethnic distribution, but also captures people's self-identification of their ethnicity rather than a potentially biased external evaluation. Secondly, we estimate the correlation between the level of economic development and its possible determinants, including ethnic diversity, at the subnational level (i.e. cross-district). Therefore, we avoid complications associated with cross-national studies, including the availability of comparable and reliable measures of ethnic distributions in different countries. Thirdly, we work with cross-section analyses, rather than time series. In other words, we compare levels of economic development spatially while controlling for time, which allows us to avoid statistical problems arising from the variation of ethnic identity and its construction over time.

Following a brief introduction to the characteristics of economic geography in Africa and the implications of ethnic bias on intra-country trade, we present the basic structure of our empirical model outlined above. The basic structure is the same as a conventional cross-national regression of economic development (see Alesina and La Ferrara 2005 for a comprehensive review), except that we conduct this regression at the sub-national (i.e. district) level. The dependent variable is the level of economic development of a district. We run two different models, one measuring development as per capita income and the other as the poverty head count within a district. The independent variables include levels of ethnic diversity – as measured by both fractionalisation or polarisation indices – and the conventional variables of infrastructure and human capital. We postulate that whether ethnic diversity is good or bad for an economy is an empirical question because it can go either way, depending on the balance of offsetting forces. It does not even depend on whether it is a rich or poor country, at least at the sub-national level. Our hypothesis is that ethnic diversity is associated with higher levels of economic development at the sub-national level.

We then include the neighbouring districts' economic indicators as explanatory variables (i.e. spillover effects) on the level of economic development of an individual district. Next, we extend this standard spatial autoregressive model by introducing the possible impact of ethnic similarity or dissimilarity of the neighbouring districts as additional spillover effects. Our hypothesis of this ethnicity-augmented spatial autoregressive model is that the more ethnically similar the neighbouring districts, *ceteris paribus*, the higher the spillover effects.

A brief summary of main findings and a short discussion of future directions of study conclude the chapter. The main points are as follows: firstly, the current consensus in the development literature – that ethnic diversity can explain poor economic outcomes – may need revision, as our regression results suggest that ethnic diversification – but not polarisation – may in fact help to raise economic development. Secondly, ethnically isolated areas exhibit poorer outcomes, which suggests that lack of trust may contribute to constraining regional (intra-country) trade, hence lowering economic growth. Measures to reduce such 'ethnic distance' or 'territorial confinement' could therefore improve economic outcomes. An extension of this paper could help guide in formulating relevant policy interventions.

Background

Africa's economic development has been affected by unfavourable economic geography (Venables 2010). On the environmental side, endowments of high-quality agricultural land with adequate rainfall are scarce. There is a high propensity of disease, both in humans and animals. In terms of the global economy, Africa's geographic location is also problematic. In addition to being a long distance from the world's main economic centres, many countries are land-locked. Sub-Saharan Africa as a whole has virtually no navigable rivers and few natural harbours, reducing its ability to trade with the rest of the world.

Collier and Venables (2010) and Venables (2010) point out that Africa's economic growth is also hampered by its fragmentation into more than fifty small nations. Because economies of scale are therefore lacking, the costs of public good provision are high and supplies of private goods are often monopolised. Moreover, these impediments to private and public economies are mutually reinforcing. Based on an empirical assessment of the degree of international market integration of Sub-Saharan African countries, Bosker and Garretsen (2008) predict that improving intra-regional market access would have a considerable positive effect on economic growth.

Moreover, market integration within each country remains low, which presents three important implications for efficiency and growth of national economies. Firstly, gains from trade based on the comparative advantages of each sub-national region will be diminished. Secondly, factor endowments, especially fixed endowments such as arable land, are unevenly distributed among regions. The consequent lack of factor mobility decreases growth prospects in those areas with fewer resources, while simultaneously diminishing returns in areas that have relatively more resources (Venables 2010). Thirdly, an economy with high inter-regional trade costs and low factor mobility is prone to geographical dispersion of population and production (Fujita *et al.* 1999). Consequently, cities and individual production units are smaller than optimal size. Insufficient agglomeration is related to lower levels of the division of labour, knowledge spillover and higher costs of shared inputs (e.g. intermediate goods and services and local infrastructure) – all leading to lower productivity.

The presence of ethnic bias is another potential roadblock to economic growth, as often identified by the political economy literature on Africa. For example, Bates (2000) observes that because public institutions are weak in Africa, people seek a better life through capitalising on private relationships, such as remittances from family members who have migrated to urban areas, or through learning skills from each other. If families organise their economic relations across generations and locations, then their ethnicity may shape particular codes of conduct that can reduce inter-ethnic interactions. Fafchamps (2004) explains that ethnic bias persists in a self-sustaining way because of *statistical discrimination* and *network effect*. The former suggests that individuals belonging to different groups might be treated differently even if they share identical observable characteristics in every other respect because of the high cost of gathering and evaluating information.[1]

---

[1] Jellal and Zenou (2005) presented a theoretical model suggesting that discrimination in the labour market might occur along ethnic lines in developing countries where people are ethnically diverse and production is highly volatile. Employers tend to hire workers of a similar ethnic background. Therefore, employees from different ethnic groups bear the risk of production volatility whereas those from a similar ethnic background to the employer earn a stable income.

The latter refers to the characteristic of market transactions in Africa, which often involve many intermediaries in sequential steps linked by a chain of trust-based personal acquaintances. However, it must be noted that ethnic diversity *per se* is not a source of inefficiency because heterogeneity (in technology, taste, etc.) forms the basis for trade as predicted by international trade theory. But when ethnic diversity and ethnic bias are combined, inefficiency can occur because the market is thus fragmented into small homogeneous markets.

It is also noteworthy that, specifically in the context of Kenya, ethnic groups have a 'blockier' geographic distribution by which ethnic identities correspond reasonably well with geographic placement (Shipton, Chapter 7). Oucho (2002: 42) points out that 'the present day provinces are largely a repeat of those created in 1924, apparently a deliberate attempt by the departing colonial administration to institutionalise tribalism or ethnocentrism in independent Kenya'. Separation along ethnic lines for historical reasons has been sustained through low labour mobility attributable to weak agglomeration economies, as described above.[2] As a result, ethnic heterogeneity at a national level co-exists with high degree of homogeneity at the local level (Ranis 2009). Therefore, we might observe high transaction costs in inter-regional domestic trade both in terms of physical infrastructure and ethnic divisions.

Basic model

We first set up a model without spatial auto-correlation. The estimated regression equation is shown as:

$$Y_i = \alpha_0 + \alpha_1 X_i + \alpha_2 D_i + e_i \qquad (1)$$

where the dependent variable Y is the level of economic development in a particular district indexed by i. Included in the independent variable set X are endowment of infrastructure, human capital and ethnic diversity. The error term is assumed to be i.i.d.

The model is operationalised in two ways. We run two separate regressions: one with the poverty headcount ratio (the proportion of

---

[2] Miguel and Gugerty (2005) suggest that relocation cost is high in rural Kenya because of thin local land markets and difficulty in obtaining approval from relatives to sell clan land.

the population under the poverty line) as Y_i and the other with log of per capita income. The two variables will present different implications when we consider the spatial auto-correlation of Y_i. Poverty may be contagious across the space because of some latent common local profiles such as agro-climatic and health–sanitary conditions. Income spillovers are expected to involve more human exchange such as trade and job searches. We expect that ethnic bias, if it exists, will be more relevant in income spillovers.

A few comments on the data will be clarifying. At the time of the study, results of the 2009 census were unavailable: the most recent comprehensive primary data source was the 1999 census, from which we obtained the district-level poverty headcount ratio. Data related to average regional income should have been obtained elsewhere because they are lacking in the census data. Fortunately, we were able to rely on the United Nations Development Programme (UNDP) estimate of per capita gross regional domestic product at the district level (UNDP 2006). We used the figure for 2005, which was the most recent.

As a measure of the endowment of infrastructure, we used access to main trunk roads. This is a dummy variable by which we assigned one to districts lying on international trunk ('class A') roads. The information derives from the geographic information system database compiled by the World Resource Institute.[3] Because the provision of trunk roads has not increased substantially since the mid-1980s in Kenya, we can consider that information related to trunk-road access is invariant over time (see Washike 2001: Table 6). Therefore, this variable is used in both poverty and income regressions. As common sense might reveal, we expect that access to roads can reduce poverty (therefore, a negative sign is assumed for the estimated coefficient) and that it has a positive impact on income.

The human capital endowment is represented by the population share having no formal basic education or the adult illiteracy ratio. For the poverty regression, we use the education data obtained from the 1999 population census; for the income regression we use the adult illiteracy rate in 2005. Different data are used merely for the sake of coherence with the dependent variable by deploying data from the same year and the same data source. Because we expect that better

---

[3] *Major roads in Kenya*, available from www.wri.org/publication/content/9291# basedata.

human capital reduces poverty and increases income, the predicted sign of the population share having no formal basic education on the poverty headcount ratio is positive and that of the adult illiteracy ratio on income level is negative.

We use two measures of ethnic diversity: ethnic fractionalisation and ethnic polarisation. As done in many studies (for example, Alesina and La Ferrara *et al.* 2005), the fractionalisation index was computed as one minus the Herfindahl index of the ethnic shares obtained from the Kenya Population Census 1989, which is the last year for which information on ethnicity of the population is publicly available. Using the same data, a polarisation index was calculated using the formula proposed by Montalvo and Reynal-Querol (2005). The two indices address the question of ethnic diversity in different contexts. Fractionalisation increases as the population is encapsulated in many small groups while polarisation intensifies when the population is split into a few (typically two) large groups. Alesina and La Ferrara (2005) point out that polarisation explains better the outbreak of conflicts such as a civil war, while fractionalisation serves better as an explanatory variable for poorer economic performance. It should be noted that the two indices should have been calculated with the 1989 population census data for the reason that the ethnicity data were not published from the 1999 census results because they were classified as politically sensitive information. This is unsatisfactory because ethnic compositions at the sub-national level can change more substantially than at the national level because of migration.[4] We assume that the ethnic diversity in each district as of 1989 includes information about what has affected the evolution of poverty and income thereafter. We adopted no preconceived notion related to the overall impact of ethnic diversity on poverty and income because it could be either positive or negative depending on the balance of offsetting forces. Ethnic diversity may be detrimental for an economy if it is linked to bias along ethnic lines for the lack of trust, or to eventual violent conflicts (Easterly and Levin 1997). Alternatively, we could argue that ethnic diversity would enhance productivity through the combination of strong points of each group, exchanging goods, job opportunities and ideas. Although previous studies (Alesina and La Ferrara 2005) have found that the ills

---

[4] However, in this way we were able to avoid the problem of possible endogeneity between economic results and ethnic diversity.

Table 6.1. *Summary statistics*

Variable	Mean	Std. Dev.	Min	Max
Poverty	0.5411905	0.1218208	0.2171581 (Kiambu)	0.808475 (Kuria)
Income	6.528851	0.7000979	5.135798 (Wajir)	8.303505 (Nairobi)
No education	0.6348116	0.1370097	0.2862105 (Nairobi)	0.9429141 (Mandera)
Adult illiteracy	0.3375797	0.1520748	0.111 (Mombasa)	0.826 (Marsabit)
Fractionalisation	0.3430435	0.2493434	0.03494 (Nyamira)	0.86518 (Mombasa)
Polarisation	0.4429359	0.2324567	0.0684938 (Gucha)	0.839626 (Busia)

of ethnic diversity outweigh its virtues, particularly in poor countries, we will find that this may not be the case at the local level.

Our data show that, among the top ten districts in terms of the poverty headcount ratio, seven are from Nyanza province, while all of the bottom ten are from either Central or Rift Valley provinces (see Table 6A.1 and Figure 6A.1 in the Appendix). In order to control for this concentration, we introduce regional dummy D referring to Nyanza, Rift Valley and Nairobi and Central to capture the level differences. We expect that the dummy assigned to Nyanza is associated positively with poverty, while the opposite is expected to be the case for Rift Valley and Nairobi and Central.

Table 6.1 presents some summary statistics. Variable definitions are listed in Appendix 6.1. The poverty headcount ratio is the lowest in Kiambu district (Central province), adjacent to the northern border of Nairobi. Kuria district (Nyanza province) had the highest intensity of poverty. Income level measured by the per capita gross domestic product (GDP) is the highest in Nairobi and the lowest in Wajir district (Northeastern province). Bordering Somalia and Ethiopia, Wajir district occupies about one-tenth of the Kenyan territory but 75 per cent of its land is semi-arid. The proportion of the population which had not completed formal education was the highest in Mandera (Northeastern province); the adult illiteracy rate was the highest in

Marsabit (Northeastern province). Mombasa is the most ethnically diverse district in Kenya. This makes sense due to its history as the major port city in Eastern Africa. In Nyamira district (Nyanza province), ethnic fractionalisation is the lowest. Ethnic polarisation was the lowest in Gucha district (Nyanza province) where Kisii people comprise 98 per cent of the population, but in Busia (Nyanza province), the district with the highest polarisation index, 90 per cent of the population was divided into two groups (Luhya 61 per cent and Teso 29 per cent).

Estimated results obtained using equation (1) are presented in Table 6.2. We set the poverty headcount ratio as the dependent variable in the first two columns. In the right-most two columns, we chose per capita GDP as the dependent variable. As expected, access to trunk roads is associated with a lower incidence of poverty although it did not work well to explain income level. A lack of formal basic education and adult illiteracy is associated with higher levels of poverty and lower income. Regional dummies reflect that poverty is more severe in Nyanza province and less in Central and Rift Valley provinces. Districts in Central province and Nairobi have significantly higher per capita income compared to others.

Our first major finding is that higher ethnic diversity as measured by the fractionalisation index has a negative association with the intensity of poverty and a positive relation to income levels.[5] In other words, after controlling for physical and human capital, higher levels of ethnic fractionalisation are related with better economic outcomes at the district level. This contradicts results from cross-national studies that followed Easterly and Levine (1997), which found correlations between higher ethnic diversity and bad economic performance. Later, Alesina and La Ferrara (2005) elaborated that there are costs and benefits of ethnic diversity: while benefits may facilitate growth in richer countries, the costs may lead to worse economic outcomes in poorer countries. Yet our finding suggests that even in a poor country such as Kenya, ethnic diversity may be beneficial for an economy at the local level. It is plausible that the higher levels of ethnic diversity in particular

[5] The polarisation index did not show a statistically significant effect here. Alesina and La Ferrara (2005) already pointed out that the polarisation index is a poorer indicator of economic outcome than the fractionalisation index. We also followed their study and did not include the two ethnicity variables together because high correlation can be expected between them.

Table 6.2. *Regression results with regional dummies*

	Poverty	Poverty	Income	Income
Road	−0.040154**	−0.0354573**	−0.0338705	−0.07589
	(0.0161025)	(0.0149134)	(0.1714399)	(0.1720885)
No education	0.2344886***	0.2394624***		
	(0.055839)	(0.0485739)		
Adult illiteracy			−1.22584*	−1.140387**
			(0.65434)	(0.5582955)
Fractionalisation		−0.0927405***		0.8152888**
		(0.032022)		(0.3860441)
Polarisation	−0.054102		0.4190911	
	(0.0412469)		(0.3717827)	
Nyanza	0.0948081**	0.0844276***	−0.0723709	0.0258334
	(0.029431)	(0.0294909)	(0.1925601)	(0.1814985)
Rift Valley	−0.0939295***	−0.0976902***	0.0072516	0.0252957
	(0.0181776)	(0.0169064)	(0.2207658)	(0.2161774)
Central	−0.2260062***	−0.2383974***		
	(0.0262816)	(0.0258739)		
Nairobi_Central			0.507424*	0.5954395***
			(0.2847261)	(0.2247545)
Constant	0.4699371***	0.4760187***	6.728047***	6.59691***
	(0.0479139)	(0.0428439)	(0.3338173)	(0.2753026)
R-squared	0.7332	0.7541	0.1708	0.2282
Prob. > F	0	0	0.0103	0.0002
Observation	69	69	69	69

* 10 per cent; ** 5 per cent; *** 1 per cent. Robust standard errors are shown in parentheses.

areas capture geographic endowments such as good agro-climatic conditions. Thus, these areas historically attracted in-migration of various ethnic groups. Alternatively, it may suggest that ethnic diversity promoted division of labour and knowledge sharing that contributed to enhance productivity and reduce poverty. This might be the case for urban areas such as Nairobi and Mombasa.

Spillover from adjacent districts

Next, we include the economies from adjacent districts as potential spillover effects on levels of poverty and income. The regression equation we estimate has the following form:

$$Y_i = \alpha_0 + \alpha_1 X_i + \rho W_i Y_i + e_i \qquad (2)$$

In this equation, W_i is the adjacency weight consisting of w_{ij}/n_i where we assign $w_{ij} = 1$ if districts i and j share the border and 0 otherwise; n_i denotes the number of districts that share a border with district i.[6] Equation (2) is called the *spatial autoregressive model* or *spatial lag model*. It assumes that situations of poverty and income level of district i (i.e. Y_i) are not only determined by its own local conditions (X_i) but also affected by the income level of neighbouring districts. This has two implications. Firstly, if spatial autocorrelation is expected, then an OLS regression that does not include this measure can yield a serial correlation in the error term. Second, the estimated parameter ρ represents the inter-district spillover effect. If ρ has a statistically significant coefficient, then we can interpret that this significance suggests the existence of interactions across space (i.e. spillover effects). Table 6.3 reports estimated results.

Estimated results of variables *road, no education, adult illiteracy, fractionalisation* and *polarisation* barely change from those presented in equation (1). The effect on income of access to a trunk road is still not statistically significant and has an unexpected sign in the last column. Focusing on estimates of parameter ρ of equation (2), we found a positive spatial autocorrelation for the district-level poverty headcount ratio (i.e. poverty spillover), although the spatial autocorrelation of per capita district GDP was not statistically significant. Hence,

---

[6] We do not include regional dummies that appear in equation (1) because correlation can be expected with the spatial lag term $W_i Y_i$.

Table 6.3. *Regression results with spatial correlation*

	Poverty	Poverty	Income	Income
Road	−0.0458996 **	−0.0409929 **	0.0118628	−0.0231559
	(0.0192405)	(0.0183548)	(0.1637239)	(0.1563547)
No education	0.167372 **	0.1798538 **		
	(0.0836058)	(0.0827373)		
Adult illiteracy			−1.540431 ***	−1.52936 ***
			(0.5801538)	(0.4984949)
Fractionalisation	−0.0595084	−0.0884833 **		0.7536241 **
	(0.0371971)	(0.0393338)		(0.3587953)
Polarisation			0.2789139	
			(0.3020793)	
W*poverty	0.9586826 ***	0.9658064 ***		
	(0.1403531)	(0.1299536)		
W*income			0.1777369	0.2890305
			(0.2745791)	(0.2589353)
Constant	−0.0238925	−0.0343925	5.771954 ***	4.935014 ***
	(0.0735505)	(0.0746591)	(1.855182)	(1.749749)
R-squared	0.5725	0.5912	0.1305	0.1901
Prob. > F	0	0	0.0609	0.0047
Observation	69	69	69	69

*10 per cent; **5 per cent; *** 1 per cent. Robust standard errors are shown in parentheses.

after controlling for conditions of physical and human capital and the degree of ethnic diversity, a district exhibits higher intensity of poverty if it is adjacent to poor neighbouring districts. However, a systematic relationship is *not* observed for the income level. Here, the lack of a clear indication of inter-district income spillovers is worth noting. Such spillovers, also known as the trickle-down process in the literature of development economics, presume backward-linkages and forward-linkages in inter-district economies. Thus, the lack of income spillover may imply a lack of economic interaction among inhabitants of the districts. If this is the case, we may further ask whether any ethnic bias could be involved in lower levels of inter-district linkages. This issue will be addressed next.

Impact of ethnicity

Now we introduce ethnicity by modifying the spatial autoregressive model of equation (2) to the following form:

$$Y_i = \alpha_0 + \alpha_1 X_i + \theta E_i W_i Y_i + e_i \tag{3}$$

where E_i is an ethnic weight matrix with i-th row elements consisting of e_{ij}/e_i where e_{ij} represents population size in district j belonging to the dominant ethnic group in district i, and where e_i is the total population of district i's dominant ethnic group in all its adjacent districts. For example, supposing that district i's dominant group is Kikuyu and it is adjacent to districts j, k and l, the total Kikuyu population in the three districts is 100,000 distributed as 25,000, 35,000 and 40,000 respectively in j, k and l. In this case we have 0.25, 0.35 and 0.40 in column j, k and l and zeros in others of the i-th row. The ethnic weight matrix differentiates the impact of spillovers from adjacent districts depending on the number of people sharing the same ethnicity. Therefore, $E_i W_i Y_i$ might be designated as the *ethnicity-augmented* spatial lag term. We will assign zero in $E_i W_i$ even for adjacent districts if no one of the same ethnicity lives there. Therefore, while ρ in the previous section identifies the effect of physical closeness, θ captures spatial spillovers occurring among *ethnically similar* adjacent districts.

Table 6.4 presents the estimated results. Basic characteristics remain almost unchanged, except that the effect of ethnic fractionalisation on poverty becomes statistically not significant. More importantly,

Table 6.4. *Regression results with ethnicity-weighted spatial correlation*

	Poverty	Poverty	Income	Income
Road	−0.043895 **	−0.042358 **	−0.016126	−0.039841
	(0.0204129)	(0.0195607)	(0.157504)	(0.1500607)
No education	0.1874827 **	0.1990724 **		
	(0.0829944)	(0.0866672)		
Adult illiteracy			−1.428324 ***	−1.465143 ***
			(0.5187375)	(0.4698105)
Fractionalisation	−0.010317			0.6030055
	(0.039874)			(0.3393688)
Polarisation		−0.032579	0.1961421	
		(0.0412908)	(0.2852494)	
E*W* pov_ratio	0.6861334 ***	0.6777612 ***		
	(0.1064225)	(0.1057059)		
E*W* pc_income			0.4395456 ***	0.4222738 ***
			(0.1560752)	(0.159973)
Constant	0.0908942	0.0936748	4.089088 ***	4.106704 ***
	(0.0703801)	(0.0700019)	(1.064078)	(1.075231)
R-squared	0.5419	0.5457	0.2172	0.2585
Prob. > F	0	0	0.0015	0.0005
Observation	69	69	69	69

*** 1 per cent, ** 5 per cent, * 10 per cent. Robust standard errors are shown in parentheses.

we found statistically significant positive coefficients of the ethnicity-augmented spatial lag term for both poverty and income. The case of income spillover is of particular interest. Although we did not find a spatial correlation in equation (2), Table 6.4 shows that the income spillover is statistically significant between ethnically similar adjacent districts. We can infer that the ambiguous result related to income spillovers in Table 6.3 results from the influence of mixed effects, with significant interactions between ethnically similar districts mitigated by the low levels of interactions (hence less spillover) between ethnically dissimilar districts. It should be noted also that the magnitude of the estimated coefficient θ is greater than ρ. Hence, we can conclude that ethnic similarity serves a role in making spatial income spillovers to become more relevant and stronger.

We can extend the following conjecture from this result. Interactions through market transactions and extra-market interaction (such as knowledge exchange and technological spillovers) will be mutually beneficial for all participants. In the case of the Kenyan regional economy, income spillovers were found only between ethnically similar adjacent districts. Overall, such effects are not statistically significant. Therefore, we cannot blame a lack of infrastructure for reduced economic outcomes, but we must conclude that some sort of ethnic bias additionally impedes interactions among geographically divided ethnic groups.

We found poverty spillovers in both the general setting (Table 6.3) and in an ethnically similar situation (Table 6.4), which suggests that ethnic similarity has no role in the context of poverty spillovers. This in turn suggests that poverty can be attributed to omitted variables that commonly affect adjacent districts but which do not affect economic interactions among people in those districts. For example, prevalence of diseases, climate (temperature, rainfall) and soil quality may all play roles in determining levels of poverty. Inclusion of these independent variables might have invalidated the spatial correlation of poverty we identified.

Summary and conclusions

In this paper, we examined the impact of ethnic diversity on levels of poverty and income through identification of spatial spillovers. Using district-level data of Kenya, we found that income spillovers depend on ethnic similarity. Assuming that spillovers result from economic interactions between people in neighbouring districts, this suggests that interactions are more likely to occur among people of the same ethnic group. This result implies that the question of inter-regional transaction costs should not focus narrowly on problems of transportation infrastructure: costs are also related to ethnic divisions. If transactions are confined along ethnic lines due to ethnic bias, then it would not be sufficient to promote internal market integration through improving physical infrastructure; policies for reducing ethnic bias and facilitating inter-ethnic economic interactions are also necessary. Alternatively, if we are to take ethnic bias as given, then policies that facilitate interactions among similar ethnic groups located in different districts would create greater scale economies and would enhance growth (Shipton, Chapter 7).

A question has been raised of whether the observed spatial spillover reflects geographic or economic similarity of adjacent districts rather than ethnic similarity. To answer this question, it may be noted that any impact of geographic or economic similarities is captured in the second stage of our regression analyses, where the standard model of spatial correlation is applied. Ethnic diversity is introduced in the third stage as an additional explanatory variable by modifying the standard model, specifically to capture the impact of ethnic similarity or dissimilarity. The result we report above relates to the spatial spillover coefficient attached to ethnic diversity variable in this third stage.

This chapter also presents a challenge to the conventional wisdom that relates high levels of ethnic diversity to poor economic outcomes. Studies supporting that conventional wisdom have often relied on cross-national data. However, our sub-national study design revealed that even in a poor country such as Kenya, ethnic diversity is associated with better economic outcomes at the local level. However, this does not necessarily contradict the conventional view of ethnic diversity as impeding economic growth. When ethnic diversity and ethnic bias are combined, inefficiency increases because the market is fragmented into small homogeneous markets, gains from trade among different groups are lacking and technical progress through exchanging different types of knowledge will be undermined. Thus, even though ethnic diversity seems to play a positive role at the local level, it may be detrimental to the economy at the national level. For more precise policy recommendations, it is indispensable to study the *microfoundation* of ethnic bias through rigorous empirical strategies. One promising direction is the formation of trust-based divisions, as have already been studied by Fafchamps (2004). Researchers can also examine which institutional frameworks promote trust among heterogeneous agents.

Appendix 6.1

Variable definitions

Poverty:	headcount ratio under the poverty line reported in *1999 Census of Population and Housing*, Kenya National Bureau of Statistics.
Income:	natural logarithm of GDP per capita in 2005 reported by the UNDP (2006: Appendix i).
Road:	dummy representing districts lying on international trunk ('class A') roads.
No education:	ratio of persons 15 years and older who have not completed primary education, calculated from microdata of the *1999 Census of Population and Housing*, Kenya National Bureau of Statistics, obtained from IPUMS-I (Minnesota Population Center, 2010).
Adult illiteracy:	1 minus the adult literacy ratio of 2005, as estimated by UNDP (2006: Appendix i).
Fractionalisation:	measure of ethnic diversity calculated using the formula of $1 - \sum_i s_{ij}$ by Taylor and Hudson (1972), where s_{ij} stands for the share of *i*th ethnic group (tribe) in district *j*. Data of ethnic composition at the district level were obtained from the *Kenya Population Census 1989*, Central Bureau of Statistics.
Polarisation:	measure of ethnic polarisation using the formula $4\sum_{i=1}^{N} \sum_{i \neq j} (s_i)^2 s_j$ introduced by Montalvo and Reynal-Querol (2005).
Nyanza, Rift Valley and *Central*:	regional dummies representing districts belonging to respective provinces. *Nairobi_Central* includes Nairobi.

Table 6A.1. *Districts ranked by poverty headcount ratio and by the log of GDP per capita*

Rank	District	Province	Poverty headcount ratio	Rank	District	Province	GDP per capita
1	Kuria	Nyanza	0.808	1	Nairobi	Nairobi	8.304
2	Homa Bay	Nyanza	0.723	2	Mombasa	Coast	8.255
3	Bondo	Nyanza	0.719	3	Kericho	Rift Valley	7.955
4	Rachuonyo	Nyanza	0.717	4	Moyale	East	7.853
5	Kilifi	Coast	0.713	5	Tharaka	East	7.570
6	Kitui	East	0.710	6	Malindi	Coast	7.507
7	Busia	West	0.683	7	Mtelgon	West	7.502
8	Nyamira	Nyanza	0.682	8	Koibatek	Rift Valley	7.228
9	Suba	Nyanza	0.669	9	Kisumu	Nyanza	7.191
10	Kisumu	Nyanza	0.663	10	Trans Mara	Rift Valley	7.151
11	Wajir	North-east	0.657	11	Kiambu	Central	7.108
12	Siaya	Nyanza	0.656	12	Nyeri	Central	7.101
13	Mandera	North-east	0.647	13	Thika	Central	7.093
14	Maltndi	Coast	0.641	14	Muranga	Central	7.084
15	Lugari	West	0.637	15	Mbeere	East	7.054
16	Kwale	Coast	0.636	16	Keiyo	Rift Valley	6.974
17	Mbeeke	East	0.634	17	Lamu	Coast	6.963
18	Tharaka	East	0.631	18	Nakuru	Rift Valley	6.947
19	Kakamega	West	0.630	19	Lugari	West	6.912
20	Central Kisii	Kyanza	0.630	20	Meru South	East	6.907
21	Gucha	Kyanza	0.624	21	Marakwet	Rift Valley	6.900
22	Makueni	East	0.624	22	Kuria	Nyanza	6.894
23	Mwingi	East	0.624	23	Isiolo	East	6.886
24	Butere/ Mumias	West	0.622	24	Suba	Nyanza	6.877
25	Moyale	East	0.620	25	Maragua	Central	6.865
26	Nyando	Nyanza	0.619	26	Embu	East	6.746
27	Garissa	Northeast	0.618	27	Marsabit	East	6.724
28	Machakos	East	0.596	28	Taita Taveta	Coast	6.655
29	Vihiga	West	0.592	29	Kirinyaga	Central	6.653
30	Taita Taveta	Rift Valley	0.589	30	Nyandarua	Central	6.629
31	Taita Taveta	Coast	0.588	31	Teso	West	6.612
32	Meru South	East	0.583	32	Narok	Rift Valley	6.558
33	Taita Taveta	Rift Valley	0.583	33	Baringo	Rift Valley	6.548
34	Embu	East	0.554	34	Bomet	Rift Valley	6.532
35	Mt. Elgon	West	0.550	35	Nyando	Nyanza	6.521

Table 6A.1 (*cont.*)

Rank	District	Province	Poverty headcount ratio	Rank	District	Province	GDP per capita
36	Lamu	Coast	0.522	36	Bondo	Nyando	6.504
37	Bomet	Rift Valley	0.521	37	Central Kisii	Nyanza	6.497
38	Narok	Rift Valley	0.519	38	Kilifi	Coast	6.455
39	West Pokot	Rift Valley	0.519	39	Laikipia	Rift Valley	6.455
40	Meru North	East	0.519	40	Kakamega	West	6.402
41	Buret	Rift Valley	0.503	41	Nandi	Rift Valley	6.377
42	Teso	West	0.503	42	Buret	Rift Valley	6.356
43	Marsabit	East	0.498	43	Uasin Gishu	Rift Valley	6.308
44	Uasin Gishu	Rift Valley	0.493	44	Homa Bay	Nyanza	6.292
45	Nandi	Rift Valley	0.490	45	Trans Nzoia	Rift Valley	6.223
46	Isiolo	East	0.484	46	Vihiga	West	6.217
47	Koibatek	Rift Valley	0.484	47	Rachuonyo	Nyanza	6.213
48	Transnzoia	Rift Valley	0.484	48	Busia	West	6.205
49	Samburu	Rift Valley	0.475	49	Meru Central	L East	6.196
50	Migoki	Nyanza	0.468	50	Gucha	Nyanza	6.194
51	Kericho	Rift Valley	0.468	51	Mwingi	East	6.186
52	Baringo	Rift Valley	0.459	52	Samburu	Rift Valley	6.105
53	Tana River	Coast	0.448	53	Kwale	Coast	6.098
54	Kajlado	Rift Valley	0.444	54	Migori	Nyanza	6.084
55	Mombasa	Coast	0.444	55	Nyamira	Nyanza	6.031
56	Nairobi	Nairobi	0.439	56	Bungoma	West	5.961
57	Laieipia	Rift Valley	0.437	57	Siaya	Nyanza	5.930
58	Meru Central	East	0.437	58	Tana River	Coast	5.829
59	Bungoma	West	0.418	59	Meru North	East	5.805
60	Marakwet	Rift Valley	0.415	60	Kitui	East	5.743
61	Keiyo	Rift Valley	0.391	61	Butere/ Mumias	Aswest	5.700
62	Nakuru	Rift Valley	0.367	62	West pokot	Rift Valley	5.666
63	Thka	Central	0.360	63	Makueni	East	5.505
64	Kirinyaga	Central	0.357	64	Kajiado	Rift Valley	5.429
65	Maragua	Central	0.346	65	Machakos	East	5.403
66	Nyandarua	Central	0.345	66	Mandera	Northeast	5.333
67	Nyeri	Central	0.302	67	Garissa	Northeast	5.252
68	Muranga	Central	0.292	68	Turkana	Rift Valley	5.142
69	Kiambu	Central	0.217	69	Wajik	Northeast	5.136

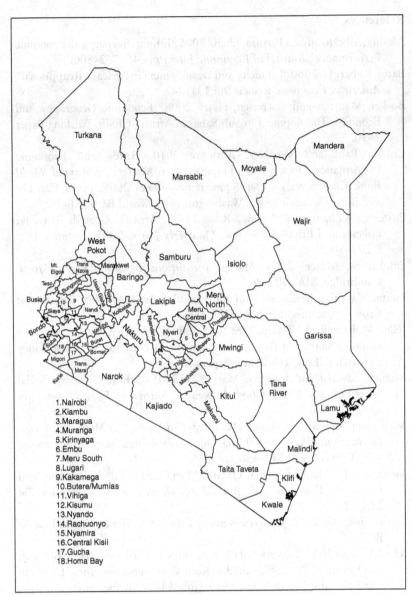

1.Nairobi
2.Kiambu
3.Maragua
4.Muranga
5.Kirinyaga
6.Embu
7.Meru South
8.Lugari
9.Kakamega
10.Butere/Mumias
11.Vihiga
12.Kisumu
13.Nyando
14.Rachuonyo
15.Nyamira
16.Central Kisii
17.Gucha
18.Homa Bay

Figure 6A.1 Kenya district map (1999)

References

Alesina, Alberto and La Ferrara, Eliana 2005. 'Ethnic Diversity and Economic Performance', *Journal of Economic Literature* 43: 762–800.

Bates, Robert H. 2000. 'Ethnicity and Development in Africa: a Reappraisal', *American Economic Review* 90: 131–34.

Bosker, Maarten and Garretsen, Harry 2008. 'Economic Geography and Economic Development in Sub-Saharan Africa', CESifo Working Paper 2490.

Collier, Paul and Venables, Anthony 2010. 'Trade and Economic Performance: Does Africa's Fragmentation Matter?' in *Annual World Bank Conference on Development Economics 2009*, Justin Yifu Lin and Boris Pleskovic (eds.). Washington, DC: World Bank, 51–76.

Easterly, William and Levine, Ross 1997. 'Africa's Growth Tragedy: Policies and Ethnic Divisions', *Quarterly Journal of Economics* 112: 1,203–50.

Fafchamps, Marcel 2004. *Market Institutions in Sub-Saharan Africa.* Cambridge, MA: MIT Press.

Fujita, Masahisa, Krugman, Paul and Venables, Anthony 1999. *The Spatial Economy*, Cambridge, MA: MIT Press.

Jellal, Mohamed and Zenou, Yves 2005. 'Ethnic Diversity, Market Structure and Risk Sharing in Developing Countries', Centre for Economic Policy Research (CEPR) Discussion Papers 5366.

Miguel, Edward and Gugerty, Mary Kay 2005. 'Ethnic Diversity, Social Sanctions, and Public Goods in Kenya', *Journal of Public Economics* 89: 2,325–68.

Minnesota Population Center 2010. *Integrated Public Use Microdata Series, International: Version 6.0* [machine-readable database]. Minneapolis, MN: University of Minnesota.

Montalvo, José G. and Reynal-Querol, Marta 2005. 'Ethnic Diversity and Economic Development', *Journal of Development Economics* 76: 293–323.

Oucho, John O. 2002. *Undercurrents of Ethnic Conflict in Kenya*, Leiden: Brill.

Ranis, Gustav 2009. 'Diversity of Communities and Economic Development: an Overview', Paper Presented at Kobe Conference on Ethnic Diversity and Economic Instability in Africa (July 13–14), Kobe University.

Taylor, Charles Lewis and Hudson, Michael C. 1972. *The World Handbook of Political and Social Indicators* (2nd Edn). New Haven, CT: Yale University Press.

UNDP 2006. *Kenya National Human Development Report 2006.* Nairobi, UNDP.

Venables, Anthony 2010. 'Economic Geography and African Development', *Papers in Regional Science* 89: 469–83.

Washike, Wilson. S. K. 2001. 'Road Infrastructure Policies in Kenya: Historical Trends, and Current Challenges', Kenya Institute for Public Policy Research and Analysis (KIPRA) Working Paper No. 1.

PART III

Relationships between ethnicity and stability

7 | Belonging, exclusion and ethnic competition

PARKER SHIPTON

Introduction

New and renewed discussion about the supposed sovereignty of nations, and about the naturalness or artificiality of their borders, raises related issues of human well-being. This chapter offers a contribution towards understanding the effects of constraints to movement on the economic lives of people whose movement is impeded, and the further effects on perceptions of ethnicity and on inter-ethnic relations within nations.[1]

In the Introduction (Ranis), Chapter 2 (Brown and Langer) and elsewhere in this book, it is supposed that ethnic diversity and ethnic discord contribute to economic instability and uncertainty. Here I wish to draw attention to something more like the reverse. This is to suggest that economic instability and uncertainty may contribute to the kinds of schism and conflict often expressed and construed in ethnic terms, and to identify movement restriction as one of the factors contributing to both economic uncertainty and ethnic disharmony in the first place. The central observations put forth here are relatively simple; the questions to which they lead on distant causes are more complex. My comments thus add to those of Lonsdale (Chapter 1), Berman (Chapter 5)

I thank the organisers of the Kobe University and Japan International Cooperation Agency (JICA) Conference on Ethnic Diversity and Economic Instability in Africa, and the editors of this volume, for their kind invitation to participate. Thanks go to Jean Ensminger, Hiroyuki Hino, Juro Teranishi and an anonymous reviewer for their insightful comments on drafts, and to Katherine Snyder for help with the diagram presented as Figure 7A.1.

[1] For recent collections of writings on the problem of blocked and constrained human movement between nations (and continents), and for a variety of opinions on what ought to be done about it, see Pécaud and de Guchteneire, 2007; and Smith 2011. Ferguson (2006) reflects broadly on African people's feelings of marginalisation from international opportunities, including chances of intercontinental migration.

and others in cautioning against any simplistic rules linking ethnicity and economy. The chapter is offered in the spirit of a reflection on accumulated impressions, not as proof. But since its observations arise from extended stays in several rural and urban settings south of the Sahara – and from locally expressed sentiments by people of all ages, both sexes and varied classes and statuses known personally in their home areas – they are in a sense empirically based.

Central to our concerns is a reality of territorial confinement in Africa within a perceived boundary of an ethnic community, a national territory, or the continent as a whole. People in Africa are acutely aware of being excluded from richer or better favoured countries, inside or outside Africa, and from opportunities that freer movement of people across borders might offer. The problem comes partly from restrictive immigration policies of richer countries (or countries with rich or specially privileged enclaves), atop challenges variously geographic, economic and political that beset people in Africa's interior especially. Population pressure on arable lands, denial of access to paying work, and territorial confinement and exclusion all aggravate economic uncertainty and general frustration. This hardens inward-looking ethnic allegiance and outward prejudice, which in turn intensify territorial confinement, perpetuating a cycle that magnifies economic uncertainty and intensifies ethnic discord. Development aid that pre-supposes that goods and money, but not people, should move freely between richer and poorer countries has reinforced this vicious cycle.

Ethnicity's facets and fluidity: 'race', language and culture

The term 'ethnic', with its extensions such as 'ethnicity', can mean many things and have many dimensions. In its various usages in English, it can refer to considerations racial, linguistic and more broadly cultural (foodways, dress, law, religion, etc.). In some usages it can refer instead to a kind of community or 'tribe' constituted by political loyalty or control instead or in addition. The entities of these sorts that humans perceive do not always coincide. In many parts of the world, including much of Africa, they coincide even less neatly than they do in, say, Denmark or Japan. (Even in these, old stereotypes of homogeneity conceal significant ethnic or national minorities, for instance Turks in Denmark or Koreans in Japan.)

Ethnicity, whether it refers to race, language, or culture, is not simply innate or immutable, nor is it entirely made up (that is, individually or 'socially constructed' or construed) or able to be fully manipulated by just anyone. Humans have different powers to name and categorise each other, and to impose their categories on others. Humans draw and redraw ethnic lines partly on the basis of what they deem timeless, and partly on the basis of circumstantial and transient conditions. These lines, and the categories we divide, are cultural products themselves, communicated by language, by other action and by graphic and other means – for instance, by dress codes, by mapping, or by the issuance of identity cards designating ethnic categories or putative home territories.

The fairest and safest human categorising takes account of people's self-expressed identities, whether racial, linguistic or cultural. This need not mean that a Saami Finn can become undeniably Han Chinese, or vice versa, merely by thinking or calling herself so. It merely means that no third person or party should be given the final word in deciding whether a person is a Saami Finn, or Han Chinese, or Navajo American. Even genetic testing, at present, can provide very little information about who we 'really' are for any constructive social, cultural, or political purposes.[2] And the possibilities and temptations for its misuse (as in modern-day counterparts to mid-twentieth century-eugenics) are legion. Hence there is marked unwillingness of many people, inside and outside Africa, to be categorised officially at all.

'Race' itself is a much-debated concept. Many anthropologists have lately considered it useless for analytical purposes, except as 'folk taxonomy', that is, as a cultural fabrication in itself, communicable as an idea but existing only in the eye of the beholder. In other informed views, race retains some residual scientific and medical utility, for instance as a way to discuss loosely the clustering of genotypic and

---

[2] One of the main reasons why genetic testing can as yet tell little about our individual ancestral origins is that it can identify origins of only *direct* lineal ascendants in the matriline or the patriline. Thus, while it can tell us something about the ancestry of one's mother's mother, or one's father's father, it cannot provide information about one's mother's father, or father's mother – let alone about one's father's father's mother's mother, or mother's mother's father's father. The farther back we go in time, the smaller is the fraction of our ancestors in any chosen generation about whom we can learn anything. Even then, we still learn only about straight lines of descent and not whole 'sides' of family trees.

phenotypic traits (for example, hair texture, skin tone and suscep-
tibility to sickle-cell anaemia), which might help in guiding clinical
practitioners to know whom to test or pre-emptively treat for what.
Scientifically grounded or not, racial stereotypes are resilient and keep
recurring, in public if not so often in scholarly or official communication. While anthropologists and other highly schooled communicators
no longer speak of culture as being transmitted 'in the blood', bones,
or other body parts or secretions, many other people in Africa, as in
China or North America, persist in doing so.

A few basics now on Africa, for any reader unfamiliar with ethnol-
ogy or with the anthropology of the continent.

Ethnicity in Africa

There was never a time in Africa without genetic, linguistic, or cultural variation between humans; and Africa is arguably the world's
most diverse continent on all these counts. In this sense, it would be
incorrect to say that all ethnicity in Africa, or all tribalism, is merely
a European colonial contrivance. Europeans sometimes fomented and
exploited it – including by creating new names for ethnic groups and
aggregations where they chose, designating 'martial races', printing
ethnic affiliations (tribes) on personal identity cards and so on. But
Europeans in Africa never had the power or interest to create linguistic
diversity such as one finds south of the Sahara.

In most of Africa, 'tribe' is *not* coterminous with country. Ethnic
differences –as locally perceived, that is – do not coincide neatly
with national territories. Most of Africa's national boundaries have
remained pretty constant since the 1884–5 Berlin Convention, when
nearly all were drawn with straight edges on maps, or else traced along
the curving courses of rivers.[3] By and large, neither the straight lines nor
the riverine squiggles tended to correspond with pre-existing or subsequent ethnic divisions, whether these be defined racially, linguistically

---

[3] While the boundaries of colonies, protectorates and later nations in Africa
have remained relatively stable since the mid-twentieth century and before,
the boundary of Eritrea, independent from Ethiopia since 1993, is a notable
exception. So too, for a brief time in the 1970s, was the shifted boundary
between Uganda and Tanzania during the Amin rule and southward invasion
of Bukoba, the home area of the Haya ethnic group. South Sudan officially
became independent from Sudan on 9 July 2011.

or culturally. Only a few African nation-states as currently recognised by the United Nations could claim anything like ethnic homogeneity in either a linguistic or a broader cultural sense (candidates might include Lesotho, Swaziland, Libya, or the otherwise sharply divided Somalia), and even these cases are debatable. Most are much more mixed.

Conversely, many are the conventionally recognised ethnic groups (or 'communities', as lately known) in Africa that overlap national borders. Examples are Luo, Kuria and Maasai, divided between Kenya and Tanzania; or Wolof, Manding, Fulbe (Fulani, Peuls) and Diola (Jola), between Senegal and the Gambia (and Guinea too); or Hutu, Tutsi and Twa now spread between Rwanda, Burundi and the Democratic Republic of the Congo. Some ethnic groups, notably Fulbe, have representatives in many nations, in this case with substantial fractions of populations in nations spanning all the way from Cameroon and the Congos in the south-east to northern Senegal in the north-west.

Some parts of Africa have much 'blockier' distributions of ethnic groups than others do. Kenya, Zimbabwe and Nigeria, for instance, are among the blockier ones. In these, self-proclaimed ethnic identity tends to correspond more clearly with geographic placement (say, between Shona and Ndebele in Zimbabwe, or between Luo, Gikuyu and Kamba in Kenya). By contrast, The Gambia is one of the ones more thoroughly mixed around. Here one tends to see more radically different ethnic composition even moving from village to village or from neighbourhood to neighbourhood within a village. In fact, however, even in the 'blockier' countries such as Kenya, one can find evidence of ethnic inter-mixture in many or even most localities, and inter-stitial zones of recent rural resettlement where the mixtures are rich and complex.

Some African 'ethnic groups' are made up of amalgamations of others. Examples include the Ako in Sene-Gambia, descending from persons enslaved and exported from Africa and more recently from others returned to it. And some groups presently perceived as ethnic blocks are made up of congeries of diverse smaller groups, including ones lumped together by outsiders or insiders for political convenience. Examples of such 'umbrella groupings' include Luhya (or Luyia) or Kalenjin in Kenya, Diola (or Jola) in the Casamance region in southern Senegal and Igbo (or Ibo) in Nigeria. Ethnic groups sometimes change names as they combine, recombine and sub-divide. That ethnic groups are redefinable over time, though, by no means implies that just anyone can become anything at will and be recognised as such.

While Africa's remarkable ethnic and linguistic diversity has led many outsiders to think of it as a continent of 'tribalist' allegiances and of endemic internecine warfare, it is less often remarked how many *peaceful* ties, how many *harmonious* arrangements and accommodations between ethnic groups, must have long occurred and endured over such a continent. Some of these take forms familiar to outsiders, including international faith communities (Islamic, Christian, other) that provide inter-ethnic stitching no less than inter-religious strife. Affinal (that is, marital) and quasi-kin ties between ethnic groups, particularly in cities (godparenthood, for instance, more celebrated in Latin America but not unknown in Africa), have received less attention than they deserve, even from anthropologists who specialise on kinship. Other sorts of arrangements and accommodations between groups or their members seem exotic or primordial to some observers – for instance, blood pacts, less often noted in recent decades than only a century ago – but have served valuable functions of easing travel, visitation and trade, and of keeping peace. Still other forms that must occur all over the continent from day to day, and that might take very local (sometimes ritualised) forms, are all but unknown abroad. They simply have been too seldom noticed or studied.[4]

One point here is crucial. *Ethnic differences (whether defined racially, linguistically or culturally) do not in themselves lead to inter-group*

---

[4] Geschiere (2009) warns against simplistic, naturalising interpretations of autochthony and belonging. Concentrating especially on Cameroonian and Dutch settings, he reminds us that soil does not speak for itself about who belongs on it or doesn't. Along other lines, Allen (1996) and Thomson (2006) describe many and varied examples of efforts made at local scale to innovate means of keeping peace across ethnic lines, in regions otherwise known for 'ethnic' strife. Lentz (2006), in her historical ethnography of a northern Ghanaian setting, shows how difficult autochthony and belonging can be to define. She shows how multiple, cross-cutting loyalties (for instance, to earth shrine territories, colonially introduced chiefdoms, and post-colonial electoral constituencies) can together mitigate tension and conflict over autochthony and belonging. But the weave can tear. Ethnographic studies vividly conveying the feel of violent inter-ethnic and class-related upheaval include those of Besteman (1999) and Little (2003) on Somalia, and Taylor (1999) and Pottier (2002) on Rwanda. Malkki (1995) treats Burundians in exile in Tanzania and their complex sentiments about belonging. Shack and Skinner (1979) and contributors discuss roles of recent and longer-established 'strangers' continent-wide.

conflict. They become the focus of inter-group strife only when and where other factors are involved, be these economic, political or psychological. The number of ethnic groups represented in a nation may have some bearing upon the nature of inter-ethnic relations within, but it would be hard to defend a clear rule (as a linear mathematical function, say) about such correspondence. It sometimes seems as though the nations with just a couple or few predominant ethnic groups, and a much larger number of much smaller ones, have proved the most politically unstable as far as national governments and regimes are concerned (Nigeria, for instance, with its 'big three' – Hausa, Igbo and Yòrubá – and its large number of coups and contrecoups d'état). But that is about as far as one can generalise.

A second point is subtler but no less crucial. *The criss-crossing of multiple allegiances (or seen another way, of multiple lines of social division) may ironically help hold a society (or society as a whole) together.*[5] Particularly noteworthy in eastern African contexts are age grades and age sets that cut across the bounds of ethnic groups.[6] But age, gender, class, caste, political party, trade guild or union membership, sport team allegiance and all sorts of other principles can operate together the same way, seemingly at crossed purposes but actually weaving society together by criss-crossing each other. Trade relations can help tie together ethnic groups (and with no one's attempt at supervision) – at least until they foster class divisions that destabilise ethnic relations too. Helping it happen are European languages, highly

[5] This idea of social cohesion through criss-crossing divisions has been familiar to social and cultural anthropologists since Lewis Henry Morgan, in 1851, reconstructed and interpreted the principles of the Iroquois Confederacy. As he noted, traditional territorial groups (to him, 'nations') and clans (or what he called 'tribes') were arranged such that each territorial group contained members of all the clans, and each clan was represented in each territory. In this system, as he noted, none of the territorial groups could fight another territorial group without straining relations within a clan, or vice versa. In an African context, Max Gluckman (1956) made use of much the same ironic idea of cross-stitching holding society together.

[6] Contributors to the Kurimoto and Simonse collection (1998) devote much attention to age and generation grading among potentially conflicting ethnic groups among north-eastern African herding people. Along other lines, the basic principle of plural allegiances in a kind of weave is also one used strategically for centuries, by European royal families for instance, who have long cemented alliances between ethno-linguistic communities, nations or even empires by arranged marriages of their young. So it works in many parts of Africa too, and not just among royals or nobles.

creolised African languages, including especially Swahili in eastern and central Africa, and lesser known pidgins concocted more locally as linguae francae for inter-ethnic relations. Trade appears here – provided it is carried out on fair terms – as one more dimension of inter-group affinity.[7]

From the foregoing, a negative corollary ensues. *When too many lines of division closely coincide, politics within a nation can become extremely unstable.* An example was Sudan for the several decades preceding the 2011 declaration of South Sudan's independence. Here some of the major divisions of race (as locally perceived – lighter skins, for instance, in the north and darker ones in the south), language (between Arabic in the north and more local languages in the south) and religion (between Muslims in the north and Christians and adherents to local faiths and religious traditions in the south) all coincided along roughly the same geographic line. These came with further distinctions of dress, foodways, modes of transport (horse versus foot travel) etc. Of course, the picture of political relations between northern and southern Sudan and its fraught, violent history can be made far more complex than this. But here as elsewhere, competition for land (and in this case, oil in it too) has seldom been irrelevant as a contributing cause for violence.

Linguistic homogeneity can help impart understanding and co-operation (as it has often done in Tanzania since independence), but it does not necessarily provide enduring stitching for a nation (as the Rwandan case shows well). 'Linguistic imperialism' in the name of national solidarity can cause resentment, too, where it threatens local language, traditional knowledge and wisdom and communicative custom.

Ethnic relations are mutable over time and space. Ethnic groups that seem to get along well at some times can compete and conflict at others. A now classic example of this, again, is the relations between Hutu and Tutsi in much of Rwanda, who spoke a common language and lived often amicably as neighbours or kin over many periods before 1994, when, soon after a presidential plane crash, large parts

---

[7] Claude Lévi-Strauss' early work on what he called the 'elementary structures of kinship' (1971 [1947]) famously hypothesised exogamy (marriage outside a group) and the exchange of women between kin groups to be not just the foundation of trade but of civilisation more generally. Few but anthropologists (and indeed few of them), though, actually read this densely written, sometimes technical opus.

of the country divided internally into both warring classes and soon ethnic groups. Some of those enmities seem to have been locally overcome since that several-month national (and international) bloodbath; others have not. Nor have the conflicts remained confined to that country's borders; eastern Congo and parts of other neighbouring countries have been deeply affected by population movements back and forth.

Ethnic discrimination and enmity come and go. Most of what journalists and other commentators have sometimes called 'ancient tribal rivalries' in Africa turn out not so ancient, enduring or general. Animosity between two groups often depends in part on the absence of common threats from third parties. Nor do political coalitions or alliances between leaders, some fickle as the wind, always indicate shared public sentiments of solidarity (which in many cases change much more slowly). In Kenya, for instance, Luo and Gikuyu politicians found themselves at odds in the late Kenyatta and early Moi regimes (up to 2002), then often and increasingly allied against the Tugen Kalenjin Moi regime, which lasted from 1978 to 2002, but bitterly at loggerheads again in 2008 after a contested election at the end of 2007, and until a coalition government could be formed by compromise. In South Sudan, Nuer (or Naath) and Dinka, whose kindred languages and whose cultures are similar in many respects, have sometimes found themselves to be allies against northern 'Arab' encroachments and aggressions, but at other times bitter antagonists themselves, each side with its own internal regional–political divisions. These things are relative, that is, like team sports in leagues; but in this case not even the relativities make a rule.

If, as is clear by now, ethnic differences do not in themselves bring about inter-group conflict, then the roots of conflicts described in ethnic terms must be sought in broader configurations of factors. But some of these are always more salient, usual or influential than others.

Roots of conflicts

Much of Africa's contemporary violence south of the Sahara, including violence that goes unreported abroad, takes place over contested lands, including farming, grazing and fishing lands, and over mineral resources concealed in and extracted from land. That competition over land is among the most usual and important root causes of fighting does not mean, though, that it is always explicitly mentioned or indicated by contestants. Many indirect routes of causation – and rationalisation – can entangle with it and overlay it, for instance when disagreement or violence is sparked by cases of perceived animal raiding, by homicide, or by electoral dispute.

Tension and sporadic fighting between farmers and herders constitute a pattern long familiar across in Africa, most notably in the Sahel, but not only there. People who mainly farm in one place, and other people more mobile who mainly herd, tend to clash over what the one need as fields and the other as grazing routes.[8] Conflicts of this sort are exacerbated when climate changes force herders and herds to verge into what farmers deem their turf, or compel farmers to block what herders deem as their accustomed access routes for seasonal or other migration. Frequently, tensions and violent confrontations between people relying on different mixes in their modes of livelihood – 'farmers' who herd or trade (like some resettled Gikuyu), 'herders' who farm (like many Fulani in West Africa or lately Maasai in East), or 'fishers' who have no more fish and have had to turn to farming, herding, or trade (like some Luo in East Africa or perhaps Serer in West) – express themselves in news media as confrontations between members of different ethnic groups. So to outsiders these conflagrations can seem like mere 'tribal warfare'. But inter-ethnic schisms and alliances shift quickly, and conflict over access to land or water remains no less at root.

Strife with land competition and related economic anxiety at root does *not* always appear first where land is most densely settled, or where poverty is direst. In Kenya, for instance, recent rural clashes pitched members of several ethnic groups at loggerheads, but they did so mainly in officially resettled zones, notably ones in the Rift Valley – places where land holdings and farms have tended to be rather larger than in many of the crowded earlier 'home' areas of contestants (for instance, in the hilly centres of Nandi or Gikuyu countries in western and central Kenya, respectively). Land claims still remained very much at issue, though, in places where members perceived as belonging to

---

[8] Farmer–herder disputes over land are a familiar pattern from the American West (forming indeed the stuff of some of the classic Western films, for instance 'Shane'), but they are an African pattern no less. See Moritz (2006) and other contributions to the same collection for numerous African examples.

more than one group had moved back and forth onto it over decades or generations of successive resettlement.

If land losses from territorial confinement and displacement are one main root cause of violence, joblessness is another. Joblessness among the schooled is particularly dangerous because it involves disappointed expectations. Frustrated young men, educated but unable to earn the means for marriage (whether this means cash, cows, or cloth in a system of marriage payments such as covers much of the African continent in its varied forms), are a volatile force. The pattern of youth combatants and vigilantes in gangs (sometimes including girls and young women) has occurred in many places in recent decades. Some of the more noteworthy cases have been in Sierra Leone, Liberia, Rwanda, Burundi, northern Uganda and eastern and northeastern Democratic Republic of the Congo.

Politicians and other government officials can and do foment ethnic conflict, sometimes for deliberate, identifiable purposes.[9] They do so particularly in times when their power is threatened by uncertain flows of funds used for patronage – conditions occasioned in turn by the intermittent stopping and starting of international 'aid'. Rulers and senior state officials whose aid funds are shut off unpredictably, but whose supporters and constituents have become accustomed to being rewarded with siphoned aid funds, may sometimes feel desperate enough to reward them instead with chunks of land taken from politically peripheral rural people they find ways to force off, or from public forests or game reserves, or other parks. Well-intentioned aid 'conditionality' may thus have perverse effects if inconsistently applied.

Other roots of ethnic strife, as yet poorly understood, are symbolic and psycho-sexual. Some of the violence has taken sexual forms or involved sexual liaisons, both within militia camps or relief camps, where members of one generation frequently take advantage of those of another, or in attacked settlements, where rape has been common.[10]

---

[9] Africa Watch (1993) reports an investigation of a Kenyan outbreak of 'state-sponsored' ethnic violence, not the first or last in that country. See also Lonsdale (1977), Maxon (1989), Okoth-Ogendo (1991), Oucho (2002) and Ogot (this volume, Chapter 3) for some historical background on ethnic group and boundary formation in western Kenya. On ways ethnic group formation has been manipulated in southern Africa, see Vail (1989).

[10] See, for instance, the sobering reports of Honwana (2005) and of Mazurana *et al.* (2005) (both comparing nations and their recent histories), and of Sverker Finnström (2008 – for northern Uganda specifically) on the often

Such news is easily sensationalised, but credible stories (for instance, from eastern Congo in the early 2000s) are too frequent to discount. Sexual violence occurs in conflicts that are also class, ethnic or religious violence (as in southern Sudan in the late nineteenth and early twentieth centuries). Often one of these three masquerades as another, but Africa's most sobering and intractable 'civil' conflicts seldom have just one such dimension.

Territorial confinement: countries as cages, and continents too

Racial, cultural and linguistic prejudices contribute to border controls and other blockages of human movement, between nations or between other polities territorially defined. Border controls and territorial confinement contribute to economic hardship and uncertainty, not least by raising competition for land. Economic uncertainty, disappointed expectations and competition – for land, jobs, marriage partners or political offices – sharpen racial, cultural and linguistic prejudices and animosities.

In Africa south of the Sahara, territorial confinement has come about in more than one way. In colonial times, and in some countries still, it has been effected with devices such as identity cards bearing racial or ethnic identifiers – the markers of categorical as well as territorial boxing-in. Currently they also take the form of border controls and immigration blockages, not just within but also outside the continent. African-born people who have lately been allowed to destroy their old identity or 'pass' cards in one country or another are now stymied by the near impossibility of obtaining passports, visas, green cards and the like for themselves or their junior kin or neighbours, to travel overseas. The reasons and motives behind these blockages, in turn, are complex and partly obscure, but racial prejudice is surely among them. Fear and prejudice, once institutionalised as laws and immigration rules,

strikingly high frequency of rape, including rape of young girls and sometimes of boys, in and around militia camps and relief or concentration camps. These last two have been practically the same thing, in northern Uganda – and in some other African settings too – in the late twentieth and early twenty-first centuries. This truth is still not widely known or understood outside. Whether rape and other sexual assault are reproductively adaptive for perpetrators, or to see it another way perhaps for their genes, remains scantly studied, but such function would hardly make such acts any less disturbing.

may become easier to ignore; but ignoring them does not make them go away, or relieve the hardships endured by people pent up.

One effect of this bottling up of human beings – within nations, within a continent – is ethnic divisiveness within smaller territories, and the direction of animosities towards closer, more identifiable targets. Local and regional conflicts contribute to economic instability and uncertainty. Territorial confinement contributes to population pressure on land, and to competition for it, as climate change further reduces land available for farming and grazing. Many and probably most wars or armed skirmishes, in the present just as in ancient times, are fought with land claims and belonging deeply at issue. But frustration erupts at whatever target is around, as lightning finds a lightning rod. This is likely to be not the person or category different by nature, but the one that has come to look or feel so under the circumstances. Resulting increased animosities and loss of trust further entrench ethnic prejudice.

Aid, trade and mobility

Strategies proposed for reducing economic hardship in the parts of the world deemed poor have tended to focus on aid and trade. Let us take them briefly in turn, and then in comparison with other measures that might eventually supplement or replace them. This will enable us to ask whether aid and trade in commodities and currencies are really longer-term, comprehensive solutions to large-scale human problems in Africa, or just partial ingredients, expedients or palliatives.

From the mid-twentieth century to the time of writing, a common presumption in the bigger aid agencies has been that a way to assist people deemed poor was to transfer good things (money, seeds, knowledge, etc.) from the better-off to the worse-off countries, usually conceived as nations, by *sending* them there. This presumption, in turn, rests on three others. One is that things are not good enough there. A second is that outsiders know what is needed to make these things better. The third is that the intended 'beneficiaries' cannot, will not, or should not travel overseas to find good things on their own. None of these is a sound general principle.

The story of international aid in the past half-century has been a story of disappointed hopes and often frustratingly perverse consequences, though one with occasional instances of genuine improvement in livelihoods and of lives, and with many mixed outcomes and unknowns remaining. This chapter comes at the end of one extended study of such systems and processes and their outcomes.[11] Over decades of studying the kinds of initiatives ostensibly meant as aid for development, I have been compelled to the conclusion that sending in money, materials, or human agents from afar is usually not a satisfactory answer for alleviating longer-term hardships of people in rural areas, or of people who move between town and country.

The presumption that aid to Africa is something to send in, not to arise in place or be brought in by people from there already, has allowed people in the sending countries to conceive of themselves as the main active agents in the process. It has also allowed them control over what gets sent – and often when, where and how. The problems of linguistic and cultural barriers, presumptuous planning and asymmetric control have refused to go away, even in periods of much lip service to participation, partnership and co-operation – all standard, approved vocabulary in aid agencies for decades.

Some writers with economic interest who have acknowledged the shortcomings of development aid have proposed strategies such as 'trade, not aid', variously intended to allow more play to market actors and forces: to supply and demand, to price and pricing policy and to the incentive of presumed self-interest.[12] The strategy of opening borders to trade, they suggest, offers promise of more symmetrical relations to replace more purely patronising ones, but also need involve

[11] The observations briefly alluded to here about entrustment, obligation and aid (or what is supposed as aid) are spelled out in more detail in Shipton (2007, 2009 and 2010) and in earlier publications cited there. These three related volumes concentrate on western Kenya but reach more broadly into African and other parts of the agrarian tropics. Among the processes investigated are state-organised land titling programmes ostensibly meant to facilitate borrowing and lending, as well as public, private and self-help loans conceived and framed as aid, for people variously gaining their livelihood in various combinations of farming, herding and fishing. The results of these initiatives, I show, have been generally disappointing for most concerned. Aspects of them, for instance where mortgaging is concerned, seriously threaten rural populations.

[12] The slogan 'trade, not aid' can be traced back at least as far as John Henry Williams' Stamp Memorial Lecture at Harvard (1954), which carried the ambitious subtitle 'A Program for World Stability'. It was adopted by the United Nations Conference on Trade and Development (UNCTAD) in 1968 and has been promoted often since then in publicity from multinational corporations and from pro-market policy think-tanks such as the Cato Institute.

less presumption on the part of donors or lenders about what might constitute 'aid' or 'development' in the first place.

Nothing inherent in commodity or currency trade, alas, guarantees fairness or any general solution to poverty, powerlessness, or other hardship. Uneven control over supplies and over terms of trade – qualities, quantities, allowable forms of compensation and prices – has a way of conferring advantages to categories of persons already privileged. It can advantage lenders over borrowers, manufacturers over growers, urbanites over rural dwellers, richer over poorer, male over female, schooled over unschooled, able-bodied over handicapped and so on. A half-century of theorists from varied schools of thought have sought to portray inequities and subtle processes by which persons or categories in positions of relative privilege can press advantages, and political and economic disparities can self-exacerbate, in market systems ostensibly open to supply and demand, to willing buyers and willing sellers.[13] Some of the critiques have been more convincing than others. But it is harder to argue against voices raised across the continent in rumour, story and song, or in graffiti or shop pillaging in times of open rebellion, or in spirit mediumship or funeral speeches, or in the street demonstrations lately so common around the times and places of aid agency and trade association summit meetings, or in the 'factual fiction' committed to stage plays or movies, or written stories destined to last longer. The discontents expressed in these together cast doubt on commodity trade in particular, on distant centres of commerce and on 'the market' more generally and abstractly, as any realistic general solution to problems of living in the lesser-privileged parts of Africa's interior.[14]

More basically, thinking about development aid *or* trade as a panacea has allowed the people of the sending and lending countries to avoid having to confront a deep and, to some, a frightening question,

[13] For one of the more comprehensive collections of theories on the social dimensions of development, trade and 'globalisation', drawn from not only anthropology but also from sociology, history, human geography, political science and economics, see Edelman and Haugerud (2005). For an Africa-specific collection on social and cultural dimensions of political economy, see Grinker *et al.* (2010).

[14] Isichei (2002) offers one of the more convenient distillations of a wide assortment of imaginative popular representations – oral no less than written – of economic systems perceived as exploitative, from around Africa south of the Sahara.

one that can open questions of racial, ethnic or religious prejudice. Why should people born in the less advantaged parts of the world *need* to stay there? What makes for the fixation on birthplace (not conception place), or the fetish about parental papers, that seem, by common consent or acquiescence, to govern so much of the life course and to hedge about life's chances and opportunities?[15] It is puzzling why the assumption should persist that anyone born in a country or continent ought to remain there for life, resting content with resources available there – an assumption that continues to deadbolt the doors that keep them there. Thinking outside that box, and finding ways to free more people to move in and out of their countries and continents – as officers of donor and lender agencies have long been free to do themselves – might allow more to find good things and ideas abroad (money, ideas, experience, trade goods, etc.) for themselves and their own, and to bring or send them back as they choose. Until people in Africa are as free to come and go as the people who purport to help them and plan for them – free politically, economically, legally – there will remain something hypocritical about aid and trade.

Movements between countries, regions or continents can take permanent or circulatory forms. Inhabitants of the richer countries, or richer pockets within them, seem often to fear both. Some fear immigrants will bring disease, squalor, incomprehensible languages and blood they deem impure. Others fear they will crowd locals out of jobs, food or land, or send away or take away money from local economies. Yet others fear the contamination of cherished political principles such as democracy, or the immigration of potential new terrorists. The immigrants they fear most are usually those they know least. It is easy to neglect the fact that countries such as the US and Canada have been built precisely on immigration, and on an inclusive and flexible concept of belonging. It is easy to neglect, too, that to the best of current genetic knowledge, the ancestors of all humans originally came from Africa.

---

[15] Indirect migration routes, following paths of acquaintances gone ahead, can be a sign of steep barriers and high risks that international migrants face. For a powerful memoir of the chutes-and-ladders game of trying to travel by any possible means, legal and otherwise, from Africa to Europe, and being sent back or partway back at intervals, see Bay Mademba's book, published in Italian as *Il Mio Viaggio di Speranza* (2006); compare Mostefa Djadjam's 2002 Algerian–French film *Borders* (Frontières). Michael Lambert's book *Longing for Exile* (2002) documents the strategies and sentiments of Diola and other Casamançais traveling to Dakar and beyond.

Belonging and sovereignty

The crux of the issue is the concept of belonging. Who belongs where, and who gets to decide it? Who is it who will presume to tell farming people in Cameroon, or herders-turned-urbanites in Mogadishu, or fishers who trade and tailor in the Niger Delta – that there are *so* many countries to which they should not even try to go? Anglophones like to answer such questions with verbiage about the sanctity of borders or the sovereignty of nations.[16] Borders may be well barricaded, but rationales about sovereignty are thin and brittle. Who is ultimately doing the blocking, and with what justification, is seldom entirely clear.

Nor does formal authority pose the only constraint to long-distance travel. Poverty, poor health and plain fear keep many put. Some just about anywhere simply enjoy their homes, or at least enjoy enough fit, routine or serenity in the order they know. Others feel duty to remain near kith or kin. Human sentiments, like human predicaments, are complex. No single answer will fit all.

But one part of an answer is clear enough. Nation-states, or rather persons acting in their name, prevent human movement. Some bottle people up within their borders by denying passports, or barricade them out by denying visas and work permits. Some regulate the kinds of water vessels, land vehicles or aircraft they can travel upon. Some impose immigration quotas, require literacy tests or insist on chest X-rays or strip searches. Some stipulate minimum amounts of cash one can bring or wealth one can hold before being permitted entry into a country, or require evidence of guarantors few will be lucky enough to secure. Some wave machine guns at stomachs around

---

[16] The concept of sovereignty is a product of only certain cultures, languages and intellectual traditions (and oft debated even there); to many African tongues it is hard to translate. Claims of nation-states and their regimes to sovereignty are historically rather recent over most of the African continent and not necessarily permanent. They often seem based no less on past or present coercion, early childhood training and indoctrination than on deliberate or explicit mutual consent of their members or member communities. That claims to exclusive sovereignty ought to be questioned need not imply, however, that the claiming entities serve no valued functions, or that their integrity and safety deserve no respect or protection from outsiders. James Scott (1999, 2009) offers some skeptical perspectives on the sovereignty of nation-states and their rulers, describing common strategies for avoiding and resisting them.

border roadblocks. Some harass immigrants they suspect have faked or hastily concocted marriages of convenience, conducting nosey interrogations that not all cultures would deem appropriate among virtual strangers. Or they send back people whose boats did not quite make it ashore before daybreak. Together, they block, persecute, incarcerate and expatriate.

Or they follow courses less active, but equally effective. They let phones ring indefinitely in consulate offices, or delay paper processing. They put up language barriers, and they authorise written testing that presumes experience with multiple-choice and no. 2 pencils. They frighten anyone who grew up in schools with no chalk, communities with no schools, or nothing like a community. They take bribes, atop fees, for issuing passports or stamping visas. Once all these obstacles to travel are taken into account, it becomes less surprising when, for instance, youth stowaways are found hiding under the planks of boats, or occasionally, pressed half-frozen in the landing gear of planes.

To suggest that things might be otherwise is not to suggest that wholesale population movements would be an answer to the world's problems, still less that such movements ought to be forced. It is simply to raise the suggestion that some persons in poverty, threatened by climate change, factory or mine layoffs or information suppression might be better off if they and their kith and kin were freer to come and go from their homes, and travel abroad – as those who have been their erstwhile aid donors and lenders have been free to do. This is in turn to raise the possibility that people may be able make better decisions on their own behalf, or on behalf of their kith and kin, than are made by agencies that may be oceans away, or by agents of these who deem themselves to be on aid missions. It is to raise a question of control, sovereignty and responsibility.

Nor should one naively assume that if national border blocks were erased, other kinds of blockages might not spring up in their stead. Persons acting on behalf of provinces, districts, chiefdoms or municipalities can, or could, put up keep-out signs just like persons acting for nations. Migrants are not always welcome where they move. Unwelcome takes not just legal or official forms, but subtle, unofficial ones too, such as job hiring discrimination, rental refusals and street gang hazing and mugging. Certainly adjustment problems can be daunting, for migrants, for their kin back home, and sometimes for migrants' host communities. Brain drains from poorer African countries to richer ones, and from within Africa to outside, are an untoward prospect already.

But people in rural tropical Africa seem less concerned about these eventualities than about being boxed in. A Luo small-scale farmer in Kanyamkago, western Kenya, seemed to speak for many others when I asked him how his many children would get by with their heritable landholdings so tiny. 'They'll manage,' he said in dead earnest; 'we'll send some of them to find work in America.' This is the way many there know, one they have helped design themselves, and one many certainly prefer to aid dependence. None of this suggests they wish to leave their homes for good. More than a few get stuck overseas who would rather come and go, but they fear the gate keepers in their host nation abroad will shut them out for good if they do.

Migration typically involves a quandary. The nicer parts of the world, however defined, are mostly settled already. People living there do not always wish to be joined by people not of their choosing. So people who migrate typically face a choice between places hard to live in materially and places hard to live in socially. The decision can be momentous for migrants or their descendants, yet it is usually taken at a distance, with limited information from contacts who have gone before, often kin. These people may have vested interest in luring familiars from the old country to the new, if only to make their own position there more secure.[17]

Migration always carries risk, however warm the welcome in the host community. Seasonal shuttling between places, as between dry-season and wet-season grazing land (to anthropologists, 'transhumance') leaves land that that is left to recover its growth as 'unused and unclaimed' (or, in a common French expression, *terre vacante et sans maître*), and therefore subject to encroachment, appropriation or seizure. Circulatory migration between town and country is easy to misunderstand as shiftiness or fecklessness when it may simply mean responsiveness to opportunity or a search for security. Moving from place to place to place, true nomadism, is anathema to officialdom

---

[17] Contributions to Allen's *In Search of Cool Ground* (1996), on north-eastern Africa, and to Ohta and Gebre's *Displacement Risks in Africa* (2005) present many vivid descriptions of complex decisions that migrants in Africa have confronted in recent decades about both moving away from civil disturbances (including inter-class and inter-ethnic violence) and moving back home in quieter times. They show that the latter is not always so easy a process either.

anywhere, as it can mean shelter from taxation, military conscription and other forms of one-sided control.

Terms for human movement carry subtle connotations. 'Migrant' and 'migration', in the island-rooted English tongue, can convey overtones of poverty, desperation, uncouthness, untrustworthiness, illegality, dirtiness or any mix of these. It can conjure fears of invasion, neighbourhood degradation, or disease. 'Refugee' adds implications such as desperation, passivity, helplessness or hopelessness – all indignities. The subtle stigmata can be hard to wear off. These are biases of sedentary peoples, a legacy of agricultural and industrial life. They imbue not just day-to-day interactions, for instance around relief camps, but also lasting laws.[18]

International law has progressed only partway to recognising a human right to movement. The United Nations Declaration of Human Rights in 1948 states, in Article 13–2, that 'everyone has the right to leave any country, including his own'. But no comparable declaration to date has recognised the reverse: the right of anyone to *enter* a country. '[W]hat value,' asks Catherine Wihtol de Wenden, 'has the right to leave without the corresponding right to enter? What does a right to travel mean without a right to settle?'[19] If caging people in denies a fundamental human right, then so, arguably, does caging them out. The only difference is the size of the cage.

Questions of belonging are questions of territoriality, and this is a topic where many mysteries remain. As of the time of writing, no one in the academy, be it in anthropology, psychology or political science, has a definitive answer to what makes humans territorial – what mix of biological, historical and cultural forces makes the hairs on our

---

[18] North Americans and South Africans who speak disparagingly of migration or flight sometimes forget how many of their own forebears were taking refuge from someone or something – economic, political or religious. Hence the common switch to more glamorous, active lingo like 'pioneer', or the Dutch and Afrikaans '*Vortrekker*' (trekker ahead).

[19] Catherine Wihtol de Wenden (2007: 61). She ties a 'right to mobility' to Immanuel Kant's universalist and individualist 'right to visit' in his 1795 essay, 'Perpetual Peace: a Philosophical Sketch'. Kant supposed such rights of visitation to be only temporary: 'A special beneficent agreement would be needed in order to give an outsider a right to become a fellow inhabitant for a certain length of time.' But Kant strongly promoted the principles of world citizenship and a shared human right to the planet. By this right, humans 'must finally tolerate the presence of each other. Originally, no one had more right than another to a particular part of the earth.' (1795: sec. 2, article 3, para. 1).

neck stand up when we feel someone is encroaching on whatever we deem our turf.[20]

Ethnic discord and economic instability

While possible causes of ethnic conflicts are many, the main point of this paper is to underscore interactions between territorial confinement, economic hardship and ethnic discord, not as a one-directional relation but rather a cyclical one. Some of the likely links in the chain of causation are shown in Figure 7A.1 in the Appendix.

Territorial confinement aggravates economic hardship as limited land is continuously over-cultivated and its productivity threatened.[21] Physical and psychological confinement inhibit trade with ethnically dissimilar communities, to the likely detriment of incomes if not also their distribution.[22] The combined effects of rising population pressure, hardening ecological conditions and ethnic isolationism are likely to further exacerbate economic instability and uncertainty. The barriers to movement that conceptual boundaries present, with all the

[20] Ethology, the study of animal behaviour, provides as yet only vague clues for explaining human territoriality, since not all mammalian species (or bird or fish species) are equally territorial: far from it. Moreover, new discoveries about variation in local animal cultures even within the same species (not least by sex and age) are emerging all the time. Indeed, we cannot confidently even call territoriality a human universal, though emerging brain science promises to shed more light on the question. These human–animal overlaps and gaps, topics of much debate and speculation, are among the ones lately being explored in *On the Human*, an online interdisciplinary forum of the National Humanities Center (http://onthehuman.org).

[21] Local population growth and demographic pressure on land may sometimes stimulate technological innovation (for instance, in terracing or irrigation, to make more intensive use of each unit of land) – but there is no guarantee that such innovation can keep up with economic needs under increasingly crowded conditions. Nor is there any guarantee that such innovations, from inside or out, will not bring their own forms of harm, as when, for instance, irrigation brings repressive water management bureaucracies, malaria-carrying mosquitoes, or salinisation that renders land barren. Other problems include division of labour skewed towards male advantage over female. These are all-too-familiar outcomes in riverine parts of rural Africa south of the Sahara where large-scale irrigation has been attempted. Influential work by Robert Chambers and by human geographers Michael Watts and Judith Carney has sketched out some of the many problems, often unanticipated, arising from such interventions.

[22] Hamaguchi (Chapter 6) discusses ethnic barriers to trade as potentially harming livelihoods.

bolstering myths and ethnic stereotypes that grow around them, may be no less restrictive than the high physical and emotional barriers that state officialdom presents with border blockages, armed patrols and visa hurdles. But these are not separate processes. The vicious cycle of territorial confinement, economic instability and ethnic isolationism continues.

A concluding caveat

Humans easily grow to overlook or neglect systemic dangers, or to blame them on more immediate, nameable or tangible causes they perceive – such as neighbours and any ethnic groups these are deemed to represent. The systems, structures and processes some humans create to increase their control over others may grow so habitual to these latter as not to be noticed for the presumptions on which they are founded. Bureaucratic and behavioural coercion can thus come to seem normal or natural. Confinement in territories is one such easily 'naturalised' process.[23] Its converse, eviction in compulsory programmes for resettlement (as occasioned for instance by construction of hydroelectric dams or establishment of plantation estates), also causes deep and lasting problems for the people needing to find or accept new homes. Both forced confinement and forced resettlement can cause problems more serious and diverse than it is easy to trace, label, describe or remember

---

[23] This way of thinking about habituation has become associated with Michel Foucault and Pierre Bourdieu in France, and also in a way with Anthony Giddens in England. But its intellectual pedigree in western Europe extends much earlier than the late twentieth century, when these three became so famous. Marcel Mauss, versed in Roman tradition and usage, wrote on 'habitus' decades before Bourdieu. Jeremy Bentham wrote about the prison (and the panopticon) as an instrument of control long before Foucault became famous for writing about both this and about subtler, more diffused mental control outside, as through language. David Hume, in writing 'Of the Original Contract' (to him, a mere fiction) in 1748 (1947), commented upon gradual habituation to a conquered condition, and about what we might today call mental denial as a common human response to subjugation. His contemporary, Jean-Jacques Rousseau, in his essay on human inequality (1967 [1762]), lamented that by his time so many people had become accustomed to nation-states (so many of which in Europe were then still new) and their laws and lawyers as not to question their authority – that is, the 'legitimacy' or moral grounding of law itself as an instrument by which some humans seek to control others.

at once – making it hard for those harmed to seek out or uproot their causes.

Finally, pluralism of allegiances, and the cross-stitching of social affiliations between different kinds of groups (or seen another way, the criss-crossing of social divisions) can be salutary. Having members of the same family, clan or age grade (for instance) on two sides of an ethnic boundary may function to temper ethnic prejudice or animosity within a nation. Between nations, marriages or even the twinning of towns or cities for cross-border civic visits or exchanges, or popular diplomacy, may foster peace and cohesion in ways that are hard to measure.

For now, for both researchers and policy makers, there are basics to get back to. Researchers still have the difficult tasks ahead of unearthing the roots of racism, ethnic prejudice and territorial emotion. Social planners and policy makers, for their part, be they established officials or aspiring radical reformers, have the task of figuring out how to bring down border blockages and visa barriers abroad. People of all interests and positions have the task of helping ensure mutual accommodation and tolerance where newly intensified human flows converge, where immigrants meet autochthons, and where erstwhile exiles return home. All have the task of helping prepare the time when more people from inside Africa become freer to come and go, and to move and live in whatever continent, country and community they choose. Until then, the old anonymous caveat remains as apt as ever: best to watch out where you're born.

Appendix 7.1

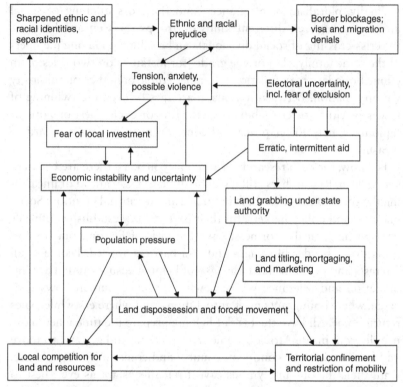

Figure 7A.1 Flow chart on interactions between territorial confinement, economic hardship and ethnic discord

References

Africa Watch 1993. *Divide and Rule: State-sponsored Ethnic Violence in Kenya*. New York: Human Rights Watch.

Allen, Tim (ed.) 1996. *In Search of Cool Ground: War, Flight and Homecoming in Northeast Africa*. Trenton, NJ and Asmara, Eritrea: Africa World Press.

Besteman, Catherine 1999. *Unraveling Somalia: Race, Violence, and the Legacy of Slavery*. Philadelphia, PA: University of Pennsylvania Press.

Djadjam, Mostefa (director) 2002. *Borders* (Frontières). Film.

Edelman, Marc and Haugerud, Angelique (eds.). 2005. *The Anthropology of Development and Globalization: from Classical Political Economy to Contemporary Neoliberalism*. Oxford, UK and Malden, MA: Wiley-Blackwell.

Ferguson, James 2006. *Global Shadows: Africa in the Neoliberal World Order*. Durham, NC: Duke University Press.

Finnström, Sverker 2008. *Living with Bad Surroundings: War, History, and Everyday Moments in Northern Uganda*. Durham, NC: Duke University Press.

Geschiere, Peter. 2009. *The Perils of Belonging: Autochthony, Citizenship, and Exclusion in Africa*. University of Chicago Press.

Gluckman, Max 1956. *Custom and Conflict in Africa*. Oxford: Basil Blackwell.

Grinker, Roy R., Lubkemann, Matthew and Steiner, Christopher (eds.). 2010. *Perspectives on Africa: a Reader in Culture, History, and Representation* (2nd edn). Oxford, UK and Malden, MA: Wiley-Blackwell.

Honwana, Alcinda 2005. *Child Soldiers in Africa*. Philadelphia, PA: University of Pennsylvania Press.

Hume, David 1947 [1748]. 'Of the Original Contract', in *Social Contract*, Ernest Barker (ed.). Oxford University Press, 145–66.

Isichei, Elizabeth 2002. *Voices of the Poor in Africa: Moral Economy and the Popular Imagination*. University of Rochester Press.

Kant, Immanuel 1795. 'Perpetual Peace: a Philosophical Sketch', last accessed 28 April 2011 at www.mtholyoke.edu/acad/intrel/kant/kant1.htm.

Kurimoto, Eisei and Simonse, Simon (eds.). 1998. *Conflict and Power in North East Africa: Age Systems in Transition*. Oxford, Nairobi, Kampala and Athens: James Currey, EAEP, Fountain Publishers and Ohio University Press.

Lambert, Michael 2002. *Longing for Exile: Migration and the Making of a Translocal Community in Senegal, West Africa*. Portsmouth, NH: Heinemann.

Lentz, Carola 2006. *Ethnicity and the Making of History in Northern Ghana*. Edinburgh University Press.

Lévi-Strauss, Claude 1971 [1947]. *The Elementary Structures of Kinship*. Boston: Beacon.

Little, Peter D. 2003. *Somalia: Economy Without State*. Bloomington: Indiana University Press.

Lonsdale, John 1977. 'When Did the Gusii (or any other group) become a "Tribe"?', *Kenya Historical Review* 5: 122–33.

Mademba, Bay 2006. *Il Mio Viaggio di Speranza: dal Senegal all Italia in Cerca di Fortuna*. Pontedera: Bandecchi e Vivaldi Editore.

Malkki, Liisa 1995. *Purity and Exile: Violence, Memory, and National Cosmology among Hutu Refugees in Tanzania*. University of Chicago Press.

Maxon, Robert. 1989. *Conflict and Accommodation in Western Kenya: the Gusii and the British, 1907–1963.* Cranbury, NJ: Associated University Presses.

Mazurana, Dyan E., Parpart, Jane L. and Raven-Roberts, Angela (eds.) 2005. *Gender, Conflict, and Peacekeeping.* Boulder, CO and Oxford: Rowman and Littlefield.

Morgan, Lewis Henry 1851. *League of the Ho-dé-no-sau-nee, or Iroquois.* Rochester, NY: Sage and Brother.

Moritz, Mark 2006. 'Introduction: Changing Contexts and Dynamics of Farmer–Herder Conflicts Across West Africa', *Canadian Journal of African Studies* 40 (1, special issue): 1–40.

Ohta, Itaru and Gebre, Yntiso D. (eds.) 2005. *Displacement Risks in Africa: Refugees, Resettlers and their Host Population.* Kyoto University Press.

Okoth-Ogendo, H.W.O. 1991. *Tenants of the Crown: Evolution of Agrarian Law and Institutions in Kenya.* Nairobi: African Centre for Technology Studies.

Oucho, John O. 2002. *Undercurrents of Ethnic Conflict in Kenya.* Leiden and Boston: E.J. Brill.

Pécaud, Antoine and de Guchteneire, Paul (eds.) 2007. *Migration without Borders: Essays on the Free Movement of People.* Paris and Oxford: UNESCO Publishing and Berghahn Books.

Pottier, Johan 2002. *Re-imagining Rwanda: Conflict, Survival and Disinformation in the Late Twentieth Century.* Cambridge University Press.

Rousseau, Jean-Jacques 1967 [1762]. 'Discourse on the Origin and the Foundation of Inequality among Mankind (Discours sur l'origine et les fondements de l'inégalité parmi les hommes)', in *The Social Contract and Discourse on the Origin of Inequality*, Lester G. Crocker (ed.) and anon. (trans.). New York: Washington Square Press, 175–258.

Scott, James C. 1999. *Seeing Like a State: How Certain Schemes to Improve the Human Condition Have Failed.* New Haven, CT: Yale University Press.

2009. *The Art of Not Being Governed: an Anarchist History of Upland Southeast Asia.* New Haven, CT and London: Yale University Press.

Shack, William A. and Skinner, Elliott P. (eds.) 1979. *Strangers in African Societies.* Berkeley: University of California Press.

Shipton, Parker 2007. *The Nature of Entrustment: Intimacy, Exchange, and the Sacred in Africa.* New Haven, CT and London: Yale University Press.

2009. *Mortgaging the Ancestors: Ideologies of Attachment in Africa.* New Haven, CT and London: Yale University Press.

2010. *Credit between Cultures: Farmers, Financiers, and Misunderstanding in Africa.* New Haven, CT and London: Yale University Press.

Smith, Rogers M. (ed.) 2011. *Citizenship, Borders, and Human Needs.* Philadelphia: University of Pennsylvania Press.

Taylor, Christopher C. 1999. *Sacrifice as Terror: the Rwandan Genocide of 1994*. Oxford: Berg.

Thomson, Steven K. 2006. 'Children of the Village: Peace and Local Citizenship in a Multiethnic Gambian Community', Doctoral Dissertation, Boston University, Ann Arbor, MI: UMI/Proquest.

Vail, Leroy (ed.) 1989. *The Creation of Ethnicity in Southern Africa*. Berkeley: University of California Press.

Wihtol de Wenden, Catherine 2007. 'The Frontiers of Mobility', in *Migration without Borders: Essays on the Free Movement of People*, Antoine Pécaud and Paul de Guchteneire (eds.). Paris and Oxford: UNESCO Publishing and Berghahn Books, 51–64.

8 | Horizontal inequalities and market instability in Africa

GRAHAM K. BROWN AND FRANCES STEWART

Introduction

In the previous chapters, we have shown that economic diversity can adversely affect economic performance as well as economic and political stability through a number of channels, including political mobilisation, segregation, territorial confinement and bias against trade with other ethnic communities. This chapter focuses on inequality among ethnic communities (horizontal inequality, HI), and reviews the links between HI and market instability in Africa. Is there a presumption that higher HIs lead to greater instability, and/or that greater instability increases HIs? In order to consider this issue, first we define HIs in general and consider what group categorisation is relevant in the African case.

There are reasons for expecting a two-way link between HIs and market instability, with greater market instability causing greater instability; and greater instability in turn increasing HIs. There are also important intervening links that account for these relationships. In particular, higher HIs are likely to be associated with greater political instability which in turn causes greater market instability, and higher HIs may be associated with lower quality of governance which also is likely to increase instability. The reverse linkage may also be mediated by conflict, political instability and poor governance.

In this chapter we provide both theoretical inferences and regression analyses to shed light on this inter-dependence. We provide some empirical evidence for the linkage from HIs to market instability, showing that in addition, higher HIs are associated with greater political instability and lower-quality governance, which both contribute to greater market instability. However, given the well-known difficulties in obtaining

We are very grateful to participants at the Yale seminar and to Hiroyuki Hino and Motoki Takahashi, for extremely helpful comments on a previous draft of this chapter.

suitable data on ethnic distribution for cross-country comparison, the endogeneity between HI and market instability and multicollinearity involving the most relevant explanatory variables, it has proved diffi- cult to provide firm evidence for a causal relationship between HI and instability or the reverse causality. It is possible, indeed, that causality goes both ways; or that the statistical relationship reflects some com- mon factors explaining both instability and HIs. Nevertheless, it is our view that the weight of the available evidence here and elsewhere points to causality running from HI to market instability. More rigor- ous exploration of this and reverse causality, perhaps with appropriate instrumentation, is a subject for future research.

The paper is organised as follows. The following section provides a definition of HIs and considers relevant group categorisations in gen- eral and in Africa. The next section then considers the potential links between HIs and market instability on the basis of qualitative reason- ing and inferences. We then provide some evidence from regression analyses, before drawing conclusions in the final section.

What are HIs?

HIs are inequalities between groups of people that share a common identity. Such inequalities have economic, social, political and cultural status dimensions (Stewart 2002, 2008). Horizontal inequality differs from 'vertical' inequality (VI) in that the latter is a measure of inequal- ity among individuals or households, not groups – furthermore, meas- urement of VI is often confined to income or consumption.

For vertical inequality, attention is usually focused on income (and occasionally assets). But in analysis of HIs a much more multidimen- sional approach is common because the importance of HIs stems from their impact on perceived well-being and on political mobilisation, and for both income is just one dimension, and by no means the most significant. Relevant HIs may be economic, social or political, or may concern cultural status.

- **Economic HIs** include inequalities in access to and ownership of assets – financial, human, natural resource-based and social. In add- ition, they comprise inequalities in income levels and employment opportunities, which depend on such assets and the general condi- tions of the economy.

- **Social HIs** include inequalities in access to a range of services such as education, health care and housing, as well as those in educational and health status.
- **Political HIs** include inequalities in the distribution of political opportunities and power among groups, including control over the presidency, the cabinet, parliamentary assemblies, the bureaucracy, local and regional governments, the army and the police. They also encompass inequalities in people's capabilities to participate politically and to express their needs.
- **Cultural status HIs** include disparities in the recognition and standing of different groups' languages, customs, norms and practices.[1]

Group categorisation

A crucial issue is to decide on group boundaries for the purpose of estimating HIs. Identities are not intrinsic, but are socially constructed. Yet they can be important to people both in their personal lives and behaviour and in relation to political mobilisation (Allen and Eade 1997; Anderson 1983; Banks 1996; Ukiwo 2005). Group identities arise partly from individuals' own perceptions of membership of and identity with a particular group – that is, the self-perceptions of those 'in' the group – but they are also determined by the perceptions of those outside the group about others. People see themselves and others in many different ways; they have many identities; hence they can be grouped in many ways, according, for example, to age, gender, location, religion and ethnicity. Some identities are fluid, short-lived and insignificant (for example, being a member of an evening class), while others are more permanent and more significant both personally and socially (for example, gender, ethnicity and religion). The identities which are important to people vary across societies: thus religion is clearly important in some contexts (at least as a label), for example in Northern Ireland or the Middle East, while ethnicity is important in others (for example, many African countries) and race in others (such as Fiji or South Africa). In some contexts, identities may overlap (for example in northern Nigeria a large majority of people are Hausa-Fulani and Muslims).

---

[1] Arnim Langer and Graham K. Brown introduced the concept of cultural status inequalities. See Langer and Brown (2008).

The significance people attribute to different aspects of their identity also varies according to context and over time. Research into self-perceptions of identity found, for example, that religion was much more important in West Africa than ethnicity as an identity in people's self-perceptions and their social lives. Yet in terms of government allocation of resources and political mobilisation, ethnicity has been viewed as much more important than religion (see below, and Langer and Ukiwo 2008).

In assessing and measuring HIs then the aim is to identify salient group categories in the particular society, which makes measurement more complex than in the case of vertical inequality. What is salient will depend on the purposes of the enquiry as well as on the nature of society and the historical evolution of identities. In fact, for two reasons this process can seem more complicated than it is in reality: firstly, because the important categories are often apparent in an actual society; and secondly, because assessment and measurement can adopt a variety of categorisations. Nonetheless, it is important to avoid 'objectifying' what are essentially socially created distinctions. However, it is essential to measure HIs in order to monitor particular situations, to identify policy needs and appropriate policies and, of course, to investigate relationships between HIs and other variables, as is the aim of this paper. Because of the importance of history and politics in forming salient identities, a country specific approach is really needed. Yet this obviously makes it difficult for cross-country comparisons.

For cross-country comparisons several approaches have been adopted: one is to use a data set compiled initially by some Russian anthropologists in the 1960s as the basis of cross-country comparisons in Africa.[2] This approach provides the foundation of most empirical research investigating relationships between ethnicity and economic and political developments (e.g. Collier and Hoeffler 1998; Easterly and Levine 1997). As noted in the previous chapters, clearly, this data set does not incorporate specific national or local perceptions, and it is historically dated. A second approach is to use region as a proxy for ethnicity, on the grounds that at least historically, different ethnic groups were located in different regions – although migration has

[2] *Atlas Narodov Mira* (1964). Moscow Miklukho-Maklai Ethnologicial Institute at the Department of Geodesy and Cartography of the State Geological Committee of the Soviet Union.

modified this relationship. Thirdly, there are modern surveys, such as the Demographic and Health Surveys (DHS), which ask people about their ethnicity. Altogether there are over 200 DHS surveys covering about seventy-five countries, over half of which ask questions about respondents' ethnicity; there are clear limitations to the DHS data, but among the available sources, these are closest to what we are looking for since they are based on people's own current perceptions of their ethnicity (see, for example, Lonsdale, Chapter 1).[3]

Relevance of ethnicity in Africa

As elsewhere, many categorisations are possible and relevant depending on the question. Surveys in West Africa by the Centre for Research on Inequality and Human Security ('CRISE') found that people generally saw themselves as having a range of identities; when asked to rank them in importance, religion was first, followed by occupation and then gender.[4] Ethnicity was given a subordinate role, said to be one of the three most important aspects of identity by less than a quarter of the respondents (Figure 8.1). However, respondents may have interpreted 'language' or 'region' as basically referring to their ethnicity. When one includes all those who mentioned either ethnicity, or language or region as one of their three most important aspects of their identity, over 40 per cent of respondents included this broad ethnic variable in Ghana and over 65 per cent of respondents in Nigeria. In both cases, it was still less than religion (at 76 per cent in Ghana and 78 per cent in Nigeria). Answers to questions about attitudes to cross-ethnic and cross-religious marriage also indicated that many more people objected to cross-religious than to cross-ethnic marriage, and socialising was also said to be greater among people of different ethnicities than among people of different religions.

---

[3] The censuses provide an alternative source of data, but many do not include an ethnicity question, and they are often out of date. For example, Burkino Faso's last census with an ethnic variable included was for 1976, whereas the DHS data for the same country with ethnicity included is available for 1993, 1998–9 and 2003 (see Stewart *et al.* 2010).

[4] These surveys included 600 interviews in two different locations in each country – Ghana and Nigeria. They were not designed to be representative of the country as a whole, although they were random samples in the selected locations. For more information, see Langer and Ukiwo (2008).

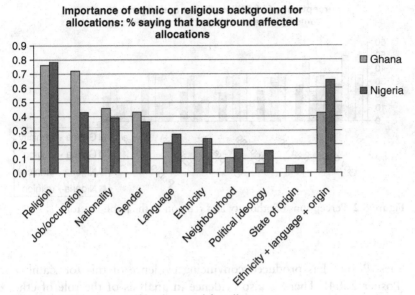

Figure 8.1 Importance of background for allocations

The subordinate personal role of ethnicity accords with histori-cal analysis which points to the construction of ethnicity in Africa: 'Modern Central Africa tribes are not so much survivals from a pre-colonial past but rather colonial creations by colonial officers and African intellectuals' (quoted in Ranger 1983: 248; Van Binsbergen 1976), and that: 'Almost all recent studies of nineteenth century pre-colonial Africa have emphasised that far from there being a single "tribal" identity, most Africans moved in and out of multiple identi-ties, defining themselves at one moment as subject to this chief, at another moment as a member of that cult, at another moment as part of this clan, and at yet another moment as an initiate in that professional guild' (Ranger 1983: 248). One example is the distinc-tion between Hutus and Tutsis, which some historians argue was largely invented by the colonial powers for administrative conven-ience (Lemarchand 1996).

Yet, despite the apparently lesser role of ethnicity (compared with religion) in *personal* or *private* life in the countries in the sample, eth-nicity seems to be generally much more powerful in terms of political mobilisation and political division (see Berman, Chapter 5). Political mobilisation in many African countries appears to occur along ethnic

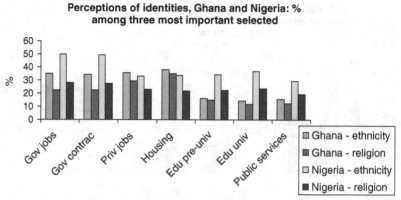

Figure 8.2 Perceptions of ethnicity and religion in the public sector

lines. Posner has produced convincing evidence of this for Zambia (Posner 2004). There is also evidence in analysis of the role of ethnicity in political appointments in Cote d'Ivoire, Ghana and Kenya, while voting patterns are often largely determined by ethnic differences (Langer 2005; Langer and Ukiwo 2008; Stewart 2010). Political offices and benefits seem to be conferred to a considerable extent along lines of ethnicity in a range of countries (Horowitz 1985; Posner 2005). The distribution of government expenditure and of aid is often biased towards particular ethnic groups. For example, in Burundi, there has been a marked concentration of government resources in the southern province of Bururi, from which many of the elite Tutsis came (Nkurunziza 2012), while in Kenya, there is evidence of aid and public expenditure more generally being distributed disproportionately to the region or group which dominates government (Cohen 1995; Stewart 2010).

The perceived *political* role of ethnicity was vividly demonstrated by the CRISE surveys, which showed that many more people felt that political benefits, such as public sector jobs and contracts, were awarded according more to ethnicity than according to religion, as presented in Figure 8.2. Moreover, when it comes to violent mobilisation, ethnicity is often the banner and unifying element (if not the motive) behind mobilisation, though there are cases where religion and ethnicity overlap and both play a role, such as in the Middle Belt in Nigeria. Ethnic militias are often active agents in violent conflicts.

To summarise, a number of different types of categorisation are relevant and salient in African countries. While ethnicity in many countries seems to be the most important from a political perspective, it does not necessarily follow that this is the case also from an economic perspective, or from the perspectives of well-being and justice, where gender and religious inequalities are highly relevant.

HIs and the market

In principle, there may be two-way links between the market (economic levels and instability) and HIs. On the one hand, HIs may affect the level of development and economic instability; on the other, market developments and instability may affect HIs. It is useful at this stage, therefore, to isolate the mechanisms through which influence might be transmitted in each direction.

From HIs to market instability

Market instability can arise from a number of sources:

(1) political instability, which undoubtedly contributes to market instability;
(2) fluctuations in commodity prices due to factors external to the country;
(3) fluctuations in commodity prices and output due to changing natural conditions (notably rainfall);
(4) domestic business cycles;
(5) inconsistent policies resulting from weak governance, inadequate technical capacity and unstable political regimes;
(6) stop–go policies often associated with negotiations with international financial institutions (IFIs).

In developing countries generally, (1), (2), (3), (5) and (6) are often sources of instability, but (4) less so since this tends to be the outcome of investment cycles, associated with accelerator–multiplier interactions and cycles in business confidence. But the much lesser role of private investment and the greater role of external aid and the state tends to reduce this source of instability in Africa. On the other hand, the very high dependence on external aid can lead to cycles particularly if the government does not follow the economic policies demanded by the IFIs. We may expect this source of instability to be associated with failure to meet international standards of 'good governance' described in (5) above.

The most obvious way that HIs can affect market stability is via channel (1), since there is considerable evidence that high HIs increase the probability of violent political eruptions (see, e.g. Barrows 1976; Gurr 1993; Kirwin and Cho 2009; Langer 2005; Mancini 2008; Ukiwo 2008).

As far as (2) and (3) are concerned, the fluctuations are caused by factors beyond the control of the country – world economic fluctuations and weather fluctuations. Nevertheless, changes in the terms of trade could well significantly impact HI as well as stability of economic policy, and hence market instability. A similar argument also applies to drought and other adverse weather conditions.

A slower transition away from dependence on primary commodities may well be associated with higher HIs, via the impact on political instability which not only causes economic instability directly but which can deter investments and lead to slow growth. Indeed there is evidence that reduced growth, certainly during a conflict and for a few years after, is a consequence of conflict (Collier *et al.* 2003; Stewart *et al.* 2001a, 2001b). While these analyses suffer from the considerable and well-known weaknesses, regression analysis of ninety-two countries using data of 1960–89 showed an annual loss of 2.2 per cent during the conflict and in the immediately following years, compared with a no-conflict situation (Collier 1999). Other cross-country regression analyses for 1960–99 yielded similar conclusions – with an average loss of growth of 2.4 per cent per annum (Hoeffler and Reynal-Querol 2003), although Imai and Weinstein (2000) suggest somewhat lower costs. Essentially such slow growth prolongs dependence on primary commodities and hence vulnerability to fluctuations via channels (2) and (3). On the other hand, slower growth may result in a larger subsistence sector which is relatively impervious to global fluctuations.

Another way in which high HIs can reduce economic growth is the tendency that, where present, high horizontal inequality results in less and asymmetrical social capital. Essentially, a (nearly) defining characteristic of a group is that interactions within the group are stronger than interactions with those outside the group.[5] The asymmetry of social capital (or networks) that results in principle means that everyone's contacts are more unbalanced than they would be in the absence of group differentiation, and this is likely to impede efficiency. This is a consequence of heterogeneity as such, as is the lesser provision of public goods. But it seems plausible that this asymmetry (and the public goods effects) is larger for conditions with more HIs, i.e. for greater social and economic distance between groups.

Having multiple ethnicities, particularly if groups are unequally treated (i.e. where there are higher HIs) might be expected to lead to weaker governance, as more groups need to be brought into decision-making and compensated where their interests suffer. Consequently, one might expect that a society with more diversity (as measured either by the ethno-fractionalisation index or by the ethno-polarisation index) *and* one with higher HIs would have weaker governance and more instability from this source.

Thus we might expect a connection between HIs and market instability through the following channels:

- HIs leading to political instability which causes greater economic instability;
- HIs leading to heavier dependence on primary commodities and consequently greater instability resulting from irregular rainfall and higher levels of political instability, as well as via reduced and asymmetric social capital which also lowers the rate of development;
- HIs (and ethno-diversity as measured by the ethno-fractionalisation index and ethnic polarisation index) leading to weaker governance, weaker public administration and consequently greater instability.

From market instability to HIs

HIs stem from the cumulative impact of a number of factors:

- Firstly, some initial inequality (which is often caused by colonial policy) leads to multiple disadvantages. For example, colonial policy often concentrated development regionally and selected certain ethnic groups for education and civil servant jobs. Thus HIs emerge initially.

[5] In his brilliant book about the consequences of heterogeneity, Blau made this a defining characteristic of a group (Blau 1977).

- Secondly, the initial inequality of incomes generates inequalities in accumulation, including both financial and human capital, resulting in further inequality in incomes.
- Thirdly, the asymmetry of social capital, already referred to, means that members of poorer groups have fewer good contacts and economic opportunities.
- Fourthly, this lack of contacts and opportunities is worsened by explicit or implicit discrimination.
- Fifthly, there is interaction in returns to different types of capital. Even if poor groups manage to send their children to school, their weak social and financial capital, as well as employment discrimination, means that returns to education are lower, leading to a disincentive to acquire education. This phenomenon is illustrated for Peru in Figure 8.3.
- Finally, often there are parallel political inequalities which reinforce the disadvantage of some groups in a variety of ways.

How does market instability bear on this? Links may not be obvious but may nonetheless be significant.

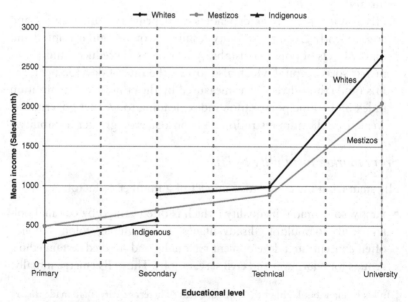

Figure 8.3 Differential returns to education in Peru by ethnicity
Source: Figueroa (2006)

(1) Market instability hits those people in the vulnerable ethnic groups harder, through loss of jobs, access to public goods, etc. This raises HI.

(2) Market instability strengthens the need for those particularly in the vulnerable ethnic groups to reinforce their identity and fortify their allegiance for self protection. This could reduce trade and other interactions between ethnic groups and hence could raise HI (see Hamaguchi, Chapter 6 and Shipton, Chapter 7).

(3) Market instability is likely to affect those without insurance mechanisms worst, and it is arguable that these would be poorer groups, especially since public insurance mechanisms are less likely in heterogeneous societies.

(4) Market instability may encourage those affected to take their children out of school, and so worsen their relative situation.

(5) Market instability may accentuate discrimination.

(6) Social protection schemes, if any, in poor countries are often highly partial, and members of richer groups are likely to have privileged access.

The possible two-way links are presented in Figure 8.4.

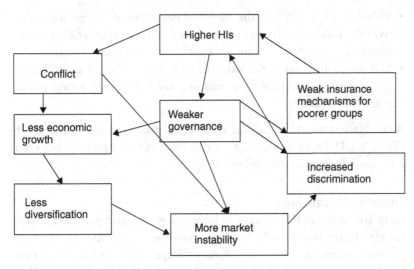

Note: Arrows show the presumed direction of causality.

Figure 8.4 Possible two-way causal links between market instability and HIs
Note: Arrows show the presumed direction of causality.

A preliminary empirical investigation

In this section we provide a preliminary empirical analysis of correlation between horizontal inequalities and market instability. The data source for horizontal inequalities is unfortunately not as solid as one might hope, and the findings of this section thus need to be treated with considerable caution. Nonetheless, there is clear confirmation here that there is a relationship between horizontal inequalities and market instability, although further investigation would be necessary to determine the precise nature of this relationship and, in particular, which of the possible mechanisms outlined above is more dominant and whether there are other mechanisms at play.

Data and Measures

Market instability

Measuring the dependent variable – economic or market instability – can be done in a variety of ways, depending on whether we are concerned with overall volatility of growth rates, or with a sudden negative shock. Here we define two alternative variables, corresponding to these two ideas.

- VOLATILITY, which is the standard deviation of the growth rates over the following five-year period, with a natural logarithm transformation to obtain a normally distributed dependent variable.
- SHOCK, which takes the value of 0 or 1; it is 1 if the growth rate in any year is 4 percentage points or more below the average of the prior four years.

A correlation matrix for all the variables is presented in Appendix 8.1 (Table 8A.1). From this we can see that there is no correlation between our two measures of instability.

Horizontal inequalities

Data for horizontal inequalities between ethnic groups, particularly in Africa, are notoriously hard to come by, except for census data in some countries. For cross-country comparisons, one data set that can be used, although with caution, is the standardised Demographic Health Surveys, which are conducted at around five-yearly intervals in many African countries, and which often contain an ethnicity question. While the surveys are targeted at women and do not ask questions about income *per se*, they do ask questions about household assets. We use the average level of asset ownership in each ethnic group as data for the calculation of horizontal inequalities. Because the surveys are not conducted every year, estimates of horizontal inequality for other years are imputed through linear interpolation. The asset index is constructed from five assets: television, car, motorbike, radio and refrigerator. This means that the measure of HIs is likely to depend partly on the aggregate per capita income since, as incomes rise, ownership of these assets spreads. HIs, using this index, are likely to rise initially and then fall as incomes rise even though a broader definition of assets or data for income might not show any such movement.

To measure the extent of HIs in a country we use two variables, starting with the group coefficient of variation of assets, weighted by group population (GCOV).[6] We also compute an alternative specification of horizontal inequality, the economic polarisation index of Esteban and Ray (ECPOL).[7] The GCOV measure estimates the coefficient of variation of asset ownership of every group in a country weighted by population size. The deviations are squared so that large differences from the average are weighted more heavily than small differences. The Esteban–Ray index of economic polarisation weights a combination of group size and economic difference between groups so that for any economic difference between groups, it tends to be highest in situations where there are two or three large groups, and lowest where there are large numbers of groups.[8] The value of the polarisation index depends on a coefficient α that determines the weight given to the size of the group distribution, which falls as α rises and the weight given to economic differences which rises as α rises. Below we set α at 1.5, as is common (Ezcurra 2009). The two measures of HIs are significantly correlated with each other, but clearly measure somewhat different phenomena, with a Pearson correlation coefficient of 0.403.

[6] See Brown and Langer (Chapter 10) for a discussion of these measures.
[7] The formulae for these measures are given in Appendix 8.1.
[8] Esteban and Ray define their approach as one in which the population 'is grouped into significantly sized "clusters" such that each group is very "similar" in terms of the attributes of its members, but different clusters have members with very "dissimilar" attributes' (Esteban and Ray 1994).

Ethnic diversity
We use the ethno-fractionalisation index (variable ETHFRAC), cal-culated on the basis of the formula for the ethno-linguistic fraction-alisation index (ELF), using the DHS data and ethnic polarisation (ETHPOL). ETHFRAC is larger the more the population is divided into a large number of small groups, while ETHPOL rises the more nearly the population is divided into two equal groups. The two measures are correlated (Pearson correlation coefficient of 0.274) but not highly. Further discussion of the measures above can be found in Brown and Langer (Chapter 2).

Level of gross domestic product (GDP) per capita, logged (GDPCAP)
This is derived from the World Bank's *World Development Indicators* (WDI). The level of GDP per capita is included to see if there are any systematic changes that occur as incomes rise.

Two measures of economic diversity
The first measure assesses the economy's reliance on primary commod-ities for exports (Primary Commodity Exports as a ratio to GDP, or 'PCOMEX', derived from WDI). The second uses agricultural value-added share in GDP (AG) (from WDI). These two measures are negatively cor-related (Pearson correlation coefficient of −0.663), presumably because the high primary exporters are exporting minerals or petroleum.

Terms of trade (TOT)
TOTs are used to identify the impact of changes in international terms of trade on market instability (derived from the WDI). This variable is indexed to the country's terms of trade in 2000.

Rainfall fluctuations (RAINSHOCK)
This is given a value of 1 if the annual rainfall falls 20 per cent or more below the average of the previous two years and 0 otherwise. The data are derived from an earlier report (Miguel *et al.* 2007). This variable is used to see how far market instability is due to weather irregularities.

Violent conflict (CONF)
This is valued as 1 where there are more than twenty-five deaths per year, according to the Uppsala data set, and 0 otherwise. Conflicts are

included where there is 'a contested incompatibility that concerns government or territory or both' and at least one party to the conflict must be the state (Gleditsch *et al.* 2002: 619).

Quality of governance (QOG)
This is a measure taken from the Quality of Governance Institute (Teorell *et al.* 2010). We use the variable 'Quality of Public Administration'.

Results

The data are limited to Sub-Saharan African countries. Country-level dummies are included (but not reported) to hold for country-specific heterogeneity.

We begin with a set of simple regressions to see whether there is any systematic relationship between horizontal inequality and the two measures of market instability, taking the various other influences into account, but excluding conflict.

Tables 8.1 and 8.2 present these results for the three measures of ethnic diversity and HI; we also include a 'base' model with no ethnic measures (equation 1 shown in the first column). In Tables 8.3 and 8.4, conflict is added as an explanatory variable. In Tables 8.1 and 8.3, the dependent variable is VOLATILITY, while in Tables 8.2 and 8.4, it is the SHOCK variable.

In Table 8.1, two variables are consistently significant – terms of trade change (positively) and quality of governance (negatively) – in relation to market volatility. Perhaps surprisingly, the RAINSHOCK variable is consistently not significant. Ethnic composition of the population is not correlated with market instability either in terms of fractionalisation or polarisation. When we introduce HIs (Table 8.1, equations 4 and 5) we find that the GCOV measure, lagged by one year, is positively related to instability but not significantly, while ethnic polarisation, also lagged by one year, is positive and highly significant. GDP per capita is significant (and surprisingly positive, with higher GDP per capita raising the likelihood of instability) in equation 1, but it loses significance once HI variables are introduced.

While these estimates should be interpreted with caution due to data problems and issues of model specification, it is interesting to contrast equations 3 and 5 in Table 8.1. Equation 3 shows that polarisation of the population in terms of ethnic groups is not correlated significantly

Table 8.1. *Ethnic diversity, horizontal inequality and economic volatility*

Dependent variable: economic volatility

Variable	1	2	3	4	5
GDPCAP	0.0067**	0.00663**	0.00213	0.00016	0.00217
	(2.32)	(2.29)	(0.678)	(0.0229)	(0.384)
AG	8.74E–05	8.87E–05	–7.84E–07	0.000681	0.000694
	(0.462)	(0.467)	(–0.00408)	(1.61)	(2.16)
PCOMEX	0.000155	0.00017	0.000171	0.000585	0.000466
	(1.38)	(1.51)	(1.52)	(2.17)	(2.15)
RAINSHOCK	–0.00232	–0.00171	0.00057	0.0101	0.000492
	(–0.39)	(–0.283)	(0.0927)	(0.817)	(0.0439)
QOG	–0.00102***	–0.00102***	–0.00094***	–0.00349***	–0.00243***
	(–7.03)	(–6.77)	(–6.41)	(–6.64)	(–5.06)
TOT	0.000106***	0.000105***	9.48E–05**	0.000183**	0.000243***
	(2.9)	(2.85)	(2.45)	(2.15)	(3.33)
ETHFRAC		0.00695			
		(1.12)			

EPOL			-0.00777		
			(-0.905)		
GCOV				0.0393	
				(1.43)	
ECPOL					0.448***
					(6.98)
CONSTANT	0.0397*	0.0354	0.0692***	0.174***	0.0485
	(1.79)	(1.54)	(2.95)	(2.92)	(0.966)
N	881	876	797	315	315
R-squared	0.0722	0.0739	0.0584	0.1212	0.2497

Notes: Dependent variable: VOLATILITY; significance designated by asterisks: * < 0.05; ** < 0.025; *** < 0.01.

Table 8.2. *Ethnic diversity, horizontal inequality and negative economic shocks*

Dependent variable: economic shock					
Variable	1	2	3	4	5
GDPCAP	−0.0256	−0.00773	0.0942	−0.88	0.0257
	(−0.189)	(−0.0568)	(0.638)	(−2.28)	(0.0904)
AG	0.0105	0.0105	0.0177	−0.00499	0.0381
	(1.18)	(1.17)	(1.91)	(−0.278)	(2.62)
PCOMEX	0.00386	0.00355	0.00683	−0.0189	0.00289
	(0.739)	(0.664)	(1.27)	(−1.21)	(0.256)
RAINSHOCK	0.132	0.0675	0.0827	−1.16	−1.41
	(0.446)	(0.217)	(0.255)	(−1.11)	(−1.35)
QOG	−0.0169**	−0.0135*	−0.0174**	−0.057**	−0.02
	(−2.36)	(−1.78)	(−2.27)	(−2.28)	(−0.872)
TOT	0.00249	0.00243	0.00298	−0.00168	−0.00536
	(1.51)	(1.46)	(1.66)	(−0.382)	(−1.32)
ETHFRAC		0.183			
		(0.614)			
EPOL			−0.275		
			(−0.645)		
GCOV				−1.53	
				(−1.12)	
ECPOL					−2.82
					(−0.851)
CONSTANT	−1.15	−1.54	−2.02	7.3	−1.18
	(−1.1)	(−1.41)	(−1.78)	(2.46)	(−0.521)
N	1170	1144	1012	354	354
Pseudo-R squared	0.0101	0.0084	0.0116	0.0913	0.055

with instability. Equation 5 shows that polarisation of the population in terms of economic inequalities among these ethnic groups *is* significantly correlated with instability. This implies that ethnic diversity does not adversely affect economic stability by itself but it does so when ethnic groups are polarised *and* economically unequal. This finding is consistent with those put forward in the previous chapters.

Table 8.3. *Impact of HIs and conflict on market instability*

Dependent variable: economic volatility

Variable	1	2	3	4	5
GDPCAP	0.0087***	0.00859***	0.00413	0.00461	0.00488
	(3.01)	(2.96)	(1.33)	(0.669)	(0.857)
AG	0.000139	0.000136	0.000055	0.000679	0.000685***
	(0.739)	(0.722)	(0.29)	(1.65)	(2.16)
PCOMEX	4.88E–05	6.33E–05	3.87E–05	0.000284	0.000333
	(0.429)	(0.552)	(0.341)	(1.05)	(1.51)
RAINSHOCK	–0.00274	–0.00235	5.24E–05	0.00719	–0.00024
	(–0.465)	(–0.393)	(0.00867)	(0.593)	(–0.0212)
QOG	–0.00076***	–0.00076***	–0.00058***	–0.00243***	–0.00198***
	(–4.83)	(–4.68)	(–3.69)	(–4.27)	(–3.92)
TOT	0.00011***	0.000109***	9.56E–05**	0.000196**	0.000242***
	(3.02)	(2.97)	(2.51)	(2.37)	(3.35)
CONF	0.0196***	0.0189***	0.0242***	0.0399***	0.0229***
	(4.44)	(4.24)	(5.44)	(4.24)	(2.66)

Table 8.3. (*cont.*)

Dependent variable: economic volatility					
Variable	1	2	3	4	5
ETHFRAC		0.0057			
		(0.925)			
EPOL			−0.008		
			(−0.948)		
GCOV				−0.00458	
				(−0.16)	
ECPOL					0.391***
					(5.81)
CONSTANT	0.0104	0.00761	0.0349	0.0954	0.0143
	(0.452)	(0.322)	(1.46)	(1.57)	(0.279)
N	881	876	797	315	315
R-squared	0.0916	0.0917	0.0833	0.1672	0.2635

Table 8.4. *Impact of HIs and conflict on economic shocks*

Dependent variable: negative shock

Variable	1	2	3	4	5
GDPCAP	-0.034	-0.0114	0.0877	-0.937**	0.0165
	(-0.248)	(-0.0825)	(0.586)	(-2.32)	(0.0552)
AG	0.0103	0.0105	0.0176	-0.00484	0.0381
	(1.15)	(1.17)	(1.9)	(-0.271)	(2.62)
PCOMEX	0.00414	0.0037	0.00709	-0.0163	0.00324
	(0.784)	(0.679)	(1.3)	(-0.998)	(0.275)
RAINSHOCK	0.134	0.0692	0.0846	-1.14	-1.4
	(0.456)	(0.222)	(0.261)	(-1.09)	(-1.35)
QOG	-0.0177**	-0.0139*	-0.0182**	-0.0634**	-0.0208
	(-2.37)	(-1.72)	(-2.22)	(-2.31)	(-0.856)
TOT	0.00243	0.0024	0.00294	-0.00183	-0.00538
	(1.47)	(1.43)	(1.63)	(-0.414)	(-1.33)

Table 8.4. (*cont.*)

Dependent variable: negative shock

Variable	1	2	3	4	5
CONF	−0.0765	−0.0313	−0.0584	−0.252	−0.0464
	(−0.366)	(−0.146)	(−0.267)	(−0.55)	(−0.104)
ETHFRAC		0.185			
		(0.619)			
EPOL			−0.272		
			(−0.637)		
GCOV				−1.3	
				(−0.911)	
ECPOL					−2.72
					(−0.786)
					−1.09
					(−0.449)
CONSTANT	−1.04	−1.49	−1.93	7.92**	354
	(−0.957)	(−1.31)	(−1.63)	(2.49)	
N	1170	1144	1012	354	
Pseudo-R squared	0.0102	0.0084	0.0117	0.0979	0.055

When we introduce conflict into the models explaining economic volatility (Table 8.3), we find that conflict has a highly significant impact on increasing volatility. Quality of governance and economic polarisation remain significant, but their significance and the value of the coefficient are reduced, indicating that part of their influence on market instability may be indirect through increasing conflict. Likewise the other measure of HIs, GCOV, loses all significance and its sign changes.

Turning to the shock measure of instability, Tables 8.2 and 8.4 show that no variable, except quality of governance, is significantly correlated with economic instability. This result suggests that it may be difficult to capture, with our model specification and data, the impact of various variables on what we have termed 'shock', namely a sudden and large drop in economic activity resulting possibly from a change in economic regime or major disruptions (discontinuity) in economic policy. Such shock is likely affected by an accumulation of social tension (high HI or economic diversity) over several years, and also negatively affects economic activity over the next few years. Our model, which assumes contemporaneous correlation between the independent and the dependent variables, is better suited to explain short-term (year-on-year) economic fluctuations as measured in our volatility variable.

Given the importance of the conflict variable, Table 8.5 presents determinants of conflict to assess the importance of these indirect effects. We see there that the quality of governance is significantly negatively correlated with conflict, while both measures of HIs, GCOV and ETHPOL are highly significantly correlated (positively) with conflict. Table 8.6 exhibits the degree to which our variables explain volatility once allowing for their indirect effects via increasing conflict. We see that both quality of governance and economic polarisation retain an additional correlation with conflict after taking into account the effects via conflict, but GCOV is not a significant variable, after allowing for its effects via conflict.

The direction of causality might be called into question in both these cases. In the first case – the conflict/HI relationship – two-way causality is probable, but it seems likely that the relationship is stronger from HIs to conflict than the reverse, as detailed case study evidence of countries suffering violent conflict shows ethnic inequalities rising in some cases but not in others, while the evidence that HIs lead to conflict is much stronger (see e.g. Stewart *et al.* 2001b). In the case of quality of governance, two-way causality is also likely since governance is

Table 8.5. *Determinants of CONF (logit)*

Dependent variable CONF		
GDPCAP	–0.0451	–0.267**
	(–0.393)	(–2.26)
QOG	–0.135	–0.0771
	(–6.84)	(–5.39)
GCOV	5.38***	
	(6.1)	
ECPOL		10.3***
		(5.7)
CONSTANT	5.42***	3.39***
	(4.55)	(2.81)
Athrho		
_cons	–0.172	–0.175
	(–1.54)	(–1.55)
Lnsigma		
_cons	–2.83	–2.9
	(–69.2)	(–72.4)
N	315	315
Log likelihood	320.23	359.62

likely to be adversely affected by the undermining of central authority associated with conflict, and this is suggested by case studies.

A summary of the findings: from HIs to market instability.

We found significant relationships for one of our measures of market instability, the volatility variable. Our findings in this regard can be summarised as follows:

Early in the chapter we hypothesised that:

(1) HIs might be related to market instability because of the impact on conflict. Our evidence supports this, although, of course, data and modelling issues mean that this is not conclusive.

(2) HIs might be related to market instability via an effect of slowing down diversification. The evidence was ambiguous on this depending on the measure of diversification and the measure of HIs. GCOV is positively correlated with the share of agriculture in

Table 8.6. *Determinants of market volatility after holding for selection bias in conflict*

Dependent variable VOLATILITY		
GDPCAP	0.00606	0.00617
	(0.881)	(1.08)
AG	0.000723	0.000685**
	(1.77)	(2.19)
PCOMEX	0.00024	0.000294
	(0.888)	(1.34)
RAINSHOCK	0.0072	−3.8E−05
	(0.603)	(−0.00347)
QOG	−0.00201	−0.00169
	(−3.21)	(−3.17)
TOT	0.000196**	0.000245***
	(2.4)	(3.44)
GCOV	−0.0216	
	(−0.709)	
CONF	0.0566***	0.0392***
	(3.98)	(2.92)
ECPOL		0.349
		(4.87)
CONSTANT	0.0631	−0.00674
	(0.991)	(−0.128)

GDP, but negatively correlated with the share of primary exports; ETHPOL shows the opposite relationships.

(3) Ethnic composition of the population and HIs might affect the quality of governance, with more diversity of population and/ or higher HIs leading to worse governance. This in turn might increase market instability. We found that more diversity as measured by the fractionalisation index, ELF, was significantly negatively associated with the quality of governance and with one of our measures of HI (ECPOL), but the other measures did not show significant correlation. We did find that lower quality of governance is closely correlated with market instability both via a correlation with conflict and also directly.

We summarise the relationships in Figure 8.5.

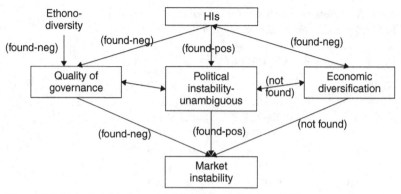

Figure 8.5 Relationship between HIs and market instability

From market instability to HIs

As noted above, what we have shown is correlation not causation. However, we do have strong reasons for thinking that one of the prime causal pathways is from HIs to instability via the political instability that HIs cause.[9] Is there also an opposite pathway with more market instability leading to higher HIs? There are plausible arguments for thinking this possible. Sudden and persistent economic depression could well lead to even stronger ethnic protectionism, including favouritism in public resource allocations, eviction and territorial confinement. In addition, market instability is likely to hurt those without insurance and those outside government protection schemes especially badly; and it may inhibit governments from taking general corrective action to address inequality. During downturns, investment expenditure is especially badly hit (Cornia *et al.* 1986), and in poor countries it is those who had previously lacked infrastructural facilities who suffer worst. Similarly, user charges which are often introduced during crises are likely to impact poor groups disproportionately. However, we lack sufficiently time sensitive data on HIs and cross-national data on social insurance schemes to be able to provide systematic supporting evidence for these connections.

---

[9] See Stewart (2008), Cederman *et al.* (2010) and Østby (2008) for other evidence on this.

Conclusions

The first part of this paper explored possible links between market instability and HIs among ethnic groups on the basis of general reasoning. We concluded that higher HIs might increase market volatility because they raise the risk of conflict and because they might reduce the growth rate and reduce diversification, not only because of there being more conflict but also for a variety of other reasons. There were also reasons for expecting market instability to increase HIs.

The middle section of the chapter provided preliminary regression results on the relationship between HIs and instability. It adopted two measures of instability: VOLATILITY, the standard deviation of the growth rates over the following five-year period; and SHOCK, which took a value of 0 or 1: 1 if the growth rate in any year is 4 percentage points or more below the value of the prior four years. For the most part we found very few significant relationships with the SHOCK variable, probably due the way the variable was defined. For the volatility variable, ethnic diversity as such had no effect, but HIs among ethnic groups, as measured by polarisation, was strongly related to instability, as was terms-of-trade change and the quality of governance index (negatively). When we introduced a conflict variable we found that this was significantly related to market instability as expected, and the impact of the HI variables and equality of governance was reduced. Investigating the determinants of conflict revealed that both quality of governance and HIs had a significant impact. Both quality of governance and HIs have direct and indirect effects on market instability, the indirect effects resulting from their association with conflict. Ethno-fractionalisation – which has no direct effect on market instability – may also have an indirect effect via its (negative) association with quality of governance.

While the above results show strong correlation, we were unable to establish causality, either from HIs to instability or from market instability to HIs. Both remain plausible hypotheses.

In conclusion then, with due respect for the caution needed given these data and model limitations, there seems to be a definite relationship between HIs and market instability, which is partially, but not fully, explained by the relationship between HIs and conflict and HIs and quality of governance.

Appendix 8.1

Table 8A.1. Correlation matrix of all variables

	VOLATILITY	SHOCK	GDPCAP	AG	PCOMEX	RAIN SHOCK	QOG	TOT	WAR	ELF	ETHPOL	GCOV	ECPOL
VOLATILITY	1.000												
SHOCK	-0.004	1.000											
	0.899												
GDPCAP	0.139	-0.051	1.000										
	0.000*	0.059											
AG	-0.109	-0.073	-0.811	1.000									
	0.000*	0.007	0.000*										
PCOMEX	0.116	-0.037	0.690	-0.663	1.000								
	0.000*	0.172	0.000*	0.000*									
RAIN SHOCK	-0.033	0.016	-0.086	0.072	-0.052	1.000							
	0.277	0.548	0.001*	0.009*	0.054								
QOG	-0.222	-0.047	-0.028	0.083	0.035	-0.010	1.000						
	0.000*	0.079	0.303	0.002*	0.195	0.718							
TOT	0.049	0.043	-0.097	0.136	-0.111	-0.029	0.038	1.000					
	0.14	0.139	0.001*	0.000*	0.000*	0.310	0.187						
WAR	0.19	0.02	-0.048	-0.041	0.043	0.028	-0.253	-0.105	1.000				
	0.000*	0.454	0.076	0.134	0.112	0.299	0.000*	0.000*					
ELF	0.054	0.032	-0.139	0.130	-0.124	0.017	-0.178	0.020	0.064	1.000			
	0.078	0.229	-0.000*	0.000*	0.000*	0.523	0.000*	0.498	0.016*				
ETHPOL	-0.021	-0.014	0.157	-0.120	0.085	0.024	-0.007	-0.104	0.046	0.274	1.000		
	0.505	-0.632	0.000*	0.000*	0.004*	0.402	0.802	0.001*	0.109	0.000*			
GCOV	0.055	-0.011	-0.286	0.208	-0.245	0.025	0.133	0.138	0.292	-0.347	-0.115	1.000	
	0.306	0.83	0.000*	0.000*	0.000*	0.620	0.008*	0.008*	0.000*	0.000*	0.028		
ECPOL	0.45	-0.1001	0.068	-0.138	-0.014	0.073	-0.443	-0.027	0.365	-0.230	0.103	0.043	1.000
	0.000*	0.039*	0.157	0.005*	0.773	0.131	0.000*	0.599	0.000*	0.000*	0.043	0.000	

Note: Pearson correlation coefficient; *-significant

References

Allen, T. and Eade, J. 1997. 'Anthropological Approaches to Ethnicity and Conflict in Europe and Beyond', *International Journal on Minority and Group Rights* 4: 217–46.

Anderson, B. R. O. G. 1983. *Imagined Communities: Reflections on the Origin and Spread of Nationalism*. London: Verso.

Banks, M. 1996. *Ethnicity: Anthropological Constructions*. London: Routledge.

Barrows, W. L. 1976. 'Ethnic Diversity and Political Instability in Black Africa', *Comparative Political Studies* 9: 139–70.

Blau, P. 1977. *Inequality and Heterogeneity: a Primitive Theory of Social Structure*. New York: Free Press.

Cederman, L.-E., Gleditsch, K. S. and Weidmann, N. B. 2010. *Horizontal Inequalities and Ethno-nationalist Civil War: a Global Comparison*. Zurich: Center for Comparative and International Studies.

Cohen, J. M. 1995. 'Ethnicity, Foreign Aid and Economic Growth in Sub-Saharan Africa: the Case of Kenya', *Development Discussion Papers*, Cambridge, MA: Harvard Institute for International Development.

Collier, P. 1999. 'On the Economic Consequences of Civil War', *Oxford Economic Papers* 51 (1): 168–83.

Collier, P. and Hoeffler, A. 1998. 'On Economic Causes of Civil War', *Oxford Economic Papers* 50 (4): 563–73.

Collier, P., Elliott, V. L., Hegre, H., Hoeffler, A., Reynal-Querol, M. and Sambanis, N. 2003. *Breaking the Conflict Trap: Civil War and Development Policy*. Washington, DC: World Bank.

Cornia, G. A., Jolly, R. and Stewart, F. 1986. *Adjustment with a Human Face*. Oxford University Press.

Easterly, W. and Levine, R. 1997. 'Africa's Growth Tragedy: Policies and Ethnic Divisions', *Quarterly Journal of Economics* 112: 1,203–50.

Esteban, J.-M. and Ray, D. 1994. 'On the Measurement of Polarization', *Econometrica* 62: 819–51.

Ezcurra, R. 2009. 'Does Income Polarization Affect Economic Growth? The Case of the European Regions', *Regional Studies* 43: 267–85.

Figueroa, A. 2006. 'Education, Labour Markets and Inequality in Peru', *Paper Presented at the CRISE Workshop*, Santa Cruz, Bolivia (18–20 September).

Gleditsch, N. P., Wallensteen, P., Erikson, M., Sollenberg, M. and Strand, H. 2002. 'Armed Conflict 1946–2000', *Journal of Peace Research* 39 (5): 615–27.

Gurr, T. R. 1993. *Minorities at Risk: a Global View of Ethnopolitical Conflicts*. Washington, DC: United States Institute of Peace Press.

Hoeffler, A. and Reynal-Querol, M. 2003. *Measuring the Cost of Conflict*. Oxford: Centre for the Study of African Economies, University of Oxford.

Horowitz, D. L. 1985. *Ethnic Groups in Conflict*. Berkeley, CA: University of California Press.

Imai, K. and Weinstein, J. 2000. 'Measuring the Impact of Civil War', *Center for International Development Working Papers no. 27*. Cambridge, MA: Harvard University.

Kirwin, M. and Cho, W. 2009. 'Weak States and Political Violence in Sub-Saharan Africa', *AfroBarometer Working Paper no. 111*.

Langer, A. 2005. 'Horizontal Inequalities and Violent Group Mobilisation in Cote d'Ivoire', *Oxford Development Studies* 33: 25–45.

Langer, A. and Brown, G. 2008. 'Cultural Status Inequalities: an Important Dimension of Group Mobilization', in *Horizontal Inequalities and Conflict: Understanding Group Violence in Multiethnic Societies*, F. Stewart (ed.). London: Palgrave, 41–53.

Langer, A. and Ukiwo, U. 2008. 'Ethnicity, Religion and the State in Ghana and Nigeria: Perceptions from the Street', in *Horizontal Inequalities and Conflict: Understanding Group Violence in Multiethnic Societies*, F. Stewart (ed.). London: Palgrave.

Lemarchand, R. 1996. *Burundi: Ethnic Conflict and Genocide*. Cambridge University Press.

Mancini, L. 2008. 'Horizontal Inequality and Communal Violence: Evidence from Indonesian Districts', in *Horizontal Inequalities and Conflict: Understanding Group Violence in Multiethnic Societies*, F. Stewart (ed.). London: Palgrave.

Miguel, E., Satyanath, S. and Sergenti, E. 2007. *Economic Shocks and Civil Conflict: an Instrumental Variables Approach African Rainfall Data Set*. New York: National Bureau of Economic Research. Data and manual available online at www.econ.berkeley.edu/~emiguel/data.shtml.

Nkurunziza, J. 2012. 'Inequality and Post-conflict Fiscal Policies in Burundi', in *Horizontal Inequalities in a Post-conflict Context*, A. Langer, F. Stewart and R. Venugopal (eds.). London: Palgrave.

Østby, G. 2008. 'Polarization, Horizontal Inequalities and Violent Civil Conflict', *Journal of Peace Research* 45: 143–62.

Posner, D. N. 2004. 'The Political Salience of Cultural Difference: Why Chewas and Tumbukas are Allies in Zambia and Adversaries in Malawi', *American Political Science Review* 98: 529–45.

2005. *Institutions and Ethnic Politics in Africa*. Cambridge University Press.

Ranger, T. 1983. 'The Invention of Tradition in Colonial Africa', in *The Invention of Tradition*, E. Hobsbawm and T. Ranger (eds.). Cambridge: Canto.

Stewart, F. 2002. 'Horizontal Inequalities: a Neglected Dimension of Development', *Queen Elizabeth House Working Paper Series* 81.

(ed.) 2008. *Horizontal Inequalities and Conflict: Understanding Group Mobilization in Multiethnic Societies*. London: Palgrave.

2010. 'Horizontal Inequalities in Kenya and the Political Disturbances of 2008: some Implications for Aid Policy', *Conflict, Security and Development* 10: 133–59.

Stewart, F., Fitzgerald, E. V. K. and Associates 2001a. *War and Underdevelopment: the Economic and Social Consequences of Conflict, Vol. I*. Oxford University Press.

2001b. *War and Underdevelopment: Country Experiences, Vol. II*. Oxford University Press.

Teorell, Jan, Charron, Nicholas, Samanni, Marcus, Holmberg, Sören and Rothstein, Bo. 2010. 'The Quality of Government Dataset', version 27 May. University of Gothenburg: The Quality of Government Institute (www.qog.pol.gu.se).

Ukiwo, U. 2005. 'The Study of Ethnicity in Nigeria', *Oxford Development Studies* 33: 7–23.

2008. 'Horizontal Inequalities and Ethnic Violence: Evidence from Calabar and Warri, Nigeria', in *Horizontal Inequalities and Conflict: Understanding Group Violence in Multiethnic Societies*, F. Stewart (ed.). London: Palgrave.

Van Binsbergen, W. 1976. 'Review of S. J. Natara "History of the Chewa"', *African Social Research* 19: 73–5.

9 | Impact of ethnicities on market outcome: results of market experiments in Kenya

KEN-ICHI SHIMOMURA AND
TAKEHIKO YAMATO

Introduction

In this final chapter, we return to the fundamental question that this book is meant to address. Namely, is it correct to presume that ethnic diversity adversely affects the market economy in general, and in Africa in particular? More precisely, does the economy, which is otherwise stable, become unstable as a result of the involvement of individuals with different ethnicities? Or, are economies in Africa less efficient because of ethnic heterogeneity?

We answer these questions by conducting a laboratory experiment. We construct a model of a pure market economy – the familiar exchange economy where two types of individuals trade two goods – and have teams of people randomly selected from the three major ethnic communities in Kenya engage in a trading simulation. The model is constructed in such a way that if the market were left to its own devices (e.g. the 'invisible hand' or 'tatonnement' in neo-classical economics), trading would bring the economy to an equilibrium at which the welfare levels of two groups of individuals are uneven, even though another equilibrium with more equitable distribution exists. We replace the invisible hand with actual people in order to determine what impact trading between people of different ethnicities has on

We thank Hiroyuki Hino, Anjan Mukherji, Shyam Sunder and Motoki Takahashi for their detailed comments and useful suggestions. We also appreciate special support in conducting experiments in Kenya and for computation of statistics by Michiharu Masui, Joseph Onjala, Tokinao Ohtaka, Kiyotaka Takahashi and Kohei Yoshida. This research was partially supported by the Japan International Cooperation Agency (JICA) and a Grant-in-Aid for Scientific Research (B) 22330085.

outcomes of market trading. We found the following. (1) Trading patterns differed depending on the combination of the ethnic groups that are engaged in trade. (2) It matters whether trading occurs between people of the same ethnicity group, or with people belonging to a different ethnic group. When trading occurs between two people of the same ethnicity, the subjects tend to settle on a trade more quickly even if the allocation is far from ideal. (3) When trading is multiethnic (i.e. between subjects belonging to two different ethnic groups), regardless of the combinations of ethnic groups, the economy converges to an equilibrium with a more equitable distribution. In other words, the experiment suggests that contrary to conventional wisdom on the negative impact of ethnic heterogeneity on economic outcomes, ethnic diversity in fact has stabilising and welfare-enhancing effects on the economy.

Larger and more rigorous experiments would have to be conducted before definitive conclusions could be drawn. Nevertheless, this experiment offers a counter-example to the popularly held view that ethnic diversity may destabilise the economy, in turn creating economic inequalities between ethnic groups. As such, it complements the historical inferences advanced by Lonsdale in Chapter 1. It also reinforces the view of Ghai (Chapter 4) that what accounts for poor economic performance in Africa is not the work of the market economy but rather government policies that have benefited the ethnic groups of those in power. This experiment thus qualifies or raises questions on the proposition advanced by Berman (Chapter 5) and others that the economic problems in Africa were caused by the imposition of neo-liberal market principles mandated by the International Monetary Fund (IMF) and the World Bank assistance packages. Finally, this experiment may be seen as a compendium to the empirical analyses of Brown and Stewart (Chapter 8) as these two studies offer quantitative approaches from different perspectives, but with results similar to our own findings.

The chapter is organised as follows. In the following section, we review relevant theory and prior experiments that inform the present study. In the next section, we present our model of an exchange economy with three competitive equilibria. We go on to explain how we transformed the theoretical model into an experimental setting. We then present the results before making our conclusions.

Background of theory and experiments

The standard neo-classical economic theory on market exchange is based on three fundamental assumptions: (1) each consumer or economic agent has an endowment of goods and a well-behaved utility function, which is a numerical representation for a selfish, non-satiated, continuous and convex preference relation over the whole set of non-negative commodity bundles; (2) each such consumer or agent chooses his consumption bundle to maximise his utility function subject to his budget constraint given prices of all goods; and (3) the market is governed by the tatonnement process, i.e. relative prices adjust according to excess demand or supply of goods being traded, and this adjustment process continues until an equilibrium is reached where supply and demand perfectly match for each good. Under these assumptions, there exists in the market at least one equilibrium, which is efficient in Pareto's sense. It is also proved, with some additional assumptions, that the equilibrium is unique and 'stable', which means that the tatonnement process leads the market outcome to the equilibrium whatever the initial prices are. This neo-classical proposition is at the foundation of the basic premise in economic policy-making that assumes markets are both fair and competitive. The Washington consensus, which espouses the reliance on these market principles, has been much debated and, in the views of many, discredited. To date, however, a theory that would replace competitive markets as the fundamental policy paradigm has not been advanced or at least has not been widely accepted.

Important advances have been made in economic theory and experiments by relaxing these two fundamental assumptions, and thus testing the robustness of the neo-classical proposition.[1] The starting point of such inquiries was an example of a well-known simple model of a two-good two-consumer exchange economy (Gale

[1] See Mukherji (2010) for a brief summary of theoretical expositions by Hildenbrand and those of Grondmont as well as discussions of his own work to introduce heterogeneity of economic preferences. While Grandmont claims that heterogeneity actually enhances the stability property of market economy, his model is so abstract that it makes it difficult to interpret in an empirical context. On the other hand, Mukherji shows that when diversity is introduced, the initial endowment must be 'just right' if tatonnement is to lead to an equilibrium with optimal quality.

1963), in which consumer preferences are represented by a utility function of the 'Leontief' type. His model, contrary to the standard neo-classical prediction, includes three equilibria: one of them is an interior equilibrium, while the other two are 'extreme' (the allocation of goods between two consumers at the equilibrium is supported by the price vector (1,0), or (0,1)). 'Walrasian' stability depends on the initial holdings of the consumers: the interior equilibrium is the only stable point in some cases, and it is unstable otherwise. The two extreme equilibria are stable in cases where the interior equilibrium is unstable.

What if totally impersonal tatonnement is replaced with, say, a double auction, in the Gale example? An answer to this question was given by Crockett *et al.* (2011), who designed and conducted an experiment of the Gale model in a double auction simulation using the computer network of an experimental laboratory.[2] The results of their experiment surprisingly confirm the predictions of the Walrasian theory. This is in line with the findings of other experiments of Charles Plott and his associates which demonstrate that classical models based on tatonnement have remarkable explanatory power even when applied to non-tatonnement, continuous, double-auction markets.[3]

Huber *et al.* (2009) conducted an experiment of another kind of non-tatonnement trading institution, using the simple two-good two-consumer exchange model of Shapley and Shubik (1977) where two consumers have 'strictly convex preferences linear in different goods' (as assumed in standard neo-classical economic theory). In the experiments, the subjects were instructed to type into a computer their offers of trade and accept those of the others only once in a given period. The subjects carried over their holdings (i.e. the outcome of the trade in the previous period) to the beginning of the next period, and repeated trading until the end of one trading session. In their model, there are three equilibria which are all interior; the intermediate equilibrium is unstable, and the two other equilibria are stable. The results of the experiment show that there is a tendency for the holdings of consumers to converge to the intermediate equilibrium.

---

[2] The double auction institution is a system of market trading in which participants are allowed to 'buy and sell' objects (doubling as a buyer and a seller) as long as their offers are accepted.

[3] See Anderson *et al.* (2004).

Our experiment, which we present below, is a substantive extension of Crockett *et al.* (2011) in that we directly introduce heterogeneity of economic agents by selecting samples of three distinct ethnic communities as the subjects of experiment, and by having each ethnic group trade with others. The methodology of our experiment is also different from that of Crockett *et al.* as ours is an experiment of manual, face-to-face trading in a pit market while theirs was an on-line experiment of double auction. Based on conventional wisdom, one could assume that the trading outcomes would converge to the intermediate equitable distribution when people of the same ethnicity engage in trade. Conversely, one could also hypothesise that when people of different ethnicities trade, the outcome would converge to an extreme equilibrium which is beneficial for one group whose members are tougher negotiators than the members of the other group. One could also hypothesise that people would be more reluctant to trade with members of a different ethnic group that had been in conflict with their particular ethnic group.[4] As it turns out, none of these hypotheses is supported by the results of our experiment.

The model

The purpose of our research is to conduct a laboratory experiment of an exchange economy with subjects of different ethnicities in order to investigate which equilibrium is selected from the multiple potential equilibria for the economy. The set-up is an exchange economy with two types of consumers, and two kinds of commodities. Three competitive equilibria exist, one intermediate 'equitable' trade and two extremes that strongly advantage (or disadvantage) one of the trading groups. One type of consumer initially owns more of the first good and less of the second good than consumers of the other type. Consumers of the same type are all rationed an identical commodity bundle of endowment.

[4] The literature of economic experiments includes findings from international comparisons about bargaining and market exchange (Roth *et al.* 1991) and public good provision (Cason *et al.* 2002), for which they conducted experiments in different places separately, but the subjects did not interact across countries. We therefore wondered where to conduct an experiment with subjects of different ethnicities.

We choose the second good as the *numeraire*, the price of which is always fixed as one, and focus on the behaviour of the relative price of the first good. There are three equilibrium prices in our exchange model. The lowest relative price is beneficial for the type of consumer having more of the second good, and the highest relative price is advantageous to the type of consumer having more of the first good. The intermediate price leads to an 'equitable' allocation.

In theory, the tatonnement dynamics predict that relative prices go up when the first good is excessively demanded, and go down when it is excessively supplied in the market. Accordingly, relative prices diverge from the intermediate equilibrium towards the lowest equilibrium or the highest equilibrium depending on the initial prices. Consequently, the market mechanism causes an income inequality and the 'invisible hand' leads the economy to an efficient but inequitable state.

We formulate the above exchange economy in terms of mathematical formula as follows.

There are two commodities, X and Y, and two types of consumers named 1 and 2. The utility functions of consumers 1 and 2 are, respectively:

$$U_1(x_1, y_1) = a_1 \min[g_1(x_1), y_1] + b_1 \text{ and}$$

$$U_2(x_2, y_2) = a_2 \min[g_2(x_2), y_2] + b_2 \tag{2.1}$$

In the experiment, we set $a_1 = 72.77$, $b_1 = 927.23$, $a_2 = 69.2$, $b_2 = 961.98$,

$$
\begin{aligned}
g_1(x_1) &= x_1 / 9.8 && \text{if } x_1 \in [0, 6.2] \\
&= 10.5x_1 - 1.6(10.5 - 1/9.8) && \text{if } x_1 \in [6.2, 7.5] \\
&= x_1 / 9.7 + 1.3(10.5 - 1/9.8) && \text{if } x_1 \in [7.5, 14.9] \\
&= 10.5x_1 - 13.6(10.5 - 1/9.8) && \text{otherwise;}
\end{aligned}
$$

and

$$
\begin{aligned}
g_2(x_2) &= x_2 && \text{if } x_1 \in [0, 7.35] \\
&= 11.3x_2 - 7.35(11.3 - 1/9.1) && \text{if } x_2 \in [7.35, 8] \\
&= x_2 / 9.1 + 16.5(11.3 - 1/9.1) && \text{if } x_2 \in [17.45, 18.45] \\
&= 11.3x_2 - 16.8(11.3 - 1/9.1) && \text{if } x_2 \in [17.45, 18.45] \\
&= x_2 / 9.1 + 16.5(11.3 - 1/9.8) && \text{otherwise;}
\end{aligned}
$$

Utility function of type 1 consumer

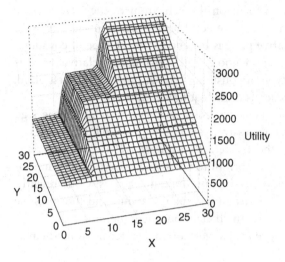

Utility function of type 2 consumer

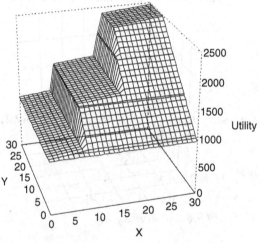

Figure 9.1 Utility functions of consumers

The above utility functions are shown graphically in Figure 9.1. The level of utility is shown vertically (height). It depends on the combination of the quantities of X and Y to be consumed.

The initial endowment of consumer 1 is given as $(\overline{x_1}, \overline{y_1}) = (25, 1)$ and the initial endowment of consumer 2 is $(\overline{x_2}, \overline{y_2}) = (5, 29)$.

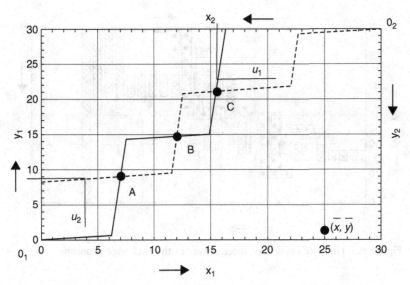

Figure 9.2 Exchange economy with three competitive equilibria

Figure 9.2 displays this economy as an Edgeworth box. The solid (respectively, dashed) piecewise linear line represents consumer 1's (consumer 2's) offer curve, derived by varying prices and asking the consumer how much she would like to trade to maximise her utility at a given price. The offer curves are given as $y_1 = g_1(x_1)$ and $y_2 = g_2(x_2)$ because the utility maximisation points are the loci of the vertices of the L-shaped indifference curves. There are three competitive equilibria indicated by the points of intersection of the two offer curves at which supply equals demand.

Consider a market excess demand function of an exchange economy. We say that a competitive equilibrium, or simply an equilibrium, is locally stable (unstable) if the market demand function is strictly decreasing (increasing) at the equilibrium price. The intermediate equilibrium B = (12.0132, 14.7432) is locally unstable, whereas the other two equilibria A = (6.99771, 9.00859) and C = (15.4803, 21.1309) are locally stable. Figure 9.2 can be also regarded as demonstrating symmetric equilibrium outcomes in a market with n traders on each side when all traders of the same type take the same action.

For our experiment, we need to convert the model from real numbers to integers because, in the experiment, subjects choose integers as trading units, not real numbers in usual theory. Figure 9.3 shows

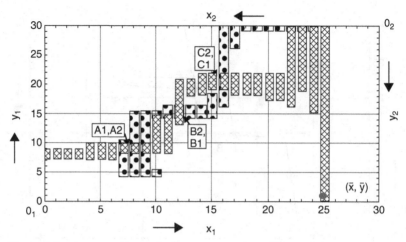

Figure 9.3 Discrete version of offer curves in the exchange economy

this discrete version of exchange economy in an Edgeworth box. The locus of circles (•) (multiplication (×)) denotes consumer 1's (consumer 2's) offer curve, which is thick, in the discrete economy. The two offer curves intersect at six points indicating competitive equilibria: A1 = (7, 9), A2 = (8, 9), C1 = (16, 20) and C2 = (16, 21) are locally stable equilibrium points with the corresponding equilibrium price ratios p_x/p_y = 0.44, 0.17, 2.11 and 2.22, respectively, while B1 = (12, 15) and B2 = (12, 16) are locally unstable points with p_x/p_y = 0.08, 1.15, respectively.[5]

To make our experiment manageable, we prohibited the subjects from trading commodities if the price ratio p_X/p_Y (which is the ratio of the amount of Y to the amount of X) was less than 1/4 = 0.25. For p_X/p_Y < 1/4, there are several competitive equilibria other than the six shown above. In Figure 9.2, we omit these equilibria and focus on the six equilibria close to the three equilibria in Figure 9.3 of the usual Edgeworth box.

---

[5] The number of competitive equilibria when only integer units are allowed in trading in experimental settings could be considerably larger than that when trading units are real numbers in theory. For a Shapley–Shubik (1977) exchange economy with two goods, only three competitive equilibria exist in theory. However, there are 198 equilibria with only integer trading units and no trading price constraint (see Masui *et al.* 2010).

Table 9.1. *Theoretical predictions about discrete equilibria*

		Allocation				Payoff	
		Type 1 (x1,y1)	Type 2 (x2,y2)	Price	Walrasian stability	Type 1 U1	Type 2 U2
	A1	(7, 9)	(23, 21)	4\9=0.44	Stable	1,582	2,415
	A2	(8, 9)	(22, 21)	8\17=0.47	Stable	1,582	2,407
Discrete	B1	(12, 15)	(18, 15)	14\13=1.08	Unstable	2,000	2,000
equilibria	B2	(12, 16)	(18, 14)	15\13=1.15	Unstable	2,000	1,931
	C1	(16, 20)	(14, 10)	19\9=2.11	Stable	2,383	1,572
	C2	(16, 21)	(14, 9)	20\9=2.22	Stable	2,455	1,572

Table 9.1 presents a summary of the equilibrium predictions. There are trade-offs between stability and 'equity' of the competitive equilibria. The equilibria A1 and A2 with low relative prices of commodity X, p_X/p_Y, are beneficial for a type 1 consumer having more of commodity Y, while the equilibria C1 and C2 with high relative prices of commodity X are advantageous to a type 2 consumer having more of commodity X. These four equilibria are locally stable, but not equitable. On the other hand, equilibria B1 and B2 with intermediate prices give allocations that generate a negligible difference between the payoffs to the two types of consumers. We say that this equilibrium is equitable. In particular, at B1, consumers of both types receive the equal payoffs. However, this equilibrium is locally unstable.

As stated above, our initial hypothesis is that (1) when each group of traders are from a different ethnicity, trading is expected to lead to an extreme and inequitable equilibrium such as A1, A2, C1 or C2; and (2) trading outcomes would converge to equilibrium B1 or B2 when the two groups of traders are of the same ethnicity.

Experimental design and procedures

Design

We selected Kenya as a place to conduct our experiment because it is well known that ethnicity plays a major role in politics and economy in Kenya, perhaps more than in most other African countries. Kenya, which has more than forty different ethnic groups with distinct identities, has a history of ethnic conflicts, the most notable of which occurred in 2008 when post-election violence claimed more than 1,000 lives.

The subjects were students of the University of Nairobi and Kenyatta University situated in major urban centres as well as those from universities located in (relatively) small towns such as Moi University, Egerton University, Mount Kenya University, Kimathi University College of Technology and Jomo Kenyatta University of Agriculture and Technology. Although ethnic identification may not be as strong among university students as for older people living in rural areas, we chose students as subjects of the experiment because of their ability to comprehend the concept of the experiment and conduct trade as stipulated in the model. Also, the number of male subjects was the same as that of female subjects.

Needless to say, it was not feasible to conduct an experiment for every possible combination of the existing ethnic identities. Thus we focused on three major ethnic groups – Luo, Kikuyu and Kalenjin. These three ethnic communities, together with Luhya, Kamba, Maasai, Somali and Swahili, have dominant roles in the political and economic landscape in Kenya.

We selected twenty-four subjects from each of the three ethnic communities for a total of seventy-two participants. We separated each ethnic group into two groups of twelve each, with one group of subjects to play the role of a type 1 consumer and the other the role of a type 2 consumer. Their roles were fixed throughout the experiment. Trade was conducted between one group of twelve belonging to one ethnicity and playing the role of either a type 1 or 2 consumer and another group of twelve belonging to one ethnicity and playing the role of either a type 1 or 2 consumer. Thus, twenty-four subjects participated in each trading session.

We conducted nine sessions during 2–4 March 2010 at the University of Nairobi. Table 9.2 (a) shows the ethnic/consumer type combination in each of the trading session names. In the table, L, Ki and Ka stand for Luo, Kikuyu and Kalenjin, respectively; 1 and 2 denote the consumer types. For example, L1-Ki2 means that the session involved trade between a group of twelve Luos playing the role of consumer type 1 and a group of twelve Kikuyus playing the role of consumer type 2. Each subject participated in three sessions.

Table 9.2 (b) shows the time schedule. In the first period each group traded with a group of the same ethnicity, and then traded with different ethnic groups in the following periods. For example, in the first

Table 9.2. *Nine laboratory sessions*

(a)

		Type 2		
Type 1		Luo	Kikuyu	Kalenjin
	Luo	Ki1-L2	L1-Ki2	L1Ka2-
	Kikuyu	Ki1-L2	Ki1-Ki2	Ki1-Ka2
	Kalenjin	Ka1-L2	Ka1-Ki2	Ka1-Ka2

(b)

	3/2/2010	3/3/2010	3/4/2010
AM	L1-L2	Ka1-Ka2	L1-Ka2
	Ki1-Ki2		Ka1-L2
PM	L1-L2	Ka1-Ki2	
	Ki1-L2	Ki1-Ka2	

period, Luo subjects of consumer type 1 faced Luo subjects of consumer type 2 in the L1-L2 session in the morning of the first day. In the second period, they traded with a group of Kikuyu subjects of consumer type 2 in the L1-Ki2 session in the afternoon of the first day. Finally, they met Kalenjin subjects of consumer type 2 in the L1-Ka2 session on the morning of the third day.

No subject had prior experience in market experiments. The three sessions in which each subject participated required approximately five hours to complete in total. Each subject received, on average, a payoff of Ksh 5,791 (about US$75 in March 2010). The maximum payoff among the seventy-two subjects was Ksh 6,277 ($82), and the minimum payoff was Ksh 4,502 ($58).

Procedures

In each session we made pairs out of the twenty-four subjects so that there were twelve trading teams in total, each with two subjects. Each team received written instructions, a record sheet, a payoff table and two name tags. The name tag of each subject indicated the subject's team name (A, B, C, ... to L), consumer type number (1 or 2) and an abbreviation for ethnicity ('L' for Luo, 'Ki' for Kikuyu or 'Ka' for Kalenjin) such as 'C-2-Ki'. Six teams (A–F) played the role of a type 1 consumer, and six teams (G–L) played the role of a type 2 consumer. Sessions, which were conducted in English, comprised five trading periods lasting ten minutes each.

During each period, each team was given pink cards and/or white cards in an envelope. One pink card was one unit of commodity X, and one white card was one unit of commodity Y. We explicitly notified every subject that they were not allowed to reveal any information regarding the payoff table or the endowment of their team to any other team.

The subjects walked around a relatively large laboratory room and found a team with which to trade. We prohibited any subject from giving any amount of commodity X or Y more than he held to the team. In addition, as explained in the previous section, the trading ratio of Y to X should be greater than or equal to 1/4 = 0.25 to exclude undesirable equilibrium allocations.

We told the subjects to trade commodity X for Y or Y for X when two teams reached an agreement. After writing the trading results in their record sheets, the teams reported them to the experimenter. The following information on the results was written on the blackboard and displayed publicly: the team name giving commodity X, the amount of the traded X, the team name giving Y, the amount of the traded Y, and the trading ratio of the commodities (=Y/X). This was the end of one trade.

During each period teams were allowed to trade as many times as they wanted within the ten-minute time limit. The teams could choose any team they wanted to trade with: they could change trading partners or return to a team with which they had previously traded. At the end of the period, the subjects went back to their seats and the experimenter collected all commodity cards. After a two-minute break, the next period started. At the beginning of the next period, the subjects received the same allocation as at the beginning of the previous period (i.e. their holdings were reset rather than carried over). Each session contained five periods of trading.

Each subject's earnings depended on the final payoff that his team earned during one randomly selected period from the experiment. This period was chosen using a randomising device after the experiment. Each member of the same team received the same earnings.

We distributed to each team a payoff table showing how their payoff depended on the amount of commodities X and Y. See Tables 9A.1

and 9A.2 in Appendix 9.1 for the payoff table of types 1 and 2, in which the column denotes the amount of commodity X and the row denotes the amount of commodity Y. We round off the decimal places of payoff values.

Experimental results

Trading Patterns

Figure 9.4 shows the distributions of the end-of-period holdings of commodities X and Y, and contrasts those in the three sessions involving type 1 of Luo and Kalenjin (Figure 9A.1 in the Appendix shows those for type 1 of Kikuyu). Each session had five periods in which six teams of subjects of each type trade, so our data consist of $5 \times 6 = 30$ consumption bundles of X and Y for each type and each session. In Figure 9.4, the XY planes of the bases of three-dimensional diagrams represent the possible holdings of goods X and Y for the subjects, and the heights denote the frequencies of the holdings observed in the experiment.

Figure 9.4 (a) shows the distributions of holdings of type 1 of Luo subjects when they traded with type 2 of Luo subjects: many different trades are observed, with no overall pattern of the trading. Figure 9.4 (b) shows the distributions of holdings of type 1 of Kalenjin subjects when they traded with the other type of Kalenjin subjects: several patterns of holdings are apparent and the data are concentrated in $(x_1, y_1) = (12, 15)$, which is the consumption bundle for type 1 at the intermediate equilibrium.

Figure 9.4 (c) shows the distributions of holdings of type 1 of Luo subjects when they traded with type 2 of Kikuyu subjects: the patterns of holdings are less pronounced than in Figure 9.4 (a) and the data are concentrated around (12, 15). Figure 9.4 (d) shows the distributions of holdings of type 1 of Kalenjin subjects when they traded with type 2 of Kikuyu subjects: the patterns of holdings are less apparent than in Figure 9.4 (c) and the trades are extremely concentrated at (12, 15).

Figure 9.4 (e) shows the distributions of holdings of type 1 of Luo subjects when they traded with type 2 of Kalenjin subjects: the patterns of holdings are much less apparent than in Figure 9.4 (c), and the data are remarkably concentrated in (12, 15). Figure 9.4 (f) shows the distributions of holdings of type 1 of Kalenjin subjects when they

(a)

Luo type 1:L1–L2.

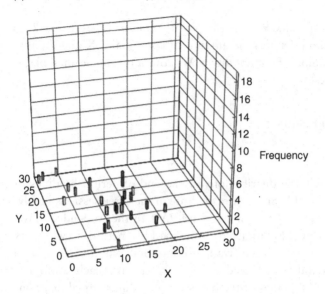

(b)

Kalenjin type 1:Ka1–Ka2

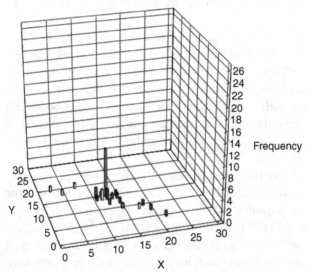

Figure 9.4 Distribution of end-of-period holdings of X and Y: Luo type 1 and Kalenjin type 1

(a) Session with Luo Type 1 and Luo Type 2

(b) Session with Kalenjin Type 1 and Kalenjin Type 2

(c) Session with Luo Type 1 and Kikuyu Type 2

(d) Session with Kalenjin Type 1 and Kikuyu Type 2

(e) Session with Luo Type 1 and Kalenjin Type 2

(f) Session with Kalenjin Type 1 and Luo Type 2

(c)   Luo type 1:L1–Ki2

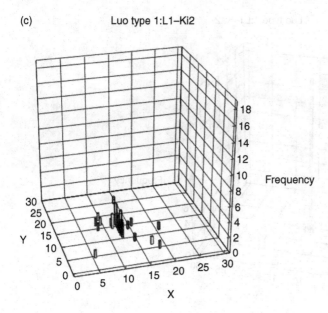

(d)   Kalenjin type 1:Ka1–Ki2

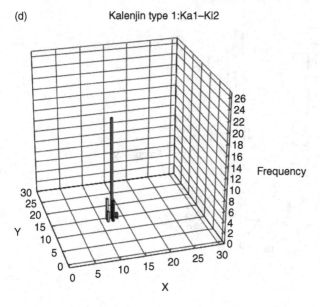

Figure 9.4 (*cont.*)

302   *Relationships between ethnicity and stability*

(e)   Luo type 1:L1–Ka2

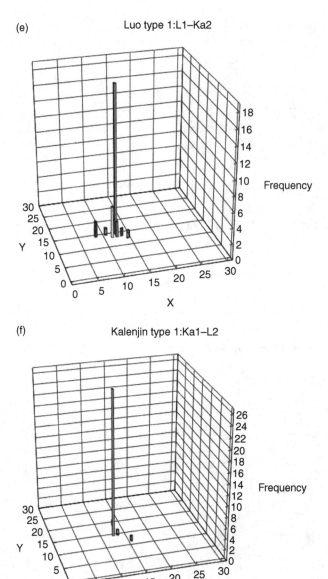

(f)   Kalenjin type 1:Ka1–L2

Figure 9.4 (*cont.*)

traded with type 2 of Luo subjects: the patterns of holdings are the least apparent of any in the six diagrams of Figure 9.4, and almost all of the data are (12, 15).

These patterns of equilibria suggest that in the sessions in which Kalenjin subjects participated, most type 1 of consumers eventually achieved the intermediate equitable equilibrium (12, 15) irrespective of their ethnicity.

Convergence to intermediate equilibrium

Figure 9.5 shows the average distance from the intermediate equilibrium B1 consumption bundle per subject for each ethnic group of subjects. Here the distance of each subject at each period is defined as the Euclidean distance between her end-of-period holdings and the consumption bundle her type of consumer receives at B1.[6] If the distance is zero, it means that trading converges completely to the intermediate equilibrium.

Figure 9.5 (a) shows that the average distances are high in the Luo group, middle in the Kikuyu group and low in the Kalenjin group in the sessions with the same ethnicity. Figure 9.5(b) demonstrates that in the sessions with different ethnicities, average distances are lower in the sessions including the Kalenjin group (i.e. sessions Ka1-Ki2, Ki1-Ka2, L1-Ka2 and Ka1-L2) than in those in the sessions consisting of trading between Luo and Kikuyu groups (i.e. sessions L1-Ki and L2-Ki2). Notably, the average distance approaches zero as periods advance; in other words, in every trading session that included Kalenjins, the allocations converge to the intermediate equilibrium allocation B1 (12, 15). We test the hypothesis that the mean distance per subject is equal between two ethnic groups by pooling the data across periods with a random effects model. The pooled distance data lead us to reject this hypothesis between each pair of Luo, Kikuyu and Kalenjin groups at the 1 per cent significance level in the first-round period with the same ethnicity. Data also lead us to reject the hypothesis between Luo and Kalenjin groups as well as that between Kikuyu and Kalenjin at the 1 per cent significance level in the second-round session with different ethnicities. On the other hand, the data do not lead us to reject the hypothesis between Luo and Kikuyu groups in the second-round

---

[6] The Euclidean distance between points (a_1, a_2) and (b_1, b_2) is
$$\sqrt{(a_1 - b_1) + (a_2 - b_2)}\, .$$

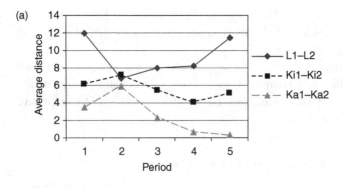

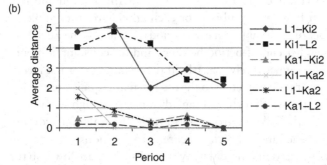

Figure 9.5 Average distances from the intermediate equilibrium allocation B1
(a) Session with the same ethnicity
(b) Session with different ethnicities

trading period between different ethnicities or that between any pair
of the three groups in the third-round period with different ethnicities
at the 5 per cent significance level.[7]

Figure 9.6 portrays the average number of transactions per subject
for each session. The number of transactions is high in the Luo group,
intermediate in the Kikuyu group and low in the Kalenjin group in the
sessions with the same ethnicity groups. In the sessions with different
ethnicities, transactions occur more often in the sessions consisting of
Luo and Kikuyu subjects than in the sessions including Kalenjin subjects in which one subject carried out only almost one transaction, on
average.

---

[7] A Wilcoxon signed rank test and a *t*-test give the same result as that obtained
using the panel data analysis.

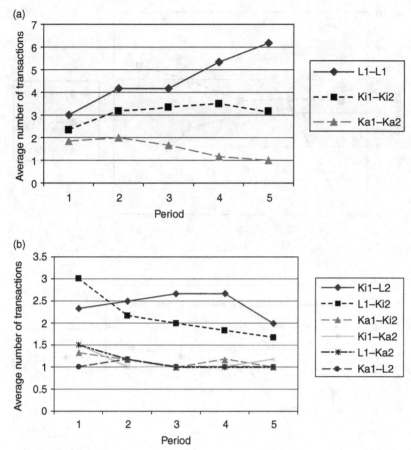

Figure 9.6 Average numbers of transactions per subject
(a) Session with the same ethnicity
(b) Session with different ethnicities

We test the hypothesis that the mean number of transactions per subject is equal between two ethnic groups by pooling the data across ethnic groups with a random effects model.

Efficiency

Next we examine a key question of whether the outcome is efficient. Here we define efficiency as the sum of realised payoffs over all subjects as a percentage of the maximum payoffs achievable.[8] Figure 9.7

---

[8] The maximum value of the sum of the payoffs of two consumer types is 4,072.

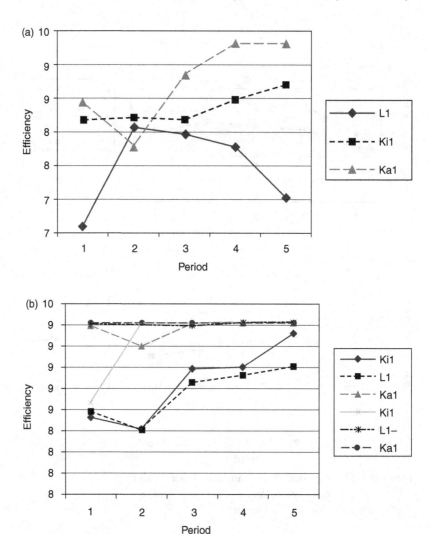

Figure 9.7 Efficiency
(a) Session with the same ethnicity
(b) Session with different ethnicities

demonstrates efficiency across periods in each session. Efficiency is low in the Luo group, intermediate in the Kikuyu group and high in the Kalenjin group in the trading periods between the same ethnicity groups. In the trading periods between different ethnicities, efficiency is lower in the sessions consisting of Luo and Kikuyu subjects than in the sessions including Kalenjin subjects.

Figures 9.6 and 9.7 together suggest an inverse relationship between the number of transactions and efficiency in our experimental market.

Why is the 'Kalenjin effect' on achieving the intermediate equilibrium so strong? Kalenjin subjects quickly began to make offers of the intermediate equilibrium only and ceased to accept other proposals although the other ethnic groups of subjects kept making small adjustments to improve their outcomes. Our results suggest that the bilateral trading does not cause large inequalities of income or welfare, and the participation of Kalenjins in this experimental market simulation significantly facilitated trading at the exact point of the intermediate equilibrium (12, 15).

To sum up, we observe the following:

(1) In the sessions with Luo and/or Kikuyu subjects only, we do not observe convergence of allocations. In the sessions with Kalenjin, however, allocations converge to the intermediate equilibrium allocation, which is equitable but locally unstable, especially in later periods.
(2) The convergence to the intermediate equilibrium B1 occurs remarkably faster with Kalenjin subjects than without them. Kalenjin subjects quickly began to make offers of the intermediate equilibrium and ceased to accept other proposals.
(3) The frequency of transactions with Kalenjin subjects is significantly lower than that with Luo and/or Kikuyu subjects only. The less frequent transactions result in the more efficient outcomes of the experimental market.

Concluding remarks

Ethnic diversity plays a central role in explaining differences in business management and local market performance within a country. We also know that in the world there are quite a few countries in which different ethnicities co-exist. It is therefore important to ask what impact ethnicity has in determining economic performance of market economies.

However, we are unable to take either a theoretical or empirical approach to consider this question because, as far as we know, there is no theoretical model in which characteristics or behavioural principles of different ethnicities are postulated. Whether the competitiveness of a market under investigation is perfect or imperfect, we always assume the 'anonymity' of traders in a market. This suggests that every participant in the market only cares about qualities and quantities of commodities traded, so the particular ethnic identity of a buyer or seller should not impact market outcomes. In addition, if we were to take an empirical approach, it would be most useful to compare market outcomes within one ethnic group with those involving different ethnic groups. But it is almost impossible to collect data that would support comparison of these two ideal market types.

We have therefore decided to take an experimental approach, and selected Kenya as a place to conduct an experiment to consider this question. We conducted experiments in Nairobi with equal numbers of Luo, Kikuyu and Kalenjin college students. We divided each ethnic cohort of the subjects into two groups, assigning them to play two types of consumers in our economic model. We had each group trade with members of the same ethnic group in their first-round session, and with different ethnic groups in the other sessions.

Our results show that the variance of individual patterns of trades was remarkably smaller in the sessions with Kalenjin subjects than in those without them. In addition, the frequency of transactions in sessions where Kalenjin subjects participated was lower than that between Luos and Kikuyus. Moreover, the lower frequency of transactions resulted in more efficient outcomes of the experimental market. The main reason is that Kalenjin subjects quickly began to make offers of the intermediate equilibrium only and ceased to accept other proposals although the other ethnic groups of subjects kept making small adjustments to be better off.

Thus, our observations suggest that face-to-face trading interactions between ethnic groups do not lead to large inequalities of income or welfare. The participation of Kalenjin people in the experimental market significantly facilitated prompt trading at the exact point of the intermediate equilibrium.

We also observe that ethnicity matters in market outcomes. In our experiment, the key players are the Kalenjin subjects. The participation of Kalenjins in the market surprisingly facilitates the fast and exact convergence to the intermediate equilibrium. Remarkable differences exist between the two data sets: data for transactions in which Kalenjin subjects participated, and data of transactions shared by Luo and Kikuyu subjects.

Appendix 9.1

Amount of Y ↓ / Amount of X →	0	1	2	3	4	5	6	7	8	9	10	11	12	13	14	15	16	17	18	19	20	21	22	23	24	25	26	27	28	29	30
30	927	935	942	950	957	964	972	1585	1970	1978	1985	1993	2000	2007	2015	2098	2862	3110	3110	3110	3110	3110	3110	3110	3110	3110	3110	3110	3110	3110	3110
29	927	935	942	950	957	964	972	1585	1970	1978	1985	1993	2000	2007	2015	2098	2862	3038	3038	3038	3038	3038	3038	3038	3038	3038	3038	3038	3038	3038	3038
28	927	935	942	950	957	964	972	1585	1970	1978	1985	1993	2000	2007	2015	2098	2862	2965	2965	2965	2965	2965	2965	2965	2965	2965	2965	2965	2965	2965	2965
27	927	935	942	950	957	964	972	1585	1970	1978	1985	1993	2000	2007	2015	2098	2862	2892	2892	2892	2892	2892	2892	2892	2892	2892	2892	2892	2892	2892	2892
26	927	935	942	950	957	964	972	1585	1970	1978	1985	1993	2000	2007	2015	2098	2819	2819	2819	2819	2819	2819	2819	2819	2819	2819	2819	2819	2819	2819	2819
25	927	935	942	950	957	964	972	1585	1970	1978	1985	1993	2000	2007	2015	2098	2746	2746	2746	2746	2746	2746	2746	2746	2746	2746	2746	2746	2746	2746	2746
24	927	935	942	950	957	964	972	1585	1970	1978	1985	1993	2000	2007	2015	2098	2674	2674	2674	2674	2674	2674	2674	2674	2674	2674	2674	2674	2674	2674	2674
23	927	935	942	950	957	964	972	1585	1970	1978	1985	1993	2000	2007	2015	2098	2601	2601	2601	2601	2601	2601	2601	2601	2601	2601	2601	2601	2601	2601	2601
22	927	935	942	950	957	964	972	1585	1970	1978	1985	1993	2000	2007	2015	2098	2528	2528	2528	2528	2528	2528	2528	2528	2528	2528	2528	2528	2528	2528	2528
21	927	935	942	950	957	964	972	1585	1970	1978	1985	1993	2000	2007	2015	2098	2455	2455	2455	2455	2455	2455	2455	2455	2455	2455	2455	2455	2455	2455	2455
20	927	935	942	950	957	964	972	1585	1970	1978	1985	1993	2000	2007	2015	2098	2383	2383	2383	2383	2383	2383	2383	2383	2383	2383	2383	2383	2383	2383	2383
19	927	935	942	950	957	964	972	1585	1970	1978	1985	1993	2000	2007	2015	2098	2310	2310	2310	2310	2310	2310	2310	2310	2310	2310	2310	2310	2310	2310	2310
18	927	935	942	950	957	964	972	1585	1970	1978	1985	1993	2000	2007	2015	2098	2237	2237	2237	2237	2237	2237	2237	2237	2237	2237	2237	2237	2237	2237	2237
17	927	935	942	950	957	964	972	1585	1970	1978	1985	1993	2000	2007	2015	2098	2164	2164	2164	2164	2164	2164	2164	2164	2164	2164	2164	2164	2164	2164	2164
16	927	935	942	950	957	964	972	1585	1970	1978	1985	1993	2000	2007	2015	2092	2092	2092	2092	2092	2092	2092	2092	2092	2092	2092	2092	2092	2092	2092	2092
15	927	935	942	950	957	964	972	1585	1970	1978	1985	1993	2000	2007	2015	2019	2019	2019	2019	2019	2019	2019	2019	2019	2019	2019	2019	2019	2019	2019	2019
14	927	935	942	950	957	964	972	1585	1946	1946	1946	1946	1946	1946	1946	1946	1946	1946	1946	1946	1946	1946	1946	1946	1946	1946	1946	1946	1946	1946	1946
13	927	935	942	950	957	964	972	1585	1873	1873	1873	1873	1873	1873	1873	1873	1873	1873	1873	1873	1873	1873	1873	1873	1873	1873	1873	1873	1873	1873	1873
12	927	935	942	950	957	964	972	1585	1800	1800	1800	1800	1800	1800	1800	1800	1800	1800	1800	1800	1800	1800	1800	1800	1800	1800	1800	1800	1800	1800	1800
11	927	935	942	950	957	964	972	1585	1728	1728	1728	1728	1728	1728	1728	1728	1728	1728	1728	1728	1728	1728	1728	1728	1728	1728	1728	1728	1728	1728	1728
10	927	935	942	950	957	964	972	1585	1655	1655	1655	1655	1655	1655	1655	1655	1655	1655	1655	1655	1655	1655	1655	1655	1655	1655	1655	1655	1655	1655	1655
9	927	935	942	950	957	964	972	1582	1582	1582	1582	1582	1582	1582	1582	1582	1582	1582	1582	1582	1582	1582	1582	1582	1582	1582	1582	1582	1582	1582	1582
8	927	935	942	950	957	964	972	1509	1509	1509	1509	1509	1509	1509	1509	1509	1509	1509	1509	1509	1509	1509	1509	1509	1509	1509	1509	1509	1509	1509	1509
7	927	935	942	950	957	964	972	1437	1437	1437	1437	1437	1437	1437	1437	1437	1437	1437	1437	1437	1437	1437	1437	1437	1437	1437	1437	1437	1437	1437	1437
6	927	935	942	950	957	964	972	1361	1364	1364	1364	1364	1364	1364	1364	1364	1364	1364	1364	1364	1364	1364	1364	1364	1364	1364	1364	1364	1364	1364	1364
5	927	935	942	950	957	964	972	1291	1291	1291	1291	1291	1291	1291	1291	1291	1291	1291	1291	1291	1291	1291	1291	1291	1291	1291	1291	1291	1291	1291	1291
4	927	935	942	950	957	964	972	1218	1218	1218	1218	1218	1218	1218	1218	1218	1218	1218	1218	1218	1218	1218	1218	1218	1218	1218	1218	1218	1218	1218	1218
3	927	935	942	950	957	964	972	1146	1146	1146	1146	1146	1146	1146	1146	1146	1146	1146	1146	1146	1146	1146	1146	1146	1146	1146	1146	1146	1146	1146	1146
2	927	935	942	950	957	964	972	1073	1073	1073	1073	1073	1073	1073	1073	1073	1073	1073	1073	1073	1073	1073	1073	1073	1073	1073	1073	1073	1073	1073	1073
1	927	935	942	950	957	964	972	1000	1000	1000	1000	1000	1000	1000	1000	1000	1000	1000	1000	1000	1000	1000	1000	1000	1000	1000	1000	1000	1000	1000	1000
0	927	927	927	927	927	927	927	927	927	927	927	927	927	927	927	927	927	927	927	927	927	927	927	927	927	927	927	927	927	927	927

Amount of X

Table 9A.1 Payoff table provided to subjects of type 1

Table 9A.2 shows the payoff to subjects of type 2 as a function of the Amount of X (columns, 0–30) and the Amount of Y (rows, 30–0).

Amount of Y \ Amount of X	0	1	2	3	4	5	6	7	8	9	10	11	12	13	14	15	16	17	18	19	20	21	22	23	24	25	26	27	28	29	30
30	962	970	977	985	992	1000	1008	1015	1526	1534	1541	1549	1557	1564	1572	1579	1587	1595	2028	2384	2392	2399	2407	2415	2422	2430	2437	2445	2453	2460	2468
29	962	970	977	985	992	1000	1008	1015	1526	1534	1541	1549	1557	1564	1572	1579	1587	1595	2028	2384	2392	2399	2407	2415	2422	2430	2437	2445	2453	2460	2468
28	962	970	977	985	992	1000	1008	1015	1526	1534	1541	1549	1557	1564	1572	1579	1587	1595	2028	2384	2392	2399	2407	2415	2422	2430	2437	2445	2453	2460	2468
27	962	970	977	985	992	1000	1008	1015	1526	1534	1541	1549	1557	1564	1572	1579	1587	1595	2028	2384	2392	2399	2407	2415	2422	2430	2437	2445	2453	2460	2468
26	962	970	977	985	992	1000	1008	1015	1526	1534	1541	1549	1557	1564	1572	1579	1587	1595	2028	2384	2392	2399	2407	2415	2422	2430	2437	2445	2453	2460	2468
25	962	970	977	985	992	1000	1008	1015	1526	1534	1541	1549	1557	1564	1572	1579	1587	1595	2028	2384	2392	2399	2407	2415	2422	2430	2437	2445	2453	2460	2468
24	962	970	977	985	992	1000	1008	1015	1526	1534	1541	1549	1557	1564	1572	1579	1587	1595	2028	2384	2392	2399	2407	2415	2422	2430	2437	2445	2453	2460	2468
23	962	970	977	985	992	1000	1008	1015	1526	1534	1541	1549	1557	1564	1572	1579	1587	1595	2028	2384	2392	2399	2407	2415	2422	2430	2437	2445	2453	2460	2468
22	962	970	977	985	992	1000	1008	1015	1526	1534	1541	1549	1557	1564	1572	1579	1587	1595	2028	2384	2392	2399	2407	2415	2422	2430	2437	2445	2453	2460	2468
21	962	970	977	985	992	1000	1008	1015	1526	1534	1541	1549	1557	1564	1572	1579	1587	1595	2028	2384	2392	2399	2407	2415	2415	2415	2415	2415	2415	2415	2415
20	962	970	977	985	992	1000	1008	1015	1526	1534	1541	1549	1557	1564	1572	1579	1587	1595	2028	2346	2346	2346	2346	2346	2346	2346	2346	2346	2346	2346	2346
19	962	970	977	985	992	1000	1008	1015	1526	1534	1541	1549	1557	1564	1572	1579	1587	1595	2028	2277	2277	2277	2277	2277	2277	2277	2277	2277	2277	2277	2277
18	962	970	977	985	992	1000	1008	1015	1526	1534	1541	1549	1557	1564	1572	1579	1587	1595	2028	2208	2208	2208	2208	2208	2208	2208	2208	2208	2208	2208	2208
17	962	970	977	985	992	1000	1008	1015	1526	1534	1541	1549	1557	1564	1572	1579	1587	1595	2028	2138	2138	2138	2138	2138	2138	2138	2138	2138	2138	2138	2138
16	962	970	977	985	992	1000	1008	1015	1526	1534	1541	1549	1557	1564	1572	1579	1587	1595	2028	2069	2069	2069	2069	2069	2069	2069	2069	2069	2069	2069	2069
15	962	970	977	985	992	1000	1008	1015	1526	1534	1541	1549	1557	1564	1572	1579	1587	1595	2000	2000	2000	2000	2000	2000	2000	2000	2000	2000	2000	2000	2000
14	962	970	977	985	992	1000	1008	1015	1526	1534	1541	1549	1557	1564	1572	1579	1587	1595	1931	1931	1931	1931	1931	1931	1931	1931	1931	1931	1931	1931	1931
13	962	970	977	985	992	1000	1008	1015	1526	1534	1541	1549	1557	1564	1572	1579	1587	1595	1862	1862	1862	1862	1862	1862	1862	1862	1862	1862	1862	1862	1862
12	962	970	977	985	992	1000	1008	1015	1526	1534	1541	1549	1557	1564	1572	1579	1587	1595	1792	1792	1792	1792	1792	1792	1792	1792	1792	1792	1792	1792	1792
11	962	970	977	985	992	1000	1008	1015	1526	1534	1541	1549	1557	1564	1572	1579	1587	1595	1723	1723	1723	1723	1723	1723	1723	1723	1723	1723	1723	1723	1723
10	962	970	977	985	992	1000	1008	1015	1526	1534	1541	1549	1557	1564	1572	1579	1587	1595	1654	1654	1654	1654	1654	1654	1654	1654	1654	1654	1654	1654	1654
9	962	970	977	985	992	1000	1008	1015	1526	1534	1541	1549	1557	1564	1572	1579	1585	1585	1585	1585	1585	1585	1585	1585	1585	1585	1585	1585	1585	1585	1585
8	962	970	977	985	992	1000	1008	1015	1516	1516	1516	1516	1516	1516	1516	1516	1516	1516	1516	1516	1516	1516	1516	1516	1516	1516	1516	1516	1516	1516	1516
7	962	970	977	985	992	1000	1008	1015	1446	1446	1446	1446	1446	1446	1446	1446	1446	1446	1446	1446	1446	1446	1446	1446	1446	1446	1446	1446	1446	1446	1446
6	962	970	977	985	992	1000	1008	1015	1377	1377	1377	1377	1377	1377	1377	1377	1377	1377	1377	1377	1377	1377	1377	1377	1377	1377	1377	1377	1377	1377	1377
5	962	970	977	985	992	1000	1008	1015	1308	1308	1308	1308	1308	1308	1308	1308	1308	1308	1308	1308	1308	1308	1308	1308	1308	1308	1308	1308	1308	1308	1308
4	962	970	977	985	992	1000	1008	1015	1239	1239	1239	1239	1239	1239	1239	1239	1239	1239	1239	1239	1239	1239	1239	1239	1239	1239	1239	1239	1239	1239	1239
3	962	970	977	985	992	1000	1008	1015	1170	1170	1170	1170	1170	1170	1170	1170	1170	1170	1170	1170	1170	1170	1170	1170	1170	1170	1170	1170	1170	1170	1170
2	962	970	977	985	992	1000	1008	1015	1100	1100	1100	1100	1100	1100	1100	1100	1100	1100	1100	1100	1100	1100	1100	1100	1100	1100	1100	1100	1100	1100	1100
1	962	970	977	985	992	1000	1008	1015	1031	1031	1031	1031	1031	1031	1031	1031	1031	1031	1031	1031	1031	1031	1031	1031	1031	1031	1031	1031	1031	1031	1031
0	962	962	962	962	962	962	962	962	962	962	962	962	962	962	962	962	962	962	962	962	962	962	962	962	962	962	962	962	962	962	962

Table 9A.2 Payoff table provided to subjects of type 2

(a) Kikuyu type 1:Ki1–Ki2.

(b) Kikuyu type 1:Ki1–L2

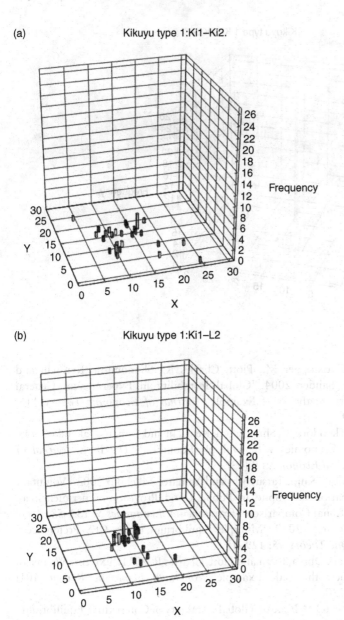

Figure 9A.1 Distribution of end-of-period holdings of X and Y: Kikuyu type 1
(a) Session with the same ethnicity
(b) Session with Kikuyu type 1 and Luo type 2
(c) Session with Kikuyu type 1 and Kalenjin type 2

(c)   Kikuyu type 1:Ki1–Ka2

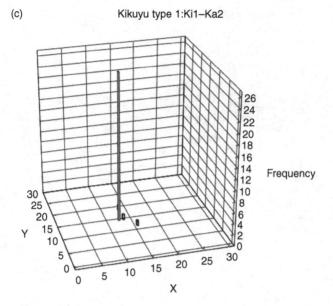

References

Anderson, Christopher M., Plott, Charles R., Shimomura, Ken-Ichi and Granat, Sander 2004. 'Global Instability in Experimental General Equilibrium: the Scarf Example', *Journal of Economic Theory* 115: 209–49.

Bergstrom, Theodore C., Shimomura, Ken-Ichi and Yamato, Takehiko 2009. 'Simple Economies with Multiple Equilibria', *The B. E. Journal of Theoretical Economics* 9 (43).

Cason, Timothy, Saijo, Tatsuyoshi and Yamato, Takehiko 2002. 'Voluntary Participation and Spite in Public Good Provision Experiments: an International Comparison', *Experimental Economics* 5: 133–53.

Chipman, John S. 2010. 'Multiple Equilibrium under CES Preferences', *Economic Theory* 45: 129–45.

Crockett, Sean, Oprea, Ryan and Plott, Charles R. 2011. 'Extreme Walrasian Dynamics: the Gale Example', *American Economic Review* 101: 3,196–220.

Gale, David 1963. 'A Note on Global Instability of Competitive Equilibrium', *Naval Research Logistics Quarterly* 10: 81–7.

Huber, Juergen, Shubik, Martin and Sunder, Syham 2009. 'Default Penalty as Disciplinary and Selection Mechanism in Presence of Multiple Equilibria', *Cowles Foundation Discussion Paper No. 1,730*, Yale University.

Roth, Alvin E., Prasnikar, Vesna, Okuno-Fujiwara, Masahiro and Zamir, Shmuel 1991. 'Bargaining and Market Behavior in Jerusalem, Ljubljana, Pittsburgh, and Tokyo: an Experimental Study', *American Economic Review* 81: 1,068–95.

Masui, Michiharu, Ohtaka, Tokitaka, Shimomura, Ken-Ichi, Takahashi, Kiyotaka and Yamato, Takehiko 2010. 'Discrete Exchange Economies: a Simulation Analysis', Discussion Paper, Tokyo Institute of Technology.

Mukherji, Anjan. 2010. 'Stability of the Market Economy in the Presence of Diverse Economic Agents', JICA-RI Working Paper No. 8.

Scarf, Herbert 1960. 'Some Examples of Global Instability of the Competitive Equilibrium', *International Economic Review* 1: 157–71.

Shapley, Lloyd S. and Shubik, Martin 1977. 'An Example of a Trading Economy with Three Competitive Equilibria', *Journal of Political Economy* 85: 873–75.

Smith, Vernon L. 1962. 'An Experimental Study of Competitive Market Behavior', *Journal of Political Economy* 70: 111–37.

Conclusion: Key findings of our interdisciplinary dialogue

HIROYUKI HINO

Introduction

Ethnicity in Africa, and its relation to the economy, has long been a subject of extensive research by anthropologists, historians, economists and political scientists. Through the contributions of anthropologists and historians, we now have a much deeper understanding of what ethnicity is – and what it is not – and how the nature of ethnicity has evolved over time. Economists and political scientists have also contributed greatly to enhance our understanding of how ethnicity affects economic performance and political discourse in Africa.

In the past, however, there has been little dialogue between anthropologists and historians on the one hand, and economists and political scientists on the other. The former saw the latter with anxiety, and perhaps even some suspicion. Historians and anthropologists were convinced that the quantitative techniques of economists were unsuitable to capture the 'contingencies' of ethnicity, and hence thought that their conclusions were often over-simplified or even misleading. Conversely, economists and political scientists saw historians and anthropologists as focusing on specific cases and circumstances, which made it difficult to come to general conclusions and policy recommendations.

Historians and anthropologists analysed ethnicity, sometimes taking the economy and the political regime as given. Economists largely neglected (or ignored) ethnicity in analysing the economy, and where they did bring it into the analysis, they took ethnicity as given. Political scientists did likewise in their work on political regimes. Even some basic concepts have meant different things to the two groups of researchers – to anthropologists, the market is where people meet, but to economists, it is where supply and demand meet.

Thus, the single most important contribution of this volume is to have initiated a genuine and productive dialogue among historians, economists, political scientists and anthropologists, i.e. those in

314

academic disciplines necessary and relevant to understanding the inter-actions between ethnicity and economy in Africa. Ogot's portrayal of the historical roots of the current expressions of ethnicity in Africa (Chapter 3) provides valuable background to the studies of econo-mists and political scientists alike throughout the volume. Lonsdale, historian, and Langer and Brown, economists, all attempt to capture the essence of ethnicity, the former from analyses of the contingen-cies of historical evidence and process and the latter with construction of quantifiable and cross-contextual measure of ethnicity (Chapters 1 and 2). The historical and socio-political expositions of the mutual dependence between ethnicity and economy by Ghai and Berman offer a context and foundation for the quantitative modelling of the eco-nomic effects of ethnic distance by Hamaguchi, and the causal rela-tions between ethnic diversity and economic instability by Brown and Stewart (Chapters 4, 5, 6 and 8, respectively).

This volume is only the beginning of an interdisciplinary dialogue and hence no definitive conclusions should be drawn at this time. Nevertheless, we were able to offer several propositions with some confidence, which together represent a major advance in understand-ing the intricacy and fluidity of the mutual dependence of ethnicity and economy, and their implications for economic instability in Africa.

Limitations of conventional wisdom

In development economics and elsewhere, it is commonly accepted that ethnic diversity, i.e. the co-existence of distinct ethnic communities in a country, is a critical factor contributing to disagreement on the alloca-tions of public goods and negatively affecting economic growth, which can lead to the emergence of civil strife. Moreover, it is often presumed that ethnic diversity is a causal factor of economic instability in Africa, although this supposed relationship has been little studied.

The papers presented in this volume have shown collectively that the above negative views on ethnic diversity should be interpreted with care and at times with skepticism. One reason is that the data and statistical methods of past quantitative studies – in which the nega-tive relationships were found – are built on the fundamental assump-tions that ethnicity can be defined quantitatively and that its definition is invariable in space and time. However, it has been illustrated in this volume and elsewhere that ethnicity is a product of historical, economic and political circumstances, and hence evolves over time. Therefore, ethnicity can properly be measured only in relation to the specific context given or to the time and place selected. It has also been demonstrated that ethnicity, politics and the economy influence each other, and that the nature of this interdependence evolves in response to changes in economic and other circumstances. This mutual dependence and the fluidity of such dependence are not accounted for in past quantitative models.

The number and relative size and strength of the ethnic groups present in a nation very likely have some bearing on the nature of inter-ethnic relations within that country, and on the influences that ethnicity may have on the economy. However, it would be presumptuous to assume that one can establish a simple mathematical rule, linear or quadratic, that cuts across all countries and which predicts the effect of ethnic composition on the rate of economic growth of a nation, irrespective of its political and historical circumstances.

This is not to deny the usefulness of quantitative approaches. Indeed, where (a) data on ethnic groups are cautiously compiled, (b) objectives of the study are prudently prescribed and (c) a mathematical model suitable to those objectives is carefully selected, quantitative techniques can yield useful insights, particularly for analysing certain specific aspects of the relationships between ethnicity and economy; see for example Hamaguchi (Chapter 6) and Posner (2011). The point is to avoid undue generalisation. 'It sometimes seems as though the nations with just a couple or few predominant ethnic groups, and a much larger number of much smaller ones, have proved the most politically unstable as far as national governments and regimes are concerned ... But that is about as far as one can generalise' (Shipton, Chapter 7).

Ethnic diversity does not by itself cause economic under-performance or political or economic instability. Historically, inter-ethnic relationships in Africa were based on gains from trade or exchange in market places and from migration impelled by economic or political circumstances. Ethnic identities constantly evolved through interactions in the market, migration and consequent integration and inter-ethnic marriages, until they were largely frozen by the boundaries set by colonial rule. Historically, African ethnicities are malleable and flexible.

In fact, an economic experiment, which was specifically designed to abstract the effects of ethnicity on the outcome of a market economy, showed that trading among certain ethnic groups *can* be welfare-improving and *can* stabilise an economy that is otherwise unstable (Shimomura and Yamato, Chapter 9). Moreover, some quantitative evidence exists that shows that trade between ethnic groups raises income and lowers poverty within the ethnic groups involved (Hamaguchi, Chapter 6), although in many instances, inter-ethnic trade is inhibited – and hence gains from trade are limited – because of the 'territorial confinement' of ethnic communities (see below).

Ethnic differences do not in themselves lead to inter-group conflict. Ethnic differences become the focus of inter-group strife only when and where other factors are involved – economic, political or cultural – or when horizontal inequalities are high. Brown and Stewart (Chapter 8) detect no significant correlation between ethnic diversity and economic instability, whether the latter is defined as fluctuations in annual rates of economic growth or as a sudden large drop in the rate of economic growth.

Alternative propositions

Yet it does appear that conflicts, economic instability and poorer long-term economic performance are observed more often in a country whose population is ethnically diverse, however that is defined. The question is why.

Many historians would answer that ethnicity in much of Africa has been transformed from an outward-looking, malleable, identity into an instrument of political mobilisation, through 'construction' by the colonial rulers and through subsequent manipulation by African political elites. Ethnic communities have become the basis for political alliance, which aims primarily to claim greater shares of the 'national pie' even at the expense of other communities, be it public goods, civil service positions, public procurements or 'allocations' of public lands (Ogot, Chapter 3; Berman, Chapter 5). A consequence is the lower overall efficiency and productivity of public resources, weaker governance and less predictable public policy, each of which contributes to lower economic growth and higher economic instability.

The macroeconomic significance of this proposition is corroborated to a degree by results of the quantitative analyses included in our interdisciplinary dialogue. Brown and Stewart (Chapter 8) have found a strong correlation between ethnic diversity and governance indicators, even giving due regard to the weaknesses of these indicators. Posner (2011) shows that the impact of ethnic political alliances on educational attainment of ethnic group(s) in power has been considerable in Kenya, although the estimated impact is not as strong as one might have suspected.

Thus, ethnicity 'mediates' state and economy through its political alliances, and it is this function that gives rise to the negative relationship between overall economic performance and ethnic diversity (Ghai, Chapter 4). The strength of the negative effects is of course not uniform across countries. It might be stronger in a nation where ethnic composition is bulkier. It might also be stronger where ethnic political alliances are influential in national affairs. The relative strength of political alliance depends on a number of factors, including history, geography, demography and leadership.

What is emerging from our research is another proposition, which runs like this. Ethnicity in Africa is driven to a large degree by the yearning for belonging. This is in a way natural because it provides the comfort of togetherness, accustomed languages and way of life and, in some cases, an escape from xenophobic fear and suspicion. But in much of Africa, with the continued economic hardship and instability, the yearning for belonging has increasingly been motivated by the desire to protect and preserve whatever little they have. Population pressure, diminishing arable land, limited mobility and hardening ecological conditions further exacerbate ethnic discord and economic uncertainty. This drives ethnic communities to antagonism, isolationism and territorial confinement, which inhibit trade and exchange with ethnically dissimilar communities. The consequent economic instability further accentuates ethnic divisiveness and territorial confinement. The vicious cycle of economic instability, ethnic isolationism and territorial confinement, and economic instability thus continues (Chapter 7, Shipton).

This vicious cycle proposition is not meant to replace the political mobilisation proposition but rather to complement it. The vicious cycle proposition appears plausible, but its validity or significance still needs to be empirically tested. Hamaguchi (Chapter 6) offers some quantitative evidence that supports some aspects of the above proposition. However, it is necessary to conduct more rigorous tests on the basis of robust measures of ethnicity and ethnic distances. Brown and Langer (Chapter 2) offer sophisticated measures, but they are still constructed from raw data which suffer from well known weaknesses. Their measures also depend on the intuition or discretion of their authors. Nevertheless, the results of Brown and Langer represent a significant advance, and will likely lead to measurements of ethnicity that could enjoy the confidence of economists, historians and anthropologists alike. Such measures could then be deployed for the careful and rigorous testing of this and other propositions.

Inequality and instability

In many African countries, inequality between ethnic communities (horizontal inequality) is believed to be high. The economy of most ethnic communities still reflects their traditional heritage and way of life. In addition, many African countries have inherited an uneven distribution of land, natural resources and social infrastructure (education and public health) between ethnic communities. Interface with the market, often underpinned by government actions, further aggravates horizontal inequality. As the disparity increases, disadvantaged communities might attempt to force radical shifts in economic policy or threaten to reject the prevailing economic regime via collective action or the expression of their grievances by political means. Such action could lead to instability, both economic and political.

Brown and Stewart (Chapter 8) provide some quantitative evidence showing that horizontal ethnic inequality is linked to economic instability, as argued above. They demonstrate that higher horizontal inequality is associated with greater political instability and lower-quality governance, each of which contributes to greater economic instability. Although this evidence must be verified by further analyses, we tentatively conclude that inequality between ethnic groups is another medium through which ethnic diversity can contribute to political and economic instability.

Our interdisciplinary dialogue underscores that ethnic diversity can be a potent force of instability particularly when high inequality between ethnic communities (horizontal inequality) coalesces with high inequality within an ethnic community (vertical inequality). In most communities, vertical inequality has increased as land has become scarcer, political patronage has become more pervasive and direct interactions with markets have become more widespread. This creates tension within an ethnic community – tension between 'moral ethnicity' and 'political tribalism'. The former is argumentative and favourably disposed to inter-ethnic social, cultural and material exchange, while the latter is despotic and predisposed to economic protectionism. When political tribalism prevails over moral ethnicity, and where horizontal inequality arouses strong resentment, ethnic conflicts and their consequent economic insta-bility are likely to ensue. See Lonsdale (Chapter 1).

The challenges of nation building

In the foregoing, we have argued that ethnicity is not inherently a constraint on market-based development. We have suggested that rather, the modes of nation building during the colonial and post-colonial periods, together with other factors, have made ethnicity an obstacle. Yet in Africa, a nation typically is composed of a number of sub-nations, each of which constitutes an ethnic community with its own language, rules and regulations, common law and a code of conduct. 'What makes a "nation" legitimately sovereign, and an ethnic group a problematic "sub-nation", is a matter of historical accident.' (Lonsdale, Chapter 1). In some countries such as Tanzania and Ghana, ethnic patriotism was subdued under a state-controlled economy dur-ing the post-colonial era, at substantial economic cost. But in others such as Kenya, the nation remains in some ways an assemblage of ethnic moral communities. 'What Britain bequeathed to Kenyans was a country with its many communities tied together by political struc-tures and with an economy devised for their subordination, but with the additional problem of finding and creating a common identity and destiny: a state without a nation' (Ghai, Chapter 4). Thus, Ogot (Chapter 3) asks rhetorically 'So who needs Kenya?'

The final proposition of our interdisciplinary dialogue in this vol-ume is that the cohabitation of national sovereignty and ethnic moral communities impedes market-based economic development. Because of this cohabitation, many countries in Africa struggle to maintain national cohesion and the purpose of unity, which facilitates a nation's drive to achieve rapid economic development. In consequence, even in a unitary state, government resembles that of a federal state or a grand coalition, with constantly shifting alliances and associated policy uncertainty, instability and inefficiency. Some African countries also have the appearance of customs unions, with their markets for labour and goods segmented by ethnic groups.

Market economy requires constitutionalism to keep the state at bay while relying on its coercive power to regulate markets, to enforce contracts and to ensure that all lawful expectations of individuals and corporations are protected (Ghai, Chapter 4). This is critical because the market economy is based on the autonomy of economic agents and on the promise of meeting future obligations. Indeed, the under-performance of African economies in the past is often attributed largely to the lack of commercial security, the unpredictability of judicial decisions, the prevalence of corruption and the failure of market institutions. In post-colonial Africa, constitutions were amended severally to establish imperial presidencies, regimes incompatible with the principles of market economy. The dominant influence of ethnic sentiment and ethnic order in society and politics, and the consequent tendency of the state to subjugate society, compromise both constitutionalism and market principles.

The way forward

This book has demonstrated the value of interdisciplinary studies in our quest to gain a deeper and more robust understanding of interactions between ethnicity and economic development in Africa. Lonsdale (Chapter 1) set out questions that we must attempt to answer: (1) how far is ethnicity inherently an obstacle to market-based 'development' or, to the contrary, how far have certain modes of nation building or trajectories of development made it so?; (2) since humanity is naturally competitive, in what circumstances, for which purposes and under what rules of the game does the cry of ethnicity become more powerful than the appeal of other identities, of gender, age, religion, ideology, social class or 'nation'?; and (3) why should that particular loyalty be deemed to be more economically destructive than others? This book has provided at least partial answers to these questions.

The next step will be to build on the diagnosis offered in this book. We should investigate institutions and policies that will help bring about sustained economic development with equity and stability in the ethnically diverse countries of Africa. Some of the useful research topics to help achieve this end could include the following.

Firstly, how does the existence of diverse ethnicities – with differing non-pecuniary preferences – affect the very properties of a market economy? Are market principles likely to lead to unstable outcomes in Africa, given the ethnic diversity in the continent? This book has offered conflicting answers. Ghai (Chapter 4) concludes that what accounts for poor economic performance in Africa is not the work of the market economy but rather of the ethnic chauvinism that encourages political forces to break the rules of market economy for personal gain. On the other hand, Berman (Chapter 5) argues that the interplay between ethnic diversity and market principles is the fundamental cause of under-performance and instability in Africa, a view that an extension of general equilibrium theory by Mukherji (2010) supports. Our own market experiments conducted in Kenya suggest that at least in certain cases, ethnicities seem to have stabilising and optimising effects (Shimomura and Yamato, Chapter 9). It would be most useful to conduct additional market experiments, drawing together economic theorists, historians and anthropologists to produce market settings in which the characteristics of each ethnic group can be demonstrated clearly.

Secondly, how does democracy's rule by majority decisions work in a country where individual preferences are mutually dependent, being bound by the social preferences of their ethnic community? How, if at all, should conventional democratic rules be modified to reflect Africa's ethnic realities? Jain (2010) suggests that in such situations, where individuals are self-regarding, rule by majority decision may itself drive minority ethnic communities to marginalisation and even extinction. For this and other reasons, Yash Ghai (2010) argues that in countries with ethnically diverse populations, it is essential to decentralise executive and legislative authorities – both horizontally (parliamentary system) and vertically (fiscal devolution) – as well as to enact strong affirmative legislation to protect minority ethnic groups. It would be helpful to develop and propose constitutional arrangements that would counter the temptation for political elites to exploit political tribalism and that would encourage socially coherent decision-making in an ethnically diverse nation.

Thirdly, what are the implications of ethnic composition within local jurisdictions in a country for the economic efficiency and stability as well as political stability of that country? Kasara (2010) demonstrated – with the data she painstakingly constructed – that in Kenya, there is a higher incidence of ethnic violence in districts where ethnicities are more mixed. On the other hand, Hamaguchi (Chapter 6) reports also for Kenya that the more the district is ethnically mixed, the higher the per capita income of that district would be. Shipton (Chapter 7) argues that the 'criss-crossing' of multiple allegiances (such as ethnicity, religion, profession, etc.) in a society may help hold that society together.

Fourthly, when and how do increases in inequality, both vertical and horizontal, damage the trust within and between ethnicities? If inequality – both horizontal and vertical – is considered excessive and/or growing, should economic growth strategies of that country be altered, and if so how? Is affirmative action appropriate and, if so, of what kind? It is generally agreed that measures which directly address the causes of inequality may be more efficient and effective. Among such causes of inequality, land tenure is of particular importance. Takahashi (2011) laid out some useful principles that can guide us in enhancing land tenure and other private property rights in the transition to a market economy in an ethnically diverse country. However, land tenure reform is a complex subject that requires additional and more extensive research before we can attempt policy recommendations.

Finally, investing in nation building – for bonding together moral ethnic communities – is a topic that calls for much further detailed research in different national and historical contexts. The case of the Taveta people of the Kenyan coast provides an interesting example of nation building (Ogot, Chapter 3). In the seventeenth century, refugee groups comprising six ethnicities fled from famine and conflict in their respective home areas and settled in the Taveta forest. By the nineteenth century, this heterogeneous group had built a distinctive common culture, and had developed land-holding clans and central institutions, which unified the migrants into a single people. A common language was adopted. Intermarriage between the clans was widespread, each of which greatly assisted in welding the clans into a cohesive nationality. It will be equally rewarding to revisit the experiences of countries with an interesting history of multiethnic living, such as India, Indonesia and Brazil, and examine their relevance to Africa.

For nation building to be truly sustainable, it should be based on fostering and cultivating ethnic diversity, rather than suppressing ethnicity. Ethnicity itself is not a problem. Managing ethnicity is the issue. After all, diversity – ethnic, religious or cultural – is an asset that we all should cherish, not least because it is characteristic of most contemporary nation-states around the world.

It is hoped that this book will serve as catalyst in further stimulating interest in the subject of ethnicity and development and in the contributions that interdisciplinary studies might be able to make. Our aim will be to deepen the understanding of ethnicity as a potentially positive force, to sustain high economic growth with stability and equity throughout Africa.

References

Ghai, Yash 2010. *Ethnicity and Nationhood: 2010 Kenya Constitution*. Mimeo.

Jain, Satish K. 2010. *Market, Democracy, and Diversity of Individual Preferences and Values*. JICA Research Institute Working Paper 7, JICA Research Institute, Tokyo, Japan.

Kasara, Kimuli 2010. *Local Segregation and Inter-ethnic Violence in Kenya*. Mimeo.

Mukherji, Anjan 2010. *Stability of the Market Economy in the Presence of Diverse Economic Agents*. JICA Research Institute Working Paper 8, JICA Research Institute, Tokyo, Japan.

Posner, Daniel 2011. *Education for All?: The Political Economy of Primary Education in Kenya*. Mimeo.

Takahashi, Motoki 2011. *Scarcity and Governance: Overcoming Ethnic Confrontation over Resources in Africa*. Mimeo.

Appendix

List of project members

James Adams	Vice President, East Asia and Pacific Region, World Bank
Bruce Berman	Director and Principal Investigator, Ethnicity and Democratic Governance Program/ Professor Emeritus, Department of Political Studies, Queen's University
Graham K. Brown	Director, Centre for Development Studies/ Senior Lecturer, Department of Social and Policy Sciences, University of Bath
Siddharth Chandra	Director, Asian Studies Center/Professor, James Madison College, Michigan State University
Yash Pal Ghai	Emeritus Professor, Faculty of Law, University of Hong Kong
Nobuaki Hamaguchi	Professor, Research Institute for Economics and Business Administration, Kobe University
Hiroyuki Hino	Professor, Research Institute for Economics and Business Administration, Kobe University/ Special Fellow, Japan International Cooperation Agency Research Institute
Satish Jain	Professor, Centre for Economic Studies and Planning, School of Social Sciences, Jawaharlal Nehru University
Michael Kremer	Professor, Department of Economics, Harvard University
Arnim Langer	Director, Centre for Peace Research and Strategic Studies/Assistant Professor, Institute for International and European Policy, Faculty of Social Sciences, University of Leuven
John Lonsdale	Fellow, Trinity College Cambridge/Emeritus Professor, University of Cambridge

Anjan Mukherji	Professor Emeritus, Centre for Economic Studies and Planning, School of Social Sciences, Jawaharlal Nehru University/ Country Director, International Growth Centre, Bihar Programme at Patna
Bethwell Allan Ogot	Chancellor, Moi University
Edward Oyugi	Professor, Department of Educational Psychology, Kenyatta University
Daniel Posner	Professor, Department of Political Science, Massachusetts Institute of Technology (MIT)
Gustav Ranis	Professor Emeritus, Economic Growth Center, Yale University
Ken-Ichi Shimomura	Director and Professor, Research Institute for Economics and Business Administration, Kobe University
Parker Shipton	Professor, Department of Anthropology, Boston University
Frances Stewart	Director, Centre for Research on Inequality, Human Security and Ethnicity/Professor, Department of International Development, University of Oxford
Motoki Takahashi	Professor, Graduate School of International Cooperation Studies, Kobe University
Juro Teranishi	Professor, College of Commerce, Nihon University

Other contributors

Ernest Aryeetey	Vice Chancellor, University of Ghana
Mamadou Diouf	Professor, Columbia University
Jean Ensminger	Professor, California Institute of Technology
Augustin Fosu	Deputy Director, United Nations University World Institute for Development Economics Research (UNU-WIDER)
Takahiro Fukunishi	Researcher, Institute of Developing Economies, Japan External Trade Organization (IDE-JETRO)
Junichi Goto	Professor, Keio University
Nahomi Ichino	Assistant Professor, Harvard University

Kimuli Kasara	Assistant Professor, Columbia University
Jane Kiringai	Senior Economist, World Bank
Carola Lentz	Johannes Gütenberg University, Mainz
Raufu Mustapha	University Lecturer, University of Oxford
Benno Ndulu	Governor, Bank of Tanzania
Takaaki Oiwa	Senior Fellow, Japan International Cooperation Agency (JICA)/JICA Representative in Singapore
Oduor Ong'wen	Southern and Eastern African Trade Information and Negotiations Institute (SEATINI), Kenya
Tavneet Suri	Assistant Professor, MIT
Keiichi Tsunekawa	Vice President and Professor, National Graduate Institute for Policy Studies (GRIPS)/ Senior Research Adviser, JICA Research Institute (JICA-RI)
Takehiko Yamato	Professor, Tokyo Institute of Technology
Toru Yanagihara	Professor, Takushoku University

Index

Printed in the United States
by Baker & Taylor Publisher Services

Printed in the United States
by Baker & Taylor Publisher Services